W9-BQD-076

Research on Written Composition

Research on Written Composition

New Directions for Teaching

George Hillocks, Jr.
Departments of Education and English
The University of Chicago

National Conference on Research in English

ERIC Clearinghouse on Reading and Communication Skills
National Institute of Education

In memory of Bernard O'Donnell and Bernard J. McCabe

NCRE Publications Committee Chair: M. Trika Smith-Burke

Consultant Readers: James R. Squire, Richard Lloyd-Jones

Staff Editor: Timothy Bryant

Book Design: Tom Kovacs for TGK Design

NCTE Stock Number 40750

Published 1986 by the ERIC Clearinghouse on Reading and Communication Skills, 1111 Kenyon Road, Urbana, Illinois 61801, and the National Conference on Research in English.

This publication was prepared with funding from the National Institute of Education, U.S. Department of Education, under contract no. 400-83-0025. Contractors undertaking such projects under government sponsorship are encouraged to express freely their judgment in professional and technical matters. Prior to publication, the manuscript was submitted to the National Conference on Research in English for critical review and determination of professional competence. This publication has met such standards. Points of view or opinions, however, do not necessarily represent the official view or opinions of either the National Conference on Research in English or the National Institute of Education.

Library of Congress Cataloging-in-Publication Data

Hillocks, George.
    Research on written composition.

    Bibliography: p.
    Includes index.
    1. English language—Composition and exercises—
Study and teaching. 2. English language—Composition
and exercise—Research. I. Title.
PE1404.H55 1986   808'.042'07   85-29276
ISBN 0-8141-4075-0

Contents

Foreword

The Educational Resources Information Center (ERIC) is a national information system operated by the National Institute of Education (NIE) of the U.S. Department of Education. It provides ready access to descriptions of exemplary programs, research and development efforts, and related information useful in developing effective educational programs.

Through its network of specialized centers or clearinghouses, each of which is responsible for a particular educational area, ERIC acquires, evaluates, abstracts, and indexes current significant information and lists this information in its reference publications.

ERIC/RCS, the ERIC Clearinghouse on Reading and Communication Skills, disseminates educational information related to research, instruction, and professional preparation at all levels and in all institutions. The scope of interest of the Clearinghouse includes relevant research reports, literature reviews, curriculum guides and descriptions, conference papers, project or program reviews, and other print materials related to reading, English, educational journalism, and speech communication.

The ERIC system has already made available—through the ERIC Document Reproduction System—much informative data. However, if the findings of specific educational research are to be intelligible to teachers and applicable to teaching, considerable amounts of data must be reevaluated, focused, and translated into a different context. Rather than resting at the point of making research reports readily accessible, NIE has directed the clearinghouses to work with professional organizations in developing information analysis papers in specific areas within the scope of the clearinghouses.

ERIC is pleased to cooperate with the National Conference on Research in English in making *Research on Written Composition: New Directions for Teaching* available.

Charles Suhor
Director, ERIC/RCS

Preface

Seven years ago when Martha King and Doris Gunderson first saw the need for a comprehensive review of research on composition, interest in teaching and learning how to write had not yet reached its present crescendo. Their foresight in encouraging the National Conference on Research in English to sponsor George Hillocks's analysis of studies completed since "The Braddock Report" now makes this unusual survey available to decision-makers in curriculum, students of language development, researchers in reading comprehension, and specialists in cognitive psychology at a time when concern with process and product in composing envelops almost every discussion of achieving excellence in English.

The impact of the National Writing Project, the New Hampshire and Iowa Centers for Writing, the Bread Loaf Institute, and similar projects elsewhere has raised the consciousness of a generation of teachers concerning the importance of writing. A decade of empirical studies has traced the interrelationships of reading and writing. The influential international movement toward writing across the curriculum impacts all discussions with colleagues in other English-speaking countries. The proposed new National Center for the Study of Writing will offer a locus for much of this activity. Yet all of these efforts are dependent on a solid knowledge base.

George Hillocks provides such a base. Comprehensive and critical reviews of research in particular areas of concern are seldom made available during the peak periods of scholarly inquiry. In providing his analysis for all of us at this time, George Hillocks assures us that tomorrow's research will be informed by yesterday's efforts.

James R. Squire
for NCRE

Introduction

Those who have worked closely with *Research in Written Composition* (1963) will be struck by the changes in research on writing over the last two decades as reported in this volume. The causes doubtless are part of overall changes in school populations and educational aims, but a few comparisons serve to establish some of the usefulness of this book as a form of intellectual stocktaking. It is clearly time to see where we have been and perhaps to chart a new course.

In a narrow operational sense, George Hillocks reports on studies that have been prepared more carefully than those of the 1940s and 1950s. Possibly researchers have simply become more fastidious in writing their reports, and possibly they have been more careful in designing studies. Whatever the cause, the more recent studies are persuasive simply because the researchers seem to take themselves more seriously. The work stands up under examination.

The methods of the last two decades are also far more varied. In the 1963 survey, error counts and comparative studies dominated the book so much that without them there would have been no review. Hillocks describes other elaborate procedures for systematically refining observations. He is as governed by empiricism as are the earlier reviewers. However, the practices he describes lead in more directions by many different routes.

Perhaps the most evident changes are based on reductions of the number of instances examined and greater emphasis on close and complicated examination of those instances. Of course, large comparative studies and error counts are still undertaken and are described, but variations in case study methods require attention because they are numerous and exciting. The hardware is occasionally complicated, but more important is the fact that researchers are willing to forego the safety of believing that errors are cancelled out in the size of the sample. Without that statistical protection, they are obliged to demonstrate other ways of controlling observer bias or rejecting atypical examples. Hillocks thus devotes special attention to the problems of studies based on small samples, helping new researchers take advantage of pioneering work. He also contemplates methods for combining the bases of separate studies so that conclusions drawn from such observations can be made more believable. Case studies, "thick description," and protocols are now part of our working vocabulary, so we need critiques to help us set the agenda for new scholarly work.

Another change implied in this survey is awareness of theoretical or philosophical bases for the studies. A pervasive worry in 1963 was that researchers had stumbled on problems—sometimes by assignment, sometimes by local program needs—and had simply worked out research exercises. By contrast, in many of the newer studies, researchers seem to be working from considered ideas of language, discourse, epistemology, writing, education, and social responsibility. One might even talk of their "world view." As a result Hillocks is obliged to give more space to examining the assumptions of the research, and his report is thus made richer.

I find these reviews rouse in me a sense of great optimism. Despite the implications of my own work in testing, I do not think of myself as an empiricist; my role with Braddock and Schoer was that of the rhetorical theorist. The material we examined forced me into empiricism, and as an academic administrator I've had to examine issues of appropriate evidence and proof. As a sometime empiricist, then, I see in Hillocks's close critical examination of new work suggestions of what can be done and what is likely to be done. In 1963 I was not sure I shared Braddock's hope that we are emerging from an age of alchemy, and I still think of lore and other forms of experiential knowledge as essential to our crafts; but Hillocks has demonstrated here how much empirical studies have to offer, and he provides useful counsel for those who wish to conduct such studies.

Richard Lloyd-Jones
Iowa City

Author's Introduction

When Braddock, Lloyd-Jones, and Schoer published *Research in Written Composition* in 1963, I was in my sixth year of teaching and chair of the Euclid Central Junior High English Department. My colleagues and I had spent several years and many hours developing a curriculum which emphasized developing higher-level skills in reading literature and writing. At the same time the curriculum deemphasized formal grammar study, relegating it to twelve weeks of instruction in structural grammar spread over three years of junior high. That dramatic shift had brought us under attack for several years by teachers at the high school our graduates attended. They demanded that we teach nouns, verbs, prepositions, introductory verbal clauses, indirect objects, retained objects, and all the other paraphernalia of traditional school grammar. The pressure was intense to give up what we considered to be a progressive and highly effective program and to return to the conventional junior high program of the time. When the Braddock report reached me, I read it avidly to find what it said about grammar and written composition. I found the now-famous statement in short order: "The teaching of formal grammar has a negligible or, because it usually displaces some instruction and practice in actual composition, even a harmful effect on the improvement of writing" (pp. 37–38). My colleagues and I rejoiced. While the study of formal grammar might have value for its own sake, there was no evidence that it improved writing. (The present report also supports that conclusion.) Unfortunately, after I found what I wanted, I put the book aside for many months. I finally returned to it and learned a great deal from it—about the problems of judging quality of writing, about research design, about needed research, and so forth. It was indeed a valuable book for me.

Effects of the 1963 Report

When my assistants and I began to develop the bibliography for this study in 1978, it became clear that *Research in Written Composition* had been important for many others in the profession. In no time at all (or so it seems writing five years later), we had compiled a preliminary bibliography exceeding, in number at least, the 504 titles listed in *Research in Written Composition*. Further, it became clear that researchers had followed a number of suggestions by Braddock, Lloyd-Jones, and Schoer for future research. For example, they posed the question "What is involved in the act of writing?" (p. 53). The first chapter of this review is devoted to studies focusing on that question. Many other questions raised by Braddock, Lloyd-Jones, and Schoer have been the foci of studies, and many of those questions require continuing research.

In addition, the recommendations for research design have had some influence. Braddock, Lloyd-Jones, and Schoer felt that few studies were exemplary. "It is an unusual study," they wrote, "which does not leave several important variables uncontrolled or undescribed" (p. 55). While many studies included in the bibliography of this report suffer from similar flaws, there are also many studies which are, I believe, exemplary and which contribute to our knowledge of composition. Without these more carefully designed studies, the meta-analysis conducted as part of this review would not have been possible. Because we had access to more carefully designed research, the essential task of this report is the synthesis of available research findings, incorporating only brief outlines of individual studies for illustration and explanation.

In 1963 Braddock and his colleagues wrote that "today's research in composition, taken as a whole, may be compared to chemical research as it emerged from the period of alchemy" (p. 5). I do not know what the next step in the analogy to the development of chemistry is (Lavoisier and the discovery of oxygen? the beginnings of the periodic table?), but the analogy may be inappropriate today anyway. We cannot expect to discover "laws" which guide practice. But we may be able to predict the effects of certain practices with some degree of accuracy. We have developed a number of instruments and techniques which will continue to be refined but which are already useful in research. We have a body of knowledge about the composing process which suggests something about teaching and which raises very interesting questions for further research. We have a good deal of knowledge about classroom practices which can serve as a basis for developing more effective programs and for developing new hypotheses for exploration and testing. And all such knowledge, tentative though some of it is, can contribute to theories of instruction in composition which will be far stronger than the highly speculative theories of the past.

Not only have we begun to develop a research tradition, but attempts to answer questions raised by Braddock, Lloyd-Jones, and Schoer have led to new breadth and depth of interest in the teaching of writing. Teachers have begun to move well beyond the narrow range of teaching strategies discovered by Braddock and his colleagues. The National Writing Project, with its over 120 affiliates around the country, has involved thousands of teachers in thinking about writing *and* about how to teach it. Here we have a grassroots movement of remarkable proportions and influence. The climate for improving the teaching of writing has never been better. In short, although many problems remain, we have reason for optimism. We have the power to teach and to continue research well beyond the stage of alchemy.

Compilation of Bibliography

The bibliography for this report was begun in 1978 with an ERIC search and searches through *Studies in Education, Education Index*, the *Annotated Index to the English Journal*, and bibliographies published by *Research in the Teaching of English, College Composition and Communication*, and the *Center for Applied Linguistics*. Also included were reviews of research published in various journals and a computer search of dissertation titles. The attempt was to be exhaustive between the years 1963 and 1982. Items included in the Braddock bibliography were not included here. However, a few items published prior to 1963 but not in the Braddock study are included. Items produced in 1981 and 1982 which did not make their way into the ERIC system, *Dissertation Abstracts International*, or one of the standard bibliographies until 1983 are probably not included.

These various searches amassed over 6,000 titles. At that point, continuing with the review seemed an impossible task. Fortunately, a grant from the Spencer Foundation allowed the continuation of the project. Many of the references were accumulated, along with brief abstracts which revealed the content and treatment of the pieces. Abstracts of all dissertations were collected from *Dissertation Abstracts International*. Other studies were examined to determine content and treatment.

Abstracts were screened throughout the project to determine whether the studies should be included in the report. For inclusion, a piece had to deal with a data set concerned with some aspect of written composition in a systematic way. However, research dealing with spelling and vocabulary, initial teaching alphabet, or English as a second language was excluded. Research dealing only with oral language and pieces which were essentially anecdotal, hortatory, historical, curricular, or literary were also excluded. Research written in languages other than English was not examined, with the exception of Wesdorp's *De Didactiek van Het Stellen* (1982), a review, written in Dutch, of selected research on written composition. Certain theoretical pieces clearly related to research concerns, for example, a model of the composing process, were included. The bibliography, then, is not limited to research, but it does not include the hundreds of nonresearch articles which a more ambitious report might have included.

The screening process reduced the available items by more than half, to the approximately 2,000 pieces which the bibliography now includes. Each of these pieces was read by at least one researcher and abstracted. Although the large number of dissertations prohibited comprehensive examination of full text, all dissertation abstracts were read, and the full texts of approximately 150 dissertations were ordered, read, and abstracted. For the most part, these were dissertations the abstracts of which indicated they would be useful in the meta-analysis discussed in Chapters 3 and 8. References to dissertations in the text are to the *DA* or *DAI* entry, with a date which may be different from that of the dissertation itself. All dissertations which were read are asterisked in the bibliography.

Classification of Studies

At the beginning of the project, I developed a set of categories which permitted the classification of most studies and a systematic approach to the material available. Studies in the first major division were concerned with various aspects of the composing process. Many of these studies dealt with what might be called the "production process," the observable behavior of writers as they compose. One subcategory of studies examined the revisions made by writers working under various conditions. A second subcategory included studies of writing apprehension, and so forth. A second major division of studies was concerned with the writer's repertoire. Many of these studies investigated syntactic patterns present in the writing of various groups. Some were concerned with modes of discourse or more precisely defined forms. A third major division consisted of studies of particular pedagogical approaches. This division included a large number of studies which, as it turned out, required many,

many hours to classify and analyze. In retrospect, those frustratingly endless hours seem worth the expenditure of time and effort.

Other divisions in the initial outline included teacher preparation and attitudes, writing in schools and in the outside world, methods of assessment, and the development of writing abilities. Studies in the last category were integrated with those in the repertoire or process categories. A decision was made to ignore teacher preparation studies and to deal with studies of school programs tangentially as it seemed appropriate. Very few studies dealt with writing outside school in business, for recreation, and so forth.

The following report includes several of the initial categories and some refinements of them. Beginning with studies of the writing process, in all their diversity, it proceeds to the writer's repertoire. Chapter 3 introduces the meta-analysis of experimental treatments. The following chapters then present narrative reviews of pedagogical studies in mode of instruction and three other categories (grammar and the manipulation of syntax, criteria, and invention). Chapter 8 presents the results of the meta-analysis of the pedagogical (or treatment) studies.

Acknowledgments

I am deeply indebted to many for their encouragement, advice, and help throughout the several years of this project: to William D. Page, who first encouraged me to undertake a review; to Doris Gunderson, whose wise comments saved me from what would have been an egregious error; to Martha King and Victor Rentel for their encouragement throughout, but especially at the beginning; and to Martha King and James R. Squire, who helped me obtain $500 from the National Conference on Research in English to help support this research. I am particularly grateful to Bernard O'Donnell, whose good Irish wit, judgment, counsel, and encouragement provided important support throughout much of the project, up to a day or two before his death. I deeply regret not finishing in time for him to read and respond to the full manuscript.

I am indebted to a host of graduate students at the University of Chicago who compiled the initial bibliography and painstakingly conducted searches and abstracted studies in the detail needed: to Gail Shea, Paris Nikolas, Jeff Bergman, Mary Zambrino, Sheila Smith, Diane Borosak, Steve Kern, Mary Schenk, Dave Elderbrock, and Betty Bidlack. I especially appreciate the dull but demanding work of screening and rescreening several hundred experimental treatment studies, which was done by Marolyn Morford and Jo Bruce Hillocks. I am grateful to Jenni Bosma and Nick Bezruzcko for their careful work in coding studies and computing effect sizes for the meta-analysis portion of the review and to George McInnes Hillocks and Jo Bruce Hillocks, who checked and rechecked calculations. Without the careful work of Larry Ludlow, currently of Boston College, the meta-analysis could not have been completed. I recommend his program for the calculation of H statistics (1983) to anyone contemplating pursuing a meta-analysis.

Several graduate students undertook not only to abstract studies but to put together narrative reviews of certain categories of studies: Larry Johannessen, Elizabeth Kahn, Nancy Mavrogenes, Peter Smagorinsky, and Michael Smith. I greatly appreciate their work.

I am grateful to all those who helped with the typing and editing of the manuscript and bibliography: to George McInnes Hillocks and Marolyn Morford for entering large chunks of the bibliography on the word processor; to Therese Chappell for her rapid typing of the manuscript; and to Elizabeth Kahn and Carolyn Calhoun Walter for editing references in the text.

From beginning to end I have had the support of colleagues at the University of Chicago. My thanks go to Charles Bidwell, who, as chair of the Department of Education, provided substantive support in the early stages and friendly but insistent proddings throughout. Special appreciation goes to Larry V. Hedges, who provided his expertise and guidance throughout the meta-analysis.

My assistant, Jo Bruce Hillocks, deserves a special note of appreciation. Not only did she help with the analysis of studies, but she typed and proofread the bibliography, read and commented on the entire manuscript, and typed parts of the final copy. Working beyond the call of duty as assistant, Jo provided succor, solace, and encouragement.

Finally, this project could not have been completed without the generous support of The Spencer Foundation.

George Hillocks, Jr.
The University of Chicago

Research on Written Composition

1 Research on the Composing Process

The decade of the seventies brought a surge of interest in the composing processes of writers. Following the recommendation of Braddock, Lloyd-Jones, and Schoer (1963), researchers set out to determine what is involved in the act of writing and of what such skill consists. Many of the studies asked small samples of students to think aloud while they composed. The resulting transcript was then combined with an observational record of some kind. One group of researchers, led by Donald Graves, situated themselves in classrooms to observe young children writing. Still another group conducted experiments with larger groups of writers to gain insight into composing processes (e.g., Bridwell 1980b, Bereiter and Scardamalia 1982). What follows examines general studies of process, studies of process in classrooms, and studies of planning, production factors, revision, and writing apprehension. Summaries of the limitations and key findings of the research on process conclude this chapter.

General Studies of Process

The early studies of process were concerned with the nature of such variables as prewriting behavior, activity during pauses, rate of writing, and what writers do when they stop. Emig (1971) attracted significant attention with her case studies of eight twelfth-grade students nominated by their English department chairs. Mischel (1974) studied the processes of a single high school senior. Stallard (1974) studied the processes of fifteen "good" student writers (those fifteen who ranked highest in their senior class on the STEP Essay Writing Test) and fifteen randomly selected students. Pianko (1979) studied seventeen college freshmen, ten of whom had been placed in remedial classes and seven of whom had been placed in "traditional" classes. Perl (1979) studied five college students whose "writing samples . . . qualified them as unskilled writers" (p. 318). Matsuhashi (1981b) studied the pauses of four competent high school writers (three seniors and one junior) chosen on the basis of teacher recommendation, grades in English, and so forth. In nearly all cases, students were

1

selected according to some standard and were asked for their cooperation.

In general, these studies involved observation of the students while writing in a situation devised by the researcher. Some of the researchers made use of audiotaping or videotaping (Emig, Perl, Pianko, Matsuhashi) in addition to their personal observations. Some (Emig, Perl, Mischel) asked that students "compose aloud." In all cases the students reported to a special room or location in order to participate in the research. In some, students wrote alone in the presence of an observer. In the Pianko study, several students participating in the research were present in the room while one was videotaped. Stallard claims that students wrote individually in a special room but were not aware of being observed. However, students were generally aware of writing for a researcher in a special environment.

Prewriting

Several of the above-mentioned researchers define prewriting as the period of time between the moment the assignment is received and the time writing begins. Emig defines prewriting as "that part of the composing process that extends from the time a writer begins to perceive selectively certain features of his inner and/or outer environment with a view to writing about them—usually at the instigation of a stimulus—to the time when he first puts words or phrases on paper elucidating that perception" (1971, p. 39). Presenting partial data for one subject, Emig claims that "prewriting is a far longer process in self-sponsored writing" (p. 92) than in school-sponsored writing (i.e., writing assigned by teachers) and, further, that "reflexive writing has a far longer prewriting period" (p. 91) than does extensive writing.

Although Emig presents a relatively clear definition of prewriting, it is difficult to interpret the application of the definition. Consider, for example, the writing of Lynn, a student in one of Emig's studies. For Lynn's first piece of writing, Emig states that the prewriting period is three minutes, a time readily measured from stimulus to writing. For the second piece, however, Lynn receives a stimulus two weeks in advance of the session in which she will write. At that point, she readily thinks of three possible subjects (p. 46). Two weeks later, Lynn reveals that she had thought, that morning, of writing about a "two-foot-high cut-out of Snoopy" (p. 129), the subject she did write about. Emig does not indicate when the prewriting period begins—whether at the session in which the assignment was made, at whatever time Lynn first thought of Snoopy as a topic, or during the actual writing session when Lynn talked about possible topics. A similar problem exists in establishing the prewriting period for a poem written by Lynn. When the assignment to write a short story or a poem is given, Lynn immediately suggests writing on one of the topics she had considered previously, and she does. But because she does the writing at home, establishing the prewriting period precisely is impossible. Further, when "Lynn describes the background to the poem, she says she first began thinking about the matter [her relationship to a boy] in April, four months earlier." Emig concludes that "the subject of the boy has had a chance to ripen, to deepen" (p. 50). There is a sense in which all of Lynn's musings about her problems with boys contribute to the poem she writes. It may be that the composing process begins well before a stimulus to write is given.

Other researchers define prewriting in terms very similar to Emig's, but in most cases "the stimulus" or the assignment is presented at the beginning of the session in which the students are to write (as is the case with Emig's first assignment). Pianko (1979) reports that the prewriting time for her subjects was even less than that of Lynn's three minutes on her first piece (1.00 minute for remedial writers and 1.64 minutes for those in traditional classes). Stallard (1974) also found very brief prewriting times, but a much longer one (4.18 minutes) for good writers than for the average group (1.2 minutes). Perl (1979) studied five unskilled community college writers in four writing sessions and one interview session. She found that prewriting time over the first two sessions averaged only four minutes. The significance of these brief prewriting times will be examined later.

What happens in the prewriting period is more important than the length of time involved. Emig shows that her subjects considered various options for writing. For example, Lynn considered three or four possibilities and chose the one which she regarded as more manageable under the circumstances, thus eliminating rather systematically those ideas which appeared too difficult to handle.

Emig claims that during the prewriting period "most of the elements that will appear in the piece are present" (p. 83). Indeed, Lynn's comments on thinking about the Snoopy composition indicate that most of the elements were present in the morning when she first considered the possibility. The same may have been the case for her poem.

Mischel (1974) indicates that the single subject, Clarence, in each

session "took no more than two or three minutes in going over the
possibilities and deciding upon a subject. . . . Clarence seemed to
have a great store of small, manageable topics. It was not difficult
for Clarence to sift through and narrate his personal experiences,
and he easily wrote on such short subjects as 'learning to play the
guitar,' 'my first year of high school.' . . ." (p. 305). While none of
these subjects is inherently "short," Clarence treated them briefly
and expediently in a single 45-minute session. Mischel makes no
comment about what elements Clarence had in mind before writing,
but the ease with which the student found a topic and began to write
suggests that he had most of the elements in mind as did Emig's
subjects.

Stallard's good writers (1974) spent an average of a bit over four
minutes in prewriting, while his randomly selected writers averaged
only a bit over one minute. Stallard apparently did not question
students about which elements were present in their minds when they
began writing. They were asked whether or not they had considered
form and purpose. None, he said, had considered form, but a majority
of both groups reported considering purpose. Does such a response
suggest that major elements were present in their thinking and that
those elements governed the forms which their compositions took, in
the way that the elements of an actual experience govern the form
that writing about it takes?

Pianko (1979) claims that her subjects used their 1.26 minutes of
prewriting time deciding whether to write on the assigned topic or
on one of their own choice, and also deciding on a particular incident
or focus and a general approach. She claims that some students also
"thought about a few ideas they might consider in the writing." But
she claims that "none had a complete conception of what they were
going to write when they began writing" (p. 9). Perhaps the same
could be said of Emig's subjects, but we cannot be sure what Pianko
means by "complete conception."

Perl (1979), who gives a clearer account of thinking during the
prewriting period, indicates that her subjects made use of three
different strategies: (1) "rephrasing the topic until a particular word
or idea connected with the student's experience," thus providing an
"event" before writing began; (2) "turning the large conceptual issue
in the topic (e.g., equality) into two manageable pieces for writing . . ."; and (3) "initiating a string of associations to a word in the
topic and then developing one or more of the associations during the
writing" (p. 328). Perl claims that "when students planned in any of
these ways, they began to write with an articulated sense of where
they wanted their discourse to go" (p. 328). She reports, however,

that frequently students had no "secure sense of where they were heading" after reading the topic. They began writing, often by rephrasing the question in the topic which "seemed to enable them to plan what ought to come next" (p. 330).

Most of the studies cited so far indicate that writers use very little "prefiguring" (Emig's term) during the prewriting period. Despite the emphasis in textbooks on note-taking and outlining, very few student writers make use of those techniques. Emig's survey of sixteen professional writers (1971) indicates that only four of them developed elaborate outlines and those only for writing in the expository mode. The majority used a set of brief phrases or even single words to indicate direction—an informal outline only. Sixty percent of eighty respondents to a questionnaire sent to technical writers by McKee (1974) indicated that they used a similar kind of topic outline made up of words and phrases. Another 30 percent used a combination of sentences, words, and phrases. Only four writers used a formal sentence outline.

These surveys suggest that most professionals do some kind of informal outlining as "prefiguring." Most students in the various studies cited so far do not. It may be that the conditions imposed by the research lead to the writing of very short pieces which can be written without an outline of any kind, while professionals write much longer pieces. For example, McKee told his respondents to consider what they do in writing an essay of 300 words, a length which may be more conducive to the use of an informal outline. A number of the studies cited above asked students to write about personal experiences. Such experiences may have been so clearly structured in the writers' minds that no outline was necessary. Indeed, several studies found that their subjects had the major elements of what was to be written *in mind* when they began writing. Another possible reason for the dearth of outlining may be that writing about personal experience shares characteristics with the writing of poetry and fiction, for which Emig found very little evidence of elaborate outlining among the professional poets and novelists she queried. At any rate, the lack of prefiguring by students is difficult to interpret. It may be dependent on length, familiarity of the subject, mode of discourse, or some other factor. Further, evidence from other studies (e.g., Flower and Hayes 1980b, 1981b) indicates that lack of prefiguring does not necessarily reflect a lack of planning.

Rate of Composing

Some of the researchers report a steady, rapid rate of composing. Pianko (1979) reports a rate of a bit over nine words per minute for both her remedial and traditional groups (p. 13). Stallard (1974) reports just under nine words per minute for his "good writers" but almost 13.5 words per minute for his randomly selected writers. That comes to two typewritten pages an hour (500 words) for Pianko's writers, a bit less for Stallard's good writers, and a whopping three typewritten pages an hour for Stallard's randomly selected writers. (By comparison, Hemingway is said to have set himself a *daily* goal of about two typewritten pages.)

How can such rapid composing be explained? None of the researchers indicate that the students were simply writing whatever random phrases came to mind. All of the students apparently wrote connected, intelligible discourse. The evidence suggests that these writers did indeed begin with the major elements in mind or thought of them soon after rephrasing the topic question in writing. Further, it suggests that the writers also had some form in mind early in the writing, if not during the prewriting period. They appeared to write rapidly and generally to know when they had reached a conclusion. No researchers report that their subjects wrote indefinitely, were puzzled about where or when to stop, or wrote several different endings. They all appeared to write steadily to what they regarded as a stopping place.

Thus, although Stallard claims that when asked his subjects were unanimous in stating they had not considered form or organization, one suspects that form must have been a subconscious element in the writing—sometimes dictated by the content itself. For example, in writing about an "experience observed," as in Pianko's topic, writers selected "an experience," thereby automatically imposing time boundaries and conceiving a beginning, middle, and end—certainly aspects of form in Aristotle's terms. That Stallard's subjects said they did not think about form or organization does not mean that knowledge of form did not somehow enter into their composing. Indeed, one is tempted to surmise that knowledge of some combination of content and form provides plans which are very important in allowing the writer to spend so little time in prewriting and to write rapidly to a definite, connected ending.

The lack of any detailed analysis of what the students actually wrote in these studies makes speculation about the brief prewriting times and rapid rate of composing difficult. It is possible that many of the writers simply used what Bereiter and Scardamalia (1982) call a "what next" strategy, writing one sentence, asking "What next?," and writing another. Without any overriding plan, the text might resemble free association more than structured discourse. However, for Emig's students, that seems not to be the case. For example, Lynn's writing, which is quoted in the text, is carefully structured. Further, Emig's subjects who wrote what she calls the "Fifty Star Theme" (the traditional five-paragraph essay) apparently did more than simply write whatever came to mind.

The data from these various studies raise questions about the idea that writing is a process of discovery. (Graves and Murray 1980, for example, hold the process view.) Some writers have suggested that a writer never knows what will come out until it's on paper. What precisely such an assertion means is probably worth examining. At one extreme, does it mean that a writer has no notion of the content or form the writing will take? Or, at the other extreme, does it mean that the writer cannot predict the full graphemic representation of what is to be written? Or does "discovery" lie somewhere in between? The data in these studies suggest that most writers have a strong conception of what they will write before they begin writing or shortly after they rephrase the assigned topic. At the same time, it is clear from Emig's discussion of students' writing process as well as from Perl's careful analysis that writers do invent or "discover" the specific details, words, syntactic structures, and perhaps some larger structures as they write. Perl (1979, p.331) states the case cogently:

> Composing always involves some measure of both construction and discovery. Writers construct their discourse inasmuch as they begin with a sense of what they want to write. This sense, as it remains implicit, is not equivalent to the explicit form it gives rise to. Thus, a process of constructing meaning is required. . . . Constructing simultaneously affords discovery. Writers know more fully what they mean only after having written it.

Observations of Process in Classrooms

Some of the most fascinating reading among studies of the writing process comes from the work of Donald Graves and his colleagues, who, under a grant from the National Institute of Education, set out to observe the writing processes of sixteen youngsters in a single rural-urban school in New Hampshire. Their observations took place four days a week during two school years and involved two groups of children. Eight children were followed from the beginning of the first grade to the end of the second grade, and eight children were followed from the beginning of the third grade to the end of the fourth. Children were selected as being of low-, middle-, or high-level writing ability, though the criteria for selection do not appear in the final report (Graves 1981f). Researchers collected data by means of video and audio recordings; direct observation; interviews which occurred before, during, and after composing; and examination of manuscripts. The researchers observed individual children directly by pulling up a chair near a child, taking notes on what the child did, and asking the child questions during the composing. When the children conferred with peers or the teacher about the writing, the researchers were there making detailed notes of what occurred. These observations resulted in a rich mass of data, which has so far appeared in the following: several narrative reports of individual youngsters as they write; a few articles which generalize across the sample, reporting data for the full sample; and several pages of "findings" in the NIE report. Unfortunately, the findings have not yet been directly and systematically tied to reports of the data, so that a reader seriously interested in evaluating them must often assume that the narrative reports of individuals are typical of the entire sample.

In the NIE report, Graves (1981f) defines the writing process as "a series of operations leading to the solution of a problem. The process begins when the writer consciously or unconsciously starts a topic and is finished when the written piece is published" (p. 4). This definition seems useful in recognizing that certain aspects of composing may take place well before writing begins and in providing for the thinking that goes on as a prospective writer first encounters, contemplates, and evaluates experience. The process is further delineated as involving "significant" subprocesses of "topic selection, rehearsing, information access, spelling, handwriting, reading, organizing, editing, and revising," which "ingredients" are "much the same for six-year-olds as they are for more advanced ten-year-olds" (p. 6). Presumably, then, a writer may rehearse even prior to topic selection. (Rehearsal is defined as "the conscious or unconscious preparation writers make for what is to follow" [p. 5].) Indeed, perhaps rehearsal instigates topic selection.

Graves examined the development of young writers along four sequences: time and space, external to internal, egocentric to sociocentric, and explicit to implicit.

Time and Space

The first aspect of development, time and space, was examined as a combination of three factors: the page, the process, and information. Graves and his colleagues examined the behavior of young writers as they first approached the task of writing. These writers sequenced letters on a page in a variety of ways: horizontally, vertically, in "indiscriminate" ways, and even in "reverse" orders (p. 7). According to Graves, as young writers begin to see the need for communicating a message, they adopt more conventional left-to-right, top-to-bottom sequences and become concerned with the cosmetic appearance of their writing. The writers erase mistakes to preserve the appearance and hesitate to add material because there is no place to put it without marring the page. Later they learn that print is temporary, that parts can be crossed out, and that new material can be added to a draft which is in the process of changing. And, at least under the tutelage of the instructors observed by the researchers, the children come to view a "messy" paper in a positive way—as an indication of constructive changes which have been made.

When children begin to write, the "parameters of the composing are narrow and writing has a tenuous connection with preceding events" (Graves 1981f, p. 7). The decision to write is often spontaneous—a decision, perhaps, to write something very much like a caption to accompany a picture. Six-year-old Toni, for example, draws a picture of a flying owl and writes below it, "I LOVE SOPPROWL," and to the left of the picture, "AND I KISS hM" (Graves 1981b, p. 229). The composing is complete. As Graves points out, "process resembles spontaneous play" (1981f, p. 7). Later, the process broadens as children extend their rehearsals of what they might compose even when not writing and when they begin to take a single piece through several drafts, thus transcending "the constraints of the present draft" (Graves 1981f, p. 7).

In beginning writing, the information presented is fragmentary, often lacks context, and has tenuous logic. Children do not consider alternative pieces of information. Rather, they write what comes to mind, secure that it has meaning for them. As they develop as writers, children write lists of attributes, making several statements about a subject. Early in the first grade, Sarah writes the following book: "I like the sun. It feels good. The sun looks nice. It looks fun. I like the fun. It feels good" (Sowers 1979, p. 831). The strategy here is a prime example of what Bereiter and Scardamalia (1982) call the "what next" strategy. The child concentrates on one piece of information at a time, linking pieces in retrospect only. There is no planning ahead. As children advance, they begin to write simple stories more frequently (Sowers 1981). This form of writing demands more planning and selectivity of information than an "attribute" list. At even more advanced stages, talented writers confront the problem of selecting only those pieces of information which will advance the story (Calkins 1979 and 1981).

External to Internal

Graves and his colleagues say that when children begin to write much of their activity is external. Many children draw as a way of rehearsing what they will write and of inventing things to write. They often speak aloud as they write, tell other children what they are writing about, and even tell the teacher what their stories say before the teacher has a chance to read them. Nearly all first-graders speak aloud as they write. The speaking aloud appears to have several functions, including saying the message to hear what is to be written, sounding out a word to check spelling, rereading what has been written so that the next word can be added appropriately, making procedural comments about what to do next, and explaining what is going on to others. As children develop, they abandon speaking aloud while writing but try to show the qualities of speech in their texts by underlining, capitalizing, darkening words, and using some punctuation, particularly exclamation points (Graves 1981c).

Calkins, in her two studies of nine-year-old Andrea's revising (1979 and 1981), shows that as Andrea learns to revise, she writes out several alternative leads for a story, then chooses one. She later uses this strategy at points in the composition other than the lead. The strategy allows her to externalize her ideas, gain some distance, and choose. By the end of the year, however, Andrea no longer produces several possibilities on paper in order to choose the best. Rather, she appears to have internalized the process.

For most children the shift from external to internal is accompanied by a shift in problem-solving focus from spelling and handwriting to topic and information. As the processes become internalized, children produce "less overt sound off the page," select information more carefully so that it is less disjointed, and relate conversation with neighbors more closely to the task, e.g., "Do you think this is a good lead?" (Graves 1981f, p. 22).

Egocentric to Sociocentric

The third shift identified by Graves and his colleagues is that from egocentric to sociocentric. Early writing of children closely resembles play. Young writers write down what they want for themselves without fear of mistakes or failures. As Graves (1981c, p. 179) puts it, "Egocentricity has its own protective cloak. . . . Children are quite pleased with their own competence and they experiment fearlessly with the new medium given a small amount of encouragement." Although Graves and his colleagues do not explore the ramifications of this finding, it is very likely important to do so, particularly in light of the findings of Benjamin S. Bloom and his colleagues at the University of Chicago. Bloom studied the development of highly talented people in a variety of fields (e.g., pianists, tennis players, mathematicians, sculptors) who were regarded by colleagues as being at the top of their respective fields. For most of these highly successful world-class professionals, the earliest experiences with their chosen fields were playful ones, without the stringent rules and practice schedules they would eventually adopt. During this apparently crucial play experience, they developed their first commitments to the activities in which they would come to excel (Bloom and Sosniak 1981, and Bloom 1984: personal communication). The same may be true for writers—that positive play experiences in early attempts at writing are important to developing high-level commitment to the task.

During their play experiences, children learn many things: how to control their pencils or crayons, how to use the space on the paper, how to separate words which flow together in speech, and eventually the need to make their messages available to others. In the egocentric beginning, children are confident that what they write, regardless of its form, will be meaningful to others. If necessary, they can simply explain the context and the intended meaning to the audience around them. Calkins (1980a) gives the example of Annie, who writes the sentence, "We kept on losing Hilary," as follows: WEN KAPTON LOSING HELARE. Annie explains to the children around her as she reads, "Hilary is only one year old, so that's why we kept on losing her. We lost her under the table cloth" (p. 209). Eventually, children discover that they themselves and their teachers cannot decode their messages or that peers have many questions about what they write. Such discoveries make their writing less playful. They begin to see writing in a broader time-and-space framework. They begin to see a need for their products to communicate beyond the context of the immediate writing situation, in which they can explain what the text does not convey. In Calkins's words, "Children no longer write solely for themselves. Writing is no longer all-process, all-present, all-personal. Children are concerned with product and with audience" (1980a, p. 213). At the same time, adds Calkins, it is necessary for children to maintain or rediscover the "playful roots" of their writing so that they will be free to change what is written, to add new material, and to expunge the inadequate.

Explicit to Implicit

The fourth dimension of change identified by Graves and his colleagues describes children as moving from a stage in which they make their messages explicit in conversation to one in which the written message conveys the full meaning. At first the writing is short, with essential information and context missing. Letters and words are run together. Context, information, and specific meanings are supplied through drawing and talk. Gradually, the child's talking aloud to accompany the writing diminishes. In the transition stage, however, children exhibit a pattern of writing, holding a conversation, and continuing to write, "suggestive of switching in conversation" (Graves 1981f, p. 22). During this transition stage, children include information non-selectively, often regardless of its relevance to any desired effect. This is a stage of over-telling, of including details just because they are there though not relevant to the effect of the central narrative.

As the writing reaches the stage which the researchers call "implicit," children choose information more selectively. Nine-year-old Andrea, the subject of Calkins's two studies (1979 and 1981), struggles with the problem of transitions. The difficulty is in moving from one event or scene to another without putting down all the steps in between. She is quoted as saying, "It is hard to go from one exciting part to another, without putting down all the stuff that comes between them. I want to write with details, but to skip from one important detail to another" (1981, p. 257). Andrea is clearly in the third stage of development, in which she struggles with bringing coherence to selectivity for an effect.

Concepts of Writing

In addition to examining the afore-mentioned sequences, the Graves team has also begun an analysis of what Graves calls "concepts" related to the writing process. The analysis categorizes the conceptual content of statements made by youngsters in commenting on their own or others' writing. The twenty-eight categories of the analysis include standard, process, information (plus three related categories), experience, experience verification, audience (plus five related categories), neatness, mechanics, drawing, feelings, motivation, action (plus two related categories), organization, topic, language, and length (plus two related categories). The researchers claim that six months of work went into defining the categories and that "the stability of definitions was then checked on several inter-rater reliability assessments" (Graves 1981f, p. 14). Neither the methods of conducting these assessments nor their results are presented, however.

The "concepts" are defined as in the following examples: "*Deletion of information*: The speaker refers to deleting information. Example: 'I didn't think it was that important and it was just a waste of time having it there' " (Rule 1981a, p. 422). "*Feelings*: Speaker refers to emotion in the writing or the experience behind the writing. Examples: 'Now what I have to figure out is how with that same feeling I could bring my father to the sofa.' 'Were you unhappy when you didn't find your luggage?' " (Rule 1981a, p. 424). "*Topic*: Speaker refers to what the whole piece is *about*, defining message or intent and reference to titles [*sic*]. Examples: 'This whole thing is about my trip to Canada.' 'Is this about red squirrels?' " (Rule 1981a, p. 425). That statements like those in the examples above are designated as reflecting concepts is somewhat problematic. If a youngster says, "Is this about red squirrels?," can we assume she is using the concept of topic? Or if the child says, "This is my fifth draft" (Rule 1981a, p. 421), can we assume the child is using the concept of process? Needed are a rigorous definition of the term *concept*, an explanation of how each category is a concept, and an explanation of the sense in which the classified statements reflect concepts.

Apparently, such work is under way. Currently available materials present a "profile" of the *topic* concept. At level I, when asked what a piece of writing is about, the child simply tells the entire story. At level II, the child specifies the topic or title and then goes on to recite the story. At level III, the child specifies the title, and may tell the story, but indicates "the beginnings of options" in selecting information and uses the concept with one other writing concept. At level IV, the child "selects the topic with other writing concepts." In addition, there is evidence that the "topic evolves, twists and turns, as the child is responsive to the dictates of the information" (Graves 1981f, p. 19). The elaboration of this and other concepts, along with an analysis of their development, promises to be a very valuable part of this research.

While the work of the New Hampshire team has considerable value, it is not without problems. One of the most serious of these is the tendency to advance explanations of cause and effect without considering alternatives. The kinds of research undertaken by Graves and his colleagues preclude the use of the systematic controls necessary to establish causation firmly. Observational case studies, of course, permit the inference of causation, but because they tend to be based on single cases which may be idiosyncratic, such inferences should be advanced very cautiously. Throughout the research by Graves and his colleagues, for example, changes in writing behavior tend to be attributed to natural development. For example, in discussing four types of revisers, Calkins (1980b) claims that "transition revisers" (one of the types) "had developed higher standards for themselves" (p. 339), the implication being that higher standards are developed internally as the natural result of efforts to write. One result of such inferences is that the researchers recommend that instruction be largely reactive, allowing children to write when and what they wish, with minimal intervention from the teacher. But the inference that children developed higher standards for themselves and by themselves may be wrong. Without controls for instructional variables, there is no way to establish the causal relationship.

The two studies of Andrea (Calkins 1979 and 1981) illustrate this problem clearly. When the case study begins in September of the school year, Andrea is writing a book about a homesick Chinese girl named Lin-Su, adding three to four hundred words per day at the rate of 15.5 words per minute, a rate somewhat faster than Stallard's (1974) randomly chosen high school seniors. Although this seems an amazing feat for a nine-year-old, we learn nothing of the Lin-Su narrative except that it is picaresque. Calkins comments that "Andrea had mastered the mechanics of writing and now it was as if there were no challenges to be met or decisions to be made" (1981, p. 243). She comments that "the subject predetermined the words. . . . Andrea's words were not only predetermined. They were final. She did not revise. . . . Print was not revisable" (p. 244).

On October 3, Calkins says, the teacher interceded, asking the children to "bring something to school which you know and care about" and then setting up interviews in which children asked each other about what they had brought. Andrea, who had brought a bird's nest, explains that she had wanted to fly and "so began to study birds" (p. 245). Calkins reports that the teacher "hoped this time Andrea's title and first lines (lead) would be focused and show a point of view. But Andrea wrote 'The Bird's Nest,' and began a long winded explanation of how she found the nest under a tree (with no birds nearby), brought it to school, and remembered trying to fly when she was younger. . . . " (p. 245). Andrea's teacher asks, "Is your story really 'The Bird's Nest?' What's important about that nest?" (p. 245). When Andrea tries to erase the title, the teacher suggests crossing it out, but Andrea gets a clean sheet and begins again, this time eliminating the material about finding the nest. However, the teacher draws a line under what Andrea has written and says, "See if you can say it differently" (p. 246). Andrea writes two more leads for a total of three: (1) "Once when I was very little I got a hank to fly so I tryed jumping of things and tryed to float up and across I tryed and tryed til my father made me and my sister big cardboard butterfly wings." (2) "I always wanted to fly, but whenever I tried, I always fell Kaboom!" (3) "Kaboom! That hurt! Why can't I fly?" (p. 246). Andrea decides she likes the third one best, but says she doesn't know why.

For the next five months, Andrea goes through a process of writing out several leads before choosing a best one. She learns to apply the same strategy to developing internal parts of the composition. She also learns to cross out words and to produce several drafts. At this stage, Andrea writes more slowly. "She often averages only six to eight words a minute and writes only one hundred words in a sitting" (1979, pp. 575–576).

Calkins claims that over the five months the externalized process of writing out several possibilities and choosing one became internalized. But she presents only slight and unsystematic evidence that Andrea considered several alternative leads without writing them out. By March, Andrea is writing 15.5 words a minute once again, as in September (1981, p. 261). She produces leads such as the following "with very little revision" (1981b, p. 259):

Washing Caspar

"Come on, Caspar," I firmly say. The dog squats down. I drag her by the collar.

In March, Andrea is also quoted as saying, "It's easier for me to start a piece of writing now. I have a better idea for topics which will work, and the leads come to me easily" (1981, p. 259).

These changes from September to March are fascinating. Even more interesting is the question of why they take place. The two studies by Calkins imply that, with the exception of the teacher's first three intercessions (telling Andrea to work on the Lin-Su story at home, asking students to bring something to school they care about, and asking Andrea to rewrite her lead for the story on learning to fly), revision is self-learned. It follows also that learning revision is a matter of learning strategies for developing alternatives and making deliberate choices (see 1981, p. 258), and that making the appropriate choice develops from some innate sense in the child. This discussion of learning minimizes the role of the teacher. As Graves states, "Until a child writes or speaks, it is difficult for a teacher to know what to do because of the inherent idiosyncrasies or variabilities of each writer. . . ." Such variability *"demands* a waiting, responsive type of teaching" (Graves 1981f, p. 29).

But the evidence available is open to other interpretations and hypotheses. Early in September Andrea demonstrates her mastery of the mechanics of writing. The evidence suggests that she is precocious, cooperative, and eager to please. She clearly has worked hard on her story of Lin-Su, producing words at a rapid rate for several minutes a day over several days and on nineteen pages. Yet when the teacher says, "I'd like you to work on your book at home, and try some shorter pieces while you are at school" (Calkins 1979, p. 571), Andrea meekly puts the book in her desk and smiles. One can surmise that a clear message to Andrea is that her hard work on this book has not won the teacher's approval. Later the teacher makes it clear that Andrea's conventional introductions to her story of trying to fly will not gain approval. The teacher hints that she should throw the first introduction out because it is not "the story" and asks her to write a second introduction in a different way. Andrea writes two more and chooses the third as the best. The question is by what criteria does Andrea decide the third is the best? She says she doesn't know why. Is there a smile or a nod from the teacher— or from the omniscient observer? (The observer does, after all, ask questions as her subjects write, perhaps providing "contentless prompts," which Bereiter and Scardamalia [1982] have shown to affect output.) A bright, cooperative child like Andrea might very well notice even minor cues.

At the early stages in October, Andrea's stories exhibit the conventional schema of stories examined by Stein and Glenn (1979) and others. Her first lead for the piece on learning to fly introduces the protagonist, tells the protagonist's goal (to fly), and relates two attempts to do so. The second lead reiterates the goal and the attempt and supplies a consequence. The third lead reiterates the consequence elliptically ("Kaboom!") and moves to the final category of the story schema, the reaction, which expresses the character's emotional and cognitive responses to the consequence. On the basis of a number of studies, Stein and Trabasso (1982) state that "under most conditions, the story teller, listener, or reader constructs a representation of events corresponding to the real-time order of occurrence rather than to the narrative time sequence" (p. 221). Andrea's set of leads about learning to fly follows the real-time order predicted by the story schema. The same is true for the set of leads she produced for another piece titled "My Dog's Heartworm Pill." Indeed, Calkins herself comments that "each lead is deeper into the sequence of events in Andrea's story" (1981, p. 250).

When Andrea's teacher encourages her to write something other than a conventional lead and when she approves that something, she is encouraging Andrea to use a drastic inversion of a conventional form. Andrea begins to use the plot that Horace and the neoclassicists would have said begins *in medias res*, in the middle of things. The conventional story schema does not serve to gain the teacher's approval. And for several months Andrea has difficulty; her words come slowly and are far fewer at a given sitting. But by March her writing speed is back to 15.5 words a minute. And she produces *in medias res* leads which are, again, "written with very little revision."

Andrea appears to have learned a new form: one that begins in the middle of things with a statement of an attempt, a consequence, or a response. She has learned to work in the exposition about settings and goals later. This new form appears to supply the criteria she needs to guide her quickly to leads which will meet the teacher's approval. (Note that in March, the teacher does not draw a line and ask Andrea to "say it differently.") Perhaps the new criteria are the reason for Andrea's production of leads with very little revision. We are told that in March she makes revisions internally. One wonders if she considered alternatives internally in writing about Lin-Su back in September. The research is silent about what attempts were made to discover internal revisions in September.

Calkins's explanation of the change in Andrea's writing is that she has learned to revise and to select the best alternatives through some innate sense. An alternative explanation appears to be at least plausible: (1) Andrea, through a process akin to trial and error and teacher reinforcement, has learned a new form; (2) the new form carries with it rules or criteria (to begin with an attempt, consequence, or response and to work in exposition about goals, setting, and protagonist later) which guide Andrea's production of leads; and (3) that knowledge eliminates the need to write out alternatives. If this alternative hypothesis is correct, then we have a model of learning and teaching considerably different from that proposed by the New Hampshire project.

In the first place, the new hypothesis states that Andrea has learned a new form, one which is rule-governed and one which she learns to generate with as much ease as she had earlier generated the conventional time-sequence form. This is considerably different from generating a series of leads with no guiding principle or rules and then choosing the *best* one on the basis of unknown criteria. In the second place, the hypothesis suggests that changes in writing behavior do not simply come about because the child develops an inner potential but that the inner potential develops as the child has positive and negative experiences with the environment. It suggests, further, that instruction need not be merely reactive (Graves's "waiting, responsive type of teaching"). Perhaps instruction can actively seek to develop or promote experiences which will allow children to move from one level of competency to higher ones. Indeed, we might ask if more direct teaching would have helped Andrea develop more quickly. If the instructor knows the rules, or some rules, for generating a stronger lead, as we do in this case, why not help the child become privy to them? That is, why not develop materials or procedures to let children examine the difference between a normal temporal sequence and an inverted, *in medias res* sequence? Why not ask them to try beginning with an "attempt" or a "consequence," working in information about setting, protagonist, and goals later? A child less precocious than Andrea might very well become frustrated and discouraged with groping about for several months trying to find the kind of lead which might gain the teacher's approval.

While the case studies of Andrea, like other materials from the New Hampshire project, are valuable in illustrating what children can do as writers, their tendencies to generalize on the basis of single cases and to ignore alternative explanations can easily lead to inadequate recommendations for instruction. Anyone concerned about developing a theory of instruction is well advised to scrutinize such materials carefully, discriminating vigorously between reported data and interpretation.

Planning

Most of the studies cited above provide general information about behavior prior to and during writing. Let us turn now to a group of studies which focus on the nature of planning and its appearance in the composing process.

The reports cited above indicate not only that writers appear to have the major elements in mind when they begin writing, but that some kind of generalized plan may be important in allowing them to write connected discourse efficiently. A number of researchers who have focused on planning make this speculation explicit. Matsuhashi (1981), for example, suggests that her writers are able to move "confidently ahead to report an event" because they are "guided by a years-long familiarity with a script for narratives of personal experience." She finds, however, that when it comes to prose involving argument and generalization, the case is different. "John's difficulties with the structure of explanatory prose are only too apparent. It is possible that John lacks an internalized script for generalizing, a script like that of a confident professional" (p. 129). Hayes and Flower (1980) also suggest the presence, in long-term memory, of "generalized writing plans, perhaps in the form of a story grammar . . . or a formula such as the journalists' questions, 'who, what, where, when, why?' " (p. 12). Such abstract forms or schemata appear to be important in guiding discourse production. The writer who lacks them may have considerable difficulty. (The nature of some of these schemata will be examined in the next chapter.)

Matsuhashi's thoughtfully designed and carefully executed study of pause length during writing in three modes of discourse (1981) provides considerable insight into planning during the writing process. Assuming that pauses indicate decision making or planning of some kind, she sought to determine whether her subjects paused for longer periods of time at certain critical syntactic and discourse junctures. To determine this she videotaped the subjects as they wrote, using two cameras, one focused on the subject and the second suspended from the ceiling and focused on the writing pad. These cameras generated a split-screen image along with the elapsing time in minutes, seconds, and tenths of a second. The finished manuscripts were segmented by T-units which were categorized by their level of abstraction: superordinate, subordinate, and coordinate. (The average rater agreement across the three discourse types was 84 percent.) T-units were coded as paragraph openers if the writer indented or used a mark to indicate a new paragraph.

The most striking results were, first, that both generalizing and persuading discourse types involved significantly greater mean pause length than did reporting. These discourse types apparently involved more complex decision making, or perhaps simply *more* decision making. Second, pauses prior to T-units in generalizing (12.56 seconds) were greater than in persuading (10.87) and reporting (7.56). Third, abstraction levels of T-units had a significant effect on pause time. The mean pause length prior to superordinate T-units was 13.52 seconds, 10.87 prior to subordinate, and 8.54 prior to coordinate. Further, superordinate T-units in generalizing were preceded by greater mean pause lengths than in either persuading or reporting. Fourth, writers paused significantly longer before T-units which began paragraphs (15.10 seconds) than those which did not (9.00 seconds).

If planning or decision making is present during the course of composing, we would expect more planning to be required in explanatory or argumentative discourse than in straightforward reporting.

If so, the total pause time and the mean pause lengths preceding T-units should be greater. They are. We would also expect the pause lengths prior to more abstract statements to be greater. They are. Similarly, if an indentation indicates some chunk of discourse (a paragraph?), we would expect pause lengths which precede them to be greater. They are. In short, sentences which govern what is to follow (superordinate sentences and paragraph openers) require more planning time than those which simply add detail or extend parallel ideas.

Perhaps even more interesting, Matsuhashi produces evidence that writers may plan sentences as abstract structures, completing specific semantic constituents for some parts but designating only a general role for other parts. While more long pauses appear prior to sentences, they sometimes appear within sentences—often after a function word introducing a clause or phrase. In fact, "in the generalizing pieces . . . the mean length of pauses following the function word was longer than the mean for pauses before the function word" (p. 128). In other words, writers apparently plan a sentence in semantic chunks, put in the function word (e.g., *because*), and then plan the specific lexical content of the clause or phrase to follow. This evidence, taken together, suggests continuous movements from high-level planning to specific word choices and back to more abstract levels.

Research on planning by Linda S. Flower and John R. Hayes shares certain characteristics with the studies cited earlier in this chapter but differs from most in a number of important ways. First, it focuses on analysis of the writing processes of competent college student writers. Second, it assigns topics which apparently typically involve writing about fairly complex problems, given complex rhetorical situations: e.g., "Write about abortion pro and con for *Catholic Weekly*" (Hayes and Flower 1979, p. 86). Compare such topics to Emig's (1971) and Pianko's (1979) relatively open-ended assignments: e.g., "Describe a single incident which involves not more than three characters taken from an experience observed" (Pianko, p. 6). Pianko's topic allows for narrative (an "incident"), although it was apparently not intended to, or description of nearly any experience, real or fictional.

Hayes and Flower's research also differs from that of others in its treatment of the resulting protocols (descriptions of "the activities, ordered in time, which a subject engages in while performing a task" [Hayes and Flower 1980, p. 4]). Hayes and Flower segment their protocols, define categories for analysis of the segments, present results of that analysis, and report data on interrater agreement.

Although, at this writing, the analysis of only one protocol is available, its presentation indicates that fairly rigorous procedures have been used by Hayes and Flower in the analysis of their data. Presumably, procedures for and results of subsequent analysis will be released.

The findings claimed by Hayes and Flower have to do primarily with the strategies used by their subjects in what they identify as three major processes of composing: planning, translating, and reviewing. The planning process consists of three subprocesses: generating, organizing, and goal setting. As Hayes and Flower see it, "the function of the *planning* process is to take information from the task environment and from long-term memory and to use it to set goals and to establish a plan to guide production of a text that will meet those goals" (1980, p. 12). The translating process produces language, guided by the writer's memory. Reviewing consists of reading and editing subprocesses. Its function is to improve the quality of the text produced "by detecting and correcting weaknesses in the text" and "by evaluating the extent to which the text accomplished the writer's goals" (p. 12).

The subprocess of generating involves searching long-term memory for items of information relevant to the topic and the audience, that is, to the task environment. Hayes and Flower assume that the process begins with information presented in the task, that "each retrieved item is used as the new memory probe," and that "items are retrieved in associative chains" (p. 13). When writers in the Hayes and Flower sample generated irrelevant or nonuseful items, they initiated new memory probes after generating no more than three irrelevant items. This behavior by competent writers is an interesting contrast to the younger, not-so-competent writers studied by Graves and his colleagues and by Bereiter and Scardamalia. Younger writers not only generated information only marginally relevant but appeared to have used it. Learning to write efficiently may involve learning to identify nonuseful items during the generating phase, to disrupt nonuseful associative chains, and to initiate new probes. The problem, of course, lies in identifying irrelevant or nonuseful material appropriately. It is possible that an apparently irrelevant associative chain, left to follow its course, might eventually lead to valuable information or to a compelling argument or metaphor. On the other hand, irrelevant associative chains might extend the generating process to the point that writing never takes place. An interesting problem for researchers might involve the examination of criteria used by writers for ending associative chains and how those criteria shift depending on the task, the mode of writing, and so forth.

In another article, Flower and Hayes (1981b) identify several types of "plans" for generating ideas. Among these are procedural and content-specific plans. When a writer decides to jot things down as they occur or to make an outline, he or she has chosen a content-free plan for generating ideas. "The chief advantage of these procedural plans is that they provide a continuing structure for the composing process," one to which the writer can return "when ideas stop *flowing* or when writing takes an unproductive turn" (1981b, p. 43). Flower and Hayes contend further that procedural plans "enable a writer to establish priorities which keep her focused on high-level goals, such as developing a broad set of ideas" (p. 43). However, they state that most idea-generating plans are "content-specific, acting on the information immediately available to the writer" (p. 44). They identify four such plans:

1. *Pursuing an Interesting Feature* involves beginning with a word, idea, or event which is explored by turning to various generating techniques "such as searching memory, drawing inferences, reasoning from examples, or matching current evidence to prior knowledge" (p. 44).

2. *Thinking by Conflict* involves finding contradictions, objections, or questions about information available. The most frequent example of *Thinking by Conflict* was the listing of pros and cons which seemed "to offer writers a way to define their own ideas, or what *is* true, by attacking what seems inadequate or untrue" (p. 44).

3. *Saying What I Really Mean* is a plan used by writers "when they want to abstract or reduce a complex body of information to its essential features" (p. 44).

4. Finally, *Finding a Focus* is an idea-generating plan "which writers rarely carried out successfully" (p. 45).

Flower and Hayes admit to problems in knowing "what *focus* actually meant to the writers [they] studied," although "it seemed to be equated at times with the fully articulated thesis statement" which textbooks recommend be formulated before writing (p. 45). Analysis of the protocols, however, indicates that writers in Hayes and Flower's sample "typically *don't* start with a thesis or well-focused body of ideas. Instead they start with a body of knowledge and set of goals, and they *create* their focus by such complex actions as drawing inferences, creating relationships, or abstracting large bodies of knowledge down to *what I really mean*" (p. 45). The common failure to develop a focus appears to be associated with a belief that a focus might be found by searching memory or a book. In such cases writers short-circuit the processes or strategies which enable them to create a focus.

Although the strategies by which writers "create" their focus remain to be defined more clearly, these findings are important. As Flower and Hayes point out, "creating a focus is one of the crucial acts that can bridge the gap between generating ideas and turning them into a paper" (1981b, p. 45). Traditional writing instruction has largely ignored the strategies used to operate on a body of knowledge, focusing instead on such matters as correctness, syntax, and form, with little effect.

The second subprocess of planning is organizing. The function of organizing is to select the most useful materials generated and to organize them into a writing plan. Hayes and Flower claim that organizing involves the use of five "elementary operators" (1980, p. 14). These include identifying a possible first or last topic, ordering with respect to a previously noted topic, and identifying a category in which "to classify a large number of topics generated separately under the same heading" (p. 15). Why these "operators" are called elementary is not altogether clear. If the decisions are not made randomly and arbitrarily, we must assume that they are made in light of some range of criteria for at least some writers. Even deciding to place a topic first or last must involve the application of some criteria. And unless a category is to be conceived whimsically, some criteria must be involved to include some topics while excluding others—even if the category is not rigorously defined. If such criteria are used, then the operators would appear to be relatively complex, rather than elementary, and worthy of more detailed description and analysis. Nonetheless, the presence of these operators in the processes of competent writers is valuable information not available from other studies of competent writers. Further research focusing on the precise nature and use of these operators is likely to be quite valuable not only for understanding the composing process but for instruction.

Hayes and Flower's third subprocess of planning is goal setting. During the generating process, some of the materials retrieved are not topics but "criteria by which to judge the text" (1980, p. 15). Hayes and Flower do not examine the nature and extent of these criteria in detail. However, they appear to be related to specialized plans which Flower and Hayes call "forming for use" (1981b). Plans in this category address the questions of what to use and how to use it. Such plans may include selecting information to be used, decisions about how to use it for particular effects, and even how to set it up on the page.

The presence of criteria in the early stages of the writing process (in generating, organizing, and goal setting) is significant. As will be seen in the meta-analysis section of this review, students who have been actively involved in the use of specific criteria and/or questions to judge texts of their own or others write compositions of significantly higher quality than those who have not. One wonders if criteria present early in the process serve not simply to "judge the text" but to guide its generation. We need studies of the criteria available to writers of different ages and backgrounds for various modes of discourse as well as studies of how those criteria function. Such studies should have significant value.

Flower and Hayes (1981b) claim that the plans used for producing a paper are of two major types: reader-based and product-based. They discovered that while "this distinction was rarely clear-cut, . . . writers did show a strong tendency to prefer either reader-based or product-based plans" (p. 48). Writers who use reader-based plans spend much time "considering who their audience is and developing plans or strategies based on what the reader might assume, object to, or need to know" (p. 48). Such planning is not completed after an initial audience analysis but rather is a recurring concern such that writers might generate a few sentences and evaluate them for the effect they are likely to have on readers.

Flower and Hayes present a portion of a single protocol which they claim shows, first, that the concern for the reader's response operates "at a number of levels, governing not only the ideas and focus of the paper, but decisions about word choice and the general impression the prose creates"; and second, that "planning for a reader is an intimate part of idea generation, one which leads the writer to go back and explore the topic itself" (p. 49). In the fraction of the protocol presented, we see a writer attempting to deal with his predictions about objections his audience might have to this subject. He generates two divergent plans for dealing with possible objections—plans which reflect quite different views of the subject and which are likely to entail quite different presentations of the subject matter. These findings have important ramifications for theories of the composing process and for instruction. For example, does concern for the reader actually "govern" the ideas and focus of a paper as well as decisions about word choice and general impression? Or does it, in conjunction with other concerns, simply influence those facets of composing? Does it result in divergent plans for all writers or only some? What is its range of influence or governance across a sample of writers? These and related questions should provide a rewarding focus for further research.

Flower and Hayes designate product-based plans as a second major type, "based on the features of the final written product" and occurring "when the composing process is governed by a concern for the form of the finished product" (1981b, p. 49). Flower and Hayes claim that when their subjects thought in terms of the final product and attempted to produce parts of that product, "the result appeared to interfere with the normal generating process that occurs during writing" (p. 51). Some of their subjects believed they should generate a manuscript in "a correctly ordered, closely reasoned manner, as well as in well-formed and elaborately linked sentences." When they could do this, they said their ideas were flowing. When they could not, they "became frustrated, and frequently abandoned the results of apparently fruitful but unstructured brainstorming. They appeared not to recognize the potential value of what they had said" (p. 51). According to Flower and Hayes, a product-based plan may tell a writer to begin with an overview which integrates ideas and presents a direction for the whole essay, a task "which is often extremely difficult . . . at the beginning" (p. 51). The process of generating information and relating and examining it appears to be disrupted by focusing on form too early. The process is unlikely to be as straightforward and direct as that implied by product-based plans. "A writer's conclusions, his main ideas, even his focus, are often the product of searching, trial and error, and inference. . . . The composing process of a typical writer appears to be erratic, jumping from high-level plans down to fragments of a sentence destined for the final draft, and up again to a series of inferences leading to the creation of a new category or major issue" (p. 51).

Not only do writers move from high-level plans to specific sentences and back up to high-level plans, but they usually entertain and keep track of a variety of plans. They sometimes switch from one plan to another and sometimes bring two plans together so that, for example, the two may generate ideas and produce a paper. Sometimes, however, plans come into conflict. This often happens when writers engage in the normally erratic generation of ideas and suddenly confront the rules for paper production, which demand a clearly stated, carefully supported thesis, with ideas moving logically from one to another. In this case, writers often find themselves befuddled, unable to proceed further until they can resolve the conflict.

It is important to note that Flower and Hayes indicate that some writers appear to have *no* plans: "For some, writing is simply a printout of the writer's mental state at the moment of composition" (1981b, p. 49). In another article, Hayes and Flower discuss a writer whom they call "Freewrite." "As he composed, Freewrite's top-level plan appeared to be 'Write whatever comes to mind.' . . . His protocol showed almost no discernable attention given to audience or purpose, and the final product, as you might guess, read rather like a transcript of free association, even though the writer considered it quite adequate" (1980, p. 46).

The Hayes and Flower model of composing (1980) includes two major processes in addition to planning: translating and reviewing. Translating, they say, involves retrieving some part of a plan, retrieving propositions (memory structures composed of concepts, relations, and/or attributes, "perhaps complex networks or images, for which the writer may or may not have names"), and expressing those propositions in language (p. 15).

The function of reviewing is to improve the quality of the written text. It consists of two subprocesses: reading and editing. The purpose of editing is "to detect and correct violations in writing conventions and inaccuracies of meaning and to evaluate materials with respect to the writing goals" (Hayes and Flower 1980, p. 16). Such a statement implies the writer's possession of criteria by which to make appropriate evaluations, although Hayes and Flower do not examine them in detail. While the editing process appears simple, it probably is not. Sometimes it must invoke the whole composing process recursively, as when a writer (1) discovers a gap that may lead to a reader's failure to comprehend, (2) generates ideas, and (3) composes whatever is needed to fill the gap. Hayes and Flower assume that editing is "triggered automatically . . . and that it will interrupt any other ongoing process" (p. 18). Although editing is called a subprocess of reviewing, Hayes and Flower "distinguish between *reviewing* and *editing* as two distinct modes of behavior" (p. 18). That is, while editing is triggered automatically, the writer decides to devote a period of time to systematic review and improvement of the text.

Hayes and Flower test this model (consisting of the three major processes of planning, translating, and reviewing) against fourteen pages of a single thinking-aloud protocol. They regard this protocol as unambiguous because of the writer's habit of commenting regularly on what he was doing and how. The writer's "metacomments" enabled them to divide the protocol into three major sections: generating, organizing, and translating. They assumed (1) that generating would be occasionally interrupted by editing, (2) that organizing would be interrupted by generating and editing, and (3) that translating would be interrupted by generating and editing. They assumed further that the major sections indicated by statements of what the writer says he is doing would be dominated by content statements of that type.

To test this hypothesis, the researchers analyzed the first 458 "segments" of the protocol (about half of it). They classified the segments as metacomments, content statements, or interjections. They then reclassified segments which they had agreed were content statements according to which writing process had given rise to the segment—generating, organizing, translating, or editing. They agreed in attributing writing processes to 84.7 percent of the 170 content segments. They agreed generally that most content statements in the first (generating) section could be attributed to generating; in the second section, to organizing; and in the third section, to translating. They further agreed that about 10 to 15 percent of the segments in each section represented editing and that about 10 to 15 percent of the segments in both the second and third sections could be attributed to generating.

Because their knowledge of labels assigned to the sections may have influenced their judgments, the authors selected forty-one content statements, typed them on cards, and presented them to two independent judges for classification without the benefit of the whole protocol's context. While the judges had difficulty in agreeing with one author on editing statements, they both agreed with the authors on about 86 percent of the generating, organizing, and translating statements. While a more rigorous test would examine more than one protocol and make more extensive use of independent judges, the results of this analysis are more convincing than the narratives so common among many case studies.

The research by Hayes and Flower is most valuable in suggesting the recursive nature of the writing process, in identifying various subprocesses and types of plans, and in demonstrating the tendency for these plans and processes to interact with each other. Their research demands that we view composing as involving a variety of plans and subprocesses which are brought to bear throughout the composing process as they are needed. The evidence they present clearly contradicts textbook approaches, which often suggest arbitrary, discrete steps in composing: formulate a thesis, develop an outline, and write. Hayes and Flower also firmly establish the importance of generating ideas prior to formulating a thesis or outlining and even during the translating and editing processes. Further, while the one formally examined protocol does proceed in stages, the research indicates clearly that even those stages are not discrete, that they are frequently interrupted by other processes. Finally, the evidence provided clearly indicates the importance of plans and implies the importance of criteria in the process. These are ideas which other studies of the writing process deal with only superficially, if at all.

A number of studies which examine the composing processes of weak writers, often in comparison to those of better writers, confirm the importance of planning. Perhaps the most universal finding across these studies is that weaker writers spend very little time in planning while skilled writers devote more time both to planning—during rewriting periods and in pauses during the writing—and to examining what they have written (Atwell 1981, M. E. Henderson 1980, Metzger 1977, Perl 1979, Pianko 1979, Sawkins 1971, Stallard 1974, Warters 1979). Further, these studies found that more skilled writers pay greater attention to matters of content and organization, while weaker writers have a tendency to be preoccupied with mechanics, particularly spelling (Bechtel 1979, Metzger 1977, Pianko 1979, Sawkins 1971, Stiles 1977). The skilled writer's concern with ideas is illustrated by Atlas's study (1979) of ten expert writers and ten college freshmen who were all given outlines of ideas to be used. Eight of the experts introduced new ideas of their own, but only two freshmen did. At the same time, weak writers (often called Basic Writers) do have strategies for beginning and for keeping them going (Perl 1979). Sweeder's (1981) six remedial writers used thirteen "heuristics" during prewriting, including "letting their subconscious work," and several "heuristics" during writing. Stiles (1977), who studied eight college freshmen "seriously deficient in basic writing skills," found that while her subjects were preoccupied with mechanics, they had a "secondary concern" for organization and arrangement. In short, weaker writers are not totally devoid of concern for content and organization.

The obvious question is one of cause and effect. Are good writers good because they plan more and are more concerned with content, organization, and even audience? Or do good writers devote more attention and energy to planning and content because they have mastered mechanics and need not be preoccupied by such matters? The parallel instructional question is whether to emphasize content and planning or to emphasize mechanics. Most of the researchers cited in this section appear to favor an emphasis engaging students in the processes of planning. But they present no research which tests such an hypothesis. We must turn to experimental treatment studies in a later section for that.

Production Factors

Although the observational and thinking-aloud-while-writing studies have provided information about the behavior of writers while writing under conditions imposed by researchers and have revealed the presence of complex subcomponents of the writing process (plans, goals, rereading, and so forth), they have revealed little about the particular cognitive operations involved. For example, what processes are involved in switching from generating prose to editing? How do writers decide whether or not to use the information they generate? How do writers produce clauses or larger chunks of discourse related to the surrounding chunks? How much advance planning of specific verbal representations are writers capable of? What are the various strategies writers use to meet the constraints imposed by the writing? Answers to such questions may be essential to an understanding of the composing process.

Carl Bereiter and Marlene Scardamalia and their associates have undertaken a series of investigations related to such questions and have produced some promising hypotheses. They have been particularly interested in production factors, those processes used in carrying out decisions arrived at through the interplay of goals, plans, strategies, and so forth. Production factors include such subprocesses as searching memory, recognizing relevant information, and evaluating verbal statements. According to Bereiter and Scardamalia (1982), researchers cannot observe and analyze these subprocesses directly. Rather, they must infer them through experimental studies. Bereiter and Scardamalia point out that naturalistic observations of children writing in classrooms or elsewhere fail to provide adequate information for such inference and that experimental interventions which permit inferences about covert mental events are necessary for developing theory about the subprocesses (in this case, production factors) which are not open to direct observation.

Conversation and Composition

Bereiter and Scardamalia begin by assuming (after Rumelhart 1980, Stein and Glenn 1979, and others) that discourse production is directed by schemata that specify kinds of things incorporated in the discourse and their relationships. By the time children reach school age, they have learned the schemata common to conversation, which are relatively "open" ones characterized by taking turns in responding to what partners say. Written composition is largely solitary or "closed." That is, the production of written discourse does not depend

upon "social inputs," although those may come after the production
of some text and prior to revision. Some oral discourse schemata are
more open than others. Oral argumentation is largely open, depending
heavily on what partners say, while oral narrative is largely closed.
Thus, while responses of partners may affect the degree of elaboration, they are likely to have little effect on the structure and major
components of a narrative. Oral narratives are simply extended turns
in conversation, consent for which must be gained by following specifiable rules.

Bereiter and Scardamalia hypothesize that children will more
readily adapt relatively closed oral schemata, such as narratives, to
writing than they will the relatively open oral schemata, such as
argument. If that is true, then children are likely to produce more
text in narrative than in argument either orally or in writing. Hidi
and Hildyard (1983) compared children's stories and opinion essays
at grades 3 and 5 for both oral and written modes. Combined data
from the two grades indicate that oral narratives averaged 127 words
compared to 54 words for oral opinion essays. Written narratives
averaged 93 words, while written opinion essays averaged 32 words.
Bereiter and Scardamalia suggest that such lengths are just about
what one would expect in a conversational "turn" for statements of
opinion and for an extended turn necessary to produce a short
narrative. The idea is an interesting one worthy of further
investigation.

Bereiter and Scardamalia (1982) are cognizant that expressive
writing sometimes produces longer texts, particularly when the experiences or issues are of great personal concern to the children. They
argue that such production does at times occur in conversation and
that it is not guided by a "closed discourse schema." One sign of the
latter is that the discourse ends not when a schema has been instan-
tiated but when the speaker or writer dissipates the need to produce.
This suggests that expressive writing tends to be additive and
associative, with elements piling up in whatever order they might
occur, rather than being ordered in accordance to some overriding
pattern. Researchers might profitably bring this hypothesis to bear
in examining the writing of students in programs which advocate
free writing.

Bereiter and Scardamalia produce additional evidence that in learning to write children appear to be adapting conversational strategies
to writing. In one study (Scardamalia and Bereiter 1979), children
in grades 4 and 6 were asked to compose under three conditions:
writing, speaking freely into a tape recorder, and composing aloud

while a researcher wrote the words at the child's own rate of writing (slow dictation). Speaking into a recorder produced the most words, and writing the fewest words. When composing under the third condition, the children produced significantly more words than in writing but fewer than in speaking freely. Interestingly, however, in the slow dictation mode the children produced 80 percent of their stories in a single burst, much like a conversational turn. They then waited for the researcher to catch up, reconstructed what they had already said, and added a bit more.

Memory Search

Another study (Scardamalia, Bereiter, and Goelman 1982) used similar subjects and the same three production modes, but this time researchers asked students to say as much as possible at the beginning and used predetermined "contentless prompts" (urgings to go on) when children stopped. The amount that children produced up to the first prompt tripled in comparison to the previous study. When urged to say even more, they produced about as much as they had before the prompt in the free speaking and writing conditions. In slow dictation the output increased, but less, so that the total was about equivalent to that in the writing condition. When the contentless prompts appeared to have exhausted what children had to say, specific questioning about the topics indicated that they had far more information on the topic than they had previously revealed. Urging the children to add more exhausted what they could retrieve from memory without help. But more specific prompts of a kind they would be likely to have in conversation helped them to produce more. In short, children appear to have much more content available than they use in composing by themselves. Conversational situations help them recall it.

In a study by Scardamalia, Bereiter, and Woodruff (1980) investigators interviewed fourth- and sixth-grade children to find topics about which the children knew a lot or a little. The children found this a difficult task and could not think of three familiar and three unfamiliar topics. The researchers had to settle for fewer topics. However, the children were able to provide significantly more content for their familiar topics than for the unfamiliar (1) when asked to plan what they would say in their compositions and (2) when asked to itemize content which was generally relevant to the topic but which they would *not include*. However, when the researchers examined the children's actual compositions according to six different dimensions, they found *no* differences between those on familiar topics and those on unfamiliar topics. An interesting finding in this study was that the children, particularly fourth-graders, found it difficult to imagine thinking of a relevant item of content and then *not* using it. Generally, if they thought of an item, they wanted to use it. When they did decide to exclude an item, it was on the grounds of triviality (e.g., dogs have claws) or distastefulness (e.g., high-sticking in hockey) rather than on some higher-level rhetorical basis.

Bereiter and Scardamalia (1982) take all these findings to be evidence of the difficulty young writers have in memory searches, a problem they do not confront in conversation because the partner's responses stimulate appropriate "memory nodes" from which they produce their own remarks. Bereiter and Scardamalia and their colleagues conducted various experiments to determine ways to help students learn to initiate and maintain their own memory searches. One of these (Anderson, Bereiter, and Smart 1980) is based on what they call the "common practice" in schools of using prewriting activities before students write on a topic, activities which activate memory nodes relevant to the topic. The research procedure, developed by Anderson, asked children to list all the single words that might be relevant to a topic before they wrote. This training consisted of twelve sessions, each an hour long, in which sixth-graders practiced with a variety of "expository and opinion" topics. In writing post-instruction compositions, the experimental group students wrote twice as much as did control group students. The experimental group also used three times as many uncommon words (assumed to be an indication of more varied content) and in opinion essays wrote an average of three arguments on an issue as compared to two for control students. Interestingly, however, there were no differences in quality between compositions written by children in the two groups. Bereiter and Scardamalia (1982) speculate that had their subjects been looking for content according to "some criterion of persuasiveness," their improved ability to recall information would have resulted in higher quality as well. Children in Bereiter and Scardamalia's studies appear to find content first and *then* work it into their texts. Indeed, they find it difficult to exclude content they have recalled.

At any rate, Bereiter and Scardamalia conclude from these studies that children must and can learn to do memory searches in connection with their composing. The same seems to be true for older students as well. Some studies, examined later in this report, indicate that discussion of a topic can affect the quality and length of writing. Discussions of particular assignments may very well serve as memory searches.

Use of Criteria

It may be, however, that students need to learn not only to conduct a memory search but to learn that writing requires it. If children are adapting conversational schemata to writing, they must also need to learn that the requirements for writing are different from those of speaking—that simply writing down the information they might provide in a conversational turn is inadequate. If that is the case, then youngsters must learn criteria which are appropriate to writing. Seeing the need to provide more content might activate memory searches of the kind Bereiter and Scardamalia suggest.

At least two studies with elementary students appear to confirm this hypothesis. Sager (1973b) and Coleman (1982) used scales to teach children to judge their own and other's writing. An important part of the instruction in the Sager study asked sixth-graders to generate additional information to fill out stories which were only the length of a conversational turn, providing a bare-bones narrative of events. Each narrative was accompanied by a set of questions which directed the students to make needed revisions (which generally required adding detail). In doing so, the children apparently were learning general requirements of written schemata, as well as particular criteria for selecting content. In both studies, the children in experimental groups made large gains in quality over the control students. It is possible, then, that when children learn that the requirements of written prose are different from those of conversation, they activate more extensive memory searches. In addition, when children learn criteria, they may seek content which results in higher-quality writing.

Planning and Nonplanning

A number of studies have attended to the planning strategies of writers. Flower and Hayes (1981b), in particular, have found abundant evidence of planning in their thinking-aloud protocols from relatively skilled adult writers. Bereiter and Scardamalia (1982), however, claim that the thinking-aloud protocols of young children provide little evidence of planning. Scardamalia (1981) adumbrates four levels of tasks and abilities in expository writing based on the number of "units of task information" which the writer can integrate. At the lowest level, when children are presented with information in a 2 × 2 matrix and asked to write about it, they write about the information available from each cell, one at a time, without integrating the information with that from any other cell. At the highest level, they

integrate the information from all four cells. However, such sophisticated integration is rare, even among older students. Similarly,
analysis of opinion essays written on the question "Should students
be able to choose what things they study in school?" reveals similar
levels. Scardamalia found only one of eighty grade-eight compositions
which coordinated assertions and reasons on both sides of the argument. Far more common were compositions in which, as Scardamalia
puts it, "staying on the topic was an achievement in itself" (p. 88).
The following composition exemplifies the difficulty (p. 89):

> Yes, I think we should. Because some subjects are hard like
> math. And because the teachers give us a page a day. I think the
> subjects that we should have is Reading. Because in social studies
> and science we have to write up notes and do experiments. I
> think *math* is the *worst* subject. And I *hate spelling* to. Because
> in spelling there are so many words to write and they are all
> *hard*. And they waste my time. I think school shouldn't be to
> 3:45. I think it should be to *2:00*. I think school is *too long*.

The youngster begins with an assertion about the subject, followed
by a list of "reasons" which are really statements of personal preferences and brief explanations which are only tangentially related.
By the middle of the piece the child has lost track of the original
topic altogether. It appears that the topic triggered one idea (math
is hard), which triggered another (the teachers give a page a day),
and so on. By the end of the composition, the writer is simply stating
a list of pet peeves.

The piece is a clear example of what Bereiter and Scardamalia
(1982) call the "what next" strategy. The planning, if it can be called
that, is similar to that in conversation, in which a statement from a
partner triggers what one will say next. In the composition above,
each statement triggers another, but there is little attention to the
whole. The strategy is additive and associative (Bereiter 1980), with
the child thinking of one item, then another, and another, without
what rhetoricians call a "controlling purpose."

In a study by Scardamalia and Bracewell (1979) children were
asked to write opinion essays using sentence openers drawn from a
prepared list, each opener implying a different structural element
(e.g., "for example," "another reason"). After each sentence the
students were asked to choose two sentence openers and to devise
alternative "next" sentences in the text. Most children in grades 4
through 8 wrote sentences using essentially the same content item,
despite the divergent force of the sentence openers. The same tendency
is apparent in the composition quoted above, in which most of the

"because" clauses do not provide actual reasons but simply statements about what the writer likes and dislikes. The children think of a content item to use, then use it regardless of the strength of its association with what has preceded it.

In a study by Hildyard and Hidi (1980), third- and fifth-grade children were given two conflicting statements appropriate for narrative and asked to write a story about them, while another group was given two conflicting statements appropriate for argument. The statements were presented in two conditions, consecutive and separated. In the consecutive condition, children were asked to use the statements as the beginning of their writing. In the separated condition, children were asked to use the first statement as the beginning and the second as the end. Only 13 percent of the children reconciled the conflicting argumentative assertions satisfactorily, while 45 percent reconciled the narrative conflicts. For narrative, however, the greatest proportion of the successful resolutions were in the separated condition. When children received the statements consecutively, they developed a story on the basis of one and ignored the other. With the argumentative assertions, 59 percent of the children reasserted or discussed one or both statements but made no attempt to reconcile the conflict between the statements. These findings also indicate the dominance of the "what next" strategy as opposed to what Bereiter and Scardamalia call the "means-end" strategy, which is apparent when a writer attempts to pull together the various elements of a discourse in order to meet particular substantive and rhetorical ends.

Higher-Level Planning and Mechanics

Scardamalia, Bereiter, and Goelman (1982) examine additional production factors. They begin with the question of what the relationship is between language planned and held in memory for production and its actual production, then move to the question of how the mechanics of text production affect other, presumably higher-level, processes. Such questions are important in light of suggestions by researchers such as Pianko (1979) and Shaughnessy (1977a) that some writers become so enmeshed in the mechanics of the textual representation that the quality of their writing is affected. That belief underlies the fairly common advice to get ideas down on paper without worrying about correctness until a later draft. But it also underlies the common curricular assumptions that young writers should learn all the mechanics of writing early so that the mechanical skills will become automatic, thus putting as little demand on the memory and other capacities as possible. The underlying premise is that the writer has a limited amount of attention to devote to the various tasks of writing and that when one subtask demands a lot of attention, another will lose attention. Scardamalia, Bereiter, and Goelman point out that, in this simple form, the generalization leaves much to be desired. The important question is what processes interfere with others and when.

To answer this question, Bereiter, Fine, and Gartshore (1979) asked fourth- and sixth-graders to write on any subject of their choice in the presence of an experimenter who would place a screen over the writing paper at irregular intervals, thus halting the writing process. When the screen covered their writing, the children were asked to say aloud whatever words they had in mind. (At the same time, they had been urged not to make up new material.) When the screen was removed, the children were to continue writing. This simple experiment provides some basic insights into the composing process. At each interruption, the subject said aloud, or "forecasted," the words he or she supposedly intended to write. The number of words per forecast averaged five to six and tended to go to the end of a "clause," suggesting that writers plan their verbal representations in clause-length chunks which are held in short-term memory while the mechanical process of graphic representation takes place. The sequence of these chunks appears to be guided by certain abstract decisions already made which enable succeeding chunks to be coherent but without having been prefabricated to any great extent.

The children in this forecasting study, for the most part, proceeded to write what they had forecast, with variations amounting to only one word in every two forecasts. Of the variations, 17 percent involved the loss of a word from forecast to written text, about half of which losses resulted in syntactic elipses (e.g., "on the way to school" became "on the to school"). The remainder of the losses cut down on the richness of detail. These data suggest that in one out of ten sentences written by children, there is some short-term memory loss affecting the content of their writing (not a very appreciable influence when one considers that some words may have been intentionally eliminated). About 5 percent of the variations involved the addition of single words. Seventy-eight percent of the variations amounted to stylistic changes from the forecast, variations which did not affect the meaning of the words. There was a tendency for these variations to be in the direction of more formal written English. The addition of words and the stylistic changes suggest the presence of an editorial process which occurs *after* the planning of the basic syntactic unit and during the time the structure is committed to writing.

If an editorial monitor comes into play after the generation of a syntactic unit as the unit is being written, or perhaps even after the unit has once been written, we can better understand why instructional programs emphasizing grammar have had so little impact on student writing: knowledge gained from such instruction comes into play only after higher-level decisions have been made. As one might suspect, knowledge of "correct forms" for punctuation and usage cannot contribute to higher-level planning.

Gould and his colleagues have conducted a series of experiments which shed some light on the effect which the mechanical processes of handwriting or typing, as opposed to dictating or speaking, have on such factors as speed, quantity, and quality of production. For example, in one study Gould and Boies (1978b) asked sixteen college graduates to compose eight "routine" business letters and eight "complex" letters on topics such as capital punishment. Production of words per minute was about twice as great in dictating and speaking as in writing. "This speed advantage had a small effect on total composition time, however, because generation time was only a small fraction of total composition time" (p. 1146). Planning (with no generation) took about two-thirds of total composing time regardless of the "output modality." Also, despite the difference in speed, there were no differences in quality across methods. Gould (1980) indicates further that these results strongly suggest that "good authors are good authors regardless of composition method, and poor authors are poor authors" (p. 109). He concludes "that output modality in composition is not the limiting factor" (p. 108).

While it is understandable that this may be true for educated adults, it may not be true for youngsters. In a study already cited by Scardamalia and Bereiter (1979) children in grades 4 and 6 were asked to compose using what Gould might call three "output modalities"—writing, dictation, and slow dictation. The children produced the fewest words in writing, about 86 percent more in slow dictation and 163 percent more in normal dictation. In summarizing the study, Scardamalia, Bereiter, and Goelman (1982) state that "there was a tendency, significant at the .06 level, for rating on quality of presentation to differ in the order writing (lowest), normal dictation, slow dictation (highest)." They conclude that "low-level requirements of writing do make a difference to children" (p. 186), e.g., children write more slowly than they speak. At the same time, quality ratings indicate that the mechanical demands have only a weak effect on higher-level components of the writing process.

Similar results were obtained in a second study (Scardamalia,

Bereiter, and Goelman 1982) using a similar methodology. In this study, however, using the same three production methods, the researchers assigned three opinion essay (argumentative) topics, made use of contentless cues to urge the children to write more when they stopped writing, and then scored the resulting compositions for quality and for coherence of premises, reasons, and elaborations. The compositions written to the point before any cues were given were scored. In addition, the whole compositions, which included what was written before and after cues, were scored as a separate batch of writings. Quality ratings of the uncued portions of the compositions did not show any significant differences by mode of production. However, quality ratings for the whole compositions (cued plus uncued portions) showed a significant difference in favor of the written mode at both fourth- and sixth-grade levels ($p < .02$). In addition, the analysis of coherence indicated that sixth-grade children composed their longest coherent strings in the written mode. Why the written mode should be superior on these two measures is not immediately apparent.

To attempt an explanation of these and other findings, Scardamalia, Bereiter, and Goelman (1982) posit a model of possible mental representations of text at different levels of abstraction, extending from "whole text plan" at the most abstract to "graphical representation" at the most concrete. In between lie what they call "text segment plan," "gist unit," "sentence plan," and "verbatim representation." While admitting the speculative nature of this model, they believe it helps explain some of their findings. For example, why did the written opinion essays have higher quality and coherence ratings when both uncued and cued portions were judged than did the dictated versions? The researchers suggest that the answer may be that writing is *not* controlled by an ever-present plan but requires continual reconstruction of higher levels of text representation. That is, when a writer concentrates attention on the graphemic representation, he or she loses track of higher-level representations and must periodically reconstruct them. Thus, the youngsters who had been writing (as opposed to dictating slowly or speaking normally) had also been periodically reconstructing representations of the whole text. When the writers were asked to write more, they reconstructed what they had been writing and added to it in a logical way, thus achieving higher quality and coherence ratings. Those who had been dictating, on the other hand, had not had to reconstruct a representation of the whole text; they had not had to pause after concentrating on a graphemic representation to say, "Let's see, where was I?" They had simply gone on in a generally associative way, thus failing to continue coherent strings of statements when asked to say more. Instead, they said something generally but not directly associated with what they had been saying. On the other hand, it may simply be that the writers had the advantage of glancing at their written texts to help them recall exactly what they had said. The authors suggest that for rereading to be effective, the child must be oriented toward reconstruction at higher levels of representation. It is interesting to note that sixth-graders were able to produce significantly longer coherent strings after cueing than were fourth-graders, which suggests that older children can reconstruct text representations more readily than younger children. This is perhaps a developmental aspect of learning to write.

Might such evidence suggest that learning to write helps children think in a fundamentally different way? Might learning to write coherently help people learn strategies for keeping many ideas in mind (by reconstructing text plans) for the purposes of drawing conclusions, extrapolating, evaluating, and so forth? Or is it the other way around? Do people have to learn strategies for reconstructing text plans (to bring many ideas to mind) in order to write more coherently?

Though the researchers do not say so, their model may help to explain the "what next" strategy, which appears to involve movement among only the very lowest levels of the model. Further, the finding that most variations between spoken forecasts and what is actually written are stylistic suggests that whatever is stored in the "output buffer" waiting to be translated into script is not fully formed language but some sort of general semantic and syntactic plans. The evidence of other researchers (e.g., Flower and Hayes 1981b, Matsuhashi 1981 and 1982), alluded to earlier, suggests strongly that more abstract levels of text representation exist, at least for more mature writers.

A more complete understanding of these levels of text representation and the micro-processes and routines by which writers switch from one to another might well provide insight into what is necessary for successful instruction. On the other hand, what we know about the effects of instruction may provide some insight into or support for some such model of text production.

Revision as Process

Revision has been a subject of concern in a variety of studies. Some examine the kinds, numbers, and quality of revisions made by writers.

Others attempt to determine the cognitive processes involved in revision.

Production studies tend to present information on the number and kinds of revisions students make. Emig (1971), who discusses "reformulation" as including editing and revising, claims that for the pieces written for her study, the students "engage in no reformulating" (p. 97). Stallard's (1974) good writers made an average of slightly over twelve revisions per paper, while his randomly selected writers made an average of only a bit over four per composition, a difference significant at $p < .01$. Interestingly, however, of 248 revisions made by all of Stallard's writers, only six were at the level of "paragraph changes (any change in the organization of the sentences of a paragraph . . .)" (p. 213). Stallard does not even include a category for higher-level changes, those involving changes in mode of discourse, point-of-view, subject matter, or what Emig calls "vantage." Pianko (1979) claims that her writers made no "major reformulations" (p. 10); indeed, her data indicate an average of only about two to four revisions per paper, with no significant difference between the number made by her "traditional" writers and those by remedial writers. Perl's (1979) five writers averaged nearly thirty-one revisions per paper, but few if any of those revisions appear to be beyond the level of individual words and sentences. At least, Perl presents no higher-level categories of revision, such as organization, point-of-view, and so forth.

A study by the National Assessment of Educational Progress (1977b) asked nine-year-olds, thirteen-year-olds, and seventeen-year-olds to write a composition and then asked some of them (unfortunately, different percentages at each grade level) to revise using a pen. While this technique ignores revisions which may have been made in pencil, it does provide useful information. The types of revisions classified are cosmetic, mechanical, grammatical, continuational, informational, stylistic, transitional, organizational, and holistic. The three categories of revisions used least by those *asked* to revise were cosmetic (used by 8 to 20.6 percent of revisers), organizational (used by 7.7 to 22.7 percent), and holistic (used by 5.3 to 11 percent). All other categories were used by considerably larger percentages of revisers, e.g., mechanical by 39 to 62.8 percent, informational by 42.3 to 61 percent, and stylistic by 43 to 67.5 percent. Although comparing categories across studies is problematic, one is tempted to guess that the NAEP study found more revision behavior than did Emig, Stallard, Pianko, or Perl, perhaps because of the built-in prompting to revise.

In a carefully designed study, one which focused on the nature, extent, and quality of revisions made by 100 randomly selected seniors in high school, Bridwell (1980b) found that, given the opportunity, students make fairly extensive revisions. For this experiment students were asked to write about a place they knew well. They were encouraged to write down facts they wished to remember on specially provided sheets which they could bring to class with them. When they wrote, they were asked to write so that another twelfth-grader reading it would "be able to recognize the thing or place if he or she ever got the chance to see it for real" (p. 202). Students were allowed three days for the writing. On the first they were given "fact sheets" on which to record any ideas they might have for the essay. On the second day they wrote a draft in blue ink, crossing out the material they changed as they wrote. In the third session they considered their first drafts, made revisions on them if they wished, and wrote a final draft, this time using black ink.

Bridwell developed a classification system composed of seven levels (surface, lexical, phrase, clause, sentence, multi-sentence, and text), each with four to ten subcategories. She trained raters in using the system and tested it, finding a reliability of 84.43 percent agreement for levels and 79.61 percent for subcategories. Over half of the disagreements were the result of omissions by a rater. This thorough and careful attention to the content analysis of protocols, like Matsuhashi's, is exemplary among studies of the composing process.

Overall, the students in Bridwell's study made 6,129 revisions, or on the average about 61 per student, almost half of which were made on the first draft. Although the design of the study suggests revisions, it demands nothing more than recopying. The large number of revisions, then, stands in marked contrast to Emig's conclusion that "students do not voluntarily revise school-sponsored writing" (1971, p. 93).

Most of the revisions (56 percent) were at the surface or lexical levels. Surface-level revisions included changes in mechanics such as spelling, punctuation, and capitalization. Word-level changes included the addition, deletion, or substitution of single words. Another 18 percent of the revisions had to do with changes at the phrase level. The remaining 19.61 percent of the revisions were at the sentence level or the multi-sentence level, which includes additions, deletions, and reordering of two or more consecutive sentences. However, no revisions appeared at the text level. The relative proportions of these revisions might be expected. The high incidence of lower-level revisions does not necessarily demonstrate a preoccupation with the trivial; there are simply many more opportunities for revision at those levels than at the sentence or multi-sentence levels.

A consistent finding throughout the afore-mentioned studies is that the subjects, most of them elementary, high school, or college students, made very few, if any, revisions at the text level—a level which, in Bridwell's system, includes changes in the function category, in the audience, or in the overall content of the essay. Perhaps such revisions go on during a prewriting phase when a writer considers a variety of topics. Or perhaps a topic which a writer generated tends to come complete with a vantage point, a way of presenting it, and so forth. That seems to be the case for Emig's subject Lynn, who enters "the material once and once only, from a given vantage; and she does not go outside again to consider another route in" (1971, p. 56).

Given the circumstances which the subjects of these studies confronted, it is not at all surprising that they did not consider another route in to solving the problems presented to them. The researcher has asked a favor of these young people—to write one or more compositions in a limited time period and under rather awkward circumstances, e.g., having to think aloud while composing, being aware of the audio or video recorder, perhaps seeing the researcher scribbling busily on a notepad. Nearly every study of the composing process examined for this review asked the young people to write one composition at a time and to write in a limited time period—not to develop plans for several approaches to the same topic. Should we be surprised when the subjects do what the researchers have requested?

On the other hand, perhaps the results would be different if the circumstances were different or if the writers were more mature. That appears to be the case in an example presented by Flower and Hayes (1981b). They quote parts of a protocol from Roger, a competent college writer, who is planning aloud a paper on Boethius. Roger is doing this for a course, not simply for a researcher. He develops one plan to write about how he himself became convinced of the logic in *The Consolations of Philosophy*. (He had previously had objections to Boethius's logic.) However, Roger rejects that plan when he realizes it will produce a narrative—not the kind of thesis and support paper his professor will expect. His second plan is to develop the paper as a dialogue between himself and Boethius, a plan which allows for thesis, antithesis, analysis, and support—a true text-level revision— but one that occurs during prewriting.

Sommers (1979) studied the revising strategies of eight college freshmen and seven experienced adult writers. She examined four levels of change (word, phrase, sentence, and thema) and four operations (deletion, substitution, addition, and reordering). The greatest number of revisions by college students were at the word and phrase levels, with lexical deletions and substitutions being the most frequent operations. For the adult writers, however, the concentration of revisions was at the sentence level and addition was the major operation. Their revisions were distributed over all levels, suggesting that experienced writers perceive more alternatives than do younger writers.

Calkins (1980b) studied the revision strategies of seventeen third-graders. She classified them into four groups which she views as developmental: random drafting, refining, transition, and interacting. The classifications were made on the basis of the children's behavior in making revisions of their own work as well as their behavior in revising a composition prepared by the researcher. The two children classified as random drafters wrote successive drafts of their own work without examining their earlier drafts. Their changes appeared to be arbitrary or accidental. When asked to insert new information into a researcher-prepared composition, they did not bother to reread the existing draft to insert the information appropriately; they simply added it at the end, where it did not belong. The eight refiners made cosmetic and lexical changes, sometimes adding sentences but retaining most of their first drafts, so that between 75 and 99 percent of final drafts made over a year were identical to the first drafts. When asked to insert new information into the prepared text, these children did examine the existing draft, apparently struggling with where to insert the new information. But then "most of them ignored the first draft completely and wrote the new one without looking back" (p. 337). Transition children (four of them) appeared to have developed higher standards for themselves than refiners, so that draft after draft did not satisfy them. But instead of revising, they began new drafts, retaining relatively little of the first draft. When asked to insert new information, they all reread the original piece and found a way to insert the information appropriately. The three interacting revisers are described as allowing what they had written to prompt new ideas and as using symbols (carets, stars, arrows, and so forth) to indicate where additional information or reformulated sentences should go. When asked to insert new information into a prepared composition, they all asked if they could change other parts and they used their symbols to indicate where new details and reformulations should go. Calkins claims that these revisers cycled between "assessing and discovering" (p. 341), that is, between examining critically what they had written and thinking of new ideas and reformulations.

Unfortunately, Calkins does not present the data on specific types or levels of revisions and operations. It would be interesting to compare the types of revisions made by the "interacting" revisers with those made by Bridwell's or Sommers's writers.

Addition appears as a major strategy in a number of studies. Kamler (1980) presents five drafts of a composition by seven-year-old Jill. The composition grows over two weeks from 57 words to 169, with 88 of the words coming in the third draft following a 30-minute individual conference with the teacher. In this piece of writing, all revisions are additions. Bridwell found that the second drafts written by her high school seniors were significantly longer than their first drafts. Sommers found that the major operation used by her adult experienced writers was addition. Presumably, the reexamination of a manuscript prompts associations or memory searches which result in additions to the original.

A major question about revision is the extent to which it results in a better piece of writing. At least one study (Hansen 1978) has concluded that revision is a waste of time. Bracewell, Scardamalia, and Bereiter (1978) found evidence that revisions by eighth-graders made their compositions worse. Bridwell's evaluation of first and second drafts by high school seniors (with raters trained to use the Diederich scale) revealed significantly higher scores ($p < .0001$) for second drafts on both general merit and mechanics. This is persuasive evidence that at least older students can use revision successfully.

These studies, taken together, provide considerable information about the kinds of revisions students make and about the effects of those revisions. We know that younger children and even many college students confine their revisions to the cosmetic, lexical, and clause or phrase levels. We know that text-level changes, at least after some written text is produced, appear to be practically nonexistent, at least among the students involved in these studies. We know that addition is a prominent revision strategy, used by Calkins's third-grade interacting revisers, Bridwell's seniors, and Sommers's skilled writers. But for the most part, these studies indicate little about the cognitive processes involved in revising.

On the other hand, several writers have proposed models of the cognitive processes. Nold (1981) describes revising as a process which involves evaluating the text against the writer's planning as related to the intended audience, persona, meaning, and semantic layout.

"The complexity of the review subprocess is bounded by the depth of the planning subprocess that has preceded it: writers cannot match the text against their intentions if they have not elaborated upon them" (p. 73). Nold points out the corollary that texts which involve minimal planning, such as free writing exercises, "can be reviewed only against criteria that are constant across all [written] communication tasks" (p. 73), e.g., spelling and legibility. Revision, of course, involves more than evaluation. The successful reviser must note deficiencies *and* "think of a good way to change them" (p. 74).

Hayes and Flower (1980) present a similar model with one major difference. They discriminate between editing and reviewing. Editing is defined as a subprocess which "is triggered automatically and may occur in brief episodes interrupting other processes." Reviewing, on the other hand, involves a decision "to devote a period of time to systematic examination and improvement of the text" (p. 18) which has already been produced. Both, however, rely on matching text to intentions *and* producing a change when needed.

Bracewell, Scardamalia, and Bereiter (1978) asked children to write a composition on the topic "Should children choose the subjects they study in school?" They then asked the children to revise their compositions. The researchers found no change in quality as a result of revision for fourth-graders. For eighth-graders, revision made the compositions worse.

Scardamalia and Bereiter (1983) point out that the usual explanation for children's inability to revise is that their egocentricity does not allow them to stand apart from their texts as critics. (See, for example, Graves 1981f and Flower 1979.) To test this explanation, Bracewell, Bereiter, and Scardamalia (1979) manipulated psychological distance. They asked children to revise one set of texts the children had written immediately and another set after a week had elapsed. They also asked the children to revise someone else's text. When children revised a text written by someone else, they identified more spelling errors, but there were no other differences. Scardamalia and Bereiter (1983) argue that the failure to revise might lie with problems in the production system. Their model posits an "executive routine" for switching from generating text to assessment. However, because writing is so complex, making that switch from generating to criticism may be very difficult for children. The model also posits the following sequence of tasks: comparison of or evaluation of the actual text against the intended text, diagnosis of the problem underlying the perceived mismatch, making a decision about whether or not to change the plan, choosing a tactic to solve the problem, and generating a change in the text. A writer's failure to revise might stem from a failure in any one of these tasks.

Scardamalia and Bereiter's experiment, designed to check the model's "fit to reality," involved training ninety children (thirty each in grades 4, 6, and 8) to use a routine intended to facilitate their evaluation of each sentence written. The children were given eleven cards, each with a possible evaluation, e.g., "People may not understand what I mean here," "This is a useful sentence." After choosing an evaluation, the children were asked to select one of six tactical choices, also presented on individual cards, e.g., "I'd better change the wording," "I think I'll leave it this way." Finally, the children revised or let their sentences stand, according to the tactic chosen.

After brief training, children managed this rather elaborate task without difficulty. Only six of the ninety consistently chose a favorable evaluation enabling them to bypass revision. Four of those were in the fourth grade. The key assumption underlying the experiment is that the routine would reduce the burden of executive control and allow the evaluative, tactical, and language production abilities of the children to appear.

Two raters assessed individual changes one at a time without knowing which version was the original. Although the raters had little agreement on scores assigned to individual changes, they did agree in assigning positive scores to them. However, when revised versions and originals were evaluated for overall quality, there were no differences. Thus, while individual sentence revisions were judged better, they did not add up to differences in overall quality. Scardamalia and Bereiter attribute this paradox to the fact that the revisions focused almost exclusively on small units of language, seldom using such evaluative phrases as "I'm getting away from the main point" which indicate attention to the whole.

Follow-up interviews indicated that the children unanimously believed that the routine had helped them evaluate their own writing in detail, a procedure which they had found difficult and in which they did not normally engage.

The researchers also compared the evaluative statements selected by children for each of their sentences to those chosen by a semi-professional writer for the same sentences. They found that most evaluations by students in all grades were either the same as those made by the writer or judged to be appropriate. Fewer than 10 percent of the children in any grade *ever* chose an evaluation judged to be altogether inappropriate.

However, the case for the students' explanations of their evaluations was different. When the explanations of the same semiprofessional writer were compared to those made by the children, the researchers found little agreement. Indeed, many children could not explain their evaluations. Further, when the choices of remedial tactics were judged as to high or low probability for alleviating the problem, the percentage of high-probability choices increased from 50 percent at grade 4 to 74 percent at grade 8. Finally, the high frequency of revisions judged to be for the worse indicates the difficulty children had in making their fairly accurate evaluations pay off.

Scardamalia and Bereiter (1983) present a detailed analysis of thirty instances in which children chose to strike a whole sentence and rewrite it. In eleven of these, the children copied nearly the entire sentence, changing only a single word or some minor detail. In five, they wrote totally different sentences. In the remaining eleven, they attempted to revise the existing sentence. In successful attempts, the children retained the basic sentence plan, adding or deleting to clarify or breaking the sentence into simpler parts. When they made a new attempt to express the same idea, their changes were unsuccessful. Most children in the sample avoided reformulating sentences altogether. When they did, they were successful only when they retained the original sentence plan. There was no instance, in the work of ninety children, of scrapping a sentence and using a different strategy to make the same point.

Elsewhere, Bereiter and Scardamalia (1982) argue that recasting an existing sentence provides its own special difficulties because of the salience of the existing sentence stimulus. Bracewell (1980) and Bracewell and Scardamalia (1979) presented children with information in sentence form or matrix form and asked them to produce sentences of a particular form using the given information. The task was significantly more difficult when the information was presented in sentences. In another series of studies by Scardamalia and Baird (1980), children were given a set of sentences and asked to produce more interesting ones. When there were no restrictions, the prevailing strategy was to shift topic, thus avoiding any need to deal with the original sentence. When required to retain the topic, children added details, a strategy which again avoided changing the original sentence plan. Only when the researchers required children to retain the topic and restricted their use of words not appearing in the original did children begin to change sentence plans. While sixth-graders met with some success, fourth-graders could not do it.

Thus, even though children have a wealth of syntactic resources (Hunt 1965a, Loban 1976), they have considerable difficulty bringing those resources to bear when faced with a competing stimulus. Bereiter and Scardamalia (1982) argue that children need to gain conscious access to their syntactic resources, perhaps through an executive procedure which would allow them to search systematically for alternative syntactic structures. But systematic search and retrieval from memory appears to depend upon the appropriate information being coded and recalled as types of alternatives. Thus, a skilled reviser may test a variety of clause structures or phrases in a given verbal environment before finding a solution to a particular syntactic problem. Bereiter and Scardamalia argue that sentence combining procedures developed and tested by Mellon (1969) and O'Hare (1973) may provide such a repertoire of alternatives.

Egocentricity, then, appears to be an inadequate explanation of children's failures to revise, at least for children of nine and older. The executive routine discussed above seems to enable children to evaluate their writing systematically and appropriately. That routine, along with the choices of evaluations and tactics, results in improvements at the sentence level. Still, children's failures in choosing appropriate tactics and in successfully executing them appear to diminish overall differences in quality and indicate the relative difficulty of these aspects of revision. In addition, the difficulty children have in reformulating sentences presents a particular problem which appears to have little to do with egocentrism.

The experiments discussed above provide some reasonably solid evidence that some model comparable to those suggested by Hayes and Flower (1980), Nold (1981), or Scardamalia and Bereiter (1983) does have some basis in reality. However, as the cliché goes, further research is needed. How, for example, do we account for changes in intentions? In the instance of the subject Roger's protocol (Flower and Hayes 1981b), we see Roger develop a plan for a narrative of his coming to accept the logic of Boethius's *The Consolations of Philosophy*. But he rejects that plan because he realizes that his audience (the professor) expects a thesis/support paper—not a narrative. His intentions change when he considers his audience, the source of a set of criteria which, when applied to his narrative plan, leads to its rejection. Do text-level revisions occur because of such conflicting sets of criteria? If so, perhaps that explains why they occur so infrequently. Perhaps novice writers simply do not have various sets of criteria to think about.

How do we account for the common revision strategy of addition? In Hayes and Flower (1980) one writer is described as realizing that the audience may not understand a sentence. Subsequently, he develops a nine-sentence explanation which was not in the first draft. Does this illustrate a change of intentions or a lapse in the application of criteria which the writer intended from the beginning? Does the complexity of the composing process make it impossible to bear all criteria in mind during initial composing? Do some additions come about because reviewing triggers associations which were not triggered in the earlier writing? Are some additions prompted because the writer consciously uses certain criteria, perhaps in the form of questions, e.g., "What examples would support this idea?" The fact that such questions exist is in no sense an indictment of the research and theory available. On the contrary, what has been done already allows the specification of new hypotheses and suggests methods for testing them. It holds great promise.

Writing Apprehension—with Michael W. Smith

For years researchers in speech and communications have studied the phenomenon of communication apprehension. It is well known that many individuals are afraid to speak in front of an audience. Relatively recently some of these researchers wanted to test whether individuals experience a general anxiety about writing. Daly and Miller, pioneers in the research, coined the term "writing apprehension" to describe that general anxiety. They developed and tested a twenty-six-item questionnaire to measure writing apprehension (1975b). This instrument enabled researchers to consider the source of writing apprehension and the way it affects student writing.

The vast majority of the published research in this area is of a similar type. Researchers administer the Daly-Miller test to the population they wish to study, often college composition students. Then they identify those students who score one standard deviation or more above the mean as "high apprehensives" and those students who score one standard deviation or more below the mean as "low apprehensives." The researchers then examine apprehension scores with other measures of student behavior or attitude. And these results have been quite interesting. Daly (1978) found significant differences between the performance of high apprehensives and low apprehensives on a variety of measures of writing aptitude. Faigley, Daly, and Witte (1981) corroborated these findings using a different set of standardized measures. Daly (1977) also found a significant difference in the rating of message quality between high apprehensives and low apprehensives. With this research in mind, Daly and his associates theorize that apprehensive writers avoid writing tasks and instruction and as a result do not get sufficient practice to develop as writers.

The research has considered more specifically the nature of the differences between high and low apprehensives. For example, Daly and Miller (1975a) report that high apprehensives use significantly less intense language than low apprehensives. Daly (1977) found that high apprehensives use fewer words and make fewer statements than low apprehensives. He found further that they use fewer words, fewer commas, and less delimiting punctuation than low apprehensives do.

Given these findings, it is not at all surprising that high apprehensives are less successful than low apprehensives. Daly and Miller (1975c) found that high apprehensives reported less writing success in the past and expected less in the future. The researchers argue that these attitudes are likely to become self-fulfilling. Of course, teachers' expectations also play a critical role in the success of students. Daly (1979) found that teachers believe that students exhibiting the behavior characteristic of high apprehensives were less likely to do well than low apprehensives. In fact, Seiler, Garrison, and Bookar (1978) found significant correlation between writing apprehension and course grades. The research also suggests a noncognitive dimension to writing apprehension. Daly and Shamo (1978) found that low apprehensives are attracted to majors that they perceive involve writing, while high apprehensives avoid such majors.

Though this research is thought-provoking and useful, some difficulties remain. First, it is impossible to argue from the research that writing apprehension causes the behaviors that the research notes. In fact, M. A. Rose (1981) suggests that fundamentally competent writers might be stymied not by emotional difficulties but by cognitive limitations and writing problems such as rigid composing rules. Daly himself recognized that more research is needed to establish whether high apprehension causes or is caused by writing difficulties. He believes that there is an interaction between the two factors.

The entire body of research is not clear about the cause of apprehension. Daly notes that a history of aversive responses might cause apprehension. T. P. Hogan (1980) notes that student interest in writing begins to fall off rapidly in the upper elementary grades. Of course, this is when the typically detailed criticism of writing generally appears. However, a definite cause has not been established. And without a clear understanding of the cause of the problem, solutions are much more difficult to provide.

In the same manner, research has not clearly established the best approach to take to reduce writing apprehension. Fox (1980) studied a treatment consisting of exercises designed to reduce anxiety about language. He made extensive use of evaluation. His treatment also featured lessons that made objectives clear and included practice in these objectives in order to increase the likelihood for success and to reduce anxiety over evaluation. Fox's treatment was especially effective in reducing apprehension for selected high apprehensives. However, he did not find an increase in writing ability for his students. Since all students are not apprehensive, an instructional program cannot be justified, though, simply on the basis of reducing apprehension.

M. O. Thompson (1979), however, does claim an increase in writing ability and a decrease in writing apprehension with her "language study" approach. She suggests that teachers can reduce the mystery surrounding language if the student gains knowledge of symbols, patterns and sentences, the history and formation of language, and standard English and dialects. She contends that teachers can reduce the mysteries surrounding the writing process if the student gains more knowledge of invention, connections between thinking and writing, and conventional order. However, lack of controls makes her findings more suggestive than compelling. Clearly, much more study is needed in this area.

A final problem with the writing apprehension research is that the Daly-Miller apprehension test cannot identify a "danger level" above which teachers should be concerned with their students' apprehension. Some apprehension may be necessary if writers are to take sufficient care with their work to produce excellent pieces. Until teachers can administer the test and have a better sense of what the scores suggest, it is unlikely that many will make full use of the construct. On the other hand, the instrument can be useful to teachers. And further research is likely to make it even more useful.

Limitations of Research on Process

Research on the composing process has provided many valuable insights, hypotheses, and points of departure for further research. At the same time, however, it is not without problems. In the case studies, there are tendencies to present data selectively rather than systematically, to interpret data without a consistent analysis, to infer cause-and-effect relationships without adequate warrant, and to ignore the range of possible effects which the presence of researchers might have on results.

Presentation of Data

While some studies present data systematically across all subjects, several do not. Emig (1971), for example, concentrates heavily on a single case, providing only limited information on seven others. Yet, presumably, her conclusions about such matters as prewriting time are based on all eight cases. When data are not presented systematically across all cases, it is impossible to determine the source of contradictions—whether the sample, the available data, the design, or the researcher. Emig, for example, claims that in reflexive writing "starting, stopping, and contemplating the product are more discernible moments; and reformulations occur more frequently . . . " than in extensive writing (p. 91). Perl's (1979) findings appear to be in direct contradiction: "On the reflexive topics, sentences were often written in groups, with fewer rereadings and only minimal time intervals separating the creation of one sentence from another" (p. 324). Such differences cannot be explained without more systematic information.

While the research of Graves and his colleagues purports to be exhaustive, no data on the frequency of writing episodes, observed and unobserved, or on the spread of observations across children of various ability levels are presented. Reading through the eighteen "research" articles presented in the 1981 report to the National Institute of Education suggests that some subjects have received considerably more attention than others (at least in the written reports). Three girls (Andrea, Sarah, and Toni) receive major attention in four to six articles each. Other subjects appear only once or twice in passing. Did the researchers observe some children more than others? If so, what is the rationale for such discrimination once the sample is selected? Or does the imbalance reflect selectivity in reporting the data? If so, what is the rationale for that selectivity and how does it affect our view of the data?

While narrative reporting on one child at a time makes for interesting reading, it provides little evidence that any one case is typical. For example, we are told that "writing is a highly external event in the beginning. Children draw, [*sic*] and talk with other children. They need to see and hear what they mean. Later external language becomes inner language" (Graves 1981f, p. 8). The data supporting the contention that children draw and talk with other children before or as they write is scattered among various narrative reports of beginning writers at work. But one might well ask what proportion of children draw before or as they write? Some data supporting the final sentence of the above quotation comes from a case study of the subject Andrea. Calkins (1981) documents Andrea's writing out a number of possibilities for leads early in the year. Eventually, however, Andrea appears to abandon the practice of writing out alternatives, but (we are told) sifts through them mentally instead. Is Andrea's progression true for all children? Perhaps it is, but evidence for the whole sample is not presented.

Content Analysis

The nonexperimental studies of process collect bodies of data (narrative observations, thinking-aloud protocols, interviews, etc.) and attempt to draw generalizations about them. When data are collected in these ways, it is important to explain the range of data collected and explain which data support or do not support the researcher's inferences. An important generalization in Matsuhashi's (1981) study, for example, has to do with pause time before superordinate T-units. In order to establish that, she classified all T-units written by her subjects, providing the definitions governing the classifications and the rater reliabilities indicating the accuracy with which the definitions were applied. In doing this, Matsuhashi used a standard method of content analysis. Hayes and Flower (1980) also present rules for analyzing protocols according to which statements represent generating, organizing, translating, or editing. They also present rater reliabilities for applying those rules.

However, some researchers do not present any rules or categories for the analysis of their data. Emig (1971), for instance, claims that her subjects "have no *aesthetic* vocabulary, no words to express joy or satisfaction in completion" (p. 87). She presents no rules for determining which words might qualify as belonging to an aesthetic vocabulary and which words qualify as belonging to some other category. Such an analysis would allow us to see how the researcher arrived at the judgment. Without it, we have no way of knowing. Without it, we cannot even be sure of what the researcher means by the term *aesthetic vocabulary*.

In the materials produced by Graves and his colleagues, two articles (Sowers 1981 and Calkins 1980b) provide rules necessary for classifying data across cases and base generalizations on the resulting classifications. Although neither reports reliability checks, presenting the criteria used to control the classification of data lends credence to the findings. As we have seen, Calkins's classification of revisers is quite interesting. Failure to provide such rules for analysis, as well as some check on their systematic application, requires the reader to question whether all instances of a given phenomenon have been coded in the same way. If they have not, then any resulting generalizations are open to question.

Cause and Effect

A third problem in the research on process is a tendency to infer cause-and-effect relationships between associated phenomena without any mechanism for determining whether a given event is a sufficient and/or necessary condition for the occurrence of the other. For example, Graves (1979a) states that "when children control their subjects, they write more, gain greater practice in writing, and ultimately care much more about the appearance of their letters on the page" (pp. 19–20). And again, "Toni writes this much because she controls the topic, spelling, and the process of discovering how to get her message down on paper" (p. 16). But can control over the subject be firmly established as the cause of writing more, gaining greater writing practice, etc.? The conditions of the research do not provide for direct comparisons with children who do not control their subjects—at least not in the data presented so far. Without such comparisons, control of the subject cannot be isolated as a cause or even as a necessary condition for writing more or caring more about appearance.

In fact, data from studies by Scardamalia and Bereiter (e.g., 1982) suggest that other conditions are more important, at least for writing more. These researchers assigned "opinion topics" to fourth- and sixth-grade students and asked them to write. When the children stopped writing, they were given "contentless prompts," mainly requests to write more. A comparison of what they had written before the prompts and after the prompts showed that the prompts doubled the amount written. In addition, Anderson, Bereiter, and Smart (1980) found that when sixth-graders were assigned various expository and opinion topics and were asked first to write a list of key words associated with the topic, they wrote twice as much as control students, used more varied vocabulary, and on opinion topics wrote significantly more elaborate arguments. These and other experiments strongly suggest that factors other than control of the subject are associated with writing more and with higher quality.

Kamler (1980) provides a narrative of one writer, a second-grader named Jill, who produced one piece of writing through four conferences: one with a peer, two with the teacher, and one with the teacher and peers. After each conference Jill added some material. The composition, which was 57 words long after the initial composing, became 169 words after four revisions. Most of the added words (88, about 50 percent of the total) came after a 30-minute conference with the teacher. Interestingly, these results are roughly comparable to those obtained by Bereiter and Scardamalia, who used "contentless prompts" as opposed to extended conferences focusing on content.

Further, when Kamler began to observe Jill, the seven-year-old had chosen to write on two topics which "had not worked" for her, because of lack of interest in one and lack of information on the other. The teacher and child then "brainstormed writing topics," with the teacher "exploring the possibilities of the topic" in which Jill "showed most interest" (p. 681). It would appear, then, that *control of the topic* does not necessarily result in longer and better compositions. The important element may well be an individual conference with the teacher, which appears to prompt the child to recall important information.

In short, while allowing children to choose their own topics may be salutary for a variety of reasons, it cannot be designated as *the*, or even *a*, cause of longer and better compositions without comparative studies and without controlling for the effects of such factors as teacher-student conferences to brainstorm topics and to prompt additions.

The assertion that school-sponsored writing results in lack of commitment to writing on the part of students is another important example of inferring cause-and-effect relationships without adequate evidence. Because it has been taken as evidence of the need for a particular type of instruction, this assertion deserves extended attention. A number of researchers comment on the lack of concern or lack of commitment their subjects display toward the writing they have been asked to do for the researchers. Pianko (1979), for example, comments on "what causes the writing process to be of shorter duration with little commitment and little critical concern." She says, "If the writing is school-sponsored and must be written within limits set by the teacher, the composing process is inhibited." In apparent contradiction, Pianko reports that 52.9 percent of her subjects "had a positive attitude toward the writing they turned in." However, in defense of her statement that "there is little commitment to [school-sponsored writing] on the student's part," she comments that "although many students had positive feelings about their writing, this was because they were not being critical or deeply concerned about what they had just written" (p. 11). She contends that self-sponsored writing (i.e., "writing experiences which evolve from within students" [p. 17]) results in greater commitment and concern.

The problems surrounding these assertions of cause and effect are manifold. In the first place, Pianko has no observations of school-sponsored writing. Her subjects write for the benefit of the researcher in afternoon sessions, voluntarily. The assumption that what Emig (1971) calls "inquiry-sponsored" writing has the same effect as school-sponsored writing is questionable, at best. There is a significant difference between writing for a researcher and writing for a teacher. The subjects have no stake in the former, but they do in the latter. For example, the protocols reported by Flower and Hayes (1981b), some of which derive from conventional assignments (e.g., a paper on Boethius), suggest a fairly high level of commitment. The number of revisions by Bridwell's subjects (1980b) also suggest a high level of commitment on a school-sponsored assignment.

Second, the researchers provide no clear definitions or measures of levels of commitment and concern. Rather, they infer them from the behavior of the writers. Emig (1971), for example, claims that for her eight subjects, "stopping, like starting, is a mundane moment devoid of any emotion but indifference and the mildest of satisfactions that a task is over." All this she infers because students end with phrases such as "Well, here it is" (p. 87). Is it possible that her students are embarrassed or modest or unsure of themselves in front of a researcher who is not a part of the normal school environment? If inferences like Emig's must be drawn, what are the rules for drawing them to safeguard against bias? Perhaps more important, what evidence can be used appropriately as the basis of the inferences?

Third, assuming the researchers had adequate measures of commitment and concern, they would still need to show that the level of concern about school-sponsored writing is the same as that for inquiry-sponsored writing and that these levels of concern or commitment vary systematically with the levels of commitment to self-sponsored writing. It is not enough to claim systematic variation; the variation must be demonstrated.

Fourth, there is a tendency for some links in these arguments to be circular. Pianko claims that over half of her subjects had a positive attitude toward what they had written—an indication of commitment, perhaps. However, Pianko explains that they were only positive "because they were not being critical or deeply concerned", thus denying the association of satisfaction with commitment. How does Pianko know that the students were not being critical or deeply concerned about what they had written? Because they expressed satisfaction with it and because she did not regard the writing as worthy of a positive attitude? To say that the students were not *being critical* is to imply that they might have been had they chosen to be. However, Pianko presents no evidence concerning the critical abilities of students in her sample. Perhaps they were being critical but were using a set of standards different from the researcher's. Indeed, the fact that students express any satisfaction, or dissatisfaction for that matter, indicates that they applied some set of standards and were, in fact, critical. Perhaps what needs changing is not the fact that the writing is school-sponsored but the standards which students use to judge their writing. If one wished to demonstrate that school-sponsored writing cannot excite commitments and engage critical abilities, then one must show (1) that some level of critical ability was present, (2) that this ability was not engaged, (3) that it was not engaged *because* the writing was school-sponsored, and (4) that no other causes for the failure are possible.

Finally, these arguments imply that school-sponsored writing is of a single type, namely, of the type and with the conditions imposed by the researchers. They assume, for example, that assignments are given without preparation, that no specific criteria for judging writing are presented, and that no specific provisions are made for feedback and revision. It may be true that most school-sponsored writing assignments do not share these characteristics. However, the experimental treatment studies examined later in this review show that some do. Indeed, the variability of the results of those studies is immense, indicating that some have the capacity to engage students, at least in improving their writing skills, which is no mean level of engagement. Demonstrating that school-sponsored writing results in a lack of commitment to writing requires that evidence be collected over a range of programs with different characteristics. The studies at hand have not done that.

In short, while it *may* be true that school-sponsored writing causes lack of commitment and deep concern, these studies have not demonstrated a causal relationship or, for that matter, a strong association between the two. Too many other explanations are not only possible but plausible. According to Pianko (1979), the alternative to school-sponsored writing, in which the teacher controls "topic, time, and place," is self-sponsored writing. Pianko contends that "writing . . . should begin with an idea developing out of students' confrontations with life" (pp. 17–18). Although Pianko and others state their contentions as conclusions, they are not. They are hypotheses open to empirical investigation and which, in fact, have been investigated in a number of studies. They make up an important dimension of the meta-analysis which appears later in this volume.

The Presence of Researchers

A final problem in interpreting the research on process involves determining what effects the presence of researchers has on results. While this is undoubtedly a problem in collecting thinking-aloud protocols, it appears to be of particular importance in the classroom observations conducted by Graves and his colleagues for two years. He states (1981c) that "the presence of the researchers had great influence. . . . In a way, we ended up having more influence on the environment than might ordinarily be expected" (p. 178). This influence, he believes, was mainly on teachers and administrators. But it is at least possible that the presence of researchers influenced the way the children developed as writers. When children prepared to write, "the researcher then [moved] to where the child [was] ready to work" (Graves 1979b, p. 79). Researchers not only recorded what the children did but conducted interviews during the child's writing, asking such questions as, "What did you almost write?" The researchers admit that the children seemed to enjoy such attention. Would their questions have the same function as the "contentless prompts" of Bereiter and Scardamalia's (1982) work?

One cannot help but wonder if the researchers, watching the same children, day after day, for two years, would not be disappointed in some writing efforts and rejoice in others. The reports of Calkins (1979, 1981) and Kamler (1980) indicate that at least disapproval and approval were present. Could these emotions be constantly disguised, the researchers wearing masks of indifference at all times? If not, then what effect might indications of approval and disapproval, *during* actual writing, have on the writing behaviors of the observed children? Graves (1981c) believes that "the order of development would not be changed . . . even though the rate of [problem] solution might be accelerated" (p. 178) by the presence of the researchers. However, the research provides no monitoring of the kinds or rate of change in children who are not under the constant surveillance of admittedly sympathetic researchers. Thus, considerable uncertainty exists about the scope and type of researcher influence.

Despite these problems in interpreting findings and claims, particularly of the case study and observational research, the research on process provides a number of tantalizing conjectures and hypotheses about development and teaching, as well as some fascinating directions for future research. It has certainly drawn our attention to the processes of composing.

Conclusion

In 1963 Braddock, Lloyd-Jones, and Schoer asked an apparently simple question: "What is involved in the act of writing?" (p. 53). The question was only apparently simple, however. Although we may never be able to provide a definitive answer, two decades later we do have the knowledge base to ask more and more penetrating questions, to formulate and explore more and more precisely stated hypotheses. And we do have some pieces of the puzzle about which we can claim to have considerable certainty.

We know, for example, that writing involves a great deal of planning, that planning involves a lot of production time, and that planning takes place at several levels of abstraction. The levels of abstraction involved are evidenced in research as divergent as that by Emig (1971), Perl (1979), the various studies by Hayes and Flower, studies by Bereiter, Scardamalia, and their colleagues, and the research of Matsuhashi (1981). At the most abstract levels, planning appears to involve rather general intentions about the kind of text to be produced, governed in part by knowledge of schemata and in part by intended content. While the role of criteria at these higher levels of planning has not been fully explored by researchers, criteria do appear to be important. Recall, for example, Roger's rejection of his first plan for an essay on Boethius (Flower and Hayes 1981b) and Andrea's learning to write leads which begin *in medias res* (Calkins 1979 and 1981).

General intentions generate more specific, but still rather generalized, content. Recall Lynn's decision to deal with various reactions to the specific image of the cardboard Snoopy (Emig 1971) or Roger's more abstract decision to relate how his original objections to Boethius's logic were overcome (Flower and Hayes 1981b). Roger presumably knew what those objections were and how he had overcome them.

These content decisions appear to be fleshed out in their semantic dimensions before they are represented first in words in short-term memory and then graphemically. Matsuhashi's (1981) finding that the mean length of pauses prior to T-units was twice that for the mean length of all pauses (9.78 versus 4.35 seconds) suggests that writers plan verbal representations in T-units or parts of T-units. When Bereiter, Fine, and Gartshore (1979) interrupted children in their writing and asked them to say aloud what they were about to write, the children forecast five to six words, usually to the end of a clause. This is additional evidence that writers plan strings of several specific words, if not clauses or T-units. Matsuhashi's finding of anomalously long pauses *following* some subordinate conjunctions suggests that writers plan at a semantic level which allows them to select a subordinate clause or phrase with a particular relationship to what has preceded it, without having stipulated the lexical content of the structure.

Finally, the finding by Bereiter, Fine, and Gartshore (1979) that children write out nearly the same words they forecast but make occasional "stylistic" changes, indicates the occurrence of an editorial process between the verbal string held in short-term memory and the graphemic level.

While the existence of some of these levels has not been demonstrated definitively, available evidence makes them worthy of hypothesis and further exploration. On the other hand, the existence of high-level planning can hardly be doubted, though some pedagogical systems appear to ignore it. What is still needed, of course, is more rigorously presented data showing how such plans operate, interact with each other, and differ by mode of discourse.

We do know, from a wide variety of studies, that composing is recursive, with writers moving back to what has been written and forward to what has not. Further, we can be fairly certain that the subprocesses of composing interrupt each other. The writer moves from high-level plans to the transcription of words and back to higher-level planning, rereading what has been written, reconstructing plans already made, making new plans, generating new data, or performing editing of some kind. This bobbing up-and-down among various levels has been examined most systematically in the work of Hayes and Flower (1980) but has been observed in a number of other studies. Together, these recursive and bobbing actions present a far different notion of composing than there is to be found in composition texts which traditionally assume that all planning precedes all transcribing and that all editing follows. That, in itself, is a finding that could have important instructional value.

Research on composing has developed many other important ideas, most of which must still be regarded as hypotheses—but hypotheses worthy of further exploration and testing. Ideas developed by Graves, Calkins, Sowers, and their colleagues are fascinating examples. In their work we see children beginning to write very early in the first year of school by using invented spellings, learning to use the space on the paper, sharing work with other youngsters and the teacher, shifting from externalized to internalized behavior in revising, moving from egocentric to sociocentric, and so forth. Researchers should examine these ideas as rigorously as possible, presenting rules for the analysis of the events observed, displaying data across cases, and using controls to account for alternative explanations.

The work of Bereiter, Scardamalia, and their colleagues in attempting to infer the cognitive processes in composing is also very promising and useful. But here also research has much to reveal. For example, is it inability to conduct memory searches or failure to do so which results in children's writing so little without the prompting of a conversational partner? Or is it that children, who are accustomed to utterances of conversational length, simply see no need to write more? Do they need to learn criteria governing written forms, criteria which would reveal the need for more information and would prompt appropriate memory searches?

Perhaps all of the research on composing in the past two decades raises more questions than it answers. But it has answered some, and in raising others, it promises to answer more. It has come a long way from the question posed by Braddock, Lloyd-Jones, and Schoer in 1963.

2 The Writer's Repertoire

In 1971 Bernard J. McCabe, in a model of elements in the composing process, posited the existence of a writer's repertoire—a knowledge of lexical, syntactic, or rhetorical forms which writers call upon in their writing. These forms might be learned or invented. Writers learn words common to the lexicon of their language but invent others, e.g., inkhorn terms of the sixteenth and seventeenth centuries and the advertising jargon of the twentieth. Writers appear to learn rules which enable them to generate an infinite variety of specific syntactic structures. Forms such as the sonnet appear to be learned from the literary heritage. Others, such as the cinquain, can be attributed to the invention of a single person. Researchers on the composing process indicate that their subjects appear to call on forms, generalized plans, or schemata to guide their writing. For example, Emig (1971) discusses the five-paragraph, or "Fifty-Star," theme, which she claims "is so tightly lodged in the American composition curriculum" (p. 97). Whether anyone likes the form or not, Emig contends that students use it to guide their writing. Hayes and Flower (1980) and Matsuhashi (1981) indicate that their subjects appear to be guided by generalized plans or schemata. What role such forms play in the composing process is not fully understood, but research on them is well under way.

In addition to such formal knowledge, the writer's repertoire might be conceived as including knowledge about such aspects of rhetoric as the relationship of audience to form. This chapter will examine research on syntactic and generic forms and audience.

Syntactic Forms

Researchers have long known that when children arrive in first grade they are capable of using nearly all grammatical structures which adults use. The difference between adults' and children's use of the structures has been known to be a matter of frequency. For some time, researchers studied these frequencies in writing over age groups rather extensively without altogether satisfying results. However, in

1965 Kellogg Hunt published a pioneering study which established clearer and more useful measures than had been available in the past. This study showed clear patterns of development, or at least change, which have been repeatedly confirmed by subsequent research. Hunt's study involved nine boys and nine girls in each of three grade levels (4, 8, and 12), for a total of fifty-four children, each of whom produced, as part of regular classroom work, 1,000 words of writing. These students attended Florida State University School but were selected so that IQ scores ranged from 90 to 110.

In order to examine differences in the syntax of students at the various grade levels, Hunt used what has become a standard measure, the minimal terminable unit or T-unit, which is simply a main clause with all of its appended modifiers, including subordinate clauses. This measure avoided the ambiguities which had plagued definitions of the sentence and provided a tool which could be used reliably. In addition to examining the mean length of T-units, Hunt also devised the ratio of clauses per T-unit to replace LaBrant's (1933) subordination ratio. In addition, Hunt examined average clause length, ratios of T-units per sentence, and average length of sentences. Four of Hunt's measures were significant for grade level at $p < .01$, while the fifth (average sentence length) was significant for grade level at $p < .05$. The most reliable indices, with the least overlap among the three grade levels, were average T-unit length and average clause length.

These findings are no longer any surprise to us, but in 1965, when Hunt published his findings, they contradicted the long-standing ideas, stemming from LaBrant's studies, that clause length did not indicate maturity and that sentence length was a better index of maturity. The differences between Hunt's and LaBrant's findings are primarily the result of Hunt's concept of T-unit (as opposed to sentence) and his more resonable and usual definition of clause. (LaBrant counted compound predicates as separate clauses. Thus, a sentence such as, "We were running and jumping," would count as two clauses because it contains an auxiliary verb and two participles, each counting as a predicate and a separate clause.) Hunt, in fact, found that the compounding of T-units was a significant index of immaturity. Fourth-graders wrote more compounded T-units than eighth-graders, and eighth-graders wrote more than twelfth-graders. This difference indicates one serious problem in using mean sentence length as an index of "maturity." Several of Hunt's fourth-graders averaged sentence lengths of over 70 words because they strung together series of T-units, usually using *and* as the coordinating conjunction. At any rate, an important result of Hunt's research was to establish two previously unused indices as major tools for researchers—average clause length and average T-unit length, both of which proved to be better predictors of grade level than any of the older measures.

In addition, Hunt examined changes in the use of various types of clauses. He found nearly a doubling of the incidence of adjective clauses from the fourth grade to the eighth and nearly a doubling again between the eighth and twelfth grades. The number of adjective clauses used by Hunt's superior adults was nearly five times that used by fourth-graders. These differences were significant ($p < .01$). Hunt also found significant increases in the use of noun clauses ($p < .05$) and nonsignificant increases in the use of adverb clauses of various kinds.

Hunt also examined nominals, finding a significant decrease ($p < .01$) from fourth to twelfth grade in the use of unmodified nominals, and concomitant and significant gains in the use of adjective and genitive modifiers ($p < .01$) and prepositional phrases modifying nouns ($p < .01$). The use of both gerunds and infinitives as nominals increased dramatically over the grade levels, with fourth-graders using only 10 percent as many gerunds as twelfth-graders. The increased use of adjective clauses, adjectives, inflected genitives, prepositional phrases, verbal phrases of various types, and other modifiers of nouns all contribute to the increased complexity of nominals. Thus, while most nouns used by fourth-graders remain unmodified, nouns used by older students take on increasingly longer strings of modifiers. Hunt developed measures of nominal complexity by assigning a count of one to each modifier of a noun head. The resulting measures were all significant ($p < .01$) for grade level, with one measure ("total number of counts given to nominals receiving counts of two or more" [p. 116]) ranking after only average T-unit length and average clause length as a reliable index of maturity.

Hunt argues convincingly that the increases in subordinate clauses, modifiers of nominals, gerunds, and infinitives are all the result of clause reductions. That is, while a fourth-grader might write two main clauses, an eighth-grader might produce a main clause and a subordinate clause, and a twelfth-grader might reduce the subordinate clause to a phrase within the main clause. Hunt quotes a fourth-grader as writing, "Once upon a time I had a cat. This cat was a beautiful cat, it was also mean." An older student would be more likely to consolidate the three T-units, thereby eliminating the repetitions of *cat* and the unnecessary use of *it* to produce a clause such as, "Once upon a time I had a beautiful but mean cat." Such reductions contribute to increased T-unit length and to greater concision.

From its initial publication, Hunt's findings suggested specific objectives for teaching. As G. Robert Carlsen put it in his introduction to the study, "Hunt's study offers a kind of operational definition of language objectives for the school: the school's program should facilitate the student's moving in the direction of mature writing patterns" (p. vi). That is, schools should facilitate the writing of longer T-units, longer clauses, more complex nominals, and so forth. Not long after the publication of Hunt's study, various scholars began experimenting with direct approaches to teaching the writing of more "mature" sentence patterns. (A later section on sentence combining will deal with these studies in detail.)

In 1967 O'Donnell, Griffin, and Norris published a transformational analysis of the syntax of elementary school children. They collected oral samples from thirty children in each of grades K, 1, 2, 3, 5, and 7, with approximately half boys and half girls in each. These children were asked to tell the story presented in a silent film orally; the children in grades 3, 5, and 7 were also asked to produce a written version of the story after they had told it.

The findings of the transformational analysis support many of the findings of the Hunt study. The authors found the T-unit to be "a sensitive measure of development toward maturity in children's language production. Without exception for any subgroup at any stage, data obtained showed increments in T-unit length from grade to grade" (p. 44). This was true for both oral and written composition. In fact, the data on T-units for this study closely parallel Hunt's data. Interestingly, however, while T-units were longer in speech than those in writing at the third grade, they were longer in writing at both the fifth and seventh grades. According to the authors, "the data suggest that as children progress through the upper grades, they learn to control their writing more strictly than their speech" (p. 46). O'Donnell, Griffin, and Norris report that the number of sentence-combining transformations per T-unit also increases from grade to grade in writing, with the significant increases appearing in grades 5 and 7, paralleling increments in words per T-unit. This finding also supports Hunt's finding that a variety of structures which may be regarded as clause reductions or sentence-combining transformations (e.g., subordinate clauses, adjectives, prepositional phrases, verbals) increase in frequency per T-unit from fourth through twelfth grade and "superior adults." Several other specific parallels with Hunt's findings are evident, particularly in types of sentence-combining transformations thought to be used in producing noun-headed nominals and nonheaded nominals. In certain instances the rate of increase is nearly identical, e.g., in the use of prepositional phrases to modify nouns.

An interesting finding of O'Donnell, Griffin, and Norris is that while control of syntax in speech exceeds that in the writing of third-graders, by fifth and seventh grade children show greater control over the syntax of writing. At both fifth and seventh grades the superior control over syntax in writing was marked "by significantly greater use of the whole classes of transformation-produced nominals, adverbials, and coordinations within T-units; by notably more frequent use of seven of the twelve specific types of nominal structures identified; by greater use of adverbial clauses and adverbial infinitives; and by much greater use of coordinate predicates, particularly in Grade 5" (p. 85). What this reversal means is not clear. It must be due to something more than simply increased facility in handwriting. Perhaps it is due to the recognition of the peculiar requirements of writing, e.g., to inform an absent reader fully of context or qualifications. Such requirements entail more fully developed syntax than do face-to-face conversational situations. Perhaps it is due to the slower rate of production, noted by Gould (1980) and by Bereiter and Scardamalia (1982), which may permit the production of more elaborate syntax as well as the higher levels of coherence and resulting quality noted by Scardamalia, Bereiter, and Goelman (1982).

A large number of other studies of the written syntax of students at various grade levels and that of adults confirm the basic findings of Hunt (1965a) and O'Donnell, Griffin, and Norris (1967a), and add new pieces of information. A study by Blount, Johnson, and Fredrick (1968), comparing 1,000-word samples from thirty-two eighth-graders and thirty-two twelfth-graders found (1) significantly greater mean T-unit and clause lengths for twelfth-graders ($p < .01$), and (2) significantly fewer coordinated T-units for twelfth-graders than for eighth-graders ($p < .01$). These findings support Hunt's. Although changes in mean sentence length were not significant in Blount's study, there was a significant ability by grade-level interaction for mean sentence length. Low-ability eighth-graders wrote longer sentences than did high-ability students, while high-ability twelfth-graders wrote longer sentences than low-ability twelfth-graders. Does this suggest that longer sentences are the product of lack of linguistic control in eighth grade but of heightened control in twelfth? Blount's findings for subordinate clauses are discrepant with Hunt's, leading Blount to believe that subordinate clause ratios are not adequate indices of maturity.

Dixon (1970b) analyzed 200-word samples taken from the middle of narratives written by fourth-, eighth-, and twelfth-graders, and by college seniors. He examined words per T-unit, intra T-unit coordinate structure, and free modifier variables suggested by Christensen (1963). Using multiple regression analysis he determined that mean T-unit length correlated more highly (.66) with grade level than any of the other variables, accounting for about 44 percent of the variance among students. Other studies by Ashida (1967), Dauterman (1970), and Dittmer (1971) generally confirm the findings already cited, although Dauterman reports a slight drop in some indices.

Some researchers have attempted to assimilate several of the syntactic features examined into single syntactic complexity scales which yield a single quotient presumed to indicate syntactic maturity (Botel and Granowsky 1972, Endicott 1973, Golub and Kidder 1974). Such indices are appealing in their apparent simplicity of yielding a single quotient which appears to "say it all." Their difficulty lies in our not knowing what exactly the quotient means. Endicott's score is based on transformational and morphemic analyses of linguistic structures. However, as Roy O'Donnell's review (1976a) suggests, the procedures for counting co-memes appear arbitrary, particularly in their assignment of complexity levels. For example, a phrase such as *the boy's dragon* would be rated as far more complex than *the omnivorous dragon*, simply because the former includes a possessive.

Golub and Kidder's syntactic density score is based on an initial analysis of how children use various syntactic structures and which of these structures predict teacher ratings of their writings. The score is computed by counting frequencies for ten types of structures (from words per T-unit to number of possessives), weighting them, and computing a final score. As O'Donnell (1976a) points out, a problem inherent in this score is its high level of redundancy. "Words per T-unit results from the combined effects of number of clauses and length of clauses; length of clauses, in turn, results in part from the remaining items on the instrument" (p. 37). Belanger (1978a) points out a problem of much greater concern inherent in the syntactic density score: the fewer T-units analyzed, the higher the syntactic density score. This is the result of combining the mean scores of the first four variables with the raw scores of the remaining six and dividing by the total number of T-units. Even with the correct procedures recommended by Belanger, there is considerable doubt about the validity of the grade level conversions.

Some investigators have focused on the variables which Christensen (1963) considered to be especially characteristic of mature style: the number of instances of final free modifiers, the number of words in such modifiers, the number of instances of free modifiers in other positions, and so forth. Wolk (1970) found that professional writers use more free modifiers in all positions and more final free modifiers than college freshmen. Faigley (1979a) found that professional writers wrote longer T-units, longer clauses and more words in free modifiers—especially those in final positions—than did the college students in his sample. The difference between the two groups on the latter two variables is very large. The professional writers examined by Faigley write 30.3 percent of their total words in free modifiers and 17.3 percent in final free modifiers alone. That is compared to 16.1 percent in free modifiers written by freshmen, and only 3.5 percent in final free modifiers. Dixon, who examined several variables suggested by Christensen, found regression coefficients of .45 for instances of final free modifiers and of .40 for words in final free modifiers regressed against grade level.

Syntactic Features and Mode of Discourse

In discussing the implications for research of his 1965 study, Hunt pointed to the need for examining the different effects which subject matter and mode of discourse have on syntactic structures. A number of studies have examined those differences, some of them well before Hunt's study. A 1933 study by Seegers, for example, focusing on the writing of fourth-, fifth-, and sixth-graders, found that argument used more dependent clauses than either exposition or narration and that exposition used more than narration. More recent studies have found similar differences at many different grade levels. Martínez San José (1973) examined the writing of forty fourth-graders in narrative, descriptive, expository, and argumentative modes. Each composition was produced not in a test situation but as a letter to be sent to another child in England. She examined thirty syntactic variables, twenty-three of which proved to be significantly different by mode, many at $p < .001$. Mean T-unit length, subordination ratio as a percent, and the use of non-clausal adverbials were all greater for argument and exposition. Argument produced the most complex syntax, followed fairly closely by exposition. Both argument and exposition were widely separated from narration and description. In another study, Crowhurst and Piché (1979) collected samples of writing from sixth- and tenth-graders who wrote three compositions in one of three modes for each of two audiences, for a total of six compositions over a period of six weeks. Three different color slides were used to prompt writing in each mode. Using the same slide across modes helped to control for subject matter, or topic. At grade 6, words per T-unit and clauses per T-unit were significantly greater for argument than for narration and description, which were not significantly different. At grade 10, T-unit length and clauses per T-unit were significantly greater for argument than for narration or description. In words per clause, argument and description were both significantly greater than narration. Interestingly, while Crowhurst and Piché found significant syntactic differences between arguments and descriptions written by sixth- and tenth-graders, there were no significant differences between narratives by sixth- and tenth-graders on words per T-unit, words per clause, or clauses per T-unit.

Schifsky (1982) examined a single mode of discourse, expressive writing, from the NAEP 1973–74 assessment, attending to eighty-one lexical and syntactic items. He found no significant differences between the expressive writing of thirteen-year-olds and that produced by seventeen-year-olds. Other researchers have examined exposition or argument in contrast to some form of personal or expressive writing. Nietzke (1972) examined the critical and personal experience writing of sixty college freshmen and found that mean T-unit length differed significantly, with critical writing displaying greater syntactic complexity. Hennig (1980) examined three pieces of writing from twenty students (a personalized journal, a letter, and a formal essay) for several indices of syntactic maturity. The essays were the most complex on several indices. C. Watson (1980) examined twelve essays from each of twenty-one twelfth-graders and twenty-one upper-level college English majors. Four essays were expressive, four persuasive, and four explanatory. She examined these essays for seventeen syntactic variables, finding significant differences among the three modes which equalled or exceeded differences in the maturity of the students. She found that expressive writing in both groups was considerably less mature by usual syntactic standards than their persuasive writing.

In general, these studies clearly indicate that different modes of discourse entail different degrees of syntactic complexity, with argument and exposition or explanation generally involving greater complexity than narrative and expressive writing.

Syntax and Other Factors

Some investigators have examined T-unit length among students with special problems. Rodrigues (1975) found that while bilingual Hispanics at the ninth-grade level wrote shorter T-units than monolingual students, the rate of increase from fourth to ninth grade was only slightly less for bilinguals. Braun and Klassen (1973) also found that monolingual students exhibited higher indices of syntactic maturity than did bilinguals. N. T. Morris (1979) found that normal students have higher levels of syntactic maturity than do learning-disabled students. Indeed, Raiser (1981) found that eighth-grade learning-disabled students' average T-unit length was comparable to that for normal fourth-graders. However, Raiser also found that as learning-disabled students grew older, they wrote longer T-units.

Several investigators have examined various syntactic factors in relation to sex. McCarthy (1954) claimed the studies available indicated that among American white children girls were characteristically ahead of boys "in nearly all aspects of language" (p. 577). The evidence available for the present review suggests that, at least in syntactic development, boys and girls are more or less even or, if not, they become even. O'Donnell, Griffin, and Norris (1967a) point out that while third- and fifth-grade girls are ahead on several measures "taken to indicate syntactic skill" in writing (e.g., less frequent coordination of main clauses, greater use of transformation-produced nominals, more frequent adverbial clauses), by seventh grade the positions of the sexes "were clearly reversed" so that "differences almost uniformly favored boys" (p. 96). Inspection of Hunt's tables suggests similar reversals, with girls ahead of boys in mean T-unit length in fourth grade (9.0 to 8.1), but with boys ahead of girls by twelfth grade (15.8 to 13.0). However, Dauterman (1970), working with seventh- through twelfth-graders found no significant differences in words per T-unit, words per clause, or subordination index. Blount, Fredrick, and Johnson (1969) with eighth- and twelfth-graders found no differences by sex in words per T-unit or words per clause. On the other hand, while a study by Baggett (1978) found no significant differences by sex between tenth-grade boys and girls in T-unit length, it did find girls significantly superior to boys in other respects, especially in the variety of sentence-combining transformations used in the production of nominals.

House and House (1980), concerned with ability and linguistic structures in writing, compared the work of students identified as remedial and those identified as ready for a regular college freshman English program. They found no significant differences between the two groups in the number of errors produced, length of T-units, clauses per T-unit, or words per clause. Such findings, of course, may attest more to the deficiencies of the selection program than to anything else. Other researchers using more extreme differences among student abilities have found differences. Leonard (1977), using scores on a standard language test, found no significant differences on a number of factors, including mean clause length and mean T-unit length, but did find significant differences favoring the high group ($p < .05$) for the number of free modifiers and the number of free modifiers in final positions. E. M. Martin (1978) found that nominees for the Georgia Governor's Honors Program wrote more words per T-unit, more words per clause, more clauses per T-unit, more adjective and adverbial clauses, and more gerund and infinitive phrases than did Hunt's seniors.

Syntactic Features and Quality Ratings

Several studies have examined differences in the syntactic features of compositions independently rated according to some quality scale. Cooper and several colleagues (1979) found that five randomly selected college freshmen scoring high on an entrance essay wrote T-units nearly four words longer than five low-scoring freshmen and that the high-scoring freshmen used over 60 percent more structures of modification per 100 T-units than did the low-scoring freshmen. R. R. Potter (1967b) found that tenth-grade papers rated good by six raters had longer sentences, longer T-units, more structures of modification and more verbals than did papers rated as lower. Marzano (1975) found significant correlations between quality ratings and a number of syntactic features. A. E. Allen (1972) found significant correlations between quality ratings and the frequency of nonfinite verb constructions and qualifying words and phrases.

In a well-designed study, Crowhurst (1980) examined the effects of syntactic complexity on rated quality in two modes (narration and argument) at three grade levels (sixth, tenth, and twelfth). Students wrote three different narratives or three different arguments, prompted by the same stimuli and under similar conditions, over a three-week period. Mean T-unit length for each composition was computed. Pairs of compositions from the same writer were selected for qualitative ratings if one member of the pair was of high syntactic complexity (.5 word or more above the mean for mode and grade level) and the other was of low complexity (.5 word below the same mean), and if the shorter of the two papers contained no fewer than 70 percent of the total words in the longer. The 284 compositions were distributed more or less equally across a complexity × grade × mode × topic matrix. Raters used two rating scales, a holistic seven-point scale and an instrument devised by Piché, Rubin, Turner, and Michlin (1978) consisting of seven subscales.

Crowhurst found no significant qualitative difference between the high-complexity and low-complexity narratives or arguments written by sixth-graders. Neither was any found between low- and high-complexity narratives written by tenth-graders. *The low-complexity narratives of twelfth-graders, however, were significantly superior to their high-complexity narratives on both measures.* For both tenth- and twelfth-graders, high-complexity arguments scored significantly higher than low (for tenth-graders on the seven-subscale measure and for twelfth-graders on both measures). This study suggests sharply differentiated effects of complex syntax by mode. Apparently, for most writers effective narrative is not dependent on the complexity of syntax. On the other hand, as Crowhurst indicates, effective argument may demand the "logical interrelationship of propositions" (p. 230) and, therefore, longer syntactic structures.

However, a number of studies indicate little or no relationship between measures of syntactic complexity (particularly T-unit length) and rated quality. Jurgens and Griffin (1970), examining compositions by seventh-, ninth-, and eleventh-graders which had been rated with reliabilities ranging from .88 to .93, found no significant differences in words per T-unit or clauses per T-unit among low, middle, and high papers at any grade level. Words per clause differed significantly for high and low papers in grade 11 only. Martínez San José (1973) examined the compositions of forty fourth-graders in four different modes (narration, description, exposition, and argument). These pieces were each rated for general interest of content and for organization by four experienced raters, whose assigned scores were summed. The researcher found no statistical relationship between syntactic maturity and content/organization scores. In argument, shorter T-unit length tended to be associated with higher content scores. Using standard rating procedures based on Diederich (1974), Belanger (1978b) found correlations ranging from .03 to .07 between average T-unit length and quality ratings in high school compositions.

Stewart and Grobe (1979) worked with a subsample of 232 compositions from the 1977 New Brunswick Writing Assessment. In this writing assessment, fifth-graders were asked to write directions for taking care of a pet, while eighth- and eleventh-graders' assignments should have produced arguments. Stewart and Grobe found a significant positive correlation between quality scores and words per T-unit only at grade 5, a correlation of .30. The correlation of words per T-unit to quality was a nonsignificant .19 at grade 8 and − .06 at grade 11. At grade 5, the researchers also found significant positive correlations of quality to words per clause (.23), and clauses per T-unit (.37). At grades 8 and 11, these correlations were low and nonsignificant. In fact, the correlation between quality and clauses per T-unit was −.19 at grade 11.

Nold and Freedman (1977) examined four essays written by twenty-two Stanford University freshmen, each written in a half-hour period. Two of the assignments were designed to produce argument and two to produce analysis involving comparison and contrast. The researchers analyzed the compositions for words per T-unit, subordinate clauses per T-unit, mean subordinate clause length, percent of words in final free modifiers, and thirteen other variables. Six experienced teachers were trained and read all eighty-eight of the resulting essays under exemplary research conditions. Their holistic four-point scale scores were summed to give a quality score to each essay. The researchers found very low and nonsignificant correlations for most of the syntactic variables with quality scores: .08 with words per T-unit, .03 for subordinate clauses per T-unit, .06 for mean subordinate clause length. The only significant and positive correlation of a syntactic variable with rated quality was the percent of words in final free modifiers (.42), a correlation which accounts for over 17.6 percent of the variance among the compositions. The only other significant positive correlation was between length and rated quality (.57), accounting for nearly 32.5 percent of the variance. Stepwise multiple regression indicated that length and the percent of words in final free modifiers were the two most important variables associated with rated quality.

Faigley (1979c) reports similar correlations between rated quality and various syntactic features: $r = .04$ for words per T-unit, −.07 for clauses per T-unit, .18 for words per clause; but .25 for percent of words in final free modifiers, .41 for percent of T-units with final free modifiers, and .30 for length. The two most important variables associated with quality were the percent of T-units with final free modifiers and length.

Wille (1982) examined a group of pretest and posttest compositions written by one experimental and one control class ($n = 43$ for eighty-six compositions) in a study conducted by Hillocks (1982). These seventh-grade compositions had been scored holistically on a scale involving specificity and focus, with rater reliabilities ranging from .80 to .95. Both groups had made gains, but the experimental group gain was greater. Wille asked three somewhat diverse raters (an experienced college English teacher, an experienced high school English teacher, and a graduate student in English) to rank-order the papers in four levels of quality as they perceived them. The raters were instructed only to ignore mechanical errors in making their judgments. The scores assigned by the three raters were summed. In addition, Wille examined T-unit length. The summed scores of the holistic ratings correlated with the earlier specificity ratings significantly (.81). However, correlations between the rated quality scores and T-unit length were only .06 (with the specificity scale) and .01 (with the holistic scale). In fact, while both sets of quality scores revealed strong gains for both groups of students, both groups wrote shorter T-units on the posttest, $-.80$ for the experimental group and $-.89$ for the control group. This regression is about one-third of the gains made between fourth grade and eighth grade in Hunt's (1965a) study.

One might suspect that the low correlations between T-unit length and rated quality reported by some studies are the result of the compositions being written at a single grade level: the compositions would exhibit a very narrow range, thereby making high correlations with rated quality unlikely. That appears not to be the case, however. The means and standard deviations reported by Stewart and Grobe (1979) for eighth grade ($\overline{X} = 13.18$ and $sd = 3.77$) and for eleventh grade ($\overline{X} = 15.45$ and $sd = 4.09$) indicate that the eighth-graders overlap both Hunt's fourth-graders and his seniors. Similarly, a good number of the eleventh-graders overlap with Hunt's skilled adults (20.3 words per T-unit) and some overlap with many eighth-graders. Faigley's standard deviations also reflect a wide range of mean T-unit length. The actual range of Wille's seventh-graders' mean T-unit lengths extends from 7.63 (below Hunt's mean for fourth-graders) to 26.86 (well above Hunt's mean for superior adults). In short, the low correlations of mean T-unit length to rated quality cannot be attributed to narrow ranges of mean T-unit lengths.

To summarize, several researchers working independently with student writing in a wide variety of modes and at a variety of grade levels have obtained extraordinarily low correlations between mean T-unit length and rated quality. Why this is so remains something of a puzzle. If mean T-unit length is the best predictor of grade level, and if we assume that grade level is associated with quality of writing, then we should be able to assume that T-unit length is also associated with writing quality. And across grade levels, it may be. However, nearly all the studies available at this writing which have examined the correlation of T-unit length with rated quality have used compositions written by students at a single grade level. The result has been correlations which, with one exception at fifth grade, show no relationship between the two. However, some of the same studies have shown strong association between measures of more specific syntactic features and rated quality (e.g., final free modifiers) and more general features (e.g., overall length of the composition). These findings suggest that T-unit length may be, on the one hand, too gross and, on the other hand, too restricted a measure to detect differences in quality. Some T-units may be long enough to be regarded as mature but vacuous enough to be regarded as ineffective. An underdeveloped theme may be a collection of lengthy but empty T-units, while a specific and effective piece of writing may be made up of relatively short T-units. To explain the variance in quality ratings, we appear to need more refined measures of syntax as well as measures of other dimensions such as overall development.

Generic Forms

While we have many studies which have examined the syntactic features of children's writing, we have far fewer which have examined the various genres, structural features, rhetorical patterns, or schemata which appear in children's writing at various ages. Some researchers have looked for the presence of various literary devices (including alliteration, hyperbole, metaphor, simile, and personification) in young children's writing and have found them (Hill 1973, Bean 1974). Some studies have examined larger aspects of structure. Willy (1975) studied 145 oral and written narratives from first-graders, claiming that 132 of them exhibited a planned and graduated crescendo of tension climaxed and released by a sudden denouement. Stahl (1977) examined the structure of compositions by children in grades 2, 5, 8 and 11 written in response to a request to write descriptions of their homes (the rooms and their contents). He proposed various means for examining the structure of those compositions and applied them, finding various differences among the students in his sample.

Melas (1975) and Bodkin (1978) both examined the types of compositions written by elementary school children. Bodkin, who sampled free writing from journals, found that girls in the third and sixth grades wrote more about themselves (their homes, families, personal relationships, etc.) than did boys, who wrote more often about sports and metropolitan, national, world, historical, and catastrophic events. Further, she found that third-graders wrote more often in the extensive mode (see Emig 1971) than in the reflexive mode, while the reverse was true for sixth-graders.

In 1975 Britton, et al. produced a lengthy study entitled *The Development of Writing Abilities (11–18)*, which focuses on the kinds of writing produced as the result of assignments given in British secondary schools but which has little to say about the development of writing abilities. The authors present and define sets of function and audience categories. The function categories include three major categories (transactional, expressive, and poetic) and several subcategories. The researchers collected many pieces of student writing, along with the assignments which generated them, and classified them according to the categories. They report that 63.4 percent of the writing (and therefore presumably the assignments) was transactional, 5.5 percent expressive, and 17.6 percent poetic. Of all pieces in the transactional category about 78 percent fall in three subcategories, with about 22 percent in the remaining six subcategories. The three heavily used categories are what the writers call "report," "low-level analytic" (which uses generalization loosely organized), and "analogic" (which makes use of classification statements organized hierarchically or logically). Perhaps the most useful contribution of this study is to provide an empirical test of a more complex set of categories of discourse than the simplistic set which has dominated composition instruction for decades.

Applebee (1978a) examined a body of oral stories by children and classified them after Vygotsky (1962) into what he believes are six basic types: heaps (a collection of statements related, perhaps, by free association), sequences (a series of statements, each linked somehow to the following statement but not necessarily to the others), primitive narrative (events surrounding a common nucleus, possibly a character, but which do not yield a linked story), unfocused chain (a series of statements each concretely linked to the next, but in which the beginning has little relation to the ending), and finally narratives (what we generally think of as a true story).

Helen King (1979) examined both oral and written stories by third-graders and found five plot forms, the most commonly occurring of which she claims to be situation plus problem plus solution. Her other types appear to be variations of the most common type.

Sowers (1981) examined 217 "published" storybooks by twenty-two first-grade children. Judging any piece ordered chronologically to be narrative, she found that in November of a school year the children wrote relatively few narratives—36 percent. By June, 78 percent of their writings were narratives. The nonnarratives "were typically attributes of the topic" (p. 192); thus, "Whales are black and some are gray. Whales are big. They can eat you in one bite. There are brown whales and there are black whales too. There are white whales. There are blue killer whales." Many of the attribute writings, especially those of girls, are highly affective—what Sowers calls "self-expressive." She comments on "the failure of Moffett's rhetorical system to predict children's early writing preferences" (p. 204), assuming that the attribute writings, in Moffett's terms, are analogic, a category of writing which Moffett argues is more abstract than narrative. She argues that Britton's rhetorical theory, while also failing to predict preference for the nonnarrative, does predict that early writing will be expressive, displaying the writer's feelings for their own sake. Indeed, many of the attribute writings presented by Sowers are expressive: for example, "Me and Chipper have lots of fun. We have fun. I love Chipper so much. I won't stop loving Chipper. It's so much fun. It is fun."

But calling such writing expressive does not satisfactorily explain pieces such as "Whales," quoted above, or the considerably longer pieces on alligators and sailboats which Sowers presents. All of these attribute writings, however, are to some extent reminiscent of Applebee's categories of "heaps" and "sequences." They are statements which are linked by association. But they clearly seem to be products of what Bereiter and Scardamalia (1982) call the "what next" strategy. The writer finds a topic, thinks of one sentence, then another, and then another, and so forth. It is also interesting to note that this form allows for considerable repetition of key words. Note that the word *whales*, in the piece by the same name, represents over 15 percent of the total words used. This may be a great asset to young writers.

Schemata and the Production of Stories

As indicated earlier, there is good reason to believe that schemata of various kinds underlie our organization of experience and help us assimilate new information more rapidly as we encounter it. Schank and Abelson (1977), for example, show that scripts are important in allowing us to understand and predict new experience. The term *script* here refers to the chain of events in common experiences of a given type such as going to a restaurant or going to the supermarket. When we have not had experiences of a particular type, e.g., going to a clinic for X-rays, we may be uncomfortable until we have learned the script for that experience. At the same time, when we know a script, we recognize violations of it, as we would if a restaurant patron ordered only a glass of water.

In the past few years, psychologists have also been asking what generalized knowledge we have of stories and how that knowledge contributes to our comprehension and production of stories. Much of that work has not dealt with story production per se but with retellings of stories, identifying characteristics of stories, or reordering scrambled events. One important result of such work is that definitions of *story* have become more precise, with investigators differentiating between essential and optional features and attempting to establish prototypical story forms and rules which allow for transformations of those forms.

Stein and Trabasso (1982) present one commonly used definition of the minimal story which consists of a setting and an episode. The setting includes the introduction of the protagonist and one or more statements about the protagonist and the physical, social, or temporal environment. The episode contains a sequence of five different categories. The first category is the *initiating event*, which contains information marking some sort of change in the protagonist's environment and which evokes a desire to achieve some sort of goal. The second category, *internal response*, includes the goal and may also include an emotional response to the initiating event. Trabasso and Stein propose this second category as the most important because they believe that story knowledge is organized around the goal of the protagonist. The third category is the *attempt* by the protagonist to achieve the goal. The *consequence*, the fourth category, indicates whether or not the goal was achieved and in more complex stories may give rise to a second episode. *Reaction* is the fifth category and may include the character's response to what has occurred, events which occur as a direct result of what has gone before, or a moral which indicates what can be learned from the character's action. Each category in this chain causes or enables the occurrence of the subsequent category.

Stein and Trabasso's definition of story, of course, represents only one type of story—that which is goal-directed. Thus, a narrative concerning the death of a victim of a natural disaster might not allow the victim to form any goal or make any attempt to achieve a goal. Such a narrative might well require its own definition. For a review and analysis of story definitions see Stein and Policastro (1984).

Using prototypical stories with clearly identifiable characteristics, researchers have demonstrated convincingly that knowledge of story form helps young children recall stories more readily. They have shown, in addition, that when stories occur in a nonprototypical form, the story is more difficult to recall and that children tend to recall it in the prototypical form rather than in the sequence in which it was presented. Evidence of this kind is accumulating very rapidly and suggests that schemata do guide the production of stories and perhaps other types of writing.

In one of the most thorough and interesting structural analyses of children's stories to date, King and Rentel (1981) used different tools to examine stories written by thirty-six children in an urban school and a suburban school at three different times (March 1979, October 1979, and May 1980) as they progressed from the end of first grade through second grade. Each observation consisted of several days during which students retold stories, dictated their own original stories, and wrote original stories. The retold and dictated stories were tape-recorded by the researchers, and all stories were coded for indicants of cohesion and for structural properties.

The analysis of cohesion was based on the work of Halliday and Hasan (1976) and involved the use of five categories of cohesive elements: reference, substitution, ellipsis, conjunction, and lexical cohesion. Also coded were instances of restricted exophoric items. (For example, a writer begins a story with "They didn't have any food" and does not identify *they*. The unidentified pronoun is an instance of restricted exophora.)

The analysis of story structure in King and Rentel's study was based on the work of Propp (1968) and involved content analysis of the children's stories for Propp's "functions," which focus on what characters do. In his analysis of Russian fairy tales, Propp identified thirty-one functions which he believed included all major plot components of the tales in his sample. Two of the most important functions are "lack" and "villainy." A story is coded for the former when a character lacks or desires something such as money, magical power, a bride, or food. Villainy occurs when one character causes "harm or injury to a member of the group or family." Types of villainy range from murder and abduction to enchantment. Other functions, which also appear in myth, include the hero's *departure* "in quest of something or in response to an action or request," the hero's *preparation* "through interrogation, trial, testing or observation," *struggle* with the villain, and the hero's *return* to the place where the action originated (pp. 221–223). These and the other functions may take a variety of forms and were liberally interpreted in King and Rentel's study (according to the researchers themselves).

Coder reliability for written and oral stories in King and Rentel's study ranged from .85 to .93. The researchers found that, over the sixteen months of the study, the greatest increase in cohesion of the written stories was lexical. Lexical cohesion involves (1) the repetition of particular terms or synonyms when they have the same referents and (2) collocation, which refers to "the co-occurrence in a text of words that display word-meaning relationships" (p. 11). The second greatest change in cohesion was the increase in conjunction. The third greatest was the decrease in restricted exophoric references, suggesting strongly that, as children mature, they learn to write for a distant audience.

King and Rentel also found that over the sixteen months the children "were able to write increasingly more ambitious stories which contained a wider range of functions . . . and a greater number of functions" (p. 75). Further, the children included significantly more functions in their retellings of stories than in their original dictated stories. However, there was no significant growth in the number of functions or function types in dictated stories over the sixteen months.

Although King and Rentel make no explicit comparisons of the complexity of retold and dictated stories with the complexity of written stories, the data in their Tables 31 and 45 (pp. 90 and 103) clearly suggest that youngsters included many more functions in retold stories than in dictated stories and many more in dictated stories than in written stories. Further, for dictated stories the difference in the number and types of functions from observation 1 to observation 3 was not significant. The children in the study did not increase their ability to invent and sustain an original oral narrative, at least in terms of functions. The significant increases in both number of functions and types of functions for written stories must be due to something other than increased knowledge of story schemata or functions and the ability to put them to use. Presumably, it is the result of increased dexterity in getting words down on paper, a dexterity which by the end of the second grade cannot yet keep pace with the children's inventive power when it is tapped orally.

An appendix of the King and Rentel study examines text length in terms of the number of T-units included, using several analyses of variance to determine the effect on text length of a variety of variables, including school, dialect, sex, mode, and observation in various combinations. The researchers report significant increases in text length from the first to the second observation for written stories and for retold and dictated stories taken together. However, when they examine the text length of dictated stories alone for the urban school, with data grouped by dialect, sex, and observation, they report no significant differences.

In contrast, when we examine the mean length in T-units of dictated stories by the twelve suburban students, we find an increase from the first to the third observation of about 33 percent for both boys and girls (Table 19, p. 267). Similarly, when we examine means by observation for all twenty-four urban students (Table 15, p. 264), we find an increase from the first to the third observation of over 100 percent, from 17.79 to 40.21 T-units. These appear to be very large gains, which may have been obscured by the researchers' conservative statistical analysis and the small cell sizes.

If we reconstitute means and standard deviations for length of dictated stories over the whole sample ($n = 36$) from the available data (Table 15, p. 264 and Table 17, p. 266), we find a difference of 18.14 T-units between the first and third observations. Because the groups have the same students in the first and third observations, a test of t for the significance of the difference between their performances on the two occasions should technically use a formula which considers the correlation between the two sets of scores. However, since that correlation is not available, and since the t-test for correlated groups is likely to be less restrictive than that for noncorrelated groups, it seems reasonable to use the latter. We can infer that a test for correlated groups is likely to indicate an even larger difference. A test of t for differences between combined population means on the first and third observations yields a t-score of 3.65, significant at $p < .001$. If we also reconstitute whole-sample means and standard deviations of Proppian functions in dictated stories (from Table 31, p. 90 and Table 40, p. 100), assuming equal cells, we find an increase of only 1.20 functions, which is not significant.

Comparison of the means and standard deviations for length and number of Proppian functions indicates clear growth for length but not for the measure based on the number of Proppian functions in dictated stories. If we assume, on the basis of significant increases in cohesion from the first to the third observation, that the additional T-units are relevant to the stories, then we must also assume that they elaborate on the functions. The ratio of T-units to functions changes from 3:1 in March of the first grade to 5:1 in May of the second grade, an increase of 66 percent. And although this change is not even over all subgroups, it is impressive, suggesting what must be an increased ability to elaborate the details of a story.

Normally, the present review would not have examined reports of oral composing, but it has done so here because doing so seemed relevant. The above comparison suggests that over time very young children's writing abilities catch up to their abilities in dictation. At the same time, the complexity of their dictated stories remains at a plateau. However, elaboration of elements in the dictated stories appears to increase dramatically. As an interesting study should, this one leaves us with a number of questions. We wonder whether children include more functions in their dictated stories as they become older, whether they increase the elaboration of written stories in the same proportion as in their dictated stories, whether there are other plateaus in their development, what the relationships are in general between story elements and elaboration or length, and what effects experience with literature and kinds of instruction have on these aspects of story writing.

Length and Elaboration

The apparent increase in length in the dictated stories examined by King and Rentel, when compared to the lack of significant change in number of functions, suggests an increase in elaboration. A number of other studies report significant correlations between length and rated quality or indicate that length is significantly related to quality in some way. Broderick (1972) found that college freshmen with high SAT scores wrote longer compositions than did those with low scores. Baggett (1978) found that the length of compositions increased with IQ.

Jurgens and Griffin (1970), studying compositions by seventh-, ninth-, and eleventh-graders, found that longer papers (in terms of total words and number of T-units) received significantly higher scores than did shorter papers at all three grade levels. O'Donnell, Griffin, and Norris (1967a) state, in regard to length, that "one may confidently report a high correlation between advances in grade and gross increases in wordage" (p. 42). A number of other studies report relatively high correlations between length and quality ratings. Stewart and Grobe (1979) report .38 for fifth grade, .47 for eighth grade, and .36 for eleventh grade; Nold and Freedman (1977) report .57 for Stanford freshmen; Faigley (1979c) reports .30 for South Dakota freshmen; and Wille (1982), reporting on work with eighth-graders, indicates correlations between length and quality of .53 and .58.

The evidence appears overwhelming that length makes a difference in quality. But as O'Donnell and his colleagues (1967a) were quick to point out, the gross number of words produced is probably, *in itself*, defective as an indicator of linguistic development. And although it appears a better indicator of quality than mean T-unit length, it still can account for only between 9 and 25 percent of the variance in quality scores. Assuming, however, that student writers do not pile up words randomly, length could be a productive area for research as an indication of the elaboration of structure. For example, assuming that the increased length of dictated stories in the King and Rentel study indicates increased elaboration of details about the functions utilized, it would be interesting to know (1) the extent to which various functions are elaborated, (2) whether some are more elaborated than others, and (3) if so, which ones. Likewise, using a story definition comparable to the one used by Stein and Trabasso, we might ask (1) whether students elaborate their settings, initiating events, internal responses, attempts, or consequences, (2) whether they do so evenly or differentially, and (3) whether the elaborations differ by age of the student or quality of the writing. We might examine the nature of elaboration in different kinds of writing. The nature of elaboration may display certain interactions with quality and certain syntactic features. Is it possible, for example, that high-quality arguments make use of narrative examples which reduce, in some instances, their mean T-unit length? Whatever the relationships are, understanding length as a reflection of elaboration beyond the restrictions of syntactic units may very well prove to be enlightening.

Because they provide clear criteria for delineating the structure of stories, some of the definitions and methods of analysis discussed above are very likely to provide considerable insight into the ways in which abstract schemata guide composing and perhaps as much insight into how teachers can help students write better stories of their own invention as well as stories about their personal experience. Such work is likely to go well beyond the analysis of schemata underlying stories. Some researchers have already begun examining the structure or skeletal frameworks which appear to undergird other genres as written by students, such as argument (Crowhurst 1983) and definition (Hillocks, Kahn, and Johannessen 1983; Litowitz 1977). Indeed, the development of primary trait scoring, because it focuses in part on the presence or absence of certain parts of the structure of what is written, contributes to this kind of analysis (see Lloyd-Jones 1977b, for example). This is an area of research likely to receive considerable attention in the next decade.

Audience—with Larry Johannessen

Only a few studies have examined the role of audience in written communication. The relative lack of research in this area is particularly surprising in light of the emphasis contemporary rhetorical theory places on the role of audience in the communication process. Most available research focuses on one of three areas. First, some researchers have attempted to describe and measure how writing changes when topics remain constant but the audience changes. Second, some research has examined factors which may influence writers' abilities to address audiences effectively. Third, a few studies have examined various instructional methods designed to enhance writers' quality of writing.

Smith and Swan (1978) studied the syntactic structures of writers to determine if writers at different ages perceive various audiences differently and thus refine their syntax to reflect this perception. Three groups of students, twenty-seven sixth-graders, eighteen college freshmen, and twenty-one upperclassmen, were given passages about bees on three different occasions (two weeks apart) with different directions each time. One set of directions asked students to rewrite the passage to make it better. The audience was assumed to be at the level of the writer. A second set of directions asked students to rewrite the passage so that it could be read by someone who had just learned how to read. The third set of directions asked students to rewrite the passage for a superior adult.

The researchers first determined the means of words per T-unit and words per clause for each grade writing for each audience. On both syntactic measures, the means increased with each successive grade on all three levels of writing. At each grade the means in passages written for new readers were less than the means in passages at the writer's level, which, in turn, were smaller than the means in passages written for superior adults. Two-way analysis of variance revealed that there were significant differences ($p < .01$) both within the levels of writing (below, at, and above) and within the grades themselves (sixth-graders, freshmen, and upperclassmen) on words per T-unit and words per clause. Scheffé contrasts indicated no significant differences among sixth-grade passages in words per T-unit or words per clause. This indicates that these subjects did not adjust their syntactic structures for a change in audience.

Both freshman and upperclassman subjects rewrote the below-level passage using significantly ($p < .05$) shorter T-units than they used in writing at their own level or for superior adults. However, passages at the writer's level and for superior adults were not significantly different. The researchers conclude that the sixth-grade students did not distinguish audience level by altering syntactic complexity. However, the college students did distinguish between their own level of writing and writing for an audience perceived as syntactically less mature.

Three studies have examined the relationship between mode of discourse, writing quality, and audience differences. Crowhurst and Piché (1979) randomly assigned 120 tenth- and sixth-grade students to one of three mode conditions: narration, description, and argumentation. Students wrote six times in each mode (three times for each of two audiences, teacher and best friend). To control for topic, the researchers showed slides which went along with each assignment. Three independent raters evaluated the papers for words per T-unit, words per clause, and clauses per T-unit. Rater reliability on sets of papers ranged from .94 to .98. The results of the analysis indicated that compositions written for the teacher audience were more syntactically complex than compositions written for a best friend. Significant differences were found for words per clause and near-significant differences for words per T-unit. The differences in words per clause were significant only for argument. Comparisons of audience by grade showed significantly more words per clause for compositions written for the teacher by tenth-grade students. There were also differences on measures for teacher and best friend for sixth-grade students. The finding that clause and T-unit lengths were greater for the teacher audience is probably due to the dimensions on which audiences were contrasted: intimacy, age, and power.

Rubin and Piché (1979) examined the syntactic and strategic structures in the persuasive writing of fourth-, eighth-, and twelfth-grade students, along with that of adults. Eighteen subjects were randomly selected, and after seeing a film on glassblowing, each subject wrote three persuasive essays on the subject to target audiences of high, intermediate, and low intimacy. The researchers analyzed the compositions for syntactic complexity and for the use of persuasive appeals. Social cognitive ability was measured by the depth of social influence manifested in social appeals. The results revealed that the age-related increases in syntactic complexity were consistent with previous research. Also, high intimacy engendered highly subordinate writing, while low intimacy engendered lengthy clauses. The effects of age on use of persuasive strategies were evident. Older writers tended to establish persuader credibility by placing the topic in a broad social and/or historical context. Expert adults used persuasive strategies differently for audience adaptation. Younger students did not. The results demonstrate that audience awareness can be manipulated in an assigned task and that adaptation to audience can be seen in syntactic complexity and the use of persuasive strategies.

Richardson (1980) studied the quality of essays written for distant and intimate audiences by high- and low-apprehensive two-year-college freshmen. Twenty-one freshmen college students were selected from a pool of fifty-eight. Each took the Daly-Miller Writing Apprehension Test. Thirteen subjects were classified as high-apprehensive and eight as low-apprehensive. Each student then wrote two essays, one to an intimate audience and the other to a distant audience. The results indicate there was no substantial difference in the overall quality of writing between high- and low-apprehensive writers. Also, there were no differences in the quality of writing for the two audiences. However, the syntactic maturity scores for the essays written for a distant audience were significantly higher ($p < .05$) than those for essays written for an intimate audience. In contrast, the coherence scores were significantly lower ($p < .05$) for essays written for the distant audience than for essays written for the intimate audience.

Conte and Ferguson (1974) examined the idea that a writer's knowledge of subject matter rather than knowledge of audience might result in more effective writing. They asked 70 drug users and 174 nonusers from the twelfth grade to write letters to a brother, sister, or best friend to convince them not to take drugs. Students were then given packets of the letters to rate in terms of their persuasive power. Each paper was rated by at least three student judges. The results indicate no significant differences between letters written by drug users and letters written by nonusers.

Plasse (1982) tested the influence of audience perspective on the assessment of student writing. The researcher first established four writing audiences: teachers, students, parents, and business people. Forty randomly selected twelfth-grade students wrote letters to one of the four randomly assigned audiences. The researcher carefully selected an argumentative topic and writing situation that were real. She also selected audience raters that were actual members of the audience categories. The raters read and rated all forty letters holistically, and wrote comments which were later analyzed and categorized. Analysis of variance determined the effect of assigned audience and rater type on the rankings. The analysis revealed significant differences among means of the holistic ratings of letters according to assigned audience. The letters written to business and teacher audiences were rated significantly higher ($p < .05$) than those written to student and parent audiences. However, no significant differences were exhibited among the means of holistic ratings of letters according to rater types. Also, there were no significant differences among the means of comment categories according to audience or rater types. The comments made by rater types showed varying degrees of sensitivity to writing characteristics but did not predict global judgments. The assigned audience type appears to be the significant factor in the holistic assessment.

Plasse admits that problems with the design of the study may explain why all rater groups rated the business and teacher letters as the best letters. However, she says that "contrary to the assumptions of rhetoricians who suggest that readers will respond more favorably to texts that specifically address them than to those that do not, writing evaluators in this study did not necessarily prefer the letters that were written to them" (p. 74).

Several studies have examined factors affecting audience awareness and writing skill. Hays (1981) had seven competent and six basic college writers write for one hour on the same topic, composing aloud on a tape recorder as they wrote. Six of the competent writers and five of the basic writers had been exposed to concepts involving revision and audience awareness. The researcher examined revisions in each student's written text and tape-recorded protocol. Each writer's sense of audience was inferred from the evidence within the protocol and from information elicited during post-composing interviews. Student papers were ranked using a primary trait scale. The results indicate that those students who composed with a strong sense of audience and purpose were less concerned with lexical and scribal matters and focused more upon the ideas they wished to convey than were the writers without this involvement. In a related study, Flower and Hayes (1981c) had four good writers and four poor writers compose aloud on a tape recorder. Analysis of the transcripts revealed that the verbal protocols of good writers focused on generating new ideas in response to the rhetorical problem, while the poor writers focused on response to the topic itself or to a current element in memory.

Prentice (1980) had thirty-six students—twelve each in grades 3, 5, and 7—describe a drawing so that a given audience could reproduce it. Each student wrote two descriptions for a first-grader and an adult reader. One description was written before the student received feedback from the intended reader, who tried to reproduce the drawing from the description. The other description was written after receiving feedback. The results show that sentence length did not vary depending on the audience. The seventh-grade writers did simplify their descriptions for the first-grade audience. Also, all writers gave more information for the adult audience and increased significantly the amount of information in their descriptions after receiving reader feedback. The researcher concludes that the results seem to contradict a great deal of research and theory which suggests that a sense of audience is developmental.

Several researchers have examined the idea that all children are egocentric at early ages and less so as they grow older. As we have seen, one of the major shifts identified by Graves (1981f) as children develop as writers is the shift from egocentric to sociocentric writing. Graves and others suggest that egocentricity prevents young writers from considering the knowledge of an audience group and hinders their ability to revise effectively. In a pilot study, Rodriguez (1976) examined egocentrism in the language of six- to seven-year-old Mexican children from three different social backgrounds. The researcher wanted to determine if children would omit important information in telling a story due to age egocentrism or due to social class differences. Seventy-nine children were selected on the basis of their fathers' occupations. Twenty were children of government employees, nineteen were children of skilled workers, and twenty were children of temporary manual laborers. A teacher showed illustrations and told groups of three students a story. Each child then told the story to two classmates, using the same illustrations. Each child's retelling was scored by how many information units were omitted. The results indicated that age and intelligence did not affect information omission. The children from the lowest social class omitted more information than children from the other two groups. This result suggests that social background may be a factor in egocentrism.

Bracewell, Scardamalia, and Bereiter (1978) examined the ability of writers to modify their writing according to the needs of different audiences and attempted to determine if this ability is related to the age of writers. The researchers asked forty-five students in each of grades 4, 8, 12, and 15 to describe two geometric shapes so that they could be redrawn by someone else: a student of the same age at a different school, a student in the same school, or a general audience. In a second experiment, forty-five students, including fifteen students in each of grades 4, 8, and 12, wrote descriptions of the same shapes to one of three audiences: someone younger, a peer, or an adult. The third group wrote the same descriptions, but their papers were returned, and they were told to revise their compositions according to one of four conditions: (1) make them clearer, (2) provide better reasons, (3) make them more interesting, or (4) make them better. Compositions were rated independently by two raters trained to look for four types of context-creating statements. The results indicate that compositions from the first two groups displayed a low incidence of context-creating statements. In grades 4 and 8, specifying audience age produced no more context statements than in the standard condition, but specifying age did produce more such statements in grade 12. The researchers report that writers' ability to use audience-orienting devices is present as low as grade 4 and that use of these devices increases between grades 4 and 12. However, the researchers also conclude that the ability to differentiate according to the needs of a specific audience is not clear until grade 12.

Several studies have tested the impact of helping writers develop audience awareness to improve the quality of their writing. In a pilot study, Bator (1980) had one section of college freshmen apply Young, Becker, and Pike's tagmemic heuristic to audience analysis. Then this class wrote compositions. A control class not trained in the heuristic also wrote essays on the same topic. A comparison of the two classes indicates that the tagmemic heuristic may be an effective way to improve the quality of a student's writing. In a case study of three college freshman compositions, H. E. Nugent (1979) utilized a procedure for increasing audience awareness. Quantitative measures of three compositions revealed an increase in students' abilities to use certain strategies. However, qualitative measures demonstrated no differences.

Loewenthal and Kostrevski (1973) had twenty-six experimental and nineteen control undergraduate engineering students take two tests of verbal skills. Both groups were then asked to write a description of an umbrella for a normal British audience who had never seen an umbrella. The experimental group then participated in role-playing activities in four different sessions. After this, the subjects again took the verbal skills test and wrote descriptions. Analysis of the results indicates that the verbal skills scores improved for the experimental group, and the experimental group did significantly better than the control group on their umbrella descriptions after role-playing.

While these few studies indicate that audience-related instruction regarding particular writing tasks can improve writing, we have little or no research showing whether attention to audience generalizes to writing tasks other than those related to the instruction. Indeed, we still have much to learn about a variety of factors related to audience. Do writers hold some sort of audience in mind as they write? If so, how specifically developed is the image? To what extent is the image a composite which includes the writer's own memories of experience as audience? Researchers have uncovered differences in syntactic complexity apparently due to audience. What aspects of form vary according to audience? To what extent does elaboration vary? When and how do writers decide to elaborate, simplify, clarify? What kinds of instruction are likely to help writers vary their writing effectively for different audiences?

Given the claims that many theorists make for the importance of audience awareness in the composing process, these and many more such questions seem well worth addressing. Relatively little has been attempted in examining writers' knowledge of audience/product relations and their use of that knowledge. It will be at least a very interesting area for some years.

3 Experimental Studies: Introduction to the Meta-Analysis

Within the past ten years or so, many researchers have turned away from experimental studies in composition, leveling criticism at these studies for a variety of reasons. Unfortunately, too many experimental studies deserve the criticisms. Too often the treatments are poorly conceived (occasionally silly), and the studies are badly designed. However, not all experimental studies are ill-conceived and badly designed. Those that are not may yield useful information, especially when we can synthesize results across studies using the techniques of meta-analysis.

This chapter examines the criticisms of experimental studies and the difficulties in doing them. It then explains the techniques used in the meta-analysis, the selection of studies, and the variables examined.

Criticisms of Experimental Studies

In 1963 Braddock, Lloyd-Jones and Schoer listed 504 items in their bibliography of works related to research in the teaching of composition. Many of those were experimental treatment studies. Twenty years later the number of experimental treatment studies outnumbers the total number of studies in their bibliography. Currently, however, among many researchers in the field of composition, such studies are in disrepute. Cooper and Odell (1978) claim that the authors included in their *Research on Composing* share "one audacious aim—that of redirecting and revitalizing research in written composition" (p. xiii). The redirection of research was away from the kind of "comparison group" studies summarized by Braddock, Lloyd-Jones, and Schoer in 1963. Cooper and Odell argue that the Braddock review was based on the assumption that "we already had a thorough understanding of written products and processes" (p. xiv), an assumption which they and their co-authors see as unwarranted. They believe that "ultimately, comparison-group research may enable us to improve instruction in writing," but not before such research is "informed by carefully tested theory and by descriptions of written discourse and the processes by which that discourse comes into being" (p. xiv). Emig (1982) sees much less promise for "comparison group" studies. Her attack is launched against the whole "positivist" research "paradigm," by which she seems to mean testing hypotheses in experimental designs in or out of laboratories.

Graves launches the most vituperative attack against experimental research. Writing in 1980, he claims that between 1955 and 1972 research on writing was in such low esteem "that eighty-four percent of all studies were done by dissertation alone." He continues, "it [writing research] was an exercise for students to apply courses in statistics to their dissertations." Later, in the same article, he charges that experimental research "is written for other researchers, promotions, or dusty archives in a language guaranteed for self-extinction" (p. 918). Says he, "The research conducted on best methods for teachers was of the worst type. We took the science model of research and attempted to remove certain variables from their context to explain two crafts, teaching and writing, by dismissing environments through statistical means" (p. 914). According to Graves, most of this research "wasn't readable and was of limited value. It couldn't help [teachers] in the classroom" (p. 914). It is, he says, "devoid of context" and concerned only with "sterile" and "faceless" data. Graves continues, "Though they purport to give direct help, persons using experimental designs have contributed least to the classroom teacher" (p. 917). Teachers, he says, "have been unable to transfer faceless data to the alive, inquiring faces of the children they teach the next morning" (p. 918). What Graves appears to mean by this curious metaphor is that findings of research studies cannot be generalized from one classroom setting to another.

Clearly, while Cooper and Odell see some value for comparison group studies in the future, Emig and Graves, along with some others of their persuasion, see none. If they are right, then we should expect to find little of value in such studies. If Graves, in particular, is right in his suggestions that the findings and/or conclusions of experimental studies cannot be used in other classrooms, then we should find that replications of experiments have results which bear little similarity to each other. In fact, many experimental trials have been replicated, e.g., sentence combining. The question of whether the results are similar remains. It will be taken up in the meta-analysis which follows. If the results are similar, (that is, homogeneous), then Graves's criticisms of experimental studies will have been inappropriate.

Even those who see value in experimental research have criticisms of specific studies as well as animadversions about tendencies within the genre. Braddock, Lloyd-Jones, and Schoer (1963) made many recommendations which they hoped would improve experimental research design. Part II of their report consists of twenty-four pages of recommendations about scoring, controlling variables which might influence outcomes, reporting results, and so forth. As the authors explain (p. 55), these suggestions became criteria in selecting the "most soundly based" studies, five of which were reviewed in detail. By implication, many of the studies reviewed did not meet most of the criteria.

Complaints and Problems in Research

Wesdorp (1982), in a study currently available only in Dutch, reviewed 158 experimental studies and, as part of the review, discusses eight common complaints about research in composition and theoretical and methodological problems associated with it. First, critics and even partisans of research often complain that research results fail to give definitive answers. Wesdorp points out that such disappointment has at least three sources: expectations which are too high for individual studies; the absence of a "general, consistent theory concerning language ability, in particular with respect to composition ability" (p. 11); and the absence of a theory of instruction in composition. The second complaint is that "sometimes research yields unexpected or unwelcome results, which are contrary to what the teacher has learned from his own experience" (p. 13). Wesdorp points out that this is the case with grammar/composition assumptions. Certainly, many teachers continue to argue on the basis of their experience and intuitions, as they perceive them, that increasing knowledge of traditional school grammar is essential to improving composition. But the mass of research even in 1963 could not support that contention.

A third complaint cited by Wesdorp is that research proves "only what was known already" (p. 14). Wesdorp cites Hagstrum's (1964) review of the Braddock report, in which Hagstrum takes the Buxton study to task. (The Buxton study is adumbrated in the Braddock report [pp. 58–70].) Hagstrum argues that we already *knew* the conclusion of this study: that an instructional method which used careful comment by the teacher, discussion of those comments, and revision would be superior to what amounted to free writing followed by generalized sentimental encouragement by the teacher. If Hagstrum knew that, a host of other researchers did not, as many studies in the ensuing decades attest. What seems to be the root of this complaint is the confusion between what one "knows" intuitively and personally with what one "knows" objectively on the basis of systematic evidence.

A fourth complaint is that research results are contradictory; one study reports significant results while another does not. Research results which are not universal may be disappointing to some, but they should not be unexpected given the diversity of student populations and teachers as well as the difficulty of controlling key variables.

Three other complaints cited by Wesdorp are (1) research tends to be fragmented, tending to ignore the results of other studies or at least failing to incorporate them meaningfully; (2) results are too detailed or trivial, tending to concentrate on molecular aspects of instruction (e.g., the effects of comments in margins as opposed to those at the end of a composition) while ignoring more important variables; and (3) research is "fashionable," with researchers often following a hunch about what effects some current educational fad may have on writing. All three of these complaints, which are valid enough, probably arise because of our lack of unified and consistent theories to guide research. Wesdorp argues that such theories are virtually nonexistent, and, depending on how one defines *theory*, I believe on the basis of this review that he is right. Certainly, there is no widely shared theory of composing nor of instruction in composition. For that matter, there seems to be no general instructional theory which can be applied to composing. Studies of teaching related to mastery learning theory deal with such areas as mathematics, science, and foreign language but have thus far avoided composition. A number of writers have commented on the lack of theory in guiding research, e.g., Gunderson (1967), Burton (1973), and M. L. King (1978).

Lack of consistent theory, however, does not imply that experimental research has been random. Researchers have identified issues and designed experiments to resolve certain controversies surrounding these issues. An example is the issue examined in the Buxton study: the question of whether specified assignments followed by careful teacher comment and supervised revision would be more effective than allowing students to write on whatever they wished and comments which praised the writing as much as possible but gave one or two suggestions for improvement. Buxton's answer favored the former. Subsequently, a number of studies have posed hypotheses about variables similar to those investigated by Buxton: freedom of choice in deciding what to write, positive general comments, detailed comments, structured and unstructured revision, and so forth. The problem has been one that Gunderson (1967) points out: the researcher's failure to build on previous research. She recommends that reviews of research show the relationship between the study at hand and previous ones, in part by indicating that "the present study follows leads uncovered by past efforts" (p. 12). Many studies examined for this review do not examine previous research with a view to uncovering leads and refining the independent variables to be tested.

Even if we lack theory, systematic and thorough reviews of research can help us to identify variables which might prove significant, to delineate them more carefully, and to develop designs which allow testing them in combination and separately. Even studies which show "no statistically significant differences" can contribute to such an effort. For example, several studies indicate that teacher comment, whether in the margins, interlinear, or terminal, has little effect on improving student writing. But most of them have apparently dealt with comments which range over a wide variety of problems from spelling to content. It is possible that these studies show not that teacher comment has little effect but that highly diffuse comments have little effect. Indeed, at least two studies suggest that comments which focus on a particular feature of writing can have a relatively strong effect. If both findings are sound, they suggest variables which might be examined in greater depth and with greater precision through the use of both case-study methods (to determine how at least some students respond to different kinds of comments) and experimental methods (to measure the effects of the types). Although the findings from such detailed research may not constitute theory, they can provide part of the basis for theory.

Burton (1973) points out a problem associated with developing designs for experimental research: "lack of trial runs or pilot studies which might eliminate the 'bugs' from designs and instruments for evaluation" (p. 75). Not only can trial runs help to eliminate "bugs," but they can help in refining the research questions and in indicating the usefulness of undertaking the study at all. Unfortunately, some studies reviewed for this report apparently used no pilot studies to test features of the design or the adequacy of the research questions.

Wesdorp (1982) sketches a series of problems in the designs he examined, including the failure to control for intervening variables such as teacher bias and aspirations, the failure to define dependent variables (which he attributes to inadequate theory), the use of indirect measures of composition ability rather than actual pieces of writing, low interrater reliabilities, the use of very small experimental groups, unclear descriptions of the population, failure to describe the treatments adequately, and finally the use of inadequate statistical procedures (a problem also noted by Burton). I found the same problems and others in this review. However, some of them deserve more specific attention than Wesdorp allots them. In the present review of over 500 experimental studies, the most pervasive problem had to do with the control of variables. The major function of an experimental design is *control*—control over variables which might intervene to make a difference where none should be expected.

Control of Variables in Experimental Studies

Because absolute standards in composition achievement (as well as in other areas of academic achievement) do not exist, the control of observations must be based on comparison. That is, the achievement of one group of students must be compared with that of another group receiving some other treatment or no treatment. Failure to include one or more comparison groups results in various threats to internal validity. That is, the function of the comparison group is to account for the effects of factors outside the experimental treatment which might influence outcomes—factors such as maturation, intervening events, methods of measurement, the effects of being tested, or statistical regression to the mean. Studies which do not include comparison groups, including case studies, cannot generalize about the effects of any particular condition. They can report only the specifics of the particular situation.

A fairly large number of the experimental studies reviewed did not take adequate steps to insure comparability of the groups or to take into account existing differences. The classic method of assuring comparability is to assign students randomly to classes. In most real school situations, particularly in secondary schools, scheduling problems make random assignment of students to treatments extremely difficult. As might be expected, very few studies made use of random assignment. The alternative is to assign treatments randomly to groups and to pretest students in order to account for differences in ability among the groups prior to instructional treatment. A surprisingly large number of studies neither assigned students randomly to treatments nor pretested using direct tests of writing similar to those used as posttests. A number of studies assumed that a multiple-choice test of reading or mechanics and usage would serve as a pretest of composition skill. Although such tests may save the researcher time, they cannot be assumed to provide an adequate index of composition ability.

Not only must differences between control groups be accounted for, but there must be at least minimal controls for the teacher variables, i.e., his or her attitudes, abilities, or experience. Such variables can never be completely controlled, but the more teachers involved, the more reliable will be the generalizations emerging from the research. Although teachers may not think they are biased toward a treatment, when only one teacher presents both treatments or when one teacher teaches the experimental class and another teaches the control, the critical reader cannot assume that any results are due to treatment. In the first instance, differences might be due to the teacher's bias in favor of one method. In the second, they might be due to differences in teacher attitude, knowledge, or experience.

The meta-analysis undertaken for this review required that for inclusion a study either used two teachers, with each teaching all treatments, or used a minimum of two teachers for each different treatment. That is to say, if teachers were crossed with treatments, the experiment required at least two of them. If teachers were nested within treatments (each teaching only one treatment), then a minimum of two was required for each treatment. My estimate is that over 50 percent of the experimental treatment studies carried out over the last twenty years did not meet this requirement.

Assuming a given treatment is controlled for teacher bias, can the researcher or the reader be sure that the treatment is in place—that it is actually occurring in classes as assumed by the researcher? In the vast majority of cases included here, no empirical evidence is presented to indicate that the treatment was carried out as described. Fewer than 5 percent of the studies present such evidence. Naturalistic studies of classrooms, e.g., Applebee (1981), describe in some detail what occurs. Experimental studies in this review, however, tend to accept on faith what has occurred. Observations of the kind conducted by Applebee and his colleagues could present detailed information on how experimental and control classes were conducted, thereby adding not only assurance that the expected treatments were in place, but considerable understanding of *how* the treatments work.

One of the most commonly occurring shortcomings of the studies reviewed is the nonrandom assignment of teachers to treatments. Several studies did not assign teachers randomly to treatments and did not have teachers teach in all treatments. In a few studies, the experimental teachers even volunteered while the control teachers did not, a circumstance thought by some to guarantee systematic differences in the experience of the groups other than those imposed by the treatments.

Reporting of Data in Experimental Studies

Braddock, Lloyd-Jones, and Schoer (1963) made a number of recommendations about the reporting of data. Their major recommendation was that "data should be described and analyzed by methods which permit a clear understanding by the reader and replication by other investigators" (p. 27). Among the data to be presented clearly, they meant instructional procedures and materials as well as "sample themes (with markings), tabulations, distributions of scores," (p. 27) and even the raw data for individuals. Some of the studies encountered in this review, far from elucidating the data, seemed bent on obscuring them. One study, for example, avoids comparisons of control and experimental groups and presents data in such a way that no comparison is possible. Another presents only an indication of differences and probability estimates but not the direction of the differences. Several present only a part of the statistical analysis but no means or standard deviations. Several failed to report the number of subjects or obscured it by presenting one n in the text and another in the tables. A small number of studies had to be excluded from the meta-analysis because they did not provide adequate data.

With the meta-analytic tools available for aggregating research results, every reasonably well-designed piece of research has greater potential value than in the past. Besides that, making basic data available allows another researcher to reexamine results, perhaps to subject them to other tests or to include them in studies which aggregate results. With all the hours spent on empirical research the researchers owe themselves the few more hours which will ensure that basic data are clearly presented.

Scoring Compositions

One of the great bugaboos of research in composition two decades ago was the unreliability of ratings. Paul B. Diederich, speaking at the 1963 conference on Research Design and the Teaching of English in San Francisco, stated, "I honestly believe that almost all experiments concerning English composition that rely on essay grades have been conducted with tape measures printed on elastic" (1964, p. 60). He claimed that at the time the usual reliability of ratings was about .5, indicating a measure so wobbly that "one could hardly expect to find a significant difference between two treatments of any sort" (p. 59). Fortunately, since that time a number of researchers have examined the sources of unreliability and, more important for experimental research in composition, have developed various scales and procedures which yield reliabilities well over .8. A detailed analysis of the many studies which investigate the bias of scores or the reliability and validity of particular scales or the relationships among them is beyond the scope of this work. What follows is a general account of some of the important trends during the past several years.

In studies of rater preference or bias there have been two major types of design. In the first, researchers have varied certain features of writing to determine how various groups of raters respond to the variations. Hake and Williams (1981), for example, varied sentences so that one version of a composition used sentences of the form they call "agent/action/goal," while in the second version they nominalized verbs and adjectives. These procedures yield contrasting sentences such as the following:

Verbal:

The board determines the company's goals in foreign operations.

Nominalized:

Determination of the company's goals takes place at the board level.

(Hake and Williams found that their subjects—high school, junior college, and senior college teachers—tended to choose the nominalized style more often than the more direct verbal counterpart.)

In the second method of examining rater bias, researchers have asked raters, often in a variety of fields, to sort compositions into some predetermined number of categories of merit and to comment on the papers individually or on papers in each category as a group. An early and important study of this type was conducted by Diederich and his colleagues at the Educational Testing Service in Princeton, New Jersey. Diederich (1964) reports that 300 college freshman compositions were given to two distinguished readers in each of six different fields. The readers included teachers of college English, social sciences, and natural science; writers and editors; lawyers; and business executives. Fifty-three readers completed the task. Correlation of their scores yielded a median correlation of .31. Factor analysis of the correlations yielded five factors. Diederich and his colleagues then tabulated the comments of the readers scoring highest on each factor to determine "what they were agreeing on" (p. 69).

The largest cluster of readers were most concerned with the clarity, quality, fertility, development and support of ideas, and with the relevance of these ideas to the topic. The next largest cluster was most influenced by errors in usage, punctuation, and spelling. The third was most concerned with organization and analysis. Two other clusters were concerned with "verbal felicity and infelicity" and with "the personal qualities of the writing," i.e., "style, interest, and sincerity," which Diederich and his colleagues call "flavor" (p. 70). The above factors were used as parts of a scale for a year by teachers in three large high schools. This additional research yielded a scale composed of the following factors (p. 71):

General merit:

Quality and development of ideas
Organization, relevance, movement
Style, flavor, individuality
Wording and phrasing

Mechanics:

Grammar, sentence structure
Punctuation, capitals
Spelling
Handwriting, neatness

Diederich presents this scale in *Measuring Growth in English* (1974), along with procedures for using it and for attaining high levels of reliability. This scale has been used in many of the studies encountered in this review and is a valid, carefully developed scale for the assessment of expository writing.

A great deal of research has been directed at establishing other kinds of scales and scoring procedures. Particularly useful are Cooper's essay on holistic scoring (1977) and Lloyd-Jones's on primary trait scoring (1977b), both of which present lucid explications of a variety of scales. Many of the studies reviewed here have made use of the scales and systems described by Cooper, Diederich, and Lloyd-Jones with reliabilities far beyond those which Diederich complained of in 1963, usually over .80. Unfortunately, some researchers continue to ignore what has been learned about scoring and continue to break basic rules. In a few cases, researchers themselves scored all papers. Compositions were not always scored blind—that is, with raters in ignorance of experimental/control and pre/post conditions. And some studies provided no information about scoring procedures at all. Nonetheless, in this reviewer's opinion, rating methods have come a long way since Diederich's comment about "elastic tape measures" in 1963.

Meta-Analysis of Experimental Treatment Studies

With the many problems which exist in experimental research, one might well ask why it is worth bothering with. Wesdorp (1982) argues that for the time being, there is little else upon which we can rely for deciding upon concrete practices to use in classrooms. He believes that "process research is still in its infancy and therefore does not yield clear recommendations for practice yet" (p. 43). He argues that several experimental studies pointing in the same direction are important for practice, despite technical problems in the research.

I would go farther. We can ill afford to ignore experimental studies for a number of reasons. First, the total number of experimental studies completed in the past twenty years exceeds the total number of studies included in the Braddock bibliography. Second, even a cursory review of the published studies indicates that many of them have heeded the advice of Braddock and his colleagues. Third, while no consistent theory of composition has been advanced, most experimental studies examined for this review were not based on whim. Many focus on issues of reasoned concern to teachers or researchers. Many present fairly detailed rationales for their experimental treatments which are sometimes based on philosophical ideas (or ideals) about education and sometimes on classroom experience or previous research. Finally, new techniques for integrating the results of research have become available in the past few years. Thus, despite the current disdain for experimental studies, it seemed wise to examine them.

For these reasons, I decided to conduct a meta-analysis of experimental treatment studies which allows comparison of results across several dimensions, including academic level, duration, mode of instruction, focus of instruction, and the effects of teacher and peer feedback.

Traditional reviews of research have grouped studies by the variables examined and have reported, for example, the number of studies with significantly positive results, the number with no significant differences, the number with mixed results, and so forth. Such box-score reviews can be useful, particularly when all studies concerned have similar results. Braddock, Lloyd-Jones, and Schoer (1963) used such a review to conclude that the study of formal grammar had no effect on the quality of writing. Wesdorp's recent study (1982) attempts to discover significant variables in composition instruction using a similar method. However, this box-score method cannot compare the power of treatments across studies, and it relies on tests of the significance of differences, which to some extent depend upon sample size. Unfortunately, the focus on the significance of differences leads one to ignore the size of gains. For example, with a sample size of several hundred, a very small gain might be statistically significant, but not meaningful in the sense that an observer would be able to examine a writer's pretest and posttest and predict treatment group membership. On the other hand, a study indicating no significant difference might obscure very large gains for both experimental and control groups. Because meta-analysis is based on the size of gains (effect sizes), it can avoid such problems.

In order to examine the size of a gain, meta-analysis converts scores from the raw scores to standard scores. If we were considering a single student, we could report his or her raw score on a given test or we could report his or her distance from the average score (the mean) of all people taking the test. Meta-analysis examines scores in terms of their distance from the mean. The mean on the SAT examination, for example, is 500. Its standard deviation is 100. A student scoring 600 is one standard deviation above the mean and may be said to have a score of $+1.00$ standard deviation. Likewise, a student scoring 400 is one standard deviation below the mean. A student who takes the SAT more than once and raises his or her score by 50 points has raised it .5 standard deviation.

Scores for groups of students can be reported in the same way. Assuming comparable pretests and posttests, let us say that a class has a mean of ten points on the pretest and a mean of fourteen points on the posttest. If the relevant standard deviation is four points, then those students have shown a gain of 1.00 standard deviation from pretest to posttest. If on the same tests a second class shows a gain of one point from pretest to posttest, then the first class may be said to have gained .75 standard deviation more than the second.

It is important to realize that while the numbers used in reporting scores in standard deviations are small in absolute terms, an increase of one full standard deviation is a very large gain. Assuming normal distribution, such a gain would signify that about 50 percent of all students involved had reached or surpassed a point previously reached by only about 16 percent of the students. At the same time, it indicates that only 16 percent of the students fall below the mean for all students on the pretest. Although gains of that magnitude are not common, they do occur in some studies.

The techniques used in this analysis are based on the work of Glass (1978) and particularly on the statistical model developed by Hedges (1981, 1982a, 1982b). A meta-analysis computes standard scores, commonly called effect sizes, for various treatment gains or losses. This analysis will examine two types of effect size: (1) those which examine the difference between control and experimental treatments in a given study and (2) those which examine pre-to-post changes for a given group.

The experimental/control effect size is computed by dividing the difference between posttest scores—adjusted for the difference between pretest scores—by the pooled standard deviation of posttest scores for all groups in the particular study. The resulting standard score, or effect size, indicates the difference between experimental and control groups in terms of standard deviations. Thus, a given treatment might be said to have an experimental/control effect size of .5 standard deviation, meaning that the gain for the average student in the experimental group is .5 standard deviation greater than for the average student in the control group.

The pre-to-post effect size is computed by dividing the difference between pretest and posttest scores for a given group by the pooled standard deviation of pretest scores for all groups. Thus, the gain for any group, experimental or control, may be reported as being x standard deviations from pretest to posttest.

Note that for experimental/control effect sizes, the denominator is the pooled standard deviation of posttest scores for all groups, because the experimental/control effect sizes are comparisons of the posttest scores of two or more groups. For pre/post effect sizes, the denominator is the pooled standard deviation of pretests for all groups, because it compares the difference between pretest and posttest scores. In a few studies, these general rules could not be followed because the necessary data were not available. Thus, in a very few cases, the pooled standard deviation of posttest scores was used to compute pre/post effect sizes.

Most meta-analyses have focused on experimental/control effect sizes because they control for various intervening variables. The major focus of this analysis will be on experimental/control effect sizes also. However, there are at least two reasons for examining pre/post effect sizes in addition. First, in composition instruction control groups are not always simply negative instances of variables ascribed to experimental groups. They often constitute treatments which are described in fairly specific detail. In some instances, a control treatment in one study will have much in common with an experimental treatment in another study. A second reason for examining treatments independent of experimental or control status is the effect which successful and unsuccessful control treatments have on the experimental/control effect sizes. For example, in one study, the experimental treatment produced no gain while the control group exhibited a large loss. The result was a significant difference in favor of the experimental group. On the other hand, gains for control groups are certainly not uncommon. When those treatments are described, they can be examined in combination with other treatments to provide us with information more complete than that available from experimental/control comparisons alone. This study, therefore, will examine experimental/control effect sizes systematically and will examine pre/post effect sizes when they can provide useful information.

Effect sizes are computed in order to accumulate and compare results across studies. They enable researchers to ask whether treatments with similar characteristics have similar effects and to ask how much one set of treatments differs from another. Using the techniques developed by Hedges (1981), this meta-analysis weights each effect size by the reciprocal of its variance so that the accumulation is not simply an average of raw effect sizes but a mean effect size dependent on the variance of its constituents.

The major goal of meta-analysis is to explain the variability among treatment effect sizes in relation to the characteristics of the treatments under analysis. That involves categorizing the treatments along various dimensions (e.g., instructional mode, focus of instruction, duration), comparing mean effect sizes of treatments grouped together, and testing the studies grouped together for homogeneity (Hedges 1982b). The simple comparison of mean effect sizes can provide useful information about the effectiveness of treatments. However, insofar as averages obscure extreme cases, which may be significantly different from the mean, some test is useful to determine the extent to which a given mean effect is representative of its constituents.

The homogeneity statistic provides such a test, asking "whether the variability in effect size estimates is greater than would be expected if all the studies shared a common underlying effect size" (Giaconia and Hedges 1982, p. 584). The test yields a *chi square* statistic which indicates the statistical significance of differences among treatments grouped together. The higher the statistic, the more significant the variability among treatments. To be labeled homogeneous in this study, a grouping must have a homogeneity statistic (H) which is not significant at $p < .01$. If a set of treatments has common, identifiable characteristics and is homogeneous, then we can assume that their mean effect size is representative of all studies in the grouping—not simply an average—and that the effects are the result of their shared characteristics. When that is the case, the explanatory power of the category is greater. Similarly, if the sum of the homogeneity statistics for categories of treatments along a given dimension is not significant, then we can assume that the dimension or set of categories fits the data well and has a high level of explanatory power.

Given the requirements of homogeneity for the explanation of effect sizes and the experience of researchers in the social and physical sciences, it will be unreasonable to expect the analysis to explain 100 percent of the data available. The question is how much of the data can be eliminated without invalidating any claim to explanatory power. Previous research indicates that the best estimations of effect size may involve elimination of 20 to 30 percent of the data (Huber 1977). The ground rules for this study will be somewhat more restrictive. For the initial stages of analysis, four studies which contribute most heavily to the heterogeneity—two with high positive effect sizes and two with high negative effect sizes—will be dropped. These four studies represent about 5 percent of the seventy-three treatments for which experimental/control effect sizes are calculable. Thereafter, for the analysis of a given dimension, no more than 15 percent of the experimental/control treatments in the categories of that dimension will be eliminated to achieve homogeneity. The total number of studies dropped will include those eliminated for substantive reasons. If homogeneity is not possible, after eliminating 15 percent, we must conclude that the dimension and the categories in it lack a high level of explanatory power. The data available do not fit the explanatory model well.

The test of homogeneity permits a test of hypotheses implicit in certain criticisms which have been leveled at experimental studies as a genre. As indicated earlier, Graves (1980) charges that "persons using experimental designs have contributed least to the classroom teacher" (p. 917) because teachers "have been unable to transfer faceless data to the alive, inquiring faces of the children they teach the next morning" (p. 918). Both Emig (1982) and Graves (1980) have accused experimental designs of context-stripping—of ignoring the context in which an experiment takes place so that even when successful the method cannot be transferred to another classroom. If these claims are true, it should not be possible to replicate experiments, and we should find that treatments with similar instructional variables have highly disparate results. That is, if the critics are right, we should find that studies grouped together—because they are described as sharing certain characteristics—will not have homogeneous effects.

Selection of Studies

This review attempts to examine every experimental study produced between 1963 and 1982. These include over 500 published studies, dissertations, studies in ERIC, and studies in mimeographed form. Three researchers, including the author, worked independently to screen all of the studies. In the case of dissertations, abstracts were first read to determine whether a particular piece met the criteria listed below. Those dissertations that did not meet the criteria were rejected. Those that met the criteria were ordered and read, with the exception of four located in 1982. All other studies were read in their entirety.

While it is possible to include all available studies in a meta-analysis, coding them for variations in design, it seemed reasonable to include only those studies which met the following minimal criteria. First, by definition, the study had to involve a treatment: some combination of conditions, instruction, practice, and/or feedback over some period of time leading to a posttest. Studies which examined the effects of certain conditions on a single piece of writing were not included in the meta-analysis. (However, they are reviewed in Chapter 7.) Thus, Bridwell's (1980b) carefully designed study of revision was not included in the meta-analysis because it does not represent a sustained treatment but rather examines the effects of a set of conditions on a single piece of writing.

Second, a study had to make use of a scale of writing quality applied to samples of writing. Studies which used only standardized test results were excluded, as were studies which involved writing samples but only counted errors or various syntactic features. This condition permits asking the following question in the meta-analysis: Which treatments appear to produce the greatest gains in writing quality? A few studies were also excluded because rating procedures did not score compositions along a scaled continuum. Rather, they used a method in which judges were presented with compositions written by matched pairs of students and asked to choose the better piece of writing. The researcher then assigned a score to each piece of writing based on the number of judges selecting it as the better of the pair. Such scores, while reasonable, appear to have a meaning substantially different from that of a scale score. For example, if two compositions lay at the upper end of the scale, say at 6 and 7, on a seven-point scale, and if seven judges consistently picked the latter paper as superior, it would receive a score of 7, while the paper scored 6 on the scale would receive a score of 0. The difference between 6 and 7 and 0 and 7 would have a powerful—and misleading—impact on effect sizes.

Third, to be included in the meta-analysis, a study had to exercise minimal control for teacher bias. Specifically, if only two teachers were involved, each must have taught one class for each treatment. If teachers did not teach all treatments, then at least two different teachers must have taught each treatment, so that the total number of teachers was at least twice the number of treatments.

Fourth, to be included, a study had to control for differences among groups of students. In a few cases students were randomly assigned to treatment groups. In one study, the students were carefully matched (Sbaratta 1975). When students were not randomly assigned to treatments or not matched, studies must have used direct pretest and posttest measures of composition ability for both experimental and control groups.[1] Reviewers also looked for evidence that treatments were assigned randomly. However, because such information was frequently absent, this criterion could not be applied systematically.

Fifth, compositions must have been scored under conditions which help to assure validity and reliability. The compositions must have been coded for scoring and precautions taken so that raters could not infer the treatment, the teacher, the time of writing, or the identity of students. Two or more raters must have rated each composition and their scores must have been summed or averaged, *or* procedures for training raters and the subsequent reliabilities must have been reported. Nearly every study reporting reliabilities indicated them to be .70 or higher. Most were over .80. All studies included used some version of holistic, analytic, or primary trait scoring.

A few studies which met the stipulated criteria were regrettably

---

1. Although it seems almost needless to say so, the pretests and posttests also had to have been administered to the same students—those who experienced the experimental and control treatments. At least one important evaluation (Keech 1979) was rejected because it administered pretests to one group of students at the end of one school year and posttests to another group taught by the same teachers at the end of the following school year. We cannot assume that the two groups of students had the same abilities as writers at the beginning of the respective school years—even though they were assigned to the same teachers.

eliminated because the data presented did not allow for the extraction of means and standard deviations for pretests and posttests.

Bringing these criteria to bear eliminated over 80 percent of the experimental treatment studies. A study was eliminated if it violated any one of the criteria, and many violated several. For example, in one study all groups were taught by the researcher. Although students were not randomly assigned to treatments, the researcher used no pretest. Finally, scoring procedures were either inadequate or reported inadequately. The most common reason for rejection was clearly lack of adequate teacher control—a problem which might easily be rectified. This reason was followed by inadequate scoring procedures, lack of pretest writing sample without randomization of students, and no writing sample (but not necessarily in that order).

These criteria for selecting studies will be viewed by some as too stringent and by others as not stringent enough. We might have drastically changed the number of studies included or excluded by simply relaxing or tightening the criterion concerning the number and distribution of teachers. We might have eliminated studies by demanding that all studies involve classes in more than one school or that all schools used have both experimental and control classes. We might have included more studies by allowing the use of standardized tests as a pretest measure. We might have, but my decision was not to. The application of the criteria resulted in 60 studies with a total of 75 experimental treatments. For two of these, experimental/control effect sizes could not be calculated. The total of experimental and control treatments for which pretest to posttest effect sizes could be calculated was 121.

Variables Examined

Initial examinations of the experimental treatment studies revealed that most treatments described in detail involved a cluster of variables. Very few treatments were controlled to examine the effect of a single variable. For example, some treatments made use of free writing, peer feedback, and revision. Others used only one of those features. The description of some studies emphasized certain features of the treatment, but an examination of teaching materials or schedules revealed others. For example, Sager (1973b) emphasizes teaching students to use a scale for evaluating writing, but an examination of the sample lessons indicates that students were working in small groups on revision and were generating ideas for revision. Therefore, revision was coded as a feature of the treatment.

The initial list of instructional features was developed only after an investigation of several hundred studies and revised after an initial careful application to thirty studies. Not all possible features appear in the list. In a few cases, some features regarded as major by the researcher appeared to be barely discriminable from the control group features. In certain cases, the features emphasized by the researcher were one-of-a-kind. For example, the treatment in Belanger (1978b) consisted of quickly reading aloud lists of nonsense words and actual words for two days—a treatment assumed to help students focus on sentence meanings as opposed to the meanings of individual words. One-of-a-kind treatments were very few in number and were coded as having some other differentiation.

Two advanced doctoral students in measurement and evaluation coded more than the total number of studies included in the final meta-analysis. Of ninety-nine decisions per study (when studies had only two groups), they agreed on 87 percent. When they did not agree, they met to discuss and resolve differences. The author reviewed all decisions, disagreeing with only 2.1 percent. Those disagreements were resolved in conference when necessary.

Some relatively unambiguous features were coded as present or not present: the study of traditional grammar, transformational grammar, sentence combining, generative rhetoric, mechanics, or the study of model compositions; the use of feedback from teachers, feedback from peers, written feedback from teachers, teacher/student conferences, taped feedback, positive feedback, negative feedback; whether feedback was stipulated as intensive, moderate, or not present, and frequent, infrequent, or undifferentiated between groups; and whether writing was regarded as frequent, infrequent, or undifferentiated between groups. Even these features required some definition. For example, any activity involving generating changes in a given manuscript was regarded as revision whether or not the writing had been done by the students who were revising. Other variables, particularly mode of instruction, were defined at some length. Those definitions appear in the appropriate sections of this report.

When variables such as sentence combining, frequency of teacher feedback, or revision were not mentioned, they were coded as being regarded as irrelevant to the study. When a treatment was not described—as was the case with a few control groups—the variables were coded 0. For example, in a study by Alloway, et al. (1979), the analysis assumes that the experimental group's use of free writing, peer feedback, revision, and natural process mode is different from the control group treatment, which is not described. In such cases,

I have assumed, with the researchers themselves, that the experimental treatment is different from the control treatment.

In order to examine variables systematically in the meta-analysis, we have divided them into various dimensions: duration, grade level, mode of instruction, focus of instruction, revision, and feedback. Each dimension is examined in terms of its own categories, and any study may be examined in one or more dimensions. Thus a study of sentence combining at the twelfth-grade level which lasted one school year would be examined under the dimensions of focus of instruction, grade level, and duration. No treatment, however, could be included in more than one category in a given dimension. Ordinarily, this presented no problem. Occasionally, however, treatments included more than one focus of instruction. Troyka (1974), for example, includes work on mechanics as well as what I have categorized as inquiry. These few conflicts were readily resolved either by deferring to the emphasis of the researchers responsible for the study, by contrasting the study with others in the same categories, or by both methods. In Clifford (1978), for example, experimental groups made use of free writing for 15 of 150 minutes of class time per week. However, they also used structured feedback sheets in small peer-group discussions of their writing for a total of 75 minutes per week—a clear difference in emphasis. Further, none of the other studies making use of free writing emphasized the use of structured feedback. For these reasons, the Clifford study was categorized with those making use of structured feedback sheets or scales.

The results of the meta-analysis are presented in Chapter 8. Chapters 4, 5, 6, and 7 define the categories included in the meta-analysis as well as certain others which could not be included for various reasons. In addition, those chapters will provide summary and narrative reviews of studies of each type. The reader may wish to proceed directly to Chapter 8 for an overview of results. However, the results will be more meaningful after a perusal of the kinds of studies included. Chapter 4 examines studies which involve modes of instruction. Chapter 5 examines studies concerned with teaching grammar and the manipulation of syntax. Chapter 6 surveys studies focusing on learning criteria for judging writing through the study of models, the use of structured feedback sheets or scales, and through teacher feedback. Chapter 7 focuses on what has traditionally been called invention.

4 Modes of Instruction

In this review, *mode of instruction* refers to the role assumed by the classroom teacher, the kinds and order of activities present, and the specificity and clarity of objectives and learning tasks. Mode of instruction is contrasted with *focus of instruction*, which refers to the dominant content of instruction, e.g., the study of model compositions, the use by students of structured feedback sheets, sentence combining, and so forth. Foci of instruction are examined in Chapters 5, 6, and 7.

One of the first studies to examine mode of instruction in relation to composition achievement was conducted by Neville Bennett (1976) and his colleagues. After a review of research, they identified six major areas of variables which permit the differentiation of progressive and traditional teaching styles. These included (1) "extent of freedom of movement and talk in classrooms"; (2) "degree of disciplinary rather than physical control"; (3) "allocation of teaching time, extent of timetabling and homework, degree of pupil choice"; (4) "type of teaching approach"; (5) "whether intrinsic or extrinsic motivation is stressed"; and (6) "type and quantity of evaluation of pupil work" (p. 38). These broadly defined variables were used to generate a twenty-eight-item questionnaire which requested self-reports of behavior and expectations. The items included such questions as "Do pupils stay in the same seats or groups for most of the day?" and "Do you expect pupils to be quiet most of the time?" Questionnaires were sent to teachers in 871 British primary schools and were completed and returned by teachers in 88 percent of the schools.

Bennett then performed a cluster analysis which located each teacher in one category or type of teaching style. The cluster analysis is such that each teacher in each cluster is more like other teachers in that cluster than like teachers in other clusters. The resulting twelve types suggest a continuum from very informal to very formal. However, types between the extremes are mixtures of formal and informal elements. Therefore, according to Bennett, the types do not really comprise a continuum. Teachers of Type 1 are informal, allowing "pupil choice of work, whether individually or in groups," and pupil choice of seating. "Less than half curb movement and talk. Assessment in all its forms—tests, grading, and homework—appears to be discouraged. Intrinsic motivation is favoured" (p. 45). Teachers in Type 12, the very formal type, teach subjects separately through teacher talk to the whole class and individual work. They allow no choice of seating, "and every teacher curbs movement and talk. These teachers are above average on all assessment procedures, and extrinsic motivation predominates" (p. 47).

Thirty-seven teachers distributed over seven types, representing informal (Types 1 and 2), mixed (Types 3, 4, and 7) and formal (Types 11 and 12) teaching styles, agreed to participate in a second stage of the research. In the second stage, observers visited the teachers' classes and researchers examined children's accounts of what they had done in school. Both methods indicated that the cluster analysis of questionnaire responses had classified teachers appropriately. Researchers tested children in the thirty-seven classes at the beginning and end of the year on standardized tests of reading, math, and English. In each case, children in "formal" classes showed superior progress over children in "informal" classes.

What concerns us here, however, is not differences on standardized test results but differences in composition skills achieved through various teaching styles. Bennett cites the Plowden Report (1967) as wholeheartedly approving "free, fluent and copious writing on a great variety of subject matter," the essence of which writing is "that much of it is personal and that the writers are communicating something that has really engaged their minds and their imaginations" (Bennett, p. 115). Bennett points out that proponents of such writing believe that "by struggling to link a vivid experience to the appropriate language in which to express it, or, more fundamentally, to explore that area of his being in which experience and language intermingle," the child undergoes "a valuable developmental experience" (p. 116). Proponents of such writing in the United States go even further, arguing that writing which is not personal, not free and self-sponsored, is restrictive and repressive. Students, they say, respond without commitment or engagement to what they call "school-sponsored" writing, that is, writing assigned by teachers (Emig 1971, Pianko 1979, Graves 1981f). Indeed, they imply that school-sponsored writing is not simply restrictive but harmful. Emig, for example, states that the kind of writing usually taught in American schools "is algorithmic, or so mechanical that a computer could readily be programmed to produce it" (p. 53). Of three of her male subjects Emig says, "It is as if the two boys . . . are so thoroughly programmed to a single species of extensive writing that they can readily and comfortably compose no other" (pp. 81–82).

Bennett quotes an opposing point of view from the Bullock Report (1975), which cites a group of teachers as believing that "over-emphasis on it [creative, personal, or free writing] has distorted a whole view of language. It usually means, in actuality, colourful or fanciful language, not 'ordinary,' using 'vivid imagery.' It is often false, artificially stimulated and pumped up by the teacher or written to an unconscious model which he has given them" (p. 116).

To determine whether informal teaching methods enhanced crea-tivity, as its proponents claimed, Bennett asked that students in the thirty-seven classes studied write two compositions. One was intro-duced by a paragraph which invited them to write a story in which they were invisible for one day. Pupils were told "that good ideas and imagination were required and that poor spelling and grammar would not be penalised" (p. 117). The second essay was descriptive: "What I did at school yesterday." For this writing, teachers instructed pupils "to be as accurate as possible, and that in this instance spelling and grammar would be taken into consideration" (p. 117). Pupils were allowed as much time as they wished for the imaginative topic but were given a half-hour for the descriptive topic. Each essay was scored holistically by three teachers: one of each style—formal, mixed, and informal (median $r = .86$).

The mean scores for the essays across teaching styles revealed that students in the formal and informal groups scored almost equally on the descriptive essay, while formal groups scored slightly higher on the imaginative essay. Students in mixed groups scored slightly lower on both pieces of writing. Bennett concludes, "The differences are quite small and indicate no clear superiority of any one teaching style. There is little in these results to support the widely held view that informal teaching produces pupils who are more likely to respond more imaginatively in writing than do those who are being taught more formally" (p. 119).

To examine punctuation and spelling, "a matched sample of forty-eight boys and forty-eight girls was drawn from each teaching style, resulting in 288 descriptive stories" (p. 123). Pupils in informal classes made significantly more punctuation errors than pupils in formal or mixed classes—nearly 50 percent more. For spelling, however, no distinct differences by teaching style emerged.

Other studies have examined certain aspects of instructional mode. D. Cooper (1966) compared analytic methods to incidental methods. Analytic methods involved the separation of English studies into component parts (spelling, usage, vocabulary, punctuation, written composition, etc.), while incidental methods treated English as a whole subject, emphasizing extensive reading and writing. Testing in several areas revealed no significant differences except in punctuation and sentence structure, in which secondary students taught by analytic methods made significantly greater progress than those taught by incidental methods.

Hillocks (1981) conducted a study of three modes of instruction in freshman English classes at a large midwestern university. On the basis of classroom observations and interviews, researchers classified instructors as presentational, nondirectional, or environmental. Students in all classes were administered an attitude questionnaire, the analysis of which revealed highly significant differences ($p < .0001$) among students taught in the three modes on eleven factors examined. Attitudes were most positive among students taught in the environmental mode and least positive among those taught by instructors classified as nondirectional.

Although Hillocks's study involved no measures of growth in composition ability, it clearly established different effects for different patterns of instructional practice. For this reason, the 1981 categories have been used to classify instructional practices described in the experimental treatment studies examined here. Both presentational and environmental modes retain their original definitions. The nondirectional mode, however, has been redefined and accordingly renamed the "natural process" mode. A fourth, the individualized mode, has been added. Each of these will be defined in what follows.

Although the studies included in this review often do not discuss mode of instruction explicitly, a perusal of them indicates that they are not only concerned with different foci of instruction but with different modes of instruction. For example, a given study may contrast a treatment which focuses on practice in developing ideas for writing with one which focuses on the analysis of rhetorical techniques in a set of essays. In addition to this clear difference in the focus of instruction, however, the treatments may contrast in another way. For example, the first may be conducted in large part through peer interaction in small groups while the analysis of models takes place under the direction of the instructor with little or no peer interaction.

Presentational Mode

The presentational mode is characterized by (1) relatively clear and specific objectives, e.g., to use particular rhetorical techniques;

(2) lecture and teacher-led discussion dealing with concepts to be learned and applied; (3) the study of models and other materials which explain and illustrate the concept; (4) specific assignments or exercises which generally involve imitating a pattern or following rules that have been previously discussed; and (5) feedback following the writing, coming primarily from teachers.

Applebee (1981) supplies a very clear example of this mode of instruction in a teacher's own words. When asked how he prepared his students for an assignment, the teacher explained (p. 78),

> I've been doing it all semester. The first day of class I gave them a two-page thing on writing. Just about every day when I lecture about anything, I talk at the end or at the beginning of the lecture about how one might go about expressing whatever it is I'm teaching during that day in a written assignment.
>
> So I gave a sermon once last semester. I read one of Jonathan Edwards' sermons, and at the end of it in talking about the content of the sermon I also talked about how you would go about relating this to religious matters, and so on, in writing.
>
> Plus I've tried always when they are going to write about something to give them a specific, logical sequence of experiences. I ask them to read it, ask them factual questions about it, and I ask them to get in groups and discuss the topic that they are going to be writing about, and then I have them write about it individually.
>
> So, I go from individual, to group, back to the individual.

Except for the use of small-group discussions on occasion, this teacher clearly dominates the talk in his classroom. He gives the students "a two-page thing on writing," presumably explaining certain characteristics he expects their writing to display or perhaps explaining processes they might or should use. *He* talks about how "one" might "go about expressing whatever it is" *he's* teaching in a writing assignment. He apparently asks his students to write about literature and by way of preparation he asks "factual questions" about the selection, sets the topic, and asks students to discuss "what they are going to be writing about." While the small-group discussion is a departure from strict presentational format, even that is apparently intended to insure that students understand the content of assigned writing rather than to help them learn strategies which they can subsequently use in dealing with other data for other compositions.

Treatments coded as presentational in the meta-analysis which follows made no mention of small-group discussions, but they claimed to have done more by way of preparation for writing than did Applebee's subjects, who spent an average of three minutes in preparation. In these treatments, the instructor lectured on or led discussions of rhetorical techniques or principles exemplified in what students read. Or the teacher gave instructions about what students were to do individually and then led "a discussion" of what they had done.

Data reported by Goodlad (1984), based on observations of over 1,000 classrooms in elementary, junior high, and senior high schools, indicate that the presentational mode dominates in all subject matters. Goodlad reports that about 70 percent of all instructional time consists of talk, with teachers—on the average—doing 75 percent of the talking. Further, he reports that at the senior high level discussions of any kind take place only 5.2 percent of the time.

What are the assumptions about teaching and learning underlying this mode of instruction? First, users of the mode assume that they have useful knowledge about writing to convey to their students. Second, they assume that this knowledge is best conveyed directly in the form of verbal formulas, rules, examples, or admonitions. Third, they assume that the referents of the rules, formulas, and examples, which the teachers have in their heads (for these are surely abstract referents), are the same ones which the learners either have in their heads already or will somehow gain. That is, the teacher who admonishes students to "support generalizations appropriately" assumes that students will have the same concepts of "generalization" and of "appropriate support" that the teacher has. Fourth, users of this mode assume that students will be able to convert the rules and examples into guides for their own writing.

Unfortunately, although more treatments were categorized as presentational than any other, only two studies included in the meta-analysis were identified as using the presentational mode in the experimental sections but *not* in the control. Caplan and Keech (1980) focused on teaching how to expand general statements into a paragraph and on practicing specific ways to select and arrange concrete details in support of the general statements. They used models to illustrate the difference between showing and telling and as guides for teacher-led discussions of student writing in class. The class as a whole evaluated the density of detail in the student writing, but the teacher presented the final evaluation: "I grade each paper immediately as the discussion of that paper concludes" (p. 9).

Clark (1968) focused on two techniques of supplying evaluations and comments: extensive written comments on a "cover sheet" and teacher-led discussion of at least one good theme and one poor one which had been reproduced or projected for student examination. The study involved three experimental treatments (extensive comments, theme discussion, and a combination of the two), all of which were classified as presentational.

Natural Process Mode

The natural process mode is characterized by (1) generalized objectives, e.g., to increase fluency and skill in writing; (2) free writing about whatever interests the students, either in a journal or as a way of "exploring a subject"; (3) writing for audiences of peers; (4) generally positive feedback from peers; (5) opportunities to revise and rework writing; and (6) high levels of interaction among students. Treatments in this mode often refer to the teacher as a "facilitator" whose role is to free the student's imagination and promote growth by sustaining a positive classroom atmosphere. They avoid the study of model pieces of writing, the presentation of criteria, structuring the treatment around sets of skills or concepts—rhetorical or other— and using the teacher as the primary source of feedback. Treatments in this mode provide a low level of structure and are nondirectional about the qualities of good writing. In fact, proponents of this mode of instruction believe that students are only stultified by exposure to what they see as arbitrary criteria, models, problems, or assignments. In the words of Parker (1979), "Writing demands usually to be preceded by a period of exploratory talk about what the students have chosen to write on, a time in which ideas and the language to express them can be generated. It demands also the freedom for students to choose the forms suitable to their material and their purposes." He continues, "Writing is learned by doing it and sharing it with real audiences, not by studying and applying abstract rhetorical principles in exercises which the teacher alone will read and judge" (p. 36).

Those who advocate such instruction see teaching composition as primarily reactive. In the words of Graves (1981f, p. 29), "the teaching of writing is a response to what a writer shows either in oral or written statements . . . on that particular day." According to this view, the teacher's role is to respond to what children produce with hints and questions that will help the child learn new ways of dealing with writing of a particular kind. Calkins (1980b), in describing her "transitional" revisers, states that they "developed higher standards for themselves" (p. 339). She posits no influences that might have caused the development of these higher standards. This position suggests that the skills of good writers are part of every child's genetic makeup and that successful instruction allows that potential to blossom and come to fruition.

Although primarily reactive, instruction in the natural process mode may also include certain prewriting activities intended to stimulate memory or imagination. Gauntlett (1978) states, "Before a student begins writing, a process of prewriting, or a procedure for stimulating thinking must take place. Prewriting involves sensing, imagining, feeling, talking, and writing. It can also include drawing, dancing, dramatizing, or sculpturing" (p. 29). Gauntlett also recommends "multimedia" to encourage or stimulate writing.

Gauntlett's study, which was undertaken with twenty-five experimental high school classes (n = 315 after attrition) and nineteen control classes (n = 257 after attrition), also enumerates other characteristics of the natural process mode included in his treatment. "Group activity," he says, "is a must, particularly . . . where students read and comment on each other's work" (p. 27). In Gauntlett's study, students wrote many drafts, reading them aloud to peers. He asserts that "as much free writing as possible should be allowed." He indicates that feedback should be frequent and expeditious but that not all writing should be graded. Grading occurred only after "much class time" had been devoted "to the initial writing of a composition and to its revision" (p. 7). Further, Gauntlett indicates that the environment for writing in the experimental classes should be comfortable and conducive to writing. To this end, the experimental teachers each "received $1,500.00 worth of furniture, equipment, and books for the classrooms" (p. 5).

Using analysis of variance on the difference between pretest and posttest scores, Gauntlett found no significant difference between the treatment groups (F = .02) after nearly four months. The experimental/control effect size is .05 standard deviation.

A study of the effectiveness of the New Jersey Writing Project conducted by Alloway, et al. (1979) examined similar instructional techniques used by teachers of grades 7 through 12 who had been trained in teaching writing during a summer institute. (The control groups were taught by teachers scheduled for Writing Project training the following summer.) The experimental group teachers, upon returning to their own classes, used a pattern of instruction similar to that used in the institute. Their students wrote for "15 or 30 minutes two or three times a week" or for "5 or 10 minutes daily" (p. 6). The institute emphasized free writing "activated to initiate the process and keep it going. As the institute progressed writing was also initiated by other stimuli" (p. 4). The teachers had their students begin keeping journals, and they set aside time "for various kinds of peer evaluations and for teacher conferences." In addition the teachers "wrote with and when their students wrote. By doing this they were able to help their students understand the theory of writing as a process in a natural and real way" (p. 6). The nature and extent of the students' understanding of "the theory of writing as a process" is not explained. Nor is it clear how the teachers' act of writing with the students conveys that understanding.

Students were pretested in October and posttested in May, indicating a duration of six to eight months. The resulting pieces of writing were scored by ETS personnel working under standard conditions for scoring. Students in control groups, whose instruction is not described, lost .07 standard deviation. Students in the experimental groups gained .25 standard deviation. The difference between the two groups is statistically significant, with an experimental/control effect size of .39.

The Gauntlett study and the Alloway study are typical of those categorized as using the natural process mode of instruction. Several assumptions undergird this mode of instruction. The assumption that writing for audiences of peers will improve writing is usually explicit. A second assumption is that writing should be "free," that is, of the students' own choice and without the restrictions of having to use certain forms, techniques, or rhetorical conventions. A third assumption is that the teacher's role should be reactive, responding to whatever the student writes on any given occasion, in contrast to an active planning of instructional experiences intended to result in learning particular writing strategies.

These three assumptions about instruction rest on other, not-so-often expressed assumptions about children's learning. First, the approach assumes that pupils will learn or invent forms as they develop their own meanings. Second, it assumes that if acquisition of knowledge about writing is necessary, that knowledge is best provided through audience response from peers while the writing is in progress and after its completion. Third, it assumes that the development of imagination is best served by these methods and, conversely, is inhibited by more structured methods.

In addition to the studies outlined above, the meta-analysis in Chapter 8 includes seven others which were categorized as using the natural process mode in the experimental groups but not in the control. These include two Writing Project assessments: Olson and DiStefano (1980) at grades 7, 8, and 9 and Wagner, Zemelman, and Malone-Trout (1981) at grades 1–12. Two studies were conducted with college freshmen classes: Walker (1974) and K. Davis (1979). The remaining studies include V. A. Adams (1971) at grade 12, Ganong (1975) at grade 9, and Wienke (1981) at grade 6.

Many other studies examined the natural process mode of instruction but did not meet the criteria required for inclusion in the meta-analysis. These include an important evaluation of the effects of the Bay Area Writing Project (Keech 1979). The Keech study was excluded because pretests and posttests were performed on different groups of students.

Environmental Mode

The environmental mode is characterized by (1) clear and specific objectives, e.g., to increase the use of specific detail and figurative language; (2) materials and problems selected to engage students with each other in specifiable processes important to some particular aspect of writing; and (3) activities, such as small-group problem-centered discussions, conducive to high levels of peer interaction concerning specific tasks. Teachers in this mode, in contrast to the presentational mode, are likely to minimize lecture and teacher-led discussion. Rather, they structure activities so that, while teachers may provide brief introductory lectures, students work on particular tasks in small groups before proceeding to similar tasks independently. Although principles are taught, they are not simply announced and illustrated as in the presentational mode. Rather, they are approached through concrete materials and problems, the working through of which not only illustrates the principle but engages students in its use. For example, an assignment might be to write about one of thirty seashells so that another student will be able to read the composition and choose the seashell described from among the thirty. This assignment illustrates both the necessity of thinking about possible audience responses and the necessity for using precise detail. While the teacher may urge students to think about the audience and to write specifically, as in the presentational mode, the immediate, concrete activity has the potential for engaging students in the use of the principles and provides feedback from peers.

In contrast to the natural process mode, the concrete tasks of the environmental mode make objectives operationally clear by engaging students in their pursuit through structured tasks. While a natural process treatment requires students to respond to each other's writing, the criteria for doing so come from the individual students. In contrast, in one environmental treatment, the teacher led a brief discussion of a sample of student writing, helping sixth-grade students to apply a set of criteria to it. Following that discussion, working in small groups, the students applied the same criteria to other pieces of writing (Sager 1973b). While the environmental mode shares an emphasis on process and student interaction with the natural process mode, it differs sharply from the latter in the structure of the materials and activities.

The presentational mode emphasizes the teacher as presenter of knowledge about writing, whereas the natural process mode emphasizes the student as generator of ideas, criteria, and forms. The environmental mode appears to place teacher and student more nearly in balance, with the teacher planning activities and selecting materials through which students interact with each other to generate ideas and learn identifiable writing skills.

Sager's experimental treatment (1973b) is a good example of environmental instruction. The instruction with sixth-graders emphasized learning to use a set of scales in evaluating compositions. In one lesson, students working in small groups were asked to read a story entitled "The Green Martian Monster"—a story which a worksheet informed the students had been scored 0 on elaboration:

The Green Martian Monster

The green Martian monster descended on the USA. He didn't have a mouth. "Who goes?" they said. There was no answer. So they shot him and he died.

After reading this story, which certainly lacks elaboration, students were asked to do the following tasks (p. 95):

(1) Quickly list all the reasons why a mouthless, green Martian monster might land in the USA.
(2) List all the places the Martian could have landed.
(3) Who could "they" have been? List all possibilities.
(4) List all the thoughts "they" could have been thinking when they saw the Martian.
(5) What could have happened between the time the Martian was shot and the time he died? List all possibilities.
(6) Look at your lists. To be interesting and easy to understand, a story needs details such as you have written. Add some of these details to the story and take turns reading the story the way you would have written it.

It is important to note that in Sager's study the youngsters did far more than simply rate a composition. They found problems with the writing, generated ideas which would help to correct those problems, and synthesized those ideas with the existing frame. Finally, they considered the principles underlying what they had done. Using such materials as the above composition, the experimental groups in the study worked with scales dealing with vocabulary, elaboration, organization, and structure.

The Sager study was conducted in two "inner city" schools which qualified for Title I funds. Instruction was conducted daily, during 45-minute periods, for eight weeks. Both experimental and control groups received the same stimuli for writing and wrote the same number of stories. Instead of working with the scale materials, however, the control group wrote in journals and worked on aspects of grammar. The experimental group pre/post gain was .84, while the control group had a loss of −.30—resulting in an experimental control effect size of .93, nearly a full standard deviation.

A. L. Thibodeau's (1964) study with sixth-graders included one treatment which was categorized as environmental. Students worked in pairs or small groups on various exercises, each of which presented a problem involving what the researcher called "elaborative thinking." In one exercise, students were presented a passage about a diver at the bottom of the sea: "Suddenly the diver realized he must fight his way back to the surface!" Students were directed to "list all the reasons he had to suddenly return to the surface" and to "describe this place where the diver was searching." In another exercise, students were given the following sentence: "Mary, feeling very hungry, wanders downstairs in the middle of the night and hears a strange sound in the kitchen." Students were then asked to list "as many ideas as possible" (p. 25) about what sounds she might have heard, who might have been there, and so forth. It is interesting to note that each of these exercises focuses on the elaboration of an element of story structure as defined by Stein and Trabasso (1982).

Troyka (1974) conducted a study with college freshman remedial composition students in twenty-five experimental classes ($n = 172$) and twenty-five control classes ($n = 181$). The experimental procedure involved what she called "simulation-gaming," in which "at the start of every game each player received a brief situation statement which gave the setting and background of the problem as well as the action and rules for the simulation" (p. 60). The situations included a pollution problem, a neighborhood crime problem, a college campus drug problem, and a problem concerning the purchase of a fleet of taxicabs. Each involved a writing task which focused on a different writing strategy: providing facts, providing reasons, describing incidents, and comparing and contrasting.

Each student received a role sheet along with whatever background information he or she might need. The games were set up so that students were associated with a subgroup: executives of a chemical plant responsible for polluting a town's beaches and recreational waters, operators of tourist services who believed that pollution harmed the town's prosperity, and so forth. Each role had built into it the task of persuading the other groups of the legitimacy of its position on the problem. As the game progressed, the action alternated between periods of group planning and periods of "cross subgroup public hearings, debates, and the like" (p. 63). Presumably, these "games" put students in the position of using strategies required by the associated writing assignments: marshalling and arranging facts, evaluating and using reasons, examining and generating examples, predicting objections and considering how to deal with them, and so forth. The control groups, on the other hand, were taught about using facts, reasons, incidents, and comparison and contrast, but in what appears to be a traditional presentational manner.

The experimental/control effect size for the Troyka study was 1.69 standard deviations, over a half standard deviation greater than the next largest experimental/control effect size. The homogeneity statistic for all seventy-three experimental/control treatments is 411.08. Removal of the Troyka study reduces H to 241. In fact, this study is one of the four removed from the meta-analysis because of its large contribution to heterogeneity. Although the study was removed, it should not be ignored. Its instructional mode is clearly environmental, focusing on specific problems and promoting student interaction in the use of strategies which will ultimately be used in writing. However, it is different from other environmental treatments. No other treatment in the screened sample uses role playing in systematically planned simulated problem situations. In addition, however, only one or two other treatments involve such small classes in both the experimental group ($\overline{X}$ = 6.9) and the control group ($\overline{X}$ = 7.2). Although class size here is clearly not responsible for the experimental/control effect size, the small class size may contribute to the effectiveness of the experimental treatment. That, of course, is an empirical question: Can comparable effect sizes be achieved using similar instructional approaches with larger classes?

Several assumptions underlie the environmental mode of instruction. One is that teaching can and should actively seek to develop identifiable skills in learners. A second is that these skills are developed by using them orally before using them in writing. A third assumption is that one major function of prewriting activity is to develop those skills. A fourth assumption is that the use of such skills (e.g., generating criteria to define a concept) is often complex, and therefore may require collaboration with and feedback from others. A concomitant assumption is that such collaboration and feedback may be achieved through the interaction of students as they work together to solve problems of various kinds.

Studies in the meta-analysis which use the environmental mode of instruction in the experimental treatment and some other mode in the control include the following: Clifford (1978), Rosen (1974), and Sbaratta (1975), all with college freshmen; Farrell (1977) with eleventh-graders; Vinson (1980) with ninth; Hillocks (1979) with ninth- and eleventh-graders, and (1982) with seventh- and eighth-graders; and A. E. Thibodeau (1964) and A. L. Thibodeau (1964), both with sixth-graders.

Individualized Mode

In the individualized mode of instruction students receive instruction through tutorials, programmed materials of some kind, or a combination of the two. The focus of instruction may vary widely, from mechanics to researching, planning, and writing papers. The chief distinction is that this mode of instruction seeks to help students on an individualized basis. For example, Murdock (1974) contrasted independent study groups with lecture/discussion groups in teaching college freshmen. In the former condition students were not required to attend class after the second week, except for seven occasions upon which required essays were written. However, instructors were available during scheduled class periods to work with students on an individual basis. In contrast, the lecture/discussion groups required attendance for all forty-five sessions during the semester. There were no significant differences between the achievement of the two groups.

A. E. Thibodeau (1964) used self-instructional materials on "practical grammar" (which included sentence combining practice) and organization. These self-instructional materials allowed teachers to work with individual students. This individualized approach was contrasted with a traditional approach which focused on letter-writing and formal grammar.

Eagleton (1974) trained eleventh- and twelfth-graders to act as tutors to sixth-graders. The tutors were to initiate writing activities, make "appropriate" placements in instructional materials, and conduct instruction. Exactly what the writing instruction consisted of is not clear. Witte and Faigley (1981b) tested two different curricular approaches to teaching freshman composition and two modes of instruction: tutorial versus whole-class instruction. The tutorial students focused on the same curricular content as did students in whole-class treatments. Other studies included in the individualized mode are A. L. Thibodeau (1964) with sixth-graders and Farrell (1977) with eleventh-graders.

Two studies categorized as testing individualized treatments against some other mode of instruction were among the four removed from experimental studies for further analysis because of their large contribution to the heterogeneity of the overall experimental/control effect size. One of these had the second largest negative effect size (−.43); the other had the second largest positive effect (1.18). The first (Loritsch 1977) tested what it called a "self-paced" method which has certain features in common with the Murdock study. Students in the self-paced treatment were required to attend only one lecture/discussion per week, while students in traditional classes were required to attend three per week. Self-paced students were also expected to spend at least one hour per week in the writing laboratory working with programmed materials and tutors.

The results of the Loritsch experiment may well have been affected by the massive attrition rate: 167 students in eight experimental classes diminished to 48 by the end of the quarter. Such attrition is almost certainly nonrandom, but one expects it to affect results positively rather than negatively. It is interesting to note that this self-paced treatment, along with those in Murdock (1974) and Eagleton (1974), does not specify the writing skills treated or the method of the treatment. And while the other studies do designate curricular treatments, the students appear to have proceeded through standard curriculums without benefit of systematic diagnosis, corrective instruction, reassessment, and so forth. One suspects that a student in one of the individualized treatments reported here would encounter much the same experience as a student in a whole-class treatment.

However, the study with the second highest experimental effect size (D. I. Smith 1974) included a pretesting to identify weaknesses, followed by remedial procedures and posttesting to determine progress. In addition, students in this individualized treatment worked with the teacher in choosing a topic of interest. They then collected data from a variety of sources, planned an organization with the teacher, produced a rough draft, analyzed it with the teacher, rewrote it, evaluated it, and arrived at a grade with the teacher. This cycle was repeated every two weeks. Unfortunately, the criteria used by the teachers in helping to plan an organization and to evaluate the first and second drafts were not stated explicitly. However, this individualized treatment appears to have taken greater advantage of the techniques of individualization than did other treatments in this category. Perhaps for that reason it achieved one of the highest experimental/control effect sizes (1.18) and contributed heavily to the overall heterogeneity.

The major assumption underlying most treatments categorized as belonging to the individualized mode is that a teacher working with a single student is more effective than a teacher working with a whole class, even when otherwise-conventional materials and procedures are used in both treatments.

Modes of Instruction Contrasted

How would teachers representing the various modes of instruction be likely to differ in their treatment of various kinds of writing assignments? This section contrasts three of the modes described above: the presentational, natural process, and environmental. Examples of the treatment of curricular goals will help to clarify the distinctions among these three modes of instruction.

Suppose a curricular goal is to write effectively about personal experience. A presentational instructor would be likely to explain the characteristics of "good" personal-experience writing, lead students in reading and discussing samples of such writing, ask students to write such compositions on their own, and finally correct and grade the compositions.

A natural process "facilitator" would be likely to ask students to write in journals several times a week and select those entries they would like to write about in extended compositions. The students might be asked to write about an entry or some other idea, "simply filling a page in order to learn how writing helps them discover what they know, what they do not know, and, in fact, what they want to write about" (Myers 1983, p. 28). Students might then be asked to discuss what they have written with peers, in an effort to generate additional ideas or questions to write about. Or they might, according to Buckley and Boyle (1983), "map" their stories, i.e., place "a controlling idea in the center of their map and use brainstorming techniques until they have many childhood memories for their paper. They select the 'best incidents' for the map, with the central idea in the middle and supporting incidents or ideas on the extensions." After completing their "maps," students would then "tell their stories to a group or a partner." Meanwhile, the "listeners are mapping to give information to the speakers, who can then reevaluate their organization" (p. 62). (Although Buckley and Boyle speak of evaluation here, they provide no criteria for evaluation of organization.) The key feature, regardless of whether students use mapping or not, is that students receive feedback from peers concerning very early ideas and after each draft, one or more of which is eventually turned in to the teacher. Feedback from peers and the teacher is usually designated as being positive. In short, students are given opportunities to explore ideas before writing, to develop a draft, to receive feedback, and so on. In this way the teacher simply facilitates the development of ideas and forms which the students have within themselves.

In contrast, the environmental teacher is likely to break the task of personal-experience writing into components, for example, writing about setting and people, developing and resolving conflict, and using dialogue effectively. Students might be asked to write as specifically as possible about faces in photographs, attempting to capture unique expressions and facial qualities. They might then meet in small groups, sharing the pictures and what they have written and applying a set of teacher-supplied questions or criteria before revising. The revisions might then receive positive feedback from the teacher on the strongest details. In a different activity, selected students might pantomime a character in a situation: waiting in the principal's or dentist's anteroom, sitting on the bench waiting to go into an important game, or walking down a dark street fearful of being followed. The rest of the class would write several sentences trying to capture the details of the bodily movements, facial expressions, and so forth of the pantomimers. Students might read what they have written aloud, with the teacher or peers reinforcing the strongest details. In a more complex activity selected students might be given a set of kernel situations involving conflicts between two people and asked to choose a situation or invent their own. They would then be asked to develop and act out a dialogue between the two characters. Their audience might supply feedback, using questions supplied by the teacher to guide their evaluations. This activity would be followed by writing out a dialogue, perhaps with details about the appearance of the characters and setting. Feedback would come from peers, the teacher, or both. Such activities would lead to the writing of an extended paper about a personal experience, and this writing might very well include brainstorming for ideas, the production of more than one draft, and feedback at various points.

In another contrast of instructional modes, let us assume that the curricular goal is argumentative writing. Presentational teachers are likely to lecture on the features and qualities of good argumentative writing, probably providing one or more examples to be examined through teacher-led discussion. The instructor would then assign a topic or ask students to choose one of special interest to them. Ordinarily students would write one draft and submit it to the instructor.

A teacher in the natural process mode would likely avoid lecturing on the characteristics and qualities of effective argument and would also avoid the analysis of examples. This instructor is likely to begin with asking students to identify issues, perhaps from journal writings or free writing of other kinds, which concern them in some way. Students might be asked to examine their own values and expectations in contrast to what they see around them and then to generate a question which is of interest to them. Once a question or issue is generated, students might be directed to compare these starting points with those of others. Following this comparison, students would list as many features of the subject as they could, determine how the subject has changed over time, and then classify the subject, indicating how it differs from other phenomena of a similar type. After more thinking about the subject, the students, at some point, would be asked to establish a focus, analyze an audience, and begin a draft with that audience in mind. At various stages of production, students would share their writing with peers and receive feedback from both peers and teachers before producing a final draft.

An environmental teacher would be likely to invent activities to help students learn how to generate the various parts of good argumentative writing, e.g., clearly stated propositions supported by appropriate data, clear categories defined by criteria and examples, and cogently examined opposing points of view. Models might be used to illustrate these points, but the instruction would focus on activities. Students might be asked, for example, to examine a set of cases describing incidents of various kinds: drug abuse, homicide, divorce, or other less traumatic problems. They might then be asked to generalize about the set of cases and to support those generalizations from the data available. Working in small groups, they might be asked to formulate recommendations for the prevention of such problems, and to develop several arguments in favor of their recommendations. They might be given sets of information about a particular problem and asked to play roles of various people with an interest in the problem, as in the Troyka (1974) study. Such an activity is intended to contribute not only to learning how to formulate and support clear propositions but to learning to predict other points of view about the issue. Students might be given flawed arguments and asked to generate revisions or elaborations to remedy the defects. After a series of such activities they would be asked to choose an issue about which to develop an argumentative paper. At various stages of production, they might receive feedback from their peers and teachers.

Working on any kind of writing, teachers in the individualized mode might use a variety of more or less conventional techniques but would work with one student at a time. Research in the future might profitably examine the effects of real tutorial situations in which diagnostic and corrective procedures are used systematically.

The meta-analysis results presented in Chapter 8 afford a comparison of the effects of the modes of instruction. Unfortunately, it does not permit assessment of modes across the different focuses of instruction examined in the following chapters. That is a matter of concern to future research.

5 Grammar and the Manipulation of Syntax

In 1963 Braddock, Lloyd-Jones, and Schoer stated that "in view of the widespread agreement of research studies based upon many types of students and teachers, the conclusion can be stated in strong and unqualified terms: the teaching of formal grammar has a negligible or, because it usually displaces some instruction and practice in actual composition, even a harmful effect on the improvement of writing" (pp. 37–38). By "formal grammar" they meant the traditional school grammar which identifies a noun as the name of a person, place, or thing and which requires the identification of several (usually eight) parts of speech, their functions in sentences, certain types of phrases and clauses, three kinds of sentences (simple, compound, and complex), and so forth. Linguists had long before shown that such grammar provided an inconsistent and inadequate description of how the English language works. In addition, linguists had developed grammars which provide a more sophisticated, precise, and less ambiguous description of how a language works. Despite the advances in linguistics and despite the strongly stated conclusions by Braddock and his colleagues, however, many elementary and secondary schools continue to make grammar a major component of their curricula. Many teachers still contend that knowledge of traditional school grammar is crucial to good writing. These same teachers tend to make no distinction between grammar (a description of how a language works) and "correctness" (adherence to accepted conventions of punctuation and usage). A number of studies have shown that when English teachers who have not been trained as raters are asked to rate compositions (cf. Diederich 1964), they tend to focus their attention on and base their ratings on "correctness" rather than on content, logic, and other features of writing.

Researchers have continued to seek a relationship between the study of grammar and composition ability. In the past two decades several studies have examined the effects of traditional school grammar on composition and several have examined the effects of more recent grammars, particularly transformational grammar. Studies of the latter led very quickly to hypotheses that students might benefit from practice in combining sentences without the paraphernalia of

133

formal grammar. This chapter will deal with studies of the effects of teaching grammar and with sentence combining and some related instructional procedures.

Grammar—with Michael W. Smith

Studies of the effects of teaching grammar on composition reviewed for the present report suffer from the same flaws as do other experimental treatment studies. Many did not include even minimal controls for teacher bias; many did not make use of pre and post writing samples even though students had not been randomly assigned to groups. Many did not rate compositions for quality. Of those that did, some did not exercise precautions to guard against rater bias. Most of the studies in this category did not qualify for inclusion in the meta-analysis. Nevertheless, the studies do shed light on what is a serious curricular issue.

Several studies examined the effects of teaching traditional school grammar as opposed to the effects of teaching no grammar: White (1965) with seventh-graders, Whitehead (1966) with high school students, Bowden (1979) with sixth-graders, J. L. Sullivan (1969) with college students, and Elley, et al. (1976) with high school students over three years. All found no significant differences between the two treatments.

The availability of the more precise and sophisticated linguistic grammars made reasonable the question of whether using a more sophisticated grammar might have a more powerful effect on writing. Many researchers addressed the question. White (1965) examined the effects of using a structural linguistics text (Roberts's *Patterns of English*) in one class of seventh-graders for 50 minutes per week. A second class studied a traditional school grammar treatment of parts of speech. A third class used the time for free reading. The structural linguistics group showed superior performance on STEP Writing Tests, STEP Essay Tests, and teacher-assigned themes. However, the differences were significant only on the STEP Writing Test, which does not involve a writing sample. Mulcahy (1974) found that one class of college freshmen who studied a linguistic grammar for one semester showed significantly greater gains in language knowledge and writing ability than another class who studied traditional grammar. Both this experiment and White (1965), however, had inadequate teacher controls.

Gale (1968) and Morgan (1971), working with intermediate-grade pupils, also compared the effects of studying structural or structural-generative grammars to the effects of teaching traditional grammar. They found no significant differences except for some gains in syntactic complexity for the groups studying linguistically based grammars. Smith and Sustakowski (1968), working with classes in twenty-one schools, found large gains for students studying a descriptive (structural) grammar on the Modern Language Aptitude Test, which measures sensitivity to phonological, morphological, and syntactic structures. One might expect that students who had studied phonology and morphology would do better on such a test than those who had studied traditional grammar. However, the researchers found no differences on measures of spelling, punctuation, usage, and so forth. Differences in the quality of writing were not examined.

An ambitious study comparing the effects of structural and traditional grammar is by Kennedy and Larson (1969). Their study, over two school years, included two classes from the time students entered sixth grade till they completed seventh grade, and two classes from the beginning of seventh grade through the end of eighth grade. The researchers' measures included the STEP Essay Test, Roy O'Donnell's (1964) test of sensitivity to syntactic structures, and the language section of the Stanford Achievement Test. They found no significant differences on the STEP Essay or Stanford Achievement tests. The difference on the test of syntactic sensitivity favored the groups studying structural grammar. It is interesting to note that the authors report a large mean loss on the essay test for the traditional grammar groups (-1.13). They report that "the STEP Essay score obtained during the post-testing situation levelled off and became more consistent with essay scores of the experimental group classes" (p. 34). Indeed, the pre-to-post effect size for the traditional grammar groups is $-.79$ standard deviation. Unfortunately, the authors do not report data on the change in scores for the experimental groups. Nonetheless, the implication is that the groups studying structural grammar made little or no gain over two years.

Kennedy and Larson do report essay pretest scores which show that traditional grammar groups scored one full point higher ($p <$ .05) than the experimental groups. They attribute this difference to previous control group instruction which had "emphasized development of creative expression, rather than the mechanical manipulation of language." The instructors, they say, had "rewarded originality of thought and expression" (pp. 33–34), which they point out are also rewarded by the STEP Essay Test scoring procedures. If the data reported are accurate, then it would seem that the emphasis on grammar eroded gains previously made by the control groups and, at the same time, contributed nothing to the experimental groups.

A number of researchers have examined the effects of studying transformational grammar, sometimes testing it against no grammar instruction, sometimes against instruction in traditional school grammar. M. W. Davis (1967) and Goddin (1969) examined the effects of teaching transformational grammar versus the effects of teaching traditional grammar—Davis with junior high school students and Goddin with third- and seventh-graders. Davis found differences favoring transformational grammar students in certain elements of sentence structure but included no measure of overall writing quality. Goddin found differences favoring students of generative grammar on standardized tests of "paragraph meaning" and language but included no measures of writing quality.

Davenport (1971), working with ninth-graders, Harter (1978) with seventh-graders, J. L. Sullivan (1969) with college freshmen, and Fry (1972) with junior high students, studied the effects of generative grammar versus traditional grammar. All made use of pretest and posttest writing samples. None report statistically different results in writing quality.

Bateman and Zidonis (1966) studied the effects of generative grammar study over a period of two years beginning when their subjects at The University School of The Ohio State University were ninth-graders. A control group studied no grammar over the two-year period. Bateman and Zidonis found increases in structural complexity favoring the experimental group, but these were largely due to gains made by four students and were not statistically significant. However, the researchers did find a statistically significant difference between the number of well-formed sentences written by the experimental students and their control group counterparts. A subsequent study by Thompson and Middleton (1973) with tenth-graders over one semester, using the Bateman and Zidonis measures, found greater gains for students studying transformational grammar than for those studying traditional grammar. However, the differences were not significant.

The most ambitious study of the effects of grammar is that conducted by Elley, et al. (1976). The sample was large (248 students at the outset; 166 after three years), the measures were many and varied, there was careful teacher control, and the three years of the experiments were enough to reveal any changes that could have been expected to occur. Students were classified into eight groups matched on the basis of four test scores, ethnic group, sex, contributing school, and subject options. Three of these classes studied the Oregon curriculum, which included transformational grammar, rhetoric, and literature strands. A second group of three classes studied the same rhetoric and literature strands as the first group. However, for them the study of transformational grammar was replaced with extra reading and creative writing. The third group of two classes studied a largely traditional and more functional grammar than the transformational grammar group. Their literature study was based on popular class sets of fiction.

The researchers used a variety of measures at the end of each year, including reading vocabulary, reading comprehension, syntactic complexity, English usage, spelling, listening comprehension, and English literature tests. In addition, the students wrote four essays at the end of the first year and three at the end of the later years which were scored by two or more raters for content, organization, style, and mechanics. Finally, at the end of each year, the students responded anonymously to questionnaires designed to assess their attitudes toward different parts of their English programs. At the end of the first year there were no significant differences among the three groups, except that the transformational group liked writing less. After the second year the traditional grammar group's essay content was better than that of the Oregon curriculum group that did not study grammar. The attitude survey showed that the transformational grammar group found English more difficult, but both Oregon groups showed a significantly more positive attitude toward literature and toward explanatory and persuasive writing ($p < .05$).

After the third year the two Oregon groups showed a statistically superior performance on the sentence-combining measure ($p < .05$). Also, the two grammar groups showed a statistically superior performance on the English usage test ($p < .02$). The errors that accounted for this difference were largely minor mechanical errors. The final attitude survey showed that the transformational grammar group found English more "repetitive and useless" while the traditional grammar group found English less "interesting and useful." In indicating their feelings about sentence study and their language textbooks, the transformational grammar students "showed predominantly negative attitudes, especially on such dimensions as 'useless,' 'unimaginative,' 'repetitive,' 'passive,' 'complicated,' and 'unpleasant.' " As the researchers put it, "clearly" the transformational grammar strand "was not popular" (p. 16).

When over thirteen measures are used over three years, one expects to find two or three significant differences (at $p < .05$). The most striking result of the Elley study is that, even after three years of work, the writing of students studying traditional or transformational grammar showed no significant differences in overall quality from that of students studying no grammar at all. Nor is the writing of grammar students different from that of nongrammar students on any of the subscales, *not even on the mechanics of writing.*

None of the studies reviewed for the present report provides any support for teaching grammar as a means of improving composition skills. If schools insist upon teaching the identification of parts of speech, the parsing or diagramming of sentences, or other concepts of traditional school grammar (as many still do), they cannot defend it as a means of improving the quality of writing.

Teachers will protest that they cannot teach "correct" usage (by which they mean standard dialect) and punctuation without teaching grammar of some kind. But even the enormous amount of time spent on grammar in the Elley study made no difference in the mechanics ratings of actual writing. The grammar groups *did* outperform the no-grammar classes on a test of usage and mechanics. However, the researchers analyzed the items of the test to determine the precise nature of the differences. They found that the differences appeared in items on the use of capitals, commas in lists, the apostrophe, possessives and contractions, commas for appositives, and so forth— all of which appear to be amenable to direct, discrete instruction. When the researchers examined items dealing with run-on sentences, they found slightly better, but not significantly better, performance for groups studying grammar. Concerning the test of usage and mechanics, they comment, "What slight superiority there was in the two grammar groups was dispersed over a wide range of mechanical conventions, *and was not clearly associated with sentence structure*" (p. 15, emphasis added).

Confronted with evidence that grammar study does not increase the quality of writing, grammar enthusiasts argue that an understanding of traditional grammatical concepts is necessary to correct punctuation and certain usage problems such as subject-verb agreement, pronoun-antecedent agreement and so forth. Even the most liberal authorities who argue for functional treatment of mechanics (e.g., Calkins 1980c) recognize a need to attend to the mechanics of writing, although they would abjure the traditional naming of parts of speech and parsing of sentences. For both conservatives and liberals, two important questions on the issue of mechanical "correctness" remain infrequently addressed and largely unanswered by the research.

First, what constitutes adequate or inadequate performance in mechanics? Is inadequate performance best defined in terms of error frequency, the qualitative effects of certain errors on communication, or on some combination of these? Some teachers have been known to give failing grades to compositions containing as few as one or two errors—very high standards when one considers that even published materials, meticulously proofread by professionals, display "errors." On the other hand, responding to alarmist reactions to National Assessment results, Mellon (1975a) points out that except for spelling, the "National Assessment results indicate that this high initial error rate is, in fact, non-existent." He argues that "there seems little reason to continue to give students in grades five through seven the especially large doses of error-correcting practice they typically receive" (p. 32). The question of what constitutes satisfactory or unsatisfactory performance in mechanics is not answerable by research. Teachers and institutions must decide for themselves on acceptable error types and rates.

Answering the first question leads to the second: What are the best instructional techniques for reducing error rates in mechanics and usage? The evidence, at best, is mixed. Elley, et al. (1976) found no significant differences between the mean judgmental scores on mechanics for students studying grammar and those who did not. Neville Bennett (1976) counted errors in samples of writing from primary students and found that those taught by informal methods which stressed free writing and creativity made significantly more errors in punctuation than did students taught by formal methods which stressed acquisition of "basic skills" and focused on matters of mechanics. The difference was significant at $p < .05$. At the same time there were no significant differences between the mean quality ratings assigned the two groups on either their descriptive writings or their creative writings. Adams (1971), who used the natural process mode of instruction (comparable to Bennett's informal style) in experimental groups and a formal style with an emphasis on mechanics in the control group, found no gain for the experimental students and a large loss for the control students. The emphasis on mechanics included red-marking every error on compositions and returning them to the students for correction.

Several studies have examined the kinds of errors made by students in their compositions. Golub (1972), DeStefano (1972), Baird (1963), and others all provide classifications of errors and frequencies for some selected population. The National Assessment of Educational Progress study *Writing Mechanics* (1975) is the most imposing study of this type, based on the "famous person" composition of 1969–70 with a nationwide stratified sample of 2,079. The researchers found only weak inverse correlations between overall quality of the essays and the frequency of errors.

Interestingly, however, Slotnick and Rogers (1973) report a corre-

lation between length and quality ratings for the same essay set of
.60 (p. 394, fn 16), suggesting that gains in quality may best be
achieved through instructional foci which emphasize the development
of ideas rather than "correctness." *Writing Mechanics* also indicates
that the majority of errors appeared both infrequently and irregularly
and that most 17-year-olds have mechanics pretty well in hand.

For conscientious teachers, the problem remains about what to do
with those students, concentrated in certain segments of the population, whose writing displays comparatively high levels of mechanical
errors as they are currently defined. As Cronnell (1980) points out,
very little research on the teaching of mechanics has been conducted.
The teaching of grammar and mechanics has had, at best, mixed
results even for teaching correctness. We do not know how much
grammar or what grammatical knowledge writers must have to
copyread with accuracy.

Kagan (1980) has taken a promising approach to this problem by
attempting to determine which syntactic structures students can or
cannot identify as complete sentences. She gave 202 remedial community college students two tests. In the first she presented sentence
fragments using fifteen different syntactic structures along with five
complete sentences randomly ordered. She asked students to indicate
which were "part of a sentence" and which were sentences. In the
second test she presented eleven run-ons of various syntactic structures and four complete sentences, asking students to indicate which
were "more than a sentence" and which were sentences. Each structure began with a capital letter but contained no punctuation marks.
Fragments most frequently identified by students as sentences were
a verb plus a subordinate clause, a verb plus a direct object and a
prepositional phrase, and two prepositional phrases. On the run-on
test Kagan found that the most common errors related to combinations of short and long sentences, in which students apparently ignored
the short sentence and attended to the long one. These structures
also contained prepositional phrases.

In a second experiment Kagan presented sixty-two students with
an eight-item test in which each item consisted of a five-word verb/
object sequence followed by a vertical line and a prepositional phrase
of five words followed by a second vertical line. Students were asked
to indicate whether the words up to the first line were a complete
sentence, whether the words up to the second line were a complete
sentence, or whether there was no sentence. In this test 65 percent
of the boundaries mistaken for the ends of sentences fell after prep-

ositional phrases. Kagan reasons that students do not mistake prepositional phrases for verb-object structures but rather that there is something about a prepositional phrase that is a "potent miscue for sentence boundaries" (p. 137).

Further research of this kind may uncover other structures which appear to mislead students systematically in their attempts to determine sentence boundaries. If such miscues do exist and if they can be discovered, it may be possible to devise far more efficient methods of teaching copyreading than are currently available.

Sentence Combining and Construction

Since the mid1960s a large number of studies have been concerned with helping students learn to write more syntactically "mature" sentences. The indices of maturity have included the number of words per T-unit, the number of words per clause, the number of clauses per T-unit, the number of words in free modifiers, and so forth. A major impetus for a pedagogy designed to help students increase the length of their syntactic structures seems to have been Hunt's (1965a) study and others like it that show writers increasing the length of their syntactic structures as they advance from grade 4 to grade 12 and beyond.

In his preface to the Hunt study, G. Robert Carlsen suggested that "the school's program should facilitate the student's moving in the direction of mature writing patterns" (p. vi). In the years since Carlsen's statement, two methods of enhancing syntactic maturity have been advanced and studied extensively: sentence combining and sentence construction. In sentence combining, students are presented with sets of two or more sentences and asked to combine them into a single effective structure. In some pedagogies the sentences are accompanied by various cues indicating the kinds of structures to be used (e.g., Mellon 1969, O'Hare 1973). In others, students receive no cues. In sentence construction, which derives from Francis Christensen's ideas about the rhetoric of the sentence (1967), students may examine model sentences, but they do not combine ready-made sentences into new structures. Rather, they generate a basic sentence about something they have observed and add details to it through the use of various structures, usually free modifiers following the basic clause (e.g., Faigley 1979c).

The following two narrative sections review studies of sentence combining and sentence construction.

Sentence Combining—with Nancy A. Mavrogenes

Although sentence combining exercises have been used for many years, as some researchers claim, they did not become a central focus of instruction until 1973, when O'Hare reported that his seventh-grade experimental groups wrote well beyond the syntactic maturity level typical of eighth-graders and in many respects at a level similar to the twelfth-graders in Hunt's study. Prior to that, sentence combining exercises were an adjunct to something else, usually to learning grammar of some kind. In Mellon's study (1969) they were used to help students better understand the various transformations and embeddings taught in a transformational grammar curriculum. Mellon hypothesized that the knowledge of transformational grammar in combination with its concrete application to sentence combining problems would result in more "mature" syntax in student writing. Using Hunt's T-unit as a measure, he found that it did. Mellon's study has been called a "pioneering experiment" which "became the first major application of Hunt's work to pedagogical research and laid the foundations for subsequent experimental research in sentence combining" (Kerek, Daiker, and Morenberg 1980, p. 1061). As O'Hare points out, the only study to advance a sentence structure hypothesis prior to Mellon's was Bateman and Zidonis (1964, 1966), which reported that the study of transformational grammar enabled students to increase significantly the proportion of well-formed sentences they wrote as well as the complexity of their writing. O'Hare also advanced a sentence structure hypothesis, but with a significant departure from earlier studies; in his study, the sentence combining activities were completely disassociated from the study of formal grammar. Students worked only with combining sets of sentences into increasingly complex structures, cued by nongrammatical terminology. O'Hare reported not only increased syntactic maturity in terms of various measures, including mean T-unit length, but also increased quality.

Another approach to sentence combining was also being explored at about the same time: the audio-lingual or oral-drill technique. James Ney (1980b) dates the inception of this idea to the summer of 1965. Several studies using this method (Ney 1966; Raub 1966, reported on by Griffin 1967; Miller and Ney 1968) have shown generally significant results.

These studies have led to a number of sentence combining texts and a host of dissertations from 1973 to the present. The overwhelming majority of these studies have been positive, with about 60 percent of them reporting that work in sentence combining, from as low as grade 2 through the adult level, results in significant advances (at least at $p < .05$) on measures of syntactic maturity. Thirty percent of the reports have recorded some improvement at a nonsignificant level or at a level which was not tested for significance. Only 10 percent of the reports have been negative, showing either no significant differences or mixed results.

More important, many studies have shown significant gains in quality for students engaged in sentence combining, gains which appear to be concomitants of increased T-unit and clause length. These studies include O'Hare (1973); Combs (1976a, 1977); Pedersen (1978); Schuster (1976, 1977); Ofsa (1975); Howie (1979); Obenchain (1979); Waterfall (1978); Daiker, Kerek, and Morenberg (1978); and M. Stewart (1978b). Others show differences in favor of experimental groups which are not statistically significant. A few studies show mixed results for quality.

To be sure, some among the over fifty studies available exhibit weaknesses. Some are preliminary reports, giving no exact numbers, no statistical tables, and no information on the pretests and posttests, or on how teachers or groups were chosen (Ney 1976a; Schuster 1976, 1977). Some experiments included no control groups (Ney 1966, 1975b; Hilfman 1970; Schuster 1976, 1977; Swan 1978; Maimon and Nodine 1978b, 1979; Obenchain 1979) or no teacher controls. Some studies involved small numbers—less than twenty, or even ten, per group (Ney 1966; Griffin 1967; Hilfman 1970; Vitale, et al. 1971; Perron 1975; Bivens and Edwards 1974; Maimon and Nodine 1978b, 1979). Some did not use pretests (J. J. Martin 1969; Vitale, et al. 1971). Some reported no tests for significance (Hilfman 1970; Ofsa 1975; Bivens and Edwards 1974; Obenchain 1979). However, in spite of these flaws, extensive reviews of the research are unanimous in concluding that sentence combining "has been proven again and again to be an effective means of fostering growth in syntactic maturity" (Kerek, Daiker, and Morenberg 1980, p. 1067). Stotsky (1975) even suggests that it "may facilitate cognitive growth as well" (p. 59), and John Mellon (1979) states that "the time for action has arrived. Sentence combining produces no negative effects, and works better than most of the activities in current composition teaching. . . . I don't know of any component in our arsenal of literacy-teaching methods that is better supported empirically than sentence combining. . . . The best advice I can give teachers today, relative to sentence combining, is— Do it!" (p. 35).

Sentence combining seems to work well with students of all levels (O'Hare 1973; Fisher 1973; Callaghan 1978; M. A. Sullivan 1978,

1979). In fact, some studies emphasize that disadvantaged or remedial students especially benefit from sentence combining instruction (Hunt and O'Donnell 1970; Ross 1971; J. D. Perron 1975; Schuster 1976, 1977; Waterfall 1978). In addition, students enjoy sentence combining. Some researchers simply report that students and sometimes teachers enjoyed the exercises (O'Hare 1973; Perron 1975; Ney 1975b; Maimon and Nodine 1978b; Daiker, Kerek, and Morenberg 1978), while others provide a quantitative analysis (Schuster 1976; Callaghan 1978; Sullivan 1978, 1979). The one clear negative report (Ney 1976a) was later rescinded as the researcher (Ney 1978) admitted that poor teaching was probably the cause of negative attitudes and results. Chappel (1977) argued that students' self-confidence could be strengthened by letting them discover that they have the creative potential for sentence combining inherent in their own linguistic competence. Kerek, Daiker, and Morenberg (1980) spell out this building of self-confidence more clearly: "Sentence combining instruction helps build confidence because it is positive in approach, it emphasizes the learning of new skills rather than the avoidance of old errors, and it subordinates every other course consideration to students' writing. After a semester of sentence combining, students usually feel better about their writing" (p. 1151).

While reporting such generally favorable results, these studies have raised some important questions. Some studies have asked whether sentence combining practice increases or reduces errors in students' writing. Ross (1971) reported that her experimental group showed an advantage over the control group in decreasing inaccurate sentences, but the difference was not statistically significant. Schuster's (1976, 1977) experimental groups exhibited fewer errors in mechanics and usage in their posttest essays than in their pretest essays as well as an improvement in handwriting. Obenchain (1979) found that sentence combining work reduced errors from an average of 5.2 per student on the pretest to 1.5 on the posttest. However, Maimon and Nodine (1978b, 1979) reported that sentence combining practice produced more errors on a rewriting passage (but not in free writing), and Hake and Williams (1979) reported a higher "flaw count" with increased T-unit length.

Another problem is the effect of mode of discourse on syntax. Martínez San José (1973), Perron (1977b), and Crowhurst and Piché (1979) all agree that argument produces the greatest number of mature grammatical structures and description the least. Howie (1979) reported a significant difference between experimental and control groups, favoring the experimental, in description but not in exposition, and Green (1973) reported that words per clause were higher in the narrative mode than in the expository mode. More experiments might concern themselves with instruction in sentence combining as it affects performance in different modes of discourse.

Several studies have asked whether the effects of sentence combining last. Some (Combs 1977; Pedersen 1978; Daiker, Kerek, and Morenberg 1978; and Maimon and Nodine 1979) found that gains in the experimental groups persisted in quality and/or syntactic fluency, after a period of some months. However, other reports have been negative (Callaghan 1978, Green 1973) or somewhat negative (Ofsa 1975, Combs 1976a, Sullivan 1978 and 1979), suggesting that without reinforcement some effects of sentence combining tend to erode. Kerek, Daiker, and Morenberg (1980) found that twenty-eight months after the completion of instruction, on both holistic and analytical ratings of quality, the differences between control and experimental groups were not statistically significant, although at posttest time the experimental group had scored significantly higher. During the twenty-eight months the experimental group's scores did not decline, but the control group gained significantly in five of six measures without any special instruction. The researchers maintain that sentence combining practice does have a positive effect on quality, "since the control group took longer to achieve the same gains in quality that the experimental students had made in one semester" (p. 1143). Such a finding, nevertheless, raises an important question: If learners will make gains in quality and syntactic complexity without special instruction, is the time spent on sentence combining practice, or any other practice, educationally and economically justifiable?

A study by Smith and Combs (1980) raises a related question, indicating that, at least among college freshmen, longer T-units and clauses may be attainable without instruction. The researchers made use of three conditions in various combinations to stimulate increased T-unit and clause length. The conditions included (1) no cue about longer structures, but simply an assignment; (2) an assignment plus a cue indicating that the audience for the writing would be a highly intelligent person influenced by long, complex sentences; and (3) a covert cue consisting of two days of sentence combining lessons prior to the assignment. The results indicate that both the overt and covert cues produced significantly longer T-units than non-cued conditions, with the means indicating greater gains in one week than those indicated by studies conducted over a semester. That is, combinations of the overt and covert cues over one week produced mean gains in words per clause comparable to those produced, in other studies, after a semester of sentence combining practice. The researchers argue that students (at least their college students) have the linguistic resources to write longer T-units but under ordinary conditions do not do so.

This finding raises a question similar to that raised by Kerek, Daiker, and Morenberg (1980): If students can write longer T-units and clauses when they are asked, is the time spent on sentence combining practice justifiable? Unfortunately, Smith and Combs present no quality rating, so we do not know how their increased mean T-unit and clause lengths are related to changes in quality.

Sentence Construction

Although relatively few studies of sentence construction have been conducted, it appears to be a promising technique for developing syntactic facility. Sentence construction is markedly different from sentence combining. Deriving from Christensen's (1967) ideas about the rhetoric of the sentence, it asks students to observe some phenomenon, generate a basic sentence, and add details about the phenomenon using various syntactic structures but particularly final free modifiers. While sentence combining exercises present students with given information in prefabricated sentences, sentence construction requires that students generate their own information prior to building syntactic structures. This difference may allow a rhetorical context for sentence construction, one in which the student writers must make decisions about which details are important and which are not, in view of the impact they wish to achieve. Several studies make claims for the effectiveness of sentence construction in increasing the use of modifiers: Palmer (1971), Walshe (1971), and L. Y. Brooks (1976). Three other studies find no significant differences (Hardaway 1969, Bond 1972, and Caldwell 1978). Most of these studies, however, lack any teacher control and display other design deficiencies.

The most carefully designed and implemented study of sentence construction techniques is Faigley's (1979c) study conducted with eight classes of college freshmen (n = 138), four of which received instruction in generative rhetoric (sentence construction) and four of which were taught from "a standard college rhetoric" (p. 199). Half of the students wrote on one of two narrative topics for the pretest, while the remainder wrote on the other. For the posttest the topics were reversed. Each paper was rated by five members of a team of experienced university teachers of composition. Extraordinary precautions were taken to guard against bias. The papers were also analyzed for certain syntactic features. Faigley reports statistically significant gains favoring the experimental groups over the control in words per T-unit ($p < .001$), words per clause ($p < .01$), percent of words in final free modifiers ($p < .001$), and in the percent of T-units having final free modifiers ($p < .001$). He also found gains in ratings of quality favoring the experimental group ($p < .05$).

However, when pretest and posttest data were added for each student and correlations of syntactic measures and rated quality were run, the results were similar to those in other studies: $r = .04$ for words per T-unit, $-.07$ for clauses per T-unit, .18 for words per clause, .25 for percent of words in final free modifiers, .41 for percent of T-units with final free modifiers, and .30 for length. Stepwise regression showed length and percent of T-units with final free modifiers to be the two most important variables associated with quality, a result corroborated by Nold and Freedman (1977), who found that length and the percent of words in final free modifiers were the most important variables associated with quality. The Nold and Freedman correlation between percent of words in free modifiers and quality rating is .42. This correlation and Faigley's are considerably higher than most of those cited between T-unit or clause length and quality.

One wonders why that should be so. Faigley (1979c) suggests that generative rhetoric addresses the problem of unelaborated discourse "by stressing the addition of specific details to abstract statements as a means of generating content" (p. 204). The pattern of instruction in Faigley's experimental treatment—asking students to observe some phenomenon, generate a sentence, and build on the sentence by adding details observed—suggests a reciprocal relationship, at least for final free modifiers, between structure and content. The structures taught demand content; content demands structuring. Elaborated discourse receives higher quality ratings than unelaborated discourse. The relatively high correlations between total length and quality which appear in several studies, including Faigley (.30) and Nold and Freedman (.57), suggest the need for elaboration of the kind produced by sentence construction. This kind of elaboration is probably more important to quality than simply conjoining sentences, which results in longer T-units and clauses but which may not produce more elaborated content.

Syntactic Measures and the Quality of Writing

Results like Faigley's (1979c) correlation of .04 between quality ratings and mean T-unit length raise what is perhaps the most important issue for research in sentence combining or generative rhetoric: the relationship between the quality of writing and various measures of syntactic maturity. O'Donnell (1976a), in his critique of indices of syntactic maturity, called mean T-unit length the "most useful and useable index of syntactic development over a wide age-range" and mean clause length "the best single measure of syntactic complexity at the high school level and beyond" (p. 38). O'Donnell's assessment of these measures appears to be widely accepted. A problem arises, however, when the descriptive measure becomes an instructional goal. All sentence combining treatments have been undertaken to increase mean T-unit and mean clause length, with most assuming that an increment in length, in itself, is a valid goal and somehow related to quality. Of over fifty studies available, over 60 percent make no attempt to judge the quality of the writing. Of those that do, the large majority show statistically significant differences in favor of the sentence combining groups.

Only one study indicates what may be interpreted as a negative result. Hake and Williams (1979) found that students whose pretest and posttest compositions were judged incompetent increased the length of their T-units significantly. Those whose pretests were judged incompetent but whose posttests were judged competent decreased their mean T-unit length significantly. On the other hand, those judged competent on both pretest and posttest essays also increased T-unit length significantly. Such results suggest that writers who are weak to begin with may be better off decreasing mean T-unit length than increasing it.

At the same time, as indicated earlier, several studies, in addition to Faigley's, have produced very low correlations between mean T-unit length and quality ratings. Belanger (1978b) found correlations ranging from .03 to .07. Stewart and Grobe (1979) found correlations of .03 for fifth-graders, .19 for eighth-graders, and − .06 for eleventh-graders. Nold and Freedman (1977) found .08 for college freshman at Stanford. Wille (1982) found correlations of .06 and .01 between mean T-unit length and two different ratings of quality for seventh-grade compositions. When they are available, the correlations between quality ratings and other measures of syntactic maturity such as mean clause length are about the same. With the single exception of Stewart and Grobe's correlation of .30 for fifth-graders, the correlations of mean clause and T-unit length to writing quality are trivial.

Yet the largely consistent findings of significantly increased quality over many studies cannot be ignored. It would appear that increased mean T-unit or clause length for an individual is *not* necessarily an indication of increased quality for that individual, despite findings that show increased syntactic maturity for groups to be a concomitant of increased quality.

How can these apparently conflicting results be explained? One possible explanation is that raters of compositions from sentence combining studies were somehow attuned to T-unit length as a criterion of excellence and thus assigned higher scores to papers with longer T-units and clauses, while in non-sentence combining studies, raters assigned grades on some other basis not related to T-unit length. Faigley's (1979c) study suggests that that is not the case, however. While not strictly a sentence combining study, it is concerned with such factors as mean T-unit length. Raters for this study were not from the university at which the study was conducted. Nor were they all English teachers, and they did not know about the experimental treatment. The experimental quality and mean T-unit length gains were significantly greater than the control gains. Still, the correlation between rated quality and mean T-unit length was only .04. Thus, while increased T-unit length was a concomitant of increased quality, it was not in itself a major determinant of the raters' judgment of quality.

Something else must be happening in the sentence combining studies. Another explanation is suggested by the work of Bereiter and Scardamalia (1982) and Shaughnessy (1977a). Bereiter and Scardamalia found that, in revising, children tend to avoid tampering with what they call "basic sentence plans." They may retain the basic sentence plan and make minor changes. They may also add material to the existing sentence, or they may replace the existing sentence with a new one. However, when children try to change the basic plan, their attempts to revise are failures. Bereiter and Scardamalia reason that an existing sentence is so salient a stimulus that it inhibits thinking of a new way to say the same thing, much as listening to a Beethoven symphony inhibits one's whistling a Sousa march. They suggest that work in sentence combining might provide a hierarchically organized knowledge of syntactic structures which would enable writers to consider alternatives.

Shaughnessy (1977a) discusses three kinds of "consolidation" errors, each of which superimposes one kind of syntactic pattern on another, consolidating them so that neither is readily interpreted by a reader. In fact, the examples Shaughnessy provides of students' attempts to revise such sentences reveal the same inability to revamp an existing sentence as described by Bereiter and Scardamalia. In one case, even a third attempt at revising a sentence blighted by a consolidation error leaves the writer with the following (p. 57): "The life of my parents and the life I am going to lead will be the opposite of their life styles." The writer has been trapped by the compound subject, which has remained constant in three tries, and is unable to think of a structure which will make the comparison work. Shaughnessy argues that sentence combining exercises are likely to help students overcome such syntactic difficulties.

Perhaps sentence combining practice provides writers with systematic knowledge of syntactic possibilities, the access to which allows them to sort through alternatives in their heads as well as on paper and to choose those which are apt. In the Hake and Williams (1979) study, incompetent writers who became competent decreased their mean T-unit length, a result which suggests that facility in making syntactic choices may be more important to quality than longer T-units. Such an explanation helps to account for the apparent contradiction between concomitant increases in T-unit length and quality for groups and the low correlation between quality ratings and mean T-unit length for individuals. That is, the syntactic facility gained through sentence combining practice results in group mean gains in T-unit length and quality. However, this result includes decreased T-unit length for certain individuals, the quality of whose writing increases, as well as increased T-unit length for others, the quality of whose writing remains low, as in the Hake and Williams study.

Whatever the answer, the question of the relationships among sentence combining practice, increased T-unit or clause length, and increased quality for individuals may continue to be a productive one for researchers. Since the Hunt study, researchers and teachers have emphasized sentence combining practice as a means of increasing "syntactic maturity," meaning increasing T-unit and clause length. Perhaps a more useful emphasis would be on *facility*. Facility would appear to involve an expanded repertoire of syntactic structures, the ability to sort through the available structures to select and test those which are feasible, and finally the judgment to select effective structures for a given rhetorical context. Development of such facility might involve working with extended or whole-discourse exercises, as Mellon (1979) and Obenchain (1979) suggest. Kerek, Daiker, and Morenberg (1980) argue that

> it is likely that the key to making a sentence combining curriculum maximally useful is through the development of new exercise formats that relate syntactic choices to rhetorical and thematic constraints. Such materials might consist of carefully modelled whole-discourse exercises and exercises of paragraph length that

focus on the effects of syntactic decisions on controlling coherence, tone, emphasis, and style. (pp. 1151–1152)

Even with so many questions left unanswered, one is tempted to agree with Charles Cooper (1975c) that "no other single teaching approach has ever consistently been shown to have a beneficial effect on syntactic maturity and writing quality" (p. 72).

6 Criteria for Better Writing

From ancient times those concerned with teaching oral or written composition have taught their students criteria for judging effective discourse. Their assumptions have been (1) that certain generic properties of certain types of discourse make a token of that type effective and (2) that those properties may be described in terms of criteria which can be used to guide the production of discourse and to judge the effectiveness of written products. For the most part such criteria have not been validated empirically. Although several studies have attended to what characteristics of writing influence the judgments of readers (e.g., Diederich 1964), fewer have varied the characteristics of discourse types systematically to determine which properties are essential to the success of some particular type, as do Stein and Policastro (1984) with simple stories. The criteria with which studies in this chapter are concerned have been established by consensus or usage, conditions which are not altogether unacceptable.

Criteria have been taught in a number of ways, which this chapter will take up in order: (1) the study of model pieces of writing thought to exemplify various properties of good writing; (2) the use of scales or sets of criteria applied to exemplary models and to other writing, including that of the students themselves; (3) the provision of teacher comments about what is good and what to avoid in the future; and (4) revision based on the comments of teachers or peers. The first two of these methods amount to prewriting instruction. Their focus is on learning criteria before writing and using that criteria. The second two methods amount to what might be called "post-writing instruction." That is, students are to learn the criteria as a result of what they have done, with the expectation that they will benefit from the instruction in their future writing.

The Study of Models

A common assumption among teachers of writing is that a familiarity with good or great writing will enhance a writer's own work. A more concrete pedagogical version of this assumption is that a developing

153

writer learns from seeing what others have done and from imitating those forms and techniques. That is, in order to write an essay of a given type, the writer must first be familiar with examples of the type and know the parts of the type and their relationships. Such an assumption appears to be undeniable. How could a writer produce a haiku or sonnet if the writer did not first know what a haiku or sonnet is? Although some studies conducted in the last twenty years have examined the effects of general exposure to "good" writing, many more studies have concentrated on the analysis of models to identify specific qualities or features which students were expected to incorporate in their own writing. In the general exposure category, Mills (1968) tested a program in which fifth-graders read samples of children's literature for one hour per week for twenty-four weeks, while control students pursued the standard curriculum. In one of two experimental treatments, Glazer (1972) had fourth-grade teachers read twenty books of high literary quality to their classes while sixth-grade teachers read twelve books to their classes. In contrast, the control classes had no planned literature program. Some experimental groups received directed lessons; others simply listened to the books read aloud. The results for this program are mixed to the extent that they are difficult to interpret.

Several experimental treatments focused on specific structural or qualitative aspects of the models used. For example, Clark (1968), Lareau (1971), and Perry (1980) all used model pieces of writing with college students. Clark used good and poor student compositions, with the instructor identifying and explaining strengths and weaknesses. Lareau used models in technical writing courses for upper-level students, while Perry used models to illustrate structural features of compositions. None of these studies produced significant differences between the experimental and control groups.

A number of studies examined the effectiveness of using models at the secondary school level. W. W. West (1967) used models with tenth-graders to illustrate features of each rhetorical mode. Sponsler (1971), also with tenth-graders, used two models, one to illustrate concrete detail and one to illustrate fixed spatial point-of-view. Caplan and Keech (1980) used models with high school students to illustrate the difference between "showing" and "telling." Vinson (1980), working with eight classes of ninth-graders, used models in experimental groups to illustrate concrete detail, sensory imagery, unnecessary detail, and single impression. Pinkham (1969), with fifth-graders, and W. D. Martin (1981), with seventh-graders, used models for imitation. None of these studies found statistically significant differences between experimental and control groups.

A few studies did find some statistically significant gains resulting from the use of models. Calhoun (1971), working with college freshmen, found significant differences in students' abilities to recognize effective techniques, but while experimental groups gained in the use of the techniques in their writing, the gains were not significant. Andreach (1976) with college freshmen, Reedy (1966) with ninth-graders, C. F. Robinson (1978) with seventh-, ninth-, and tenth-graders, Rothstein (1970) with college freshmen, Stefl (1981) with third-graders, A. E. Thibodeau (1964) with sixth-graders, and B. W. Wood (1978) with tenth-, eleventh-, and twelfth-graders all report significant gains in writing for groups studying models. In all these cases, the models were relatively brief (as opposed to the extended essays used in many college freshman composition readers) and were selected to illustrate relatively few but specific points about good writing. However, the same appears to be true of some studies which did not produce significant gains.

This narrative review can conclude only that the results for the use of models are mixed. At the same time, it is clear that the study of models has potential for helping writers at a variety of grade levels. However, available research does not permit fine discriminations among the effects of various types of models on students of various ages and levels of ability, or among the variety of ways in which they may be used.

A model or models may be used to illustrate a single characteristic of effective writing, such as the use of concrete detail, as in Stefl (1981), Vinson (1980), and Sponsler (1971). While Sponsler used only one model (from Dickens's *Bleak House*), Stefl and Vinson used several. Stefl presented third-graders with two descriptive paragraphs about an unusual animal and asked that they (1) choose the more descriptive paragraph, (2) discuss why the one chosen was more descriptive, and (3) rewrite the other paragraph while viewing a slide of the animal. On each of the eight occasions the activity was used, the experimental students added details to an existing framework, which was a more limited task than in Sponsler and Vinson, in which students had to produce an entire discourse after examining a model and, further, to do it from their personal resources without benefit of a slide to prompt them. Stefl's third-graders gained significantly over the control group in descriptive writing. Vinson's experimental students made greater gains than her control students, but the differences were not statistically significant. Sponsler, who used only a single model, showed no significant differences.

The variations in these three studies suggest only some of the treatment variables in the use of models which may warrant systematic examination in future studies: the type and number of models, the types of student tasks accompanying the use of models, and the complexity of those tasks.

The Use of Scales

In the past two decades several experiments have tested the use of what I have called *scales* or *sets of criteria*. In all of these experiments students received sets of criteria and applied them to their own writing or to the writing of others. Sometimes the criteria were in the form of scales. In all cases students were asked to examine pieces of writing in terms of a set of questions about the extent to which the writing exhibited certain characteristics. In many of these studies, questions were also directed at finding ways to improve the piece of writing under examination, and, in fact, asked students to invent revisions. Most of the studies involved found statistically significant differences between students using the sets of criteria and those taught through some other technique. Many of these treatments, but by no means all, used model pieces of writing to illustrate the criteria. However, in contrast to studies in the preceding section, studies in this group used models incidentally rather than centrally. In the "scale" studies, models simply illustrated the sets of criteria which students then proceeded to use. Major portions of the instructional time were spent in applying the criteria or discussing how the criteria could be met, or in actually trying to meet them through appropriate revisions.

Sager (1973a, 1973b) and Clifford (1978, 1981) qualify as archetypes of the scale category. Sager's experimental and control groups were sixth-grade children in inner-city schools. She developed scales concerned with aspects of writing quality: elaboration, vocabulary, organization, and structure. Students worked with one scale at a time, learning on one day what features earned a score of 0 and on other days what features earned scores of 1, 2, or 3. In introducing each scale, the teacher presented a specific composition and led a discussion of the features which it did or did not exhibit. Following the teacher-led discussions, students worked in small groups and individually rated the compositions. When the composition was not rated 3, they suggested improvements and made actual revisions. A specific example of Sager's exercises appears in Chapter 4 of this review (see "Environmental Mode").

Sager reports that students became quite expert in judging compositions according to four scale components, achieving estimated rater reliabilities of between .96 and .98. According to Sager (1973b), "Even the most reluctant students became eager, accurate, and vociferous judges. It was not at all unusual for heated debates over scoring to be continued on the playground or in the lunchroom long after the language arts period had ended" (p. 6). However that may be, one suspects that simply judging the compositions may not have been adequate to achieve the statistically significant gains of this study. That is, probably both the judging *and* the revising are necessary for large gains. That, of course, is an interesting empirical question.

At any rate, the gains made by Sager's experimental students are significantly greater than those of the control students, who lost ground. Indeed, although this study was not included in the meta-analysis because of inadequate teacher controls, the effect sizes were calculated and are impressive. The experimental/control effect size is .93, enlarged by losses for the controls. The pre-to-post effect size for the experimental groups is .82, quite large for forty 45-minute classes in an eight-week period. A study by D. R. Coleman (1982) confirmed Sager's results. Coleman's experimental second- and third-grade gifted students used the Sager scales to evaluate their own writing. These students also made significantly greater gains than did the control students.

Clifford (1978, 1981) also used sets of criteria to guide students in rating their own writing and that of others. In Clifford's study, classroom instructors used what he calls an "invariant sequence" for each of thirteen compositions. The sequence began with a structured assignment, followed by teacher-led "oral brainstorming" to explore ideas and possible approaches, then ten minutes of free writing in response to the assignment without regard to mechanics. The period of free writing was followed by small-group discussion of ideas produced in the period.

Clifford (1981) indicates that a "feedback sheet" was used in these discussions, with small-group members responding "to their ideas and feelings about the content, but also offer[ing] suggestions about what details to leave out or stress, what to put first or last" (pp. 42–43). Such informal feedback implies a set of criteria for deciding what to include, what to stress, and so forth. The actual feedback sheet used at this stage (1978, p. 250), however, neither states nor implies any necessity to discuss what to include, exclude, or stress. Rather, it calls for highly personal reactions to the free writing, e.g., "pretend this was written by a stranger. Guess what he or she is like." Following small-group discussion, students "reported to the class on tentative plans" (1981, p. 43), including points to be made and organization.

For the following class, students prepared a first "good" draft and made five copies for use in small groups. For the first nine weeks of the course, group members responded to each other's writing using three sets of questions, one each on sentence structure, organization, and support. During the last five weeks of the course, instructors "elicited criteria against which student essays would then be judged" (1981, p. 43).

Clifford's feedback sheet for sentence structure includes such questions as the following: "Is each sentence a completed thought? Are there fragments of sentences? Are there misspellings, errors in punctuation? Where? Should parts of sentences be combined? Are unnecessary words used?" (1978, p. 252). The feedback sheet for organization includes such questions as the following: "What are the parts of this piece? Are the parts related? Should they be? Is the movement of the essay logical? Is there a conclusion? Does it follow what comes before?" (1978, p. 253). The feedback sheet for support includes such questions as "Is there a central idea, an abstraction; a generalization reducible to a sentence? Where is it? Is the writer trying to prove or disprove this idea? Illuminate it? Are reasons, examples or explanations given to support the idea? Where? What do you think of the writer's support? Evaluate it" (1978, p. 254).

Following the small-group discussion of the compositions and responses in writing by group members, the essays were returned to the writers. The groups then "exchanged their work for evaluation. Each student carefully read one essay and filled out an evaluation sheet indicating the strongest and weakest parts while also making concrete suggestions for revision" (1981, p. 43). In the course of every two class sessions, then, students applied the sets of criteria to six compositions other than their own and made suggestions for revisions. According to Clifford's precise account, the application of the various sets of criteria and the suggestions that they generated were the dominant foci of instruction, consuming 80 percent of the class time— twenty-eight of thirty-five hours during the semester.

Although some critics might quibble with the form and focus of Clifford's questions, there is little doubt as to their effect. His experiment shows an experimental/control effect size of .61 and a pre-to-post effect size of 1.12 for experimental groups. Apparently, the active application of criteria and subsequent suggestions for improvement in their own and others' writing enabled the students to internalize criteria which then served as guides for their own independent writing.

Several other studies made use of sets of criteria to guide in developing or evaluating pieces of writing or both. Working with eighteen classes of junior high school students over ten weeks, N. L. Benson (1979) experimented with two different sets of criteria to guide peer group evaluations of student writing followed by revision. Both treatments proved significantly superior to the control, which consisted of feedback from the teacher followed by revision. The two experimental treatments were not significantly different. Farrell (1977) contrasted peer evaluation guided by sets of experimenter-devised criteria with (1) classes which were tutored by trained high school students, (2) classes taught through teacher lecture, and (3) one class which received no instruction in writing. The three instructed groups all made gains significantly higher than those made by the no-instruction group. Farrell reports that boys in the peer-group evaluation treatment made significantly greater gains than boys in any other groups.

Rosen (1974) used sets of criteria focusing on organization and development of ideas with remedial college students. Students used the guide sheets as they developed each piece of writing. Classes were small (ten or fewer), and teachers were able to assist students in editing and evaluating. During the semester the teacher read several compositions by each student to the class and conducted discussions of them.

Wright (1976) and Kemp (1979) also used sets of criteria with college students. Kemp used sets of questions to help students generate ideas and sets of criteria for self-evaluation. Both Wright and Kemp, however, indicate that students used the criteria individually with little peer group interaction. In both studies the experimental groups made greater gains than the control groups, but the differences were not significant.

Cohen and Scardamalia (no date) conducted a study with twenty-one sixth-graders in which they taught students what they call "diagnostic statements" for use in the modification of the children's own texts. These statements serve as criteria and include the following (from Table 2 of the researchers' report): "(1) too few ideas, (2) part of the essay does not belong here, (3) introduction does not explain what the essay is about, (4) idea said in a clumsy way, (5) conclusion does not explain ideas, (6) incomplete idea, (7) ignored a strong point on the other side, (8) weak reason, (9) needs an example to explain the idea." These criteria were introduced and taught over five teaching sessions. In each session, the children wrote their own "opinion essays," following which the teacher introduced two of the criteria and led the students in applying them to and revising an essay written for the purpose by the experimenters. After this teacher-led class revision, the children revised their own essays, making use of the criteria available. Cohen and Scardamalia report significant gains in the quality of revisions made and in the frequency of revisions, especially in "idea" revisions.

As a group, these studies indicate rather clearly that engaging young writers actively in the use of criteria, applied to their own or to others' writing, results not only in more effective revisions but in superior first drafts. That is, most of these studies evaluate their effectiveness through pre and post writing samples, rather than through pre and post revisions. Most of them show significant gains for experimental groups, suggesting that the criteria learned act not only as guides for revision but as guides for generating new material.

Teacher Comment

Over the past two decades several researchers have turned their attention to the effects which teacher comment has on the writing skills of students. The need for such research is almost self-evident. Conscientious English teachers spend large proportions of their available time marking papers. An important question is whether or not the comments and the time they take are worthwhile. Some of the research undertaken in the past has examined the effects of teacher marking and comment as a single variable, while other studies have examined the effects of comment in conjunction with variables such as revision and amount or frequency of writing.

A number of studies have examined the effects of teacher comment alone. Gee (1972) tested the effects of praise, negative criticism, and no comment. Using IQ scores, he divided 139 high school juniors into low-, middle-, and high-ability groups. One third of the students in each ability group received praise, one third criticism, and one third no comment on each of four compositions on assigned topics written over a four-week period. No particular instruction in composition was provided. The no-comment group received only a check mark to "indicate that their papers had been read." Students in the praise and criticism groups received from five to eight comments each. The praise group received compliments for "originality, sound and thoroughly developed ideas, good grammar, etc." (p. 215). The papers receiving criticism were marked for errors in grammar, spelling, organization, and usage. Suggestions for improvement were also given. One week after the papers were written, they were returned to the students, who were asked to examine their papers (with or without comments) and to think of ways to improve in the next essay. They were also given the next topic to write on. The students, then, had the benefit of the teacher's comments immediately prior to writing.

Although Gee was able to find no difference in the quality of the writing between the first and final compositions, he did find a difference in the mean number of T-units written from the first to final compositions. Students in all treatment groups wrote fewer T-units. However, while the praised group lost only an average of about two T-units (declining from 16.57 to 14.78), the criticized group lost nearly six (declining from 18.88 to 13.00), and the group with no feedback lost about five (declining from 18.40 to 13.69). Such losses may not necessarily be detrimental. It is at least conceivable that fewer T-units are indicative of students' attempts to put more effort into each T-unit and to tighten the writing by eliminating the unnecessary. However, coupled with the finding that praised students had significantly more positive attitudes toward their writing than either the criticized or no-comment group, the loss in T-units becomes more meaningful. We can infer that the negative attitudes may be a result of the teacher's lack of comment or negative comment and that such feedback results in less enthusiasm for writing and, therefore, in less writing.

Gee's experiment reflects the common practice of teaching writing through assigning a topic and supplying feedback after the writing has been completed. It is possible that under different instructional conditions the comment types examined in Gee's study would have far different effects.

Seidman (1968) investigated the effects of three types of feedback: (1) selective, supportive, and informative comments; (2) all-inclusive negative comments; and (3) no comments. Two classes from each of five secondary English teachers participated, the students being randomly assigned to the three comment/treatment groups. Each teacher presented a sequence of eight composition assignments and provided comments (or no comments) on the papers which the students produced. Seidman made no attempt to gauge changes in the quality of the students' writing but reports that students receiving positive comments wrote significantly ($p < .025$) more optional rough drafts and revisions than either the negative-comment group or the no-comment group.

Stevens (1973) examined the effects of positive and negative comments on the writing of low-performing tenth- and eleventh-grade males. Students wrote five compositions over a period of ten weeks, each in response to a question about a one-page typed article which had been discussed in a previous class period. The evaluator then typed six to eight positive or negative comments on each composition along with a "general statement of praise or reproof" depending on the group to which the student had been assigned. While Stevens found no difference in the quality of compositions written by the negative and positive groups, he did find a significant difference in the attitudes toward composition. The negative-comment group had significantly more negative attitudes toward writing than did the group receiving positive comments.

Hausner (1976) investigated the effects of teacher comment on composition ability in relation to personality factors such as sensitivity to criticism. The subjects were 163 eleventh-graders in eight English classes who were taught six sequential composition lessons. The students were divided into two groups: an experimental group who received teacher comments, one negative and two positive or the reverse over a total of six compositions—for a total of nine negative and nine positive comments; and a control group who received no teacher comments. The only statistically significant difference to emerge was the difference in the posttest scores for students in the total group identified as sensitive to criticism and those identified as not sensitive to criticism ($p < .05$), with the latter having the higher scores. Such a result, based on data from the total group, is difficult to interpret, because only half of those sensitive to criticism received any comment at all.

Investigators have also been concerned about the effects of negative and positive comments and lack of feedback on the writing of younger children. Taylor and Hoedt (1966), for example, in what appears to be a carefully designed study, were concerned with the effects of negative versus positive comments on the creative writing of 105 fourth-grade youngsters in three classes. Pupils in each of the classes were assigned randomly to negative- or positive-comment groups. Each class was taught a creative writing lesson once a week for ten consecutive weeks. The teacher placed written comments on the creative writing papers each week, assigning comments to the negative group only as earned. For each negative comment assigned, care was taken to insure that a matching positive comment was assigned to a paper in a positive group. Thus, if a student in the negative group was assigned the comment, "Please rewrite this paragraph," then a student in the positive group would be assigned the comment, "A very good paragraph."

Although both groups showed progress in the quality of the compositions they produced over the ten weeks, the investigators detected no difference in quality between the two groups. However, a number of attitudinal and behavioral measures indicate that the difference in affective response between the two groups was significant. Children receiving negative comments actively sought praise directly from the teacher more often than did those receiving positive written comments. Children receiving negative comments also indicated far greater frustration and dissatisfaction than did the positive group. Upon the return of papers to their writers, children in the positive group seemed pleased and shared their papers with others. Children in the negative group folded or hid their papers from sight. Fifty-three papers from the negative comment group were "excessively wrinkled or torn," while only one paper from the positive group was in such condition.

Schroeder (1973a) was concerned with the effects of positive and corrective comments and no feedback on the writing of fifty-five fourth-graders who wrote two compositions per week over a period of three-and-a-half months. The children wrote in response to a variety of stimuli and topic suggestions. Comments were concerned with the use of direct discourse, descriptive passages, capital letters, and terminal punctuation. "Positive" comments noted and praised the presence of desirable features. "Corrective" comments noted the absence of desirable features and indicated how they might have been included. Although a higher level of performance was more often associated with corrective feedback than with positive comments, the difference between the groups was not significant. Both positive and corrective feedback, however, resulted in a significant increase in the inclusion of descriptive passages over the control group who received no feedback.

Alpren (1973) investigated the effects of using scales to provide feedback about originality in fifth-graders. Three classes were pooled and stratified according to reading comprehension and divided by sex. The children were then randomly assigned to three treatment groups which met separately with the investigator on Friday morning when they wrote in response to one of three stimuli: a worn sneaker, an apple, and a white mouse. On the following Monday the investigator returned the compositions to the children. Group 1 also received a thirty-six-item scale evaluating the writing from Friday. Group 2 received a simplified twenty-item scale, while group 3 received no feedback. Groups 1 and 2 were given ten minutes to examine their evaluations. All three groups were asked to write about one or all of the same stimuli again. The same procedure was followed two weeks later with all groups. All stories written on each of the four occasions were evaluated by three independent judges using the scale comprising thirty-six separate items which provided Group 1 with feedback.

Results indicate that children with the thirty-six-item scale failed to make any significant improvement over the four occasions. Group 2 (with the twenty-item scale) made a gain significant at .01, and Group 3 (with no feedback made) also showed a gain significant at .05. In interpreting these results Alpren suggests that youngsters may interpret no feedback as equivalent to "right." Alpren does not discuss the differences between the two rating instruments in relation to their effects on the children's writing. Yet, inspection of the scales contained in each instrument indicates two clear differences: the number of items and the ease with which youngsters may comprehend the language of the individual items. The thirty-six-item scale is nearly twice as long as the twenty-item version, and its language less likely to be clear to fifth-graders. Combined, these two factors seem likely to have a depressant effect on writing. Too much evaluation which is unclear may very well be interpreted as negative, an effect which might very well have overpowered the practice effect apparent in Group 3.

Although none of these studies has been able to show a difference in quality in writing between groups receiving positive comments and negative comments, the effects on the attitudes of writers seem clear. Students receiving negative criticism wrote less and developed negative attitudes about themselves as writers and about writing as an activity. Positive and/or corrective comments appear to be preferable to negative comments or to lack of feedback. But the effects of lack of feedback remain ambiguous, with Alpren's study standing in contradiction to other studies which make use of such a control group.

Other investigators have examined various modes of feedback. V. B. Coleman (1973) and Judd (1973) examined the difference between written comments and tape-recorded comments but found no consistent significant differences.

Stiff (1967) and Bata (1973) studied the effects of marginal, terminal, and mixed marginal-terminal comments on the writing of college students over the period of a semester. Both researchers report no significant differences among the various groups and, more interestingly, no significant differences from pretest to posttest.

Other studies have examined the effects of teacher comment in relation to frequency of writing. Burton and Arnold (1964) examined the effects of frequent writing (one 250-word composition per week) versus infrequent writing (three 250-word compositions per semester) and the effects of intensive evaluation (marking every error and writing detailed comments) versus moderate evaluation (grading only an occasional paper or correcting only errors related to skills students were studying at the time). The study found no significant differences among the four groups, concluding that neither frequent practice nor intensive marking will necessarily result in increased writing skill.

In another study, Sutton and Allen (1964) studied 112 college freshmen divided randomly into six treatment groups. One group did no writing at all. Another wrote one theme per week which was evaluated by peers, while still another wrote one theme per week which was evaluated by professors. All students wrote six pretest compositions and six posttest compositions. Each composition was evaluated by five raters using the Diederich scale. The mean composition scores for all sections declined significantly ($p < .01$).

Clopper (1967) also studied frequency of writing in relation to teacher comment. Seven experimental classes wrote two compositions per week for fourteen weeks and received detailed comments from lay readers. Seven control classes wrote one composition every two weeks in the same period and received comments from the teacher. Despite the fact that experimental students received four times more practice and roughly four times more comment than the control groups, there were no significant differences.

The results of all these studies strongly suggest that teacher comment has little impact on student writing. None of the studies of teacher comment discussed above show statistically significant differences in the quality of writing between experimental and control groups. Indeed, several show no pre-to-post gains for *any* groups, regardless of the type of comment. Certainly, none show gains comparable to those achieved in studies such as Sager's and Clifford's, in which students actively applied criteria to writing and made their own suggestions for revision.

However, a comparison of the studies suggests that in most of them the comments by teachers are diffuse; they range over substance, development, organization, style, mechanics, and so forth. The variables examined have to do with negative versus positive, frequent versus infrequent, marginal versus terminal, but ordinarily not with diffuse comments versus those which are focused or concentrated on one or two key aspects of writing.

Schroeder (1973a), however, specified comments concerned with the use of direct quotations, description, capitalization, and terminal punctuation. The fourth-graders who received positive or corrective feedback increased their use of description significantly over the control students. It may be, then, that focused feedback can have an effect on certain aspects of writing.

Feedback and Revision

Beach (1979) examined the effects of a between-draft evaluation on revisions made by high school students. Using three groups of randomly assigned students, he asked one group to revise without intervening evaluation, the second to revise after receiving evaluation from a teacher, and a third to revise after using a form to evaluate their own writing. Teacher evaluations were made on a form which included five five-point scales for rating "focus, sequence, support, overall quality, and need-for-change" (p. 114) and which also required clarifying comments. Students who evaluated their own writing used a form which paralleled the teacher evaluation form. The first and revised drafts were mixed and submitted to three judges for degree-of-change rating and for quality ratings on various dimensions.

The teacher evaluation group received significantly higher degree-of-change ratings and significantly higher quality ratings on support than either of the other two groups. There were no significant differences among the groups on quality ratings of sequence, sentences, language, flavor, or focus. It is interesting to note that the teacher evaluation forms did not provide for feedback on sentences, language, or flavor. Further, it is interesting to speculate that, of the five dimensions specified on the teacher evaluation form, *support* is probably the most specific and the most amenable to revision. In commenting on the higher quality ratings for support, Beach suggests that "the teacher focused more attention on matters of support in the rough drafts than on focus or sequence" (p. 118).

The important findings in Beach's study are (1) that students make more revisions in response to teacher comments than in response to their own evaluations—at least when they have not been taught to evaluate as in Sager (1973b) or Clifford (1981); (2) that those revisions are associated with significantly higher quality ratings—at least on one dimension; and (3) that comments focused on a single dimension, in this case *support*, may be more effective than those which are sporadic or diffuse.

Hillocks (1982), working with seventh- and eighth-grade classes, required that all comments be concentrated on increasing the specificity, sharpness of focus, and impact of personal-experience writing.

The four instructional conditions included (1) observational activities, assignment, teacher comment, revision; (2) observational activities, assignment, teacher comment, no revision; (3) assignment, teacher comment, revision; and (4) assignment, teacher comment, no revision. Students in each of the twelve classes (four for each of three teachers) were divided into two groups using a table of random numbers. One group received short comments consisting of at least one compliment and one or more brief suggestions for increasing specificity or focus. Cooperating teachers were asked to keep short comments to ten or fewer words. The short comments actually averaged nine to ten words for two of the teachers and just over fourteen for the third. The second group received long comments of one or more compliments and very specific suggestions for improvement. In practice, the long comments averaged about forty-one words for one teacher, thirty-eight for the second, and twenty-two for the third.

The results of this experiment indicate that focused comments coupled with the assignment and revision produced a significant quality gain, as did the assignment with no revision. However, the gain for students doing revision (1.57) was nearly twice that for students receiving comments but doing no revision (.89). Further, analysis of covariance revealed a significant interaction between comment length and instructional pattern ($p < .009$). For students engaged in observational activities and writing, the gains for students receiving longer comments were greater—but not significantly. For students who did *not* engage in observational activities, however, longer comments were less effective than shorter comments. Indeed, for the classes doing the writing assignments only, the short comments were twice as effective as the long comments (1.12 versus .55, $p < .02$).

Hillocks's study also asked teachers to record the amounts of time they spent in commenting on the compositions. Although long comments by all three teachers required approximately twice as much time as short comments, they were never significantly more effective than short comments. However, when long comments were not accompanied by instructional prewriting activities or by revision, they were significantly less effective than short comments. Thus, a teacher who spends ten hours a week making focused comments on matters of specificity and focus on the compositions of seventh- and eighth-graders might expect to achieve comparable if not better results with only five hours of work.

The available research suggests that teaching by written comment on compositions is generally ineffective. Certainly, no results for teacher comment comparable to those of Sager (1973b) and Clifford

(1981) are available, and many studies indicate no significant differences in the quality of student writing as a result of varying the options available in making comments. It may be, however, that when comments are focused and tied to some aspect of instruction, either prewriting or revision, they do increase the quality of writing. Teacher comments related specifically to prewriting instruction or to revision might at least help students understand more clearly the criteria the teacher has in mind in assigning grades.

There is reason to suspect that students are unaware of or fail to understand teachers' evaluative criteria. Zirinsky (1978) investigated whether or not students shared with their teachers an understanding of what was expected when they were asked to write. The researcher had 100 students from ten tenth-grade classes write two essays. Then, students rated each other's papers holistically according to their personal rating and how they thought their teachers would rate them. Teachers then rated the compositions. The results indicated high correlations between personal and predicted teacher ratings. However, there was no correlation between any student ratings and actual teacher ratings. Such a finding, in itself, indicates the need for teachers to tie their comments to instruction capable of clarifying the criteria they use. It also suggests the need for focusing on one or two key features of writing until students have learned them. Such inferences, of course, remain empirical questions.

In summary, of the four foci for teaching criteria for guiding the production of written language and its revision, using sets of criteria appears to be the most effective. At best, results for the study of models have been mixed, while results for various aspects of teacher comment, in and of themselves, tend to show no differences (although positive comments appear more effective than negative comments). Some combination of the study of examples, the active use of criteria by students, teacher comment, and revision may prove optimal. However, those combinations may differ widely by grade level and have yet to be thoroughly examined.

7 Invention

In ancient rhetoric, invention had to do with the development of arguments. The term *invention* is used more generally in this chapter to encompass a variety of approaches thought to be useful in generating and/or processing the substance of a piece of writing. These approaches include the following: variations in the conditions of writing assignments, free writing, heuristics, and inquiry.

Assignment Conditions

A fairly large number of studies have been concerned with how the conditions of a writing assignment affect the writing produced. And for good reason. There is a widespread belief that finding the right topic is the key to teaching writing, as witnessed by the popularity of booklets which list 1,000 or even 7,000 topics for writing but do nothing more. Mellon (1975a) has argued from a more theoretical point of view that teaching and assessing writing are very much alike—in that a good topic for assessment, like a good topic for teaching, will indicate the full rhetorical context for the piece of writing. The assumption in these cases is that working through the topic enables the writers to learn.

Assignment condition studies have examined not only the effects of variations in the phrasing and framing of topics but the effects of a variety of other conditions ranging from size of paper for writing (Ackerman 1976)[1] to various types of music used as stimuli for writing (Donlan 1976a). These studies have not been categorized in this review as treatment studies because they usually involve single writing assignments for which particular initial writing conditions are varied, as opposed to treatments lasting over a few to many days

---

1. The apprehensive reader may be relieved to learn that Ackerman found no significant differences in the quality of writing among students using 6-1/2″ × 8″, 8-1/2″ × 11″, and 11″ × 14″ paper. Clearly, the differences in paper size are not extreme. Some ambitious researcher may wish to contrast the effects of postage-stamp-size paper with newsprint size.

from which students are expected to learn new writing skills. The assignment condition studies assume certain skills on the part of the students and ask whether variations in certain conditions elicit those skills to greater or lesser degrees.

Framing of Topics

As Hoetker's informative review (1982) indicates, the phrasing or framing of topics is of particular interest to those concerned with writing assessment because they wish to insure that a given topic will elicit a writer's best work and that topics used over time in testing situations will be comparable. Such research is also important to instruction, for if particular topic characteristics consistently produce better writing, then those characteristics incorporated into a treatment might help to bring about increased proficiency.

Such studies of topics have been concerned with differences in cognitive demands, background information supplied, and rhetorical context supplied. Greenberg (1981) examined the effects of topics which she differentiated as low- or high-cognitive demand tasks and low- or high-experiential demand tasks. As Hoetker (1982) points out in his review, however, the actual differences among the topics are minor. For example, one of Greenberg's topics, classified as a high-cognitive demand task, supplies a thesis which can readily be adapted to the essay written by the student. With this version of the topic, writers have to decide for themselves on strategies to be used in defense of the supplied thesis. In the low-cognitive demand version, no thesis is supplied but alternative strategies are provided for developing the essay. With this version of the topic, writers would have to decide on a thesis—or at least a point-of-view—before electing one of the strategies professed.

It may be that college freshmen find developing a thesis as difficult as deciding on strategies for developing the essay. Or it may be that in a test situation, college freshmen respond in a global fashion to writing tasks, taking little or no notice of hints provided. Whatever the case, the differences in Greenberg's assignments did not elicit significant differences in the quality of the student responses.

Brossell (1983) tested the effects of topics which he varied by "information load." The lowest level of information consisted of a brief phrase, e.g., "violence in the schools." The highest level consisted of a paragraph which provided a fictional situation (membership in a school council at a time when the incidence of violence had increased) and a somewhat clearer purpose (a personal opinion about the cause of school violence). The "moderate information load" topic informed the writer about the increase in violence in schools and called for a personal-opinion essay about the causes of the increase.

Brossell experimented with six topics, each with three versions which twenty college seniors wrote on for a total of 360 essays. He found no significant differences among the six topics. More important, he found no significant differences among the levels of information load, or rhetorical context. He observes, however, that the topics with the most complete statements about the rhetorical context received the lowest mean scores and had the shortest mean length. Further, he points out that in the 200–400 word range, the longer an essay was, "the likelier it was to get a high score" (p. 168). These and other findings, Brossell says, "are grounds for questioning the presumed superiority of full rhetorical specification in essay topics for large-scale writing assessments" (p. 172).

Metviner (1981) examined what she calls "rhetorically based" and "rhetorically deficient" topics. In the first assignment, ninth-graders were asked to write an opinion paper on the use of drugs for submission to the school newspaper for possible publication. Students given the "rhetorically deficient" assignment wrote on the same topic, but they knew they would submit it to a teacher for a grade. Such assignments are thought to be rhetorically deficient because they are for a teacher and for a grade (see, for example, Britton, et al. 1975 and Emig 1971). In this case, however, the rhetorically deficient assignment proved to be more effective ($p < .001$). Presumably, for the ninth-graders in this study teachers are realistic audiences and grades are appropriate purposes.

Woodworth and Keech (1980), working with ninth- and eleventh-graders, also tested topics differentiated by rhetorical context. In each assignment, students were directed "to think of an experience in which [they] did something for the first time." In the first version students were asked simply to describe the experience, writing "a story, a journal entry, or any other form." The second version specified an imaginary audience: "Imagine you are writing this description for someone who is about to experience the activity for the first time." The third version specified a real audience: "Write about this experience for a particular person (brother, sister, friend, etc.) who has not had such an experience. . . . Sometime between now and Christmas, after this paper has been returned to you, plan to deliver your paper to your reader so that he or she may respond" (p. 63). In addition, the writers were asked to identify their readers on the back of their papers.

After students had begun writing, the teacher visited students writing the third version of the topic "to assure them that their papers would be delivered to their real audience and they would receive credit for the responses they received from their readers" (p. 22). The authors do not indicate that similar assurances were given the writers of the first and second versions. Despite this added personal encouragement, however, the ratings of the third-version papers were not significantly different from those of the first and second versions. The third versions had the highest mean rating, but the first version with no specification of rhetorical context fared better than the second with its imaginary audience. One wonders whether the more heavily specified topic would have fared less well (as in the Brossell study) had the teacher not paid special attention to the students writing on it.

Kahn and Johannessen (1982) also conducted a study of topics concerned in part with the specification of rhetorical situation and developed from various sources of hypotheses. The first topic simply asked that students "write a composition about an event and its consequences that concerned you or someone you know." The second topic included the first and asked that the writer "be as specific as you can . . . so that a reader of your composition will see what you saw and feel what you felt" (p. 9). (This topic does not specify much about the rhetorical context, but it does indicate that writers should consider the effect that the writing has on the audience.) The third topic stipulated the teacher as audience and indicated that the students would have some real stake in their efforts at writing. The topic explained that the teacher wanted to know students better in order to provide "recommendations about [them] concerning whether [they should] receive certain school privileges, awards, honors, or memberships on athletic teams or in other activities." The assignment stated that the teacher felt that the incident the students were to write about would help the teacher in understanding the student. It concluded, "I want you to use the incident to explain to me something you think I should know about you that will help me understand you better" (pp. 6–7).

A fourth topic stipulated the audience as a friend whom students had not seen for a long time. They were asked to write so that the audience would understand the impact which some experience had had upon the writers. In addition, the assignment suggested several steps that students might take in preparing to write: jotting details describing the place, listing what people said, and listing details about feelings and reactions.

Kahn and Johannessen's topics were distributed randomly to students ($n = 127$) in eleventh- and twelfth-grade classes. Three raters rated all papers holistically using a five-point scale so that summed scores ranged from 3 to 15. One-way analysis of variance revealed no significant differences ($p < .069$). However, the differences do approach significance. The highest mean rating (9.06) was for the fourth assignment, which provided prewriting instructions. The lowest mean (6.94) was the result of the third topic, designed to suggest that the writers had something real at stake.

Over the several studies reviewed, even extensive variations in the framing of topics—particularly in the specification of rhetorical situations—resulted in no significant differences. The topic which may come closest to helping students do their best work is that which provides suggestions for prewriting. Researchers concerned with assessment may find it beneficial to study such topics in detail.

For instructional purposes, however, the variations in topics examined here provide little of promise, despite the widespread belief in the importance of selecting the "right" topics. Variations in topics which produce insignificant effects on one occasion are not likely to produce significant differences, even when repeated over a period of weeks or months—at least not in themselves. Perhaps prewriting instructions accompanying a topic might prove effective over a period of time. But the experiments reviewed above provide little evidence that "the two activities, teaching and assessing, are in large measure identical" (Mellon 1975a, p . 34).

Effects of Various Stimuli

Several studies attempted to determine the differences in the effects of various types of stimuli as part of the assignment. Golub and Frederick (1970a) gave fourth- and sixth-graders ten concrete and ten abstract pictures—some black and white, some in color. The researchers examined sixty-three linguistic variables in the resulting compositions but found no significant differences among the groups of compositions. Ewing (1968), working with third-graders, found that an assignment accompanied by no stimulus produced better results than the assignment accompanied by a variety of sensory stimuli, including music and pictures. Kafka (1971), with fourth-, fifth-, and sixth-graders, also found no stimulus to be superior to visual, auditory, and tactile stimuli. R. P. King (1974), with fourth-, sixth-, and eighth-graders found no significant differences in creativity ratings through increasing the level of sensory stimuli. St. Romain (1975) also found no significant differences on ratings of creativity between elementary pupils' compositions written in response to pictures and those written without pictures.

Mahoney (1982), working with college students who were previously classified as extreme right- or left-hemispheric dominant thinkers, tested the effects of music and guided imagery, music and no imagery, imagery and no music, and no music and no imagery on "creative imagination imagery" in writing. She found no significant differences between the mean scores of right- and left-hemispheric dominant individuals. However, she did find that students who received music and "guided imagery" also received the highest scores on fluency, flexibility, originality, and quality. Donlan (1976a), who studied the effects of several types of music on the spontaneous writing of high school juniors and seniors, found that orchestral music appeared to produce writing of higher quality and greater length than did vocal music. In comparing the effects of different types of vocal music, he found that "popular foreign language appeared to stimulate the highest quantity and quality." At the same time he reports that the "independent evaluator noted that the majority of students (1) despised all the [vocal] selections and (2) didn't seem able to concentrate on writing to music, resorting to evaluative judgments, such as 'dumb,' 'stupid,' 'I am getting sick of this,' [and] 'I think I'm going to quit smoking' " (p. 126).

What we are to make of such research on stimuli for writing is not altogether clear, at least to this reviewer. It tells nothing about the processes of writing or instruction and little about the conditions conducive to better writing. It is often atheoretical and provides only answers to discrete questions. As such, this avenue of inquiry can proliferate studies endlessly. Think of the possibilities for types of music as stimuli for better writing. But little of that research would tell us much worth knowing.

Memory Search, Free Association, and Peer Discussion

Another set of assignment condition studies concerns activities which encourage students to recall what they know about a topic before writing about it. These activities include memory searches, free association, and discussion with peers. Kock (1972) presented experimental and control groups with three stimulus words which became topics. The experimental students were required to "free associate" to the stimuli and to use the response terms in their compositions. Control students received the stimuli but were not required to free-associate. Students who were required to free-associate wrote qualitatively better essays ($p < .05$). This experiment is similar to one conducted by Anderson, Bereiter, and Smart (1980). During twelve training sessions, students were asked to list key words which they associated with a topic before writing. These students wrote more and with more varied content than did their control counterparts. The experimenters called this experimental procedure a "memory search" rather than "free association."

Several studies examined the effects of peer group discussion of a topic prior to writing. Reff (1966) asked experimental classes to discuss a topic for 20 to 30 minutes before writing on it for 45 minutes. Control groups did no prior discussion. He then examined forty-one quantitative variables in the two sets of compositions (e.g., number of adverbial clauses and length), finding only four significant differences, which are not readily explicable. St. Romain (1975) found no qualitative differences between the creative writing of students who had or had not discussed topics. Mayo (1976) found that brief discussion did not significantly affect the quality of descriptive writing. However, Brusling (1973) reports an experiment in which third-graders who held a 10-minute discussion of a 5-minute tape recording of nature sounds produced essays scored significantly higher on organization ($p < .025$) and imagination ($p < .01$) than did those who only listened to the tape. Such differences might simply indicate that the discussion helped students make some sense of the tape recording.

Beeker (1970) asked fifth-graders to write about three films under three conditions: no discussion, whole-class discussion, and paired discussion. The study, which used only quantitative measures, revealed that writers in the condition with no discussion produced the fewest T-units, while those in paired discussion produced the most.

B. J. Craig (1982) investigated the effects of peer discussion at three different points in the composing process of college freshmen: (1) discussion of initial ideas for a paper, (2) discussion of rough drafts prior to revision, and (3) discussion of final drafts. She found no significant differences among the three methods.

Meyers (1980) conducted the most extensive examination of prewriting discussion. Two college freshman teachers each taught experimental and control classes. All classes wrote four compositions: one each in the descriptive, narrative, expository, and argumentative modes. In the four 45-minute class sessions following each assignment, students in the experimental groups worked in pairs discussing the ideas they intended to write about. During similar class periods, the control students studied grammar, punctuation, and outlining. The narrative, expository, and argumentative essays of the experimental students were rated superior to those of the control students ($p < .05$).

Although the results of the above studies are mixed, discussion or some other provision for insuring that students do some sort of thinking about what they will write appears to result in more extensive and possibly better writing than when students are asked to write without an explicit provision for thinking about ideas. Most of these results, of course, do not suggest that providing an opportunity to plan increases writing skill, merely that the opportunity allows or encourages students to utilize whatever skills they already have. Further research will be needed to determine whether or not the stipulation of a planning activity such as discussion or free association, in itself, can bring about increased skill over time. It is interesting to note that the Anderson, Bereiter, and Smart (1980) study did more than provide opportunities for planning. Over twelve sessions, it required a simple procedure for retrieving important ideas from memory—a procedure which is apparently learned and which results in more extensive writing. The studies of the effects of prewriting discussion reviewed above, however, do not appear to teach a procedure. They simply examine a condition.

Free Writing

Free writing is widely approved by authorities as a means not only of thinking through ideas but of enhancing creativity and increasing skill in writing. Moffett (1968) and Emig (1971) suggest that free writing increases verbal fluency and provides a means of gathering material. Many hold that free writing is the means to discover new ideas. Donald M. Murray (1978), for example, asserts that "writers much of the time don't know what they are going to write or even possibly what they have written. Writers use language as a tool of exploration to see beyond what they know" (p. 87). Murray provides an example of his own experience. He claims that while listening to an interesting lecture, he began doodling with writing, and the doodling turned into a story. He says he had no intention to write a story: "I want to repeat that there was absolutely no intent in what I was doing" (p. 89). He writes, as a professor at a state university, "Surely my governor would think I ought to know what I'm doing when I sit down to write . . . and yet I don't. And I hope I never will" (p. 89). To write stories, poems, or essays "that say something," Murray claims, "you have to allow language to lead you to meaning" (p. 88). For Murray and others of his persuasion, the act of doodling with language (free writing) leads to meaning. They believe that invoking intentions, assignments, criteria, or forms will abort the free flow of language.

According to Myers (1983), proponents of this pedagogy teach students "to use writing as a means of self-discovery, not just a means of communicating something to someone else. Therefore, students are given extensive practice in free writing, simply filling a page in order to learn how writing helps them discover what they know, what they do not know, and, in fact, what they want to write about" (p. 28). Gauntlett (1978) says that "as much free writing as possible should be allowed" (p. 29). The insistence on free writing usually translates to daily journal writing or free writing two or three times per week. Donlan (1976a) and others focus on free or spontaneous writing prompted by music or other specific stimuli.

A very few studies used instruction beginning with a structured assignment sheet to which students responded (e.g., Clifford 1981). In these, free writing appears to mean writing all the ideas one can think of in relation to a given topic and might be more appropriately thought of as memory search than spontaneous writing.

Most studies of free writing, however, are generated in part as a response against presenting specific topics, a practice believed to be inhibiting. Graves (1981f) and Staton (1982) both argue that presenting topics deprives students of the "right" to generate and develop their own ideas. Staton writes, "It should be no surprise that college students and adults often find it difficult to write when they are not told what to write about. They have not only had little practice in a crucial component of the writing process . . . but have come to believe that they are *not able* to choose their own topics, or to write about personally meaningful experiences in an interesting and effective way" (p. 73). It is assumed that free writing will provide not only practice in choosing topics but the incentive and practice necessary to write in effective and interesting ways.

Most of the studies using free writing also include frequent peer feedback and revision or drafting, usually with the latter following peer feedback. Indeed, most have been included in the natural process mode described earlier. It is impossible, therefore, to estimate the effect of free writing independent of other aspects of the treatment.

Several studies which used free writing as a focus of instruction in their experimental treatments achieved significant gains in contrast to their control treatments. These include three Writing Project studies: Alloway, et al. (1979) with grades 7–12 in the New Jersey Writing Project; Olson and DiStefano (1980) with grades 7–9 in the Colorado Writing Project; and Wagner, Zemelman, and Malone-Trout

(1981) with grades 1–12 in the Chicago Area Writing Project. In addition, Wienke (1981) with grade 6, Hilgers (1981), and Cummings (1981) with college freshmen show significant gains for free writing treatments. Neither Hilgers nor Cummings used a pretest of writing, however. Of these studies the largest effect sizes are those for the experimental groups in Olson and DiStefano (1980) and Wienke (1981), as indicated in Table 13 in Chapter 8. Both of these treatments suggested topics for writing. Indeed, Olson (personal communication) reports the use of "focused free writing" in which students received an assignment and discussed it with the teacher and class before writing down related ideas.

A fairly large number of studies report no significant differences in the quality of writing between experimental groups using free writing and peer feedback and their control groups. These include Arthur (1981) with grade 3, Ganong (1975) with grade 9, Gauntlett (1978) with grades 10–12, and V. A. Adams (1971) with grade 12. In addition, several studies using free writing at the college freshman level show no significant differences in quality of writing: Robert Baden (1974a), Ken Davis (1979), Delaney (1980), Dreussi (1976), Fox (1980), Norwood (1974), Reynolds (1981), J. P. Walker (1974), and Witte and Faigley (1981b).

This box-score review suggests that even a steady diet of free writing (daily or several times per week) does not accomplish what its proponents hope for. The results of the meta-analysis in Chapter 8 provide a clearer picture of results for free writing in comparison to other instructional foci.

Heuristics

Heuristics stand in sharp contrast to free writing and the various stimuli discussed above as a means of promoting invention. A heuristic may be defined as a systematic guide for investigating a phenomenon and may be as simple as the newswriting heuristic of who, what, when, where, why. More complex heuristics provide guidelines or procedures for analysis. For example, Young, Becker, and Pike (1970), in their chapter entitled "Preparation: Exploring the Problem," present the well-known tagmemic heuristic which asks students to view phenomena from the perspectives of particle, wave, and field and in terms of contrastive features, variation, and distribution. Each intersect of the resulting 3 × 3 matrix involves the use of complex strategies. Thus, the juncture of "particle" and "contrast" in the matrix (p. 127) generates the question, "What are its [the unit's] contrastive features, i.e., the features that differentiate it from similar things and serve to identify it?" Each juncture of the matrix generates such a question as a guide for exploring a subject.

Young and Koen (1973) examined the effectiveness of the tagmemic heuristic on the writing of twelve students in a rhetoric course. They report that by the end of the course students' essays were rated higher and students were better able to state problems and examine them more thoroughly. In an interesting related study, Odell (1974) examined the effects of Pike's "tagmemic discovery procedures" on the writing of freshman English students who wrote five essays about problems they discerned in literary works. In addition, three class discussions of student essays, two conferences with individual students, and presumably teacher comment on the essays focused on five questions: "Does the writer state a problem? Are there any ambiguous terms in the statement of the problem? Does he speak to the problem he poses? In proposing a solution to his problem, does he support his assertions with evidence? Does he make any unwarranted assumptions?" (p. 230).

By examining the first and last essays written by students, Odell discovered that while students did not perform *more* of the intellectual operations suggested by Pike's theory, they did perform *most* of the intellectual operations significantly more times. Further, they showed a significant increase in the use of evidence. One is forced to wonder, as Odell himself suggests, whether these results are due to the use of the tagmemic heuristic or to the instructor's teaching methods.

Other studies generally report significant gains in writing quality for groups dealing with heuristics over a period of ten weeks or more. Lamberg (1974) developed a heuristic consisting of seven questions which he claims define narrative form. Thirty-five students (twenty tenth-graders on independent study and fifteen volunteer seventh- to tenth-graders) were involved in the "process" of writing narratives to answer the questions. Twenty-seven completed both pretest and posttest narratives, which were judged by two raters using six criteria. Lamberg reports that nineteen or more of these students showed increases in completeness (number of questions answered to any degree and the completeness of those answers), development (number of words carrying specific information), and length (total number of words). No increases were demonstrated on the criteria having to do with unity, point-of-view, and chronological order. Various problems with the study (the character of the sample, the lack of controls for teacher and practice effect, and the lack of information on rater reliability), however, make the results difficult to interpret.

Burns (1980), who tested three different heuristics—including the Young, Becker and Pike tagmemic matrix—reports significant gains within all of three groups of college freshmen in "insightfulness, comprehensiveness, intellectual ability, and overall qualitative performance" (p. 21). There were no significant differences among the experimental groups, however.

Ebbert (1980), working with nine classes of sixth-graders for ten weeks in six schools, tested a tagmemic heuristic in three classes and a heuristic based on Burke's pentad (agent, action, instrumentality, recipient, and cause) in three classes against three control classes which worked with the standard curriculum of the local school. Pretest and posttest compositions were rated with a modified Diederich scale on the criteria of audience analysis, organization, and detail. Analysis of scores revealed that (1) the control group's scores were significantly higher than the tagmemic group on two of three criteria (organization and detail), (2) the pentadic group scored significantly higher on detail than the tagmemic group, and (3) there were no significant differences between the pentadic and tagmemic groups on audience analysis and organization.

Dutch (1980), with 144 students in five sections of freshman English in a thirteen-week course, examined the use of a three-to-five question student-generated heuristic in three sections against the Larson heuristic (1968) in two sections. He found that students trained to use the Larson heuristic performed significantly better on the posttest ($p < .05$) than those who generated their own heuristic. However, a sharp difference in the pretest/posttest measures (compositions requiring the use of examples and illustrations versus comparison-contrast themes) makes it difficult to judge whether the students made any progress from pretest to posttest. Mean scores for the students generating their own heuristic declined, while those for students using the Larson heuristic remained virtually the same.

While the results for studies teaching heuristics are mixed, some are encouraging and suggest that additional research with better controls might be useful.

Inquiry

The instructional focus which I have labeled *inquiry* is sharply differentiated from both free writing and heuristics. While free writing avoids specific topic suggestions, inquiry does not. While free writing requires students to recall more or less distant experience, inquiry tends to focus on immediate and concrete data of some kind during instruction and practice. While free writing implicitly requires students to use whatever strategies they have available, inquiry attempts to teach specific strategies. On the other hand, inquiry differs from heuristics in beginning with a set of data, rather than a system of analysis, and focuses on particular strategies—usually one or a few at a time—rather than on a complex matrix of strategies as in the Young, Becker, and Pike (1970) tagmemic approach.

The question from Young, Becker, and Pike quoted earlier, for example, subsumes a number of strategies: "What are its [the unit's] contrastive features, i.e., the features that differentiate it from similar things and serve to identify it?" This apparently simple question requires that one first identify and report the unit and its features, discover or imagine (generate) similar units, generate criteria for discriminating the unit from similar things, and finally apply the criteria to provide the necessary discriminations. Yet the question is only one of several even more complex questions. A treatment involving inquiry might deal with such questions but is likely to begin with a data set and involve students in using one or two strategies such as identifying and reporting the features of various units.

Inquiry and Description/Narration

Hillocks (1979) asked ninth- and eleventh-graders to observe a variety of phenomena carefully and to write about them as specifically as possible. The phenomena included seashells, objects with various textures, odors, sounds, bodily sensations, the actions of people, and so forth. Lessons usually involved teacher-led or small-group discussion prior to writing. Thus, in an exercise calling on students to describe sounds, teachers played a tape-recorded sound and called for students to suggest several words and phrases to describe it. This procedure was repeated with several sounds before students were asked to write about sounds on their own. Eventually students wrote about some experience or place in a composition which incorporated sounds and other sensations. Teachers were asked to praise effective detail, clear focus, and overall impact. These implicit criteria were emphasized in class and in comments and suggestions on writing.

In addition, students regularly shared their writing with small groups or in pairs, often in view of some rhetorical context. For example, small groups wrote a composition about one of two seashells, then passed the writing and the shells to a second group. The second group identified the shell described by the first group and picked out vivid details in the writing as well as details they found confusing. In another exercise each student wrote a description of a shell. The teacher then placed all the shells on a table and delivered each composition to another student, who had to pick out the shell described. The reader then commented on effective detail and metaphor before returning the paper to the writer.

Evaluations in the Hillocks study were based on two pretest and two posttest compositions. Independent evaluators judged the two pretest and posttest compositions using a scale for specificity, focus, and impact. Compositions by students in the experimental groups were judged significantly superior to those by control-group students, who studied model paragraphs. A second panel of five judges, using their own criteria, rated a subset of pretests and posttests from the same students for creativity. Their combined scores correlated highly with the earlier scale scores ($r = .83$), suggesting that creativity can be stimulated (if not taught) by such classroom experiences. A second study (Hillocks 1982) used observing and writing activities in one set of experimental classes of seventh- and eighth-graders with similar results.

Fichteneau (1968), working with third-, fourth-, fifth-, and sixth-grade students, emphasized invention, arrangement, and style in experimental groups while the control group followed the regular school program, which included grammar and usage. The children had scored at the eightieth percentile or above on one of two standardized tests. Lessons on invention emphasized observation of a variety of objects and pictures as well as places within walking distance of the classroom, e.g., a house near the school, the school kitchen, and the kindergarten room. Students were encouraged through discussion to develop questions about the things observed, but not a specific set of questions as in heuristics.

In addition students talked about experiences, trying to recall details of sights, sounds, smells, and conversations. They then wrote about those experiences. They examined sample compositions with and without details and were given practice in "expanding" generalities such as "a nice day" into detailed statements. The children in experimental groups scored significantly better than those in control groups.

Inquiry and Argument

McCleary (1979b) conducted a complex study with five treatments to determine the effects of Aristotle's and Toulmin's logic, each taught in two different ways, on the logical writing of college freshmen. Each logic was taught to three classes as an isolated subject and to another three classes in connection with writing. Three control classes were taught no formal logic. While results indicate no significant differences among the treatments, all treatment groups had very large pre-to-post effect sizes—all greater than 1.5 standard deviations, making them among the largest in the meta-analysis.

Closer examination of the study reveals that each treatment group received specified instruction, which may well have been responsible for the large pre-to-post gains, with the experimental groups' instruction in logic making no particular difference. The pretest and posttest essays both involved writing logical arguments about ethical dilemmas presented to the students for analysis. Instruction in all groups included examination of several ethical problems with a view to learning the strategies involved in such analysis. The problems which students analyzed and debated were concrete scenarios about actions in particular situations. For example, one scenario, paraphrased below, was a conflict between a father (Fred) and his daughter (Alice):

> Fred agrees to pay Alice's expenses to college, stipulating only that she maintain a C average. Alice maintains a B average. However, during her junior year she moves into an apartment with a male friend, using the money her father sent her to pay her share of expenses. When Fred discovers the situation, he demands that Alice, who is now twenty-one, move. He threatens to cut off her expense money if she does not.

In addition to this basic scenario, students received other information. The problem for students was to determine whether or not Fred would be ethically justified in cutting off his daughter's support and then to develop a logical argument using whatever information was relevant.

To analyze such situations, students were asked to identify the ethical principles or ideals involved (e.g., people should keep their bargains) as well as exceptions to those principles. In addition, they identified obligations, consequences of actions, and the conflicts among these. As they examined the problems, they were to (1) generate a thesis based on the analysis of ideals, obligations, and consequences of acts; (2) decide what information was relevant, (3) predict opposing arguments, and (4) attempt to dispatch them. Analysis of the problems, in short, involved students in strategies basic to the development of ethical arguments. Since all students in the control and experimental groups worked with such strategies, it is not surprising that all made similar significant gains in the rated quality of essays from pretest to posttest.

Troyka (1974), working with college freshmen in a remedial writing program, conducted a study with twenty-five experimental and twenty-five control classes. These classes were taught by thirteen teachers, with twelve teaching two classes of each group and one teaching one class of each group. (All classes were small because they were remedial.) The experimental treatment included four "simulation game" experiences. Each of these presented students with a problem requiring some policy decision: e.g., what action to take in a community pollution problem, what to do in the case of a prison uprising, what automobiles to buy for a fleet of taxicabs, and so forth. (See Troyka and Nudelman 1975 for complete materials.) The Troyka study has been discussed in Chapter 4. It is classified here as using inquiry because students received data sets related to various aspects of a problem, worked with the data, and in the process learned specifiable strategies which are important in argumentative writing: supporting generalizations, predicting opposing arguments, and so forth. As pointed out earlier, the results for the experimental groups in this study are not only significantly greater than those for the controls, but they are among the largest effect sizes in the meta-analysis.

Inquiry and Definition

Hillocks, Kahn, and Johannessen (1983) conducted a study in which both experimental and control groups were taught to write extended definitions of abstract concepts. Pretest and posttest definitions written by students were scored for (1) the presence of criteria which specified the range of the target concept and differentiated it from related but different concepts, (2) examples of the target concept, and (3) contrasting examples which served to clarify the criteria. The raters also judged the clarity of examples and criteria and the adequacy of simple introductory analytical definitions.

The control group studied nine model definitions, including three student-written definitions of varying quality. The group then wrote four definitions and planned one. All of this followed a conventional textbook treatment of definition. The experimental groups did not use the conventional textbook treatment. They studied only the three student-written models, wrote out criteria for defining freedom of speech, chose one example to illustrate the criteria, and planned the same extended definition as did the control group. Instead of studying more models and writing additional definitions, the experimental groups used the remaining instructional time in small-group discussions of three sets of scenarios, each of which described incidents illustrating some features of a target concept but which varied from it in certain essentials. For example, the set of scenarios entitled

"Courageous Action: What Is It?" included incidents which Aristotle might have viewed as examples of "seeming" courage: one in which a soldier enters a village and secures part of it, unaware that it is held by the enemy; one in which an officer leads a direct frontal attack despite reports of heavy enemy concentration at that point; one in which a gang initiate is forced to confront and taunt a member of a rival gang; and so forth. Working in small groups, students were asked to consider each scenario and to determine by what criterion the principal actor should or should not be considered courageous.

Students in both control and experimental groups showed significant pre-to-post gains in overall scores. However, the gains achieved by experimental students were significantly greater than those achieved by control students ($p < .01$). More detailed analysis indicated that students in the experimental treatments showed significant increases in the use of criteria and examples ($p < .005$), while control group students did not.

Inquiry and Analysis

Widvey (1971) and D. I. Smith (1974) both involved students in the collection and analysis of data. Widvey worked with 286 eleventh-graders who were randomly assigned to ten classes. Five teachers each taught one experimental and one control group for eighteen weeks. Students in experimental classes were involved in formulating hypotheses, gathering and analyzing data, and making inferences in order to "structure discourse." Learning was viewed as a process of inquiry designed to involve students in clarifying and solving problems. Unfortunately, specific details about the instructional materials are not reported. Control students were in the traditional curriculum, which appears to have been presentational. Differences on essay quality in favor of the experimental groups were significant ($p < .01$).

Smith (1974), who also involved eleventh-grade students in the collection of data, did so in a tutorial situation contrasted with instruction to whole classes. All students received the same three composition assignments over a six-week period: extended definition, comparison and contrast, and process analysis. Students were allowed to choose their own topics but were required to write the kind of composition indicated. In definition papers, for example, they were asked to tell what the subject was, what it did, and how it operated.

Students in the experimental (tutorial) groups chose a topic, read about it, listened to relevant radio programs and records, watched relevant television programs and movies, interviewed people about the topic, discussed it with others, and/or took trips to gather information. After students individually discussed their data with the teacher, the student and teacher agreed on an organization, and the student developed a rough draft. The teacher and student analyzed the draft together, and the student rewrote it. The teacher and student evaluated the strengths and weakness of the final draft together. This process was repeated three times during the six weeks—once for each of the three assignments. Control group instruction focused on whole-class presentations making use of two standard grammar/composition textbook series.

Studies which make inquiry an integral part of their experimental treatments all show significant effects for inquiry either in pre-to-post effects, in experimental/control effects, or in both. Although the number of treatments is relatively small, the number of students and teachers involved and the findings are robust. Indeed, two of the studies removed at the outset of the meta-analysis because of large positive residuals and heavy contributions to heterogeneity involved experimental treatments classified as inquiry: D. I. Smith 1974 and Troyka 1974. If the results of these studies are valid and reliable, they appear to point up a hitherto largely unrecognized aspect of the composing process—the ability to process data using strategies required by particular kinds of discourse. The free writing and natural process treatments examined above assume that students either can call on those strategies as they are required or will develop them as they write and rewrite drafts about topics of their own choosing. That may be the case *if* students are willing to write on topics involving unfamiliar or difficult strategies and *if* peer and teacher comment can effectively teach the strategies as they are demanded by the topic and mode of discourse. Informal comparison of the results in this narrative review, however, indicates that while free writing/natural process treatments *occasionally* achieve results significantly greater than their controls, the inquiry treatments contrasted with some other treatment *always* do.

8 Results of the Meta-Analysis

Using the criteria listed in Chapter 3, we selected studies for inclusion in the meta-analysis and coded them for the variables described in detail in Chapters 4, 5, 6, and 7. This chapter presents the results for the dimensions examined: grade level, duration of the treatment, mode of instruction, focus of instruction, revision, and feedback.

All Treatments

The application of the criteria described in Chapter 3 located sixty studies with seventy-five experimental/control treatments, for which seventy-three experimental/control effect sizes could be calculated. The experimental groups included 6,313 students, while control groups included 5,392. The seventy-three experimental/control treatments have a mean effect size of .28. The homogeneity statistic (H) is 411.08, indicating an extremely high degree of variability in effects. Thus, while the average student in an experimental group gained about three-tenths of a standard deviation more than those in control groups, the actual treatments in which students found themselves were likely to have highly different effects on them. Some average students lost .50 standard deviation more than their control counterparts (Ebbert 1980), while others gained 1.69 standard deviations (Troyka 1974). When we lump all the treatments together, the mean gain of .28 obscures the extremes. At the same time, the extreme cases add considerably to the heterogeneity.

Pre-to-post effect sizes could be calculated for sixty-five of the experimental treatments, with the mean effect size being .46. The homogeneity statistic (H) is 616.33, indicating a very high degree of heterogeneity. The control group treatments have a mean pre-to-post effect size of .17. H for these treatments is 290.42, considerably less than H for experimental treatments—but still indicating a very high degree of heterogeneity. The average student in control groups, which are often described as using traditional teaching methods, made some progress in writing quality, but this progress is less than half that achieved by students in experimental classes.

The results of all treatments, taken together, whether we look at experimental/control or pre-to-post effect sizes, are highly heterogeneous. Certain treatments with very high gains and very high losses are responsible for much of the heterogeneity. Of the two positive treatments, one involved simulation-gaming among college freshmen in need of remedial work (Troyka 1974). The other involved a tutorial treatment with high school students (D. I. Smith 1974). Of the two negative treatments, one involved a "self-paced" instructional treatment for college students, who were required to attend classes only when they felt they needed to (Loritsch 1977). The second involved the use of tagmemic heuristics with elementary school students (Ebbert 1980). These four experimental/control treatments were removed from the subsequent statistical analysis. Removing the treatments reduced the mean effect size for all experimental/control treatments to .24 and H to 161.06. The H statistic still represents highly significant heterogeneity. In fact, for the remaining sixty-nine experimental/control treatments to be considered homogeneous, H must be under 100. In short, the statistics for all treatments, taken together, tell us little other than that they vary considerably.

A very important function of a meta-analysis is to help determine what treatment variables account for the heterogeneity of the results. Simply stated, the concern in this analysis was what makes a difference in increasing the quality of student writing. The coding of treatment characteristics discussed in Chapter 3 allowed us to group treatments by their shared characteristics and to ask whether their results were similar (i.e., homogeneous).

Dimensions Examined

As one might expect, most treatments are composites of variables (e.g., mode of instruction, source of feedback, duration) and no two treatments share precisely the same sets of characteristics. To contend with this problem, studies were considered as exhibiting several variables on different dimensions simultaneously. Each dimension could then be examined independently of others. For example, a study of less than thirteen weeks in duration could be grouped with others of comparable duration and contrasted with those of thirteen or more weeks. The same study might then be examined on the dimension of mode of instruction and again on focus of instruction. On any given dimension, however, the categories of studies had to be independent. That is, a single study could appear in only one category. Fortunately, studies appeared in more than one category only in the focus-of-instruction dimension and then only in a few instances. When a treatment used more than one focus of instruction, the coders categorized it according to the focus judged to be dominant. Faigley (1979c), for example, involved students in observing phenomena to generate details—a focus that might qualify as inquiry; however, since the main focus of the treatment is clearly on sentence construction, it was categorized with sentence combining treatments.

The dimensions examined below include grade level, duration, mode of instruction, focus of instruction, and post-writing treatment variables including revision and certain characteristics of feedback. When we examined the categories of studies on any given dimension, it was necessary to ask three questions: (1) Do the treatments in a category yield homogeneous results? (2) Do the categories over the whole dimension yield homogeneous results? That is, does the model implied by the categories in the dimension fit the data? (3) Are the differences among results for the various categories significant? We hoped that the answers to these questions, taken together, would help to explain the high level of heterogeneity in the results of the treatments.

Grade Level

Of the seventy-three experimental/control treatments for which effect sizes could be calculated, ten were at the elementary level (eight at the sixth-grade level), thirty-one were from grades 7 to 12, thirty were at the college freshman level, and two were mixed elementary and secondary. Removal of the four outliers left nine treatments at the elementary level, thirty at the secondary level, twenty-eight at the college level, and two mixed. Table 1 summarizes the results of these treatments by level.

The elementary treatments have a mean experimental/control effect size of .38. Somewhat surprisingly, these treatments are homogeneous ($H = 16.4$, $df = 8$), despite a range in effect size from $-.09$ (Eagleton 1974) to .77 (Fichteneau 1968). The thirty secondary studies have a mean experimental/control effect size of .26 but are not homogeneous ($H = 80.68$, $df = 29$). The twenty-eight college treatments yield an experimental/control effect size of .14 but are not homogeneous ($H = 49.52$, $df = 27$). The dimension overall is not homogeneous ($H = 146.60$). With sixty-four degrees of freedom, H would have to be under 94 to attain homogeneity at $p < .01$.

The columns in Table 1 labeled "95% Confidence Interval" indicate the lower and upper limits of the 95 percent confidence interval, which estimates the probability that the mean gain of infinite replications

Table 1

Mean Effect Size and Homogeneity by Grade Level of Treatment

Grades	n	Mean Effect	95% Confidence Interval		H	df	Maximum H for nonsignificance at $p < .01$
			Lower	Upper			
1 - 6	9	.38	.29	.47	16.40	8	21.66
7 - 12	30	.26	.21	.31	80.68	29	49.58
13	28	.14	.07	.21	49.52	27	46.95
Total	67[a]				146.60	64	92.60

[a]Two mixed elementary and secondary treatments have been omitted.

of the experiments will fall within the designated interval. That is, if we repeated all the experiments in a given classification, the chances would be 95 out of 100 that their mean experimental/control effect size would lie between the upper and lower limits of the confidence interval.

A glance at the upper and lower extremes of the 95 percent confidence intervals suggests that differences among the effect sizes will be significant. The extremes just barely overlap. In fact, all differences are significant. The difference between elementary and secondary of .12 is significant ($z = 2.24$, $p < .02$), as is the difference of .12 between secondary and college ($z = 2.66$, $p < .01$). The difference between elementary and college is .24 and is clearly significant ($z = 4.18$, $p < .0001$).

Because the results drop significantly in equal decrements from elementary to college, one is tempted to speculate that as students become older, they have less to learn about writing; or that, as students become older, they are less amenable to instruction; or that the scorers of compositions are more demanding at higher levels than lower. Unfortunately, there is no evidence to support or deny such speculations. The homogeneity statistics indicate highly significant variability at both secondary and college levels, and across the dimension as a whole, indicating that grade level cannot be regarded as a satisfactory explanation of the results. Before speculating further about reasons for the differences, it will be useful to examine treatment variables.

Duration

It is commonly believed that many experimental treatments show no significant change in comparison to their control groups because their duration is too short. Burton (1973), for example, in lamenting the state of research, comments that experimental treatments "over a period of only a few weeks or months have been predestined to conclusions of 'no significant differences,' since one thing that is known, at least, is that improvement in general aspects of writing ability is a slow gradual process" (p. 177). Wesdorp (1982) states that "besides the frequent unreliability of crucial measures, the main reason for findings of non-significant differences" is that experimental treatments "are of very short duration" (p. 37). If these claims are true, then we should find that effect size varies with the duration of the treatment.

This hypothesis was tested in two ways. First, studies were grouped according to their duration. Those under thirteen weeks in duration were compared to those over thirteen weeks, presuming the twelfth week to mark a secondary or college-length quarter. Studies under seventeen weeks were compared to those over sixteen weeks, presuming the sixteenth week to mark a semester. When the four outliers are included in the data, there is virtually no difference among the treatments of various durations.

When the outliers are removed, greater differences appear, but they are inconsistent. When we divide the treatments between twelve and thirteen weeks, nearly equal numbers of treatments appear in each group. As indicated in Table 2, the mean for those under thirteen weeks is .28 ($H = 71.76$, $df = 35$). The mean for those over twelve weeks is .20 ($H = 93.04$, $df = 32$). Neither group of treatments approaches homogeneity. However, the difference is statistically significant ($z = 2.08$, $p < .05$).

When we compare treatments under seventeen weeks with those over sixteen, the results are reversed. The mean effect size for treatments under seventeen weeks is .21 ($H = 129.70$, $df = 53$); for those over sixteen weeks, the mean effect size is .31 ($H = 34.48$, $df = 14$). This difference is also significant ($z = 2.26$, $p < .05$). Again, neither group of treatments is homogeneous. When we compare treatments under thirteen weeks with those over sixteen weeks, the difference of .03 is not significant ($z = 0.62$). In short, these comparisons do not enable us to link duration with increased effect size with any confidence.

The second test of the hypothesis that length of treatment is related to increased effect size was a Pearson product moment correlation between experimental/control effect size and duration in weeks. The resulting correlation was $-.02$, suggesting no relationship between effect size in this group of treatments. Apparently some short treatments are effective, while some are ineffective. The same is true of treatments of longer duration. The problem is to discover what characteristics of treatments, aside from duration, appear to be responsible for differences in the effect sizes.

Mode of Instruction

Chapter 4 defined and discussed four modes of instruction: presentational, natural process, environmental, and individualized. A mode of instruction may be defined as the configuration of relationships and activities in which teachers and their students characteristically engage.

Table 2

Mean Experimental/Control Effect Sizes and Duration: Some Comparisons

Duration	n	Mean Effect	95% Confidence Interval		H	df	Maximum H for nonsignificance at $p < .01$
			Lower	Upper			
Under 13 weeks	36	.28	.22	.34	71.76	35	50.28
Over 12 weeks	33	.20	.15	.25	93.04	32	53.44
Under 17 weeks	54	.21	.17	.25	129.70	53	79.80
Over 16 weeks	15	.31	.24	.39	34.48	14	29.13

Very briefly, the presentational mode is dominated by lecture and teacher-led discussion about the characteristics of good writing, with feedback coming in written comments from the teacher. Treatments included in the presentational mode are summarized in Table 3.

The natural process mode is characterized by free writing about whatever interests the students, feedback from peer groups and the teacher, and opportunities to revise or redraft in light of peer or instructor comment. The instructor is seen as a facilitator whose responsibility is to help students find their own meanings and the forms in which to express them. Thus, teachers in this mode tend to eschew the study of models or criteria and to avoid highly structured activities. Natural process treatments are summarized in Table 4.

The environmental mode is characterized by peer-group activity also. However, such activity involves highly structured problem-solving tasks which involve students in specific strategies parallel to those they will encounter in writing. Environmental treatments are summarized in Table 5.

The individualized mode in the treatments examined here uses teacher-student conference as the primary mode of instruction, along with programmed materials in some treatments. Individualized treatments are summarized in Table 6.

The descriptions of treatments did not always present adequate information for identifying the mode of instruction. Nearly all ambiguities involved making a choice between environmental and presentational. For example, a description might present the kinds of problems and materials appropriate to environmental instruction but say nothing to indicate the presence of student interaction or small-group work. In such cases the instructional mode was coded as "unclear." In the case of several control treatments, no description was provided. These were coded 0. In what follows, experimental/control effects were analyzed for the presence of a treatment in the experimental condition but some other in the control. Codings of unclear or 0 were assumed to be some treatment other than that identified in the experimental condition.

The ground rule that one mode of instruction be present in the experimental treatment with some other mode in the control limited the number of treatments available for analysis of experimental/control effects to twenty-nine. Many treatments were coded as presentational or unclear in both experimental and control treatments.

Table 7 summarizes statistics for (1) all 73 treatments, including the four outliers; (2) all treatments without the outliers; (3) those treatments involving one mode of instruction in the experimental

Table 3

Mode of Instruction: Presentational

Mean Effect Size = .02; H = 0.92

Treatment	Grade	Duration in weeks	n Exper.	n Control	g^a	$\sigma^2(g)^b$	$g_{\cdot(j)}{}^c$	$H_{(j)}{}^d$	g Exper.	g Control
Caplan and Keech 1980*	12	12	73	56	.12	.032	−.05	.39	.01	−.12
Clark 1968	13	10	30	30	−.13	.067	.06	.50	.26	.38
Clark 1968	13	10	30	30	−.10	.067	.05	.66	.29	.38
Clark 1968	13	10	30	30	.08	.067	.01	.86	.44	.38

[a] g = effect size
[b] $\sigma^2(g)$ = variance of the effect size
[c] $g_{\cdot(j)}$ = mean effect size with particular treatment removed
[d] $H_{(j)}$ = homogeneity with particular treatment removed
*Effect size is the average for narrative and argument assignments.

Table 4

Mode of Instruction: Natural Process

Mean Effect Size = .19; H = 23.15

Treatment	Grade	Duration in weeks	n Exper.	n Control	g[a]	$\sigma^2(g)$[b]	$g_{\cdot(j)}$[c]	$H_{(j)}$[d]	g Exper.	g Control
Adams 1971	12	18	70	65	.56	.031	.17	18.02	.00	−.56
Alloway, et al. 1979	7-12	36	105	120	.39	.018	.17	20.30	.25	−.07
Davis 1979	13	16	100	202	.00	.000	.20	20.28	.30	.30
Ganong 1975	9	8	77	58	.06	.030	.19	22.26	.27	.23
Gauntlett 1978	10-12	16	420	371	.05	.005	.23	17.89	.09	.05
Olson and DiStefano 1980	7-9	36	195	195	.40	.011	.15	17.71	.53	.10
Wagner, Zemelman, and Malone-Trout 1981	1-12	24	585	294	.19	.005	.18	22.79	.31	.14
Walker 1974	13	16	41	36	−.27	.053	.20	18.76	−.34	−.10
Wienke 1981	6	32	85	72	.36	.026	.18	21.56	.62	.25

[a]g = effect size
[b]$\sigma^2(g)$ = variance of the effect size
[c]$g_{\cdot(j)}$ = mean effect size with particular treatment removed
[d]$H_{(j)}$ = homogeneity with particular treatment removed

Table 5

Mode of Instruction: Environmental

Mean Effect Size = .44; H = 12.83

Treatment	Grade	Duration in weeks	n Exper.	n Control	g^{a}	$\sigma^2(g)^{b}$	$g_{.(j)}^{c}$	$H_{(j)}^{d}$	g Exper.	g Control
Clifford 1981	13	16	43	49	.61	.046	.43	11.61	1.12	.43
Farrell 1977	11	11	49	42	.27	.045	.44	11.67	.66	.36
Hillocks 1979	9 & 11	3-5	97	94	.75	.022	.40	7.35	1.13	.20
Hillocks 1982	7 & 8	4	72	64	.43	.030	.44	12.31	1.09	.54
Hillocks 1982	7 & 8	4	75	64	.18	.029	.46	9.87	.77	.54
Rosen 1974	13	16	40	29	.82	.064	.42	9.92	2.34	.95
Sbaratta 1975	13	15	60	60	.48	.034	.43	12.25	---	---
A. L. Thibodeau 1964	6	6	136	266	.35	.011	.46	11.49	.23	-.11
A. E. Thibodeau 1964	6	6	142	266	.34	.011	.46	11.25	.21	-.11
Vinson 1980	9	6	61	48	.58	.039	.43	11.74	.91	.38

[a] g = effect size
[b] $\sigma^2(g)$ = variance of the effect size
[c] $g_{.(j)}$ = mean effect size with particular treatment removed
[d] $H_{(j)}$ = homogeneity with particular treatment removed

Table 6

Mode of Instruction: Individualized

Mean Effect Size $= .17$; $H = 14.68$

Treatment	Grade	Duration in weeks	n Exper.	n Control	g[a]	$\sigma^2(g)$[b]	$g_{.(j)}$[c]	$H_{(j)}$[d]	g Exper.	g Control
Eagleton 1974	6	14	43	44	-.09	.046	.18	13.15	.27	.36
Farrell 1977	11	11	42	42	.29	.048	.16	14.34	.64	.36
Murdock 1974	13	16	112	111	.02	.018	.20	13.24	----	----
A. L. Thibodeau 1964	6	6	97	266	.31	.014	.13	12.82	.19	-.11
A. E. Thibodeau 1964	6	6	100	266	.45	.014	.09	7.20	.33	-.11
Witte and Faigley 1981b	13	16	144	216	-.06	.012	.25	8.66	.32	.38

[a]g = effect size
[b]$\sigma^2(g)$ = variance of the effect size
[c]$g_{.(j)}$ = mean effect size with particular treatment removed
[d]$H_{(j)}$ = homogeneity with particular treatment removed

treatment and another in the control, and (4) each mode of instruction. As we have already noted, the H statistic is significant for all treatments and for treatments with the outliers removed. The 29 treatments examined in the dimension of mode of instruction have a mean effect size of .24—no different from that for the 69 treatments remaining after removal of the outliers. The H statistic for the 29 treatments taken together is highly significant at 73.83. For the heterogeneity to be nonsignificant at $p < .01$, an H statistic below 48.27 is required.

Inspection of the statistics for each mode of instruction reveals a different story. Three of the modes (environmental, presentational, and individualized) are homogeneous. Only natural process exhibits significant heterogeneity, with an H statistic of 23.15—somewhat greater than the 20.08 required for nonsignificance with eight degrees of freedom.

The mean effect size (.44) for treatments in the environmental mode is much greater than the mean effects for other modes. Note the lower and upper limits of the 95 percent confidence intervals in Table 7. The lower limit for environmental effect size (.34) does not overlap with the upper limits of the others.

Natural process and individualized modes share second place in mean effect, with sizes of .19 and .17 respectively. Their confidence intervals overlap almost entirely. Trailing behind these modes is the presentational mode, with an experimental/control effect size of .02. Its 95 percent confidence interval overlaps the intervals of both the natural process and individualized modes. While there is clearly no significant difference between the natural process and the individualized modes, the differences between presentational and both the natural process and individualized modes are also not significant ($z = 1.36$ and 1.17 respectively, $p > .05$). The mean effect size for the environmental mode, however, is significantly greater than both the natural process mode ($z = 4.15$, $p < .0001$) and the individualized mode ($z = 3.66$, $p < .0005$), as well as the presentational ($z = 3.37$, $p < .0005$).

Three problems with this dimension remain. First, the natural process mode exhibits significant variability. Second, the homogeneity statistic for all groups ($H = 51.58$) is significant at $p < .01$ ($df = 25$). Third, results for the presentational mode are based on only two studies, which are summarized in Table 3. One of these (Clark 1968) includes three treatments. More important, the mode of instruction in the control treatments for these studies could not be identified. Because considerable research indicates that the presentational mode

Table 7

Mode of Instruction

Summary of Experimental/Control Effect Size Statistics

	n	Mean Effect	sd	95% Confidence Interval		H	df	Maximum H for nonsignificance at p < .01
				Lower	Upper			
All Meta-Analysis Treatments	73	.28	.018	.24	.32	411.08	72	102.60
Treatments (4 Outliers Removed)	69	.24	.019	.20	.27	169.28	68	98.00
Treatments Included in Mode of Instruction Analysis	29	.24	.025	.19	.29	73.83	28	48.27
Presentational	4	.02	.114	−.20	.24	0.92	3	11.33
Natural Process	9	.19	.037	.11	.26	23.15	8	20.08
Environmental	10	.44	.050	.34	.53	12.83	9	21.66
Individualized	6	.17	.064	.06	.28	14.68	5	15.08
Treatments Categorized by Mode of Instruction	29	---	---	---	---	51.58	25	44.30

is ubiquitous, the safest assumption is that undescribed control groups are taught in the traditional presentational mode. Thus, the two studies with presentational teaching in the experimental sections probably have presentational teaching in the controls as well, thus providing no true control of the presentational mode with some other mode. (This is not a problem with other modes of instruction because we can safely assume that an undescribed treatment is not one of them.)

The heterogeneity of natural process treatments, summarized in Table 4, can be reduced without affecting the mean effect size appreciably by removing the studies with the largest positive and negative effect sizes. The study with the largest positive effect size of .56 (Adams 1971) should be removed for the substantive reason that it does not represent a real gain for students taught in that mode. As can be seen in Table 4, the entire effect size is due to a loss of $-.56$ for Adams's control groups. The experimental treatment made no gain at all. The loss for the control group is easy to speculate about. Every mechanical or structural error in every composition written by students in the control group was marked. Final comments were brief and directed to errors in organization. Apparently, no positive comments were included. The students were expected to correct their errors and turn in the revised compositions. Such a treatment ought to be negative enough to result in a substantial loss. It did. Removal of this study changes the effect size to .17 and reduces H to 18.02, a level which is not significant at $p < .01$.

A second study contributing greatly to the heterogeneity of the natural process group (Walker 1974) had losses in both the experimental and control groups. However, the experimental group, based on Macrorie's *Telling Writing*, had a substantially greater loss than did the control, resulting in an experimental/control effect size of $-.27$. (The reasons for that loss are not so apparent as they are in the Adams study.) Removal of the Walker treatment raises the mean effect size of the natural process mode to .20 and reduces H to 18.76, which is nonsignificant at $p < .01$. Removal of both the Walker study and the Adams study reduces the mean effect size only to .18 (from .19) but reduces H to 14.44, a level at which heterogeneity is not significant at $p < .01$. With both Walker and Adams removed, H for the dimension (all modes of instruction) is 42.87, which is not significant at $p < .01$.

Environmental treatments, in Table 5, are well within the limit for homogeneity ($H = 12.83$, $df = 9$). Since three of the environmental treatments are from my own studies, there was some question as to whether they should be included. Without these treatments, the experimental/control mean effect size would be .42 and heterogeneity would still be nonsignificant ($H = 5.56$, $df = 6$). Because my treatments did not change the significance of H appreciably, there seemed no reason to reject them.

In the individualized group (see Table 6), one study contributes heavily to both the mean and the heterogeneity (A. E. Thibodeau 1964). Its removal reduces the mean effect size to .09 from .17 and H to 7.20 from 14.68. Speculation about its relatively high experimental/control effect size of .45 is possible. The individualized treatment is the same as the study's other experimental treatment, which was categorized as environmental. The only difference is that students in the individualized treatment did not work in groups with other students. Instead, they dealt with the same kinds of problems but with individual attention from the teacher.

In the dimension of mode of instruction, the removal of any two of the experimental/control treatments responsible for high levels of heterogeneity (Adams, Walker, or A. E. Thibodeau) reduces the heterogeneity to homogeneity (not significant at $p < .01$). The dimension explains 93 percent (well within limits set earlier) of the twenty-nine treatments categorized as having an identifiable instructional mode in the experimental group and some other in the control. The homogeneity of each category of treatments and of the dimension as a whole indicates that the criteria used to classify instructional mode identify treatments which have common effects and explain a major aspect of instruction.

Pre/post effect sizes were calculated for every treatment group (except for those that used no pretest) and are summarized in Table 8. These results permit inspection of mean pre-to-post effect sizes regardless of experimental or control status. The mean pre-to-post effect for thirty-two presentational treatments is .18, higher than might be expected from the original analysis of experimental/control effects; for nine natural process treatments, .26; for nine environmental treatments, .75; and for seven individualized treatments, .24. Examining the treatments in this way indicates that their relative positions have changed only slightly, with the presentational and environmental treatments being somewhat stronger in relation to the others. While the differences among the presentational, natural process, and individualized modes are not significant, the environmental gain is three times the gain for the others and is significantly different from them at $p < .001$. Note that the lower limit of the 95 percent confidence interval for environmental treatments is about .3 standard deviation

Table 8

Mode of Instruction

Summary of Mean Pretest to Posttest Effect Size Statistics

Mode	n	Mean Effect	sd	95% Confidence Interval		H	df	Maximum H for nonsignificance at $p < .01$
				Lower	Upper			
Presentational	32	.18	.026	.13	.23	95.65	31	52.16
Natural Process	9	.26	.035	.19	.33	29.24	8	21.66
Environmental	9	.75	.053	.64	.85	101.75	8	21.66
Individualized	7	.24	.060	.12	.36	8.32	6	16.80

above the upper limits for other modes. In short, these pre-to-post results help to confirm and clarify the results of the analysis of the experimental/control effect size.

Focus of Instruction

Foci of instruction include types of content or activities which teachers of composition expect to have a salutary effect on writing. These include the study of traditional grammar, work with mechanics, the study of model compositions to identify features of good writing, sentence combining, inquiry, and free writing. These share the supposition that they precede writing and prepare for it or occur early in the writing process (e.g., free writing). For that reason, they are examined separately from instructional treatments which follow writing, namely feedback and revision.

For inclusion in the analysis of this dimension, the focus of instruction had to appear in the experimental treatment but not in the control. To insure independent sets of treatments, studies had to be grouped by their primary focus if more than one focus were included in an experimental treatment. In two cases, for example, studies included a modicum of practice in sentence combining. In the first case, free writing received greater emphasis and far more instructional time. In the second, inquiry received more emphasis and time. Accordingly, the first was grouped with free writing and the second with inquiry. In most cases, such decisions were not necessary.

Characteristics of the instructional foci were generally explicit in the description of treatments. However, at times, instructional foci were essentially the same in both experimental and control groups, contrasting, for example, somewhat different ways of using model pieces of writing (West 1967). In some cases, instructional focus was the same in both treatments, while the study examined some other aspect of instruction, for example, the type or placement of feedback (e.g., Judd 1973; Bata 1973). Occasionally, treatments were unique or were comparable to only one or two other treatments (e.g., Belanger 1978b). Such studies could not be examined for instructional focus. Exclusion of these treatments resulted in the classification of thirty-nine experimental/control treatments in one of six categories.

The six categories have been discussed in earlier chapters. Grammar and sentence combining were discussed in Chapter 5, models and scales in Chapter 6, and free writing and inquiry in Chapter 7. In what follows, each focus will be defined only briefly. (The reader may wish to examine the appropriate chapter for a more extensive discussion of the treatments as they appear in a variety of studies.) The results of the analysis of the foci of instruction are discussed in the main section following the present one.

Grammar and Mechanics

Grammar, defined as the study of parts of speech and sentences, remains a common treatment in composition instruction in schools and colleges. Only one study (with two treatments) included in this meta-analysis, however, used grammar as an experimental treatment not present in the control (Elley, et al. 1975). A treatment was coded as including mechanics if it attended to matters of usage and punctuation through the use of set classroom exercises or a particular text. Three treatments used grammar, mechanics, or a combination in the control but not the experimental groups. Further, their experimental treatments did not overlap with other foci listed below. For purposes of comparison, these three treatments were reversed such that the grammar/mechanics treatments were considered experimental while their opposite treatments were taken as controls. This provided a total of five experimental/control treatments focusing on grammar/mechanics in one treatment but not in the other. These treatments are summarized in Table 9.

The set of grammar/mechanics treatments comprises only three studies, with two of them including two treatments each. One wonders, however, if A. E. Thibodeau and A. L. Thibodeau, both completing dissertations at Boston University in 1963, actually used two different control groups of 266, treated here as experimental groups, or if they used the same control group. Even in the latter case, however, we can examine the performance of a large number of students (266) studying grammar and mechanics, in contrast to three smaller groups engaged in other approaches to learning to write.

Sentence Combining

The sentence combining treatment is one pioneered by Mellon (1969) and O'Hare (1973), who showed that practice in combining simple sentences into more complex ones resulted in greater T-unit length— a T-unit being a traditionally defined main clause and all of its appended modifiers. That this treatment results in students writing longer T-units is hardly open to question. However, a number of critics question that it produces writing of higher quality.

Only four studies of sentence combining (of over fifty) met the criteria for inclusion in this meta-analysis. (Although many studies

Table 9

Focus of Instruction: Grammar/Mechanics

Mean Effect Size = -.29; H = 8.85

Treatment	Grade	Duration in weeks	n Exper.	n Control	g[a]	$\sigma^2(g)$[b]	$g \cdot_{(j)}$[c]	$H_{(j)}$[d]	g Exper.	g Control
Elley, et al. 1975	11	96	42	62	.03	.039	-.32	6.11	---	---
Elley, et al. 1975	11	96	60	62	.08	.033	-.32	5.39	---	---
A. L. Thibodeau 1964	6	6	266	136	-.35	.011	-.26	8.38	-.11	.23
A. L. Thibodeau 1964	6	6	266	97	-.31	.014	-.28	8.70	-.11	.34
A. E. Thibodeau 1964	6	6	266	100	-.45	.014	-.23	6.26	-.11	.33

[a] g = effect size
[b] $\sigma^2(g)$ = variance of the effect size
[c] $g \cdot_{(j)}$ = mean effect size with particular treatment removed
[d] $H_{(j)}$ = homogeneity with particular treatment removed

were well-designed, they did not include scaled judgments of writing quality.) A fifth study by Faigley (1979c) was included with these four because, while it traces its ancestry to a different source (Francis Christensen 1967), it focuses on the manipulation of syntax, not so much by combining sentences but by adding free modifiers to main clauses. The five studies included in this set, each with one experimental/control treatment, are summarized in Table 10.

Models

The study of model pieces of writing or discourse is one of the oldest tools in the writing teacher's repertoire, dating back to ancient Greek academies which required that their students memorize orations. In today's composition curricula, use of models of excellence is still common. Usually, students are required to read and analyze these pieces of writing in order to recognize and then imitate their features. Occasionally, this treatment involves the examination of inadequate pieces alongside more adequate ones (e.g., Clark 1968). Six studies with seven treatments focused on the use of models in experimental treatments but not in controls. The treatments are summarized in Table 11. It is interesting to note that these treatments range in grade level from 6 to 13.

Scales

Seven studies, each with one experimental/control treatment, were categorized as involving students in the use of scales (defined as a set of criteria embodied in an actual scale or a set of questions for application to pieces of writing). Depending on the study, students applied the criteria to their own writing, to that of their peers, to writings supplied by the teacher, or to some combination of these. The scale had to be manifest in some concrete form, not simply exist in the mind of the teacher and used as part of class discussion. Generally, the instructional use of scales analyzed here engaged students in applying the criteria *and* formulating possible revisions or ideas for revisions. These treatments are summarized in Table 12.

Although the treatments extend from grades 10 to 13, the reader should not conclude that such treatments are inappropriate at lower grade levels. The experimental/control effect size for Sager (1973a), who used the treatment at grade 6, was .93. The Sager study was not included in the meta-analysis because it did not meet all criteria for inclusion. Also, D. R. Coleman (1982) claims to have replicated the Sager experiment with second- and third-grade gifted students and to have found comparable results.

Table 10

Focus of Instruction: Sentence Combining

Mean Effect Size = .35; H = 1.89

Treatment	Grade	Duration in weeks	n Exper.	n Control	g[a]	$\sigma^2(g)$[b]	$g_{\cdot(i)}$[c]	$H_{(i)}$[d]	g Exper.	g Control
Faigley 1979c	13	15	70	68	.51	.029	.30	0.80	.68	.20
Howie 1979	9	18	51	40	.21	.045	.38	1.36	----	----
Morenberg, Daiker, and Kerek 1978	13	15	151	139	.34	.014	.36	1.87	.55	.22
Pedersen 1978	7	15	18	18	.45	.114	.35	1.80	.89	.31
Waterfall 1978	13	10	19	19	.12	.106	.37	1.35	.62*	.50*

[a] g = effect size
[b] $\sigma^2(g)$ = variance of the effect size
[c] $g_{\cdot(i)}$ = mean effect size with particular treatment removed
[d] $H_{(i)}$ = homogeneity with particular treatment removed
*It was necessary to use pooled posttest standard deviation to compute the pretest to posttest gains in this study.

Table 11

Focus of Instruction: Models

Mean Effect Size = .22; H = 5.31

Treatment	Grade	Duration in weeks	n Exper.	n Control	g[a]	$\sigma^2(g)$[b]	$g_{-(i)}$[c]	$H_{(i)}$[d]	g Exper.	g Control
Calhoun 1971	13	10	64	58	.16	.033	.22	5.21	.16	-.01
Caplan and Keech 1980*	12	12	73	56	.12	.032	.23	4.99	.01	-.12
Clark 1968	13	10	30	30	-.13	.067	.23	3.43	.26	.38
Clark 1968	13	10	30	30	-.10	.067	.23	3.74	.29	.38
J. E. Reedy 1966	9	3	193	217	.26	.009	.20	5.03	.26	.00
A. E. Thibodeau 1964	6	6	142	266	.34	.011	.17	3.34	.21	-.11
Vinson 1980	9	6	70	48	.18	.035	.22	5.27	.57	.38

[a]g = effect size
[b]$\sigma^2(g)$ = variance of the effect size
[c]$g_{-(i)}$ = mean effect size with particular treatment removed
[d]$H_{(i)}$ = homogeneity with particular treatment removed

*Effect sizes are pooled results for narrative and argument. The grade level is not clear but apparently is 12.

Table 12

Focus of Instruction: Scales

Mean Effect Size = .36; H = 6.89

Treatment	Grade	Duration in weeks	n Exper.	n Control	g^a	$\sigma^2(g)^b$	$g_{\cdot(i)}{}^c$	$H_{(i)}{}^d$	g Exper.	g Control
N. L. Benson 1979	10	22	192	96	.28	.016	.41	6.24	.19*	-.09*
Clifford 1981	13	16	43	49	.61	.046	.32	5.30	1.12	.43
Farrell 1977	11	11	49	42	.27	.045	.37	6.69	.66	.36
Kemp 1979	13	4	40	40	.37	.051	.36	6.89	.24	-.01
Rosen 1974	13	16	40	29	.82	.064	.31	3.24	2.34	.95
Wright 1976	13	5	38	47	.08	.048	.40	5.02	.31	.24

[a] g = effect size
[b] $\sigma^2(g)$ = variance of the effect size
[c] $g_{\cdot(i)}$ = mean effect size with particular treatment removed
[d] $H_{(i)}$ = homogeneity with particular treatment removed
*Based on pooled standard deviation of posttests.

Free Writing

Free writing is a treatment commonly prescribed in the professional literature, particularly since the early seventies. Generally, it involves asking students to write about whatever they are interested in. The writing may be in journals, which may be considered inviolate, or in preparation for sharing ideas, experiences, and images with other students or with the teacher. Such writing is free in two senses: (1) topics are not prescribed, and (2) the writing is ordinarily not graded. The idea underlying this treatment is simply that allowing students to write without restrictions will help them discover both what they have to say and their own voices in saying it. Nine studies with nine experimental/control treatments, extending over grades 1 to 13, met the requirements for this group. They are summarized in Table 13.

Inquiry

A treatment was coded as focusing on inquiry when it presented students with sets of data (or occasionally required them to find data) *and* when it initiated activities designed to help students develop skills or strategies for dealing with the data in order to say or write something about it. Ordinarily, such activities are designed to enhance particular skills or strategies such as formulating and testing explanatory generalizations, observing and reporting significant details to achieve an effect, or generating criteria for contrasting similar phenomena. In this sense, instruction in inquiry is different from instruction which presents models illustrating already-formed generalizations, significant details, or criteria and which may demand that students produce such features in their own writing. It is also different from instruction which provides stimuli for writing (e.g., films, music, cartoons, charts, or graphs) but which does not focus on strategies for analyzing data at some level. Five studies with six experimental/control treatments met the requirements for this group. They are summarized in Table 14.

As with the environmental treatments, there was some question about including my own studies in this category. If all three treatments are removed, the effect size for the remaining three is .70 and H is 0.23. However, since the H statistic is clearly nonsignificant at $p < .01$ even with the studies included (five degrees of freedom allows a maximum of $H = 15.08$ for nonsignificance at $p < .01$), the treatments were retained in this analysis. It is interesting to note that the six treatments span grades 3 to 12.

Table 13

Focus of Instruction: Free Writing

Mean Effect Size = .16; $H = 27.25$

Treatment	Grade	Duration in weeks	n Exper.	n Control	g^a	$\sigma^2(g)^b$	$g_{\cdot(j)}{}^c$	$H_{(j)}{}^d$	g Exper.	g Control
Adams 1971	12	18	70	65	.56	.031	.14	21.87	.00	-.56
Alloway, et al. 1979	7-12	36	105	120	.39	.018	.14	24.16	.25	-.07
Davis 1979	13	16	100	202	.00	.015	.18	25.36	.30	.30
Ganong 1975	9	8	77	58	.06	.030	.17	26.90	.27	.23
Gauntlett 1978	10-12	16	420	371	.05	.005	.20	24.03	.09*	.05*
Olson and DiStefano 1980	7-9	36	195	195	.40	.011	.13	21.06	.53	.10
Wagner, Zemelman, and Malone-Trout 1981	1-12	24	585	294	.19	.005	.15	27.03	.31	.14
Walker 1974	13	16	41	36	-.27	.053	.17	23.63	-.34	-.10
Wienke 1981	6	32	85	72	.36	.026	.15	25.65	.62	.25
Witte and Faigley 1981b	13	16	252	108	-.07	.013	.18	22.80	.35	.42

[a] g = effect size
[b] $\sigma^2(g)$ = variance of the effect size
[c] $g_{\cdot(j)}$ = mean effect size with particular treatment removed
[d] $H_{(j)}$ = homogeneity with particular treatment removed

*Based on pooled standard deviation of posttests.

Table 14

Focus of Instruction: Inquiry

Mean Effect Size = .56; H = 8.73

Treatment	Grade	Duration in weeks	n Exper.	n Control	g[a]	$\sigma^2(g)$[b]	$g_{\cdot(j)}$[c]	$H_{(j)}$[d]	g Exper.	g Control
Fichteneau 1968	3-6	32	160	40	.77	.033	.52	7.13	1.44	.89
Hillocks 1979	9 & 11	3-5	97	94	.75	.022	.50	6.61	1.13	.20
Hillocks 1982	7-8	4	72	64	.43	.030	.59	8.02	1.09	.54
Hillocks 1982	7-8	4	75	64	.18	.029	.66	2.49	.77	.54
Pisano 1980	11 & 12	18	30	30	.66	.070	.55	8.59	.84	.10
Widvey 1971	11	18	36	36	.64	.058	.55	8.62	---	---

[a] g = effect size
[b] $\sigma^2(g)$ = variance of the effect size
[c] $g_{\cdot(j)}$ = mean effect size with particular treatment removed
[d] $H_{(j)}$ = homogeneity with particular treatment removed

College-level studies categorized with a focus on inquiry are Troyka (1974) and McCleary (1979b). Troyka has a very high effect size and was eliminated as an outlier. McCleary's various experimental and control treatments were all categorized as focusing on inquiry, but did not contrast inquiry and non-inquiry. All, however, have very high effect sizes.

Results for Focus of Instruction

Table 15 summarizes the experimental/control effect sizes for each focus of instruction. Students in the grammar and mechanics treatments scored .29 standard deviation *less* than their peers in no grammar or mechanics treatments. The mean effect size of $-.29$ is homogeneous ($H = 8.85$, $df = 4$). These results are supported by the pre-to-post mean effect for all treatments using grammar in experimental or control conditions. The pre-to-post mean effect size for those fourteen studies is .06. In contrast, the mean pre-to-post effect size for the seventy-five treatments which do not mention grammar[1] of any kind have a mean effect size of .44. This difference is very large ($z = 9.27$, $p < .000001$). Braddock and his colleagues (1963) argued that grammar study may have a possibly negative effect on composition ability. These data certainly support their contention, in the sense that nearly anything else is more effective in increasing the quality of writing.

Further, twenty-seven treatments (experimental or control) incorporated mechanics, yielding a pre-to-post mean effect size of .268 ($H = 207.35$). A single study is responsible for much of the heterogeneity. Its removal lowers H to below 81.00 and the pre-to-post mean effect size to about .18. The seventy-four treatments which do not mention mechanics have an effect size of .40 ($H = 1016.19$). The difference between treatments with mechanics and those without is significant ($z = 3.88$, $p < .0001$). Clearly, as with grammar, treatments including mechanics predict significantly lower qualitative change in writing than those which regard mechanics as irrelevant.

Sentence combining activities do not focus on the identification of parts of speech or parts of sentences but on the manipulation of syntactic elements, and, in the case of Faigley (1979c), on the generating of the elements as well. The mean experimental/control effect

---

1. Grammar was coded as traditional, transformational, purposely excluded, irrelevant (when the description of the treatment made no mention of grammar) or zero (when no description of the treatment was available). The effect size here is based on treatments coded with grammar as irrelevant or purposely excluded.

Table 15

Focus of Instruction

Summary of Experimental/Control Effect Size Statistics

Focus	n	Mean Effect (g.)	sd	95% Confidence Interval		H	df	Maximum H for nonsignificance at p < .01
				Lower	Upper			
Treatments Included in Focus of Instruction Analysis	39	.26	.023	.21	.30	84.48	38	62.4
Grammar and Mechanics	5	−.29	.059	−.40	−.17	8.85	4	13.27
Sentence Combining	5	.35	.083	.19	.51	1.89	4	13.27
Models	7	.22	.057	.11	.33	5.31	6	16.80
Scales	6	.36	.078	.21	.51	6.89	5	15.08
Free Writing	10	.16	.035	.09	.23	27.25	9	21.66
Inquiry	6	.56	.076	.41	.71	8.73	5	15.08
Treatments Categorized by Focus of Instruction	39	--	--	--	--	58.92	33	54.70
With 2 Outliers Removed	37	--	--	--	--	49.90	31	52.15

size for the five studies focusing on sentence combining activities is .35 and is also homogeneous ($H = 1.89$, $df = 4$). While the effect size is not significantly different from that for the study of models, it certainly is significantly greater than that of the grammar treatments ($z = 6.28$, $p < .0001$).

As indicated earlier, a clear concern in teaching writing has been with learning the characteristics of good writing. These criteria have been taught through the study of models and the application of what I have called scales or sets of criteria. The mean experimental/control effect size for studies focusing on models in the experimental groups but not in the control is .22, significantly higher than the grammar experimental/control effect size. The seven treatments in six studies are homogeneous ($H = 5.31$, $df = 6$). The mean experimental/control effect size for the use of scales is .36 and is homogeneous ($H = 6.89$, $df = 5$), higher than that for models but not significantly. It is, however, significantly higher than the effects for grammar ($z = 6.63$, $p < .001$) and free writing ($z = 2.31$, $p < .05$).

Two foci of instruction are related to what has traditionally been known as invention: free writing and inquiry. The mean effect size for the ten treatments using free writing as a major instructional tool is .16. It, however, is not homogeneous ($H = 27.25$, $df = 9$). Although free writing has a significantly stronger effect than grammar and mechanics ($z = 6.53$, $p < .001$), it is not significantly different from the treatments using models. It is significantly lower than sentence combining ($z = 2.20$, $p < .05$), scales, and inquiry.

The mean experimental/control effect size for the six treatments focusing on inquiry is .56—the highest mean effect size for any instructional focus. It is also homogeneous, with $H = 8.73$ and $df = 5$. It is significantly higher than grammar, models ($z = 3.75$, $p < .002$), scales ($z = 1.96$, $p < .05$), sentence combining ($z = 1.98$, $p < .05$), and free writing ($z = 4.99$, $p < .0001$). One treatment (Hillocks 1982) contributes heavily to the existing heterogeneity. Its removal lowers H to 2.49 and raises the mean effect size for the remaining five treatments to .66. However, the presence of that treatment does not produce significant heterogeneity in the set.

The dimension of focus of instruction includes thirty-nine treatments. Taken together, without classifying them by particular focus, they yield an H of 84.48 (see Table 15), considerably higher than the 62.4 required for homogeneity with $df = 38$. When the studies are classified by focus, the treatments in all but one focus lie well within the limits for homogeneity. Only the free writing treatments display significant heterogeneity, 27.25 ($df = 9$) when 21.66 is the maximum for nonsignificance. Several studies in this mode are responsible for the high levels of heterogeneity. The removal of any one study, however, will not bring the H statistic to the maximum allowable for homogeneity, 20.08 ($df = 8$).

The treatment contributing most heavily to the heterogeneity of the free writing category is Olson and DiStefano (1980). As far as can be told from available data, that study differs from other free writing studies in two possibly significant ways. First, the free writing it advocates is "focused" free writing, which according to the researcher (personal communication with Miles Olson, March 2, 1983) comes only after some discussion of a topic introduced by the teacher. Second, teachers were encouraged to use sentence combining practices—not as a major treatment but as part of revision. At any rate, the experimental/control effect size of this study (.40) is considerably higher than the group mean of .16. Its removal reduces H to 21.06 and the mean effect size for the nine remaining treatments to .13.

Adams (1971) also contributes heavily to the heterogeneity and the mean for the free writing group, but for different reasons. In this case, as we have seen, a loss in the control group accounts entirely for the study's positive effect size. Its removal reduces H to 21.87 and the mean effect size for the remaining treatments to .14. Two negative treatments also contribute heavily to the heterogeneity: Walker (1974) and Witte and Faigley (1981b). Removal of either reduces H and increases the mean effect size for the group.

Removal of any two of these four studies reduces the remaining treatments to homogeneity. The removal of Adams (1971) and Witte and Faigley (1981b) raises the mean slightly to .17 but reduces H to 18.23. This, in turn reduces H for the dimension to 49.90, which is not significant with $df = 31$.

In short, the dimension of instructional focus explains nearly 95 percent of the treatments classified within it. The homogeneity of each focus and of the dimension overall, as well as the significant differences among certain of the foci, indicate that the dimension has a high degree of explanatory power. The focus of instruction in teaching writing has a significant impact on changing the quality of student writing.

Removal of Outliers

While the results reported above are clear, the critical reader may ask about the extent to which removal of outliers distorts the results.

Four treatments were removed initially because of their contribution to heterogeneity, reducing the number of treatments from seventy-three to sixty-nine. Subsequently, three treatments were removed from the dimension of instructional mode and two from instructional focus to achieve homogeneity. As we have seen, the removal of the latter did not appreciably change the mean effect sizes. However, a question remains about the four studies removed initially. Did their removal change the results significantly?

Two of those studies (Troyka 1974 and D. I. Smith 1974) were classified as using inquiry. Their inclusion in the results for inquiry increases the mean effect size from .56 to .97 but also increases H from a nonsignificant 8.73 to a highly significant 87.37. The Troyka experimental treatment was also classified as environmental. Its inclusion with other environmental treatments raises the mean effect size from .44 to .65. Both changes are clearly quite large.

The Loritsch (1977) and D. I. Smith (1974) treatments were both classified as individualized treatments. Their inclusion increases the mean effect size slightly from .17 to .24. The Loritsch study could not be classified for instructional focus. It provided programmed materials and individual conferences which were not described but which college freshmen could utilize as they felt the need.

The treatment with the greatest negative effect size (Ebbert 1980) provided instruction in heuristics and remained a one-of-a-kind treatment. It could not be classified for instructional mode.

Clearly, the removal of the above studies did not distort the direction of the findings. On the contrary, those that can be explained tend to reinforce the findings.

Post-Writing Treatments: Revision and Feedback

What I have called foci of instruction include treatments which explicitly or implicitly assume that the materials and activities prepare students in advance of the actual composition writing. Thus, studying grammar is intended to help students formulate better sentences, and free writing is intended to help writers explore ideas in preparation for more formal drafts. Another tradition in the teaching of writing emphasizes instruction *after* students have written something. That is, students write and then receive comments from teachers or peers about what was effective or ineffective. These comments constitute instruction which is presumed to help students become more effective in their next writing. This feedback is sometimes coupled with revision and sometimes not. Observations suggest that in some American classrooms instruction is predominantly of the post-writing type, with little or no prewriting instruction outside the teacher's finding and assigning a topic (A. Applebee 1981).

Most treatments included in the meta-analysis which include feedback and revision also include some focus of instruction prior to writing. The studies available to the meta-analysis, therefore, do not permit examination of the effects of revision alone or of feedback alone. But we *can* examine the mean effect sizes of those studies which emphasize revision and feedback.

Revision

Thirteen treatments regularly asked students in experimental groups to revise while students in the control groups did not. The mean experimental/control effect size for these is .185, below the mean experimental/control size (.28) for all treatments. The effect size is not homogeneous ($H = 35.33$, $df = 12$).

Feedback

The studies included in the meta-analysis stipulate various dimensions of feedback as part of a treatment: written feedback from teachers, conferences with teachers, audiotaped feedback from teachers, peer feedback, positive feedback versus negative feedback, frequent versus infrequent feedback, and so forth. Unfortunately, too few studies deal with many of these aspects to provide very reliable information.

Three relatively frequent modes of feedback include (1) written comments from teachers, (2) conferences with teachers, and (3) a combination of peer and teacher feedback. Unfortunately, several treatments specifying teacher comment as the principal mode of feedback do not describe the control treatment in detail. Because some form of written teacher comment appears to be pervasive, we cannot assume that the control treatments are different. Three treatments specify student-teacher conferences in the experimental groups but not in the control groups. The largest group of treatments which provides a contrast in mode of feedback consists of those which specify a combination of peer and teacher feedback in the experimental groups as opposed to only teacher feedback in the control groups. These eighteen experimental/control treatments have a mean effect size of .21, indicating a small advantage for peer-group feedback. However, the group of studies are not homogeneous ($H = 149.32$, $df = 17$). Some experimental treatments using a combination of teacher and peer feedback have much higher gains than their control groups (e.g., Clifford 1981, R. L. Miller 1968, and Rosen 1974). However, three treatments have lower gains than their control groups (Lareau 1971, J. P. Walker 1974, and Witte and Faigley 1981b). The experimental/control effect sizes for the above treatments range from .82 (Rosen 1974) to − .27 (Walker 1974). In short, the combination of peer and teacher feedback does not explain the results for these studies. Other factors are at work.

It seems reasonable to assume that teacher and peer comments are directed at helping students meet certain goals in writing. That is, feedback represents the objectives of instruction to some extent. It also seems reasonable to hypothesize that if objectives are operationally clear to students, feedback will be more effective than when the objectives are not operationally clear. Treatments were categorized as having operationally clear objectives when they indicated that students were involved in activities which provided practice in the use of specific skills, such as using particular syntactic constructions in sentence combining treatments (O'Hare 1973), using specific detail in describing a range of phenomena (Hillocks 1982), and using specified strategies in developing arguments (McCleary 1979b, Troyka 1974).

Unfortunately, it was not possible to examine this hypothesis using experimental/control effects. Too few were available. It is possible, however, to make some comparisons using pre-to-post effect sizes for treatments if their experimental or control status is ignored. Eight treatments were categorized as displaying a combination of teacher and peer feedback and as having operationally clear objectives. Their mean pre-to-post effect size is .74. They are not homogeneous ($H = 102.06$, $df = 7$). Ten treatments were categorized as displaying a combination of teacher and peer feedback but *without* operationally clear objectives. Their mean pre-to-post effect size is .24, and they come close to being homogeneous ($H = 29.48$, $df = 9$). Removal of one study reduces the mean effect size to .20 and the H statistic to 20.09 ($df = 8$), which indicates homogeneity. Only two treatments with teacher feedback only (no peer feedback) were classified as having operationally clear objectives. Results for so few treatments must be ignored. However, twelve treatments were categorized as having *only* teacher feedback without operationally clear objectives. Their mean effect size is .05. They are homogeneous ($H = 23.81$, $df = 11$).

Only two comparisons are possible. Treatments with operationally clear objectives appear to be more effective than those without such clarity. When objectives are not operationally clear, however, it appears that treatments with a combination of teacher and peer feedback have a small but consistent advantage over those with teacher feedback only.

Few of the available studies stipulate positive feedback in one treatment and negative in the other. However, several indicate negative or positive feedback in at least one treatment. Comparisons are possible using pre-to-post effect sizes for treatments regardless of their experimental or control status. Nine treatments stipulate the use of positive comments. Their mean pre-to-post effect size is .45. However, they are *not* homogeneous ($H = 54.56$, $df = 8$), ranging in effect size from $-.34$ (Walker 1974) to 1.09 (Hillocks 1982). Removal of these two treatments, which produce the highest and lowest standardized residuals, reduces the mean effect size only slightly to .43 but reduces the H statistic to 26.92—a level which comes closer to homogeneity. (Six degrees of freedom requires an H below 16.81.) The 95 percent confidence interval is virtually the same with or without the two studies. Without them it extends from .35 to .51.

Four treatments indicate negative comments, that is, the marking of all or nearly all errors with no positive comments. The mean pre-to-post effect size for these treatments is $-.20$. It is homogeneous ($H = 6.31$, $df = 3$). The 95 percent confidence interval ranges from $-.38$ to $-.01$.

The confidence intervals for negative and positive comments are widely separated by .36 standard deviation, suggesting a large difference in effect size. In fact, the difference is highly significant ($z = 6.04$, $p < .001$). While we might wish for more treatments using negative comments, these results seem to be clear. Negative comments have negative effects, and positive comments—on the average—have positive effects.

9 Validity, Implications, and Recommendations

The past several years of research have provided us with a collection of findings and hypotheses about the composing process. In addition, the meta-analysis of experimental treatment studies provides a set of findings about the relative effectiveness of instructional procedures in improving writing. A crucial question is the extent to which findings about process are compatible with findings about instruction. If the two are not compatible, then we are faced with serious questions about the validity of both bodies of research. If they *are* compatible or, more than that, mutually supportive, then we have added assurance of their validity. Although none of the experimental treatment studies examined here were designed to test hypotheses generated by research on process, many may be interpreted as testing such hypotheses. And, although the process studies were not designed to explain the findings of experimental treatment studies, certain of the process findings may help to explain experimental results. It will be useful, then, to examine findings from the meta-analysis of treatment studies in light of findings and hypotheses from process studies.

Validity: Mode of Instruction

Research by Bereiter and Scardamalia (1982) helps to explain why instructional modes vary in effectiveness as they do. Bereiter and Scardamalia distinguish three kinds of instructional roles: substantive facilitation, teaching new knowledge and skills, and procedural facilitation. In substantive facilitation the teacher facilitates the task by doing some part of it for the student. Suggesting revisions, laying out a plan for writing, indicating errors to be corrected, using brainstorming sessions to prepare for a particular piece of writing— all of these involve the teacher in substantive facilitation. Teaching new knowledge and skills involves demonstrating or showing examples of new forms, criteria, and strategies. Procedural facilitation, on the other hand, has to do with reducing what Bereiter and Scardamalia call the "executive demands" of a task. It involves teaching students procedures which will help them to put knowledge they already have to work.

223

The presentational mode of instruction emphasizes providing new information about writing and then expecting students to put that knowledge to work. However, such instruction does not provide opportunities for learning the procedures necessary for putting the knowledge to work. Thus, while presentational instructors might explain what a thesis statement is, and while their students might learn to identify and define them, they do not teach procedures for generating thesis statements. Consequently, their students may not be able to generate their own.

Natural process instruction, on the other hand, appears to provide only substantive facilitation. In commenting on Graves's recommendations for teaching, Bereiter and Scardamalia (1982) point out that conversations about a draft between the writer and teacher or between the writer and other students prompt ideas and plans for incorporation in particular pieces of writing. The youngsters involved, however, do not have to develop their own ideas and plans autonomously. Bereiter and Scardamalia point out that substantive facilitation tends to protect the learner from those parts of the task most important for mastery. It may be for the same reason, at least in part, that teacher comments on compositions appear to have so little effect on improving writing. That is, students may be told what is strong or weak but may not have criteria for identifying problems and strengths themselves. Further, they may not have the procedures for correcting or avoiding the problems.

One might argue that natural process instruction *does* involve students in procedures: free writing, discussing writing with others, giving and receiving feedback, and revising. But these procedures are highly generalized, with all of them capable of being fulfilled through low-level strategies, e.g., the "what next" strategy discussed earlier, the prompting that comes from conversation about a topic, or even with contentless prompts—which Bereiter and his colleagues found capable of doubling writing output.

Environmental instruction appears to focus on procedural facilitation. At the same time, unlike natural process instruction, it is not averse to presenting new forms, models, criteria, and so forth. When it does, however, the emphasis is on facilitating the *use* of that information in various writing situations. Sager (1973b), for example, not only presents information about scales and criteria but, more important, provides many opportunities to apply that information in judging writing, in generating new information, and in synthesizing those ideas—all according to the criteria. The students appear to gain a procedural or operational knowledge of the criteria which influences their own independent writing.

Arthur Applebee (1981) and his colleagues describe the characteristics of the best writing lessons they observed in 300 classroom visits. The description of the better lessons indicates clearly that those lessons have much in common with the environmental mode. Applebee writes (p. 105),

> In the better lessons, and even more so in the few that were really exceptional, the students were faced with problems that had to be solved out of their own intellectual and experiential resources. Often they would work together to solve problems posed by the teacher; this forced the students both to articulate their solutions more clearly and to defend them in the face of opposing opinions. The subject of the discussion seemed less important than the openness of the approach; what mattered was the sense that the students could offer legitimate solutions of their own rather than discover a solution the teacher had already devised.

If the problems in these lessons were devised to teach strategies and provide practice in their use—strategies which would be applied in later writing—then they would indeed illustrate the environmental mode.

Validity: Focus of Instruction

It is useful to examine each instructional focus in terms of research findings about process.

Grammar

One of the strongest findings of this study and the review by Braddock, Lloyd-Jones, and Schoer (1963) is that grammar study has little or no effect on the improvement of writing. The same is true for emphasis on mechanics and correctness in writing. In fact, some studies indicate that when correctness is heavily emphasized in marking papers, the quality of student writing diminishes significantly (e.g., V. A. Adams 1971). Studies of the composing process suggest at least two explanations of this result. First, studies by Graves and his colleagues indicate that at least certain aspects of correctness may be developmental, at least in young children. Children invent spellings at first, gradually bringing them into conformity with orthographic conventions. Further, as children realize that punctuation helps to convey the sound of speech, they begin to use it and gradually bring those uses into conformity with accepted usage. It may be that grammar and mechanics may only be useful to writers as they are ready for it.

A second, more important explanation, however, comes from research by a large number of scholars which indicates, in combination, that composing takes place at various levels of abstraction: from deciding general text plans and intentions to producing the graphemic representations. The work of Flower and Hayes (1980b, 1981b, 1981c) indicates that the transcription of specific sentences generally comes as the result of many other operations (e.g., generating, organizing). That is, competent writers do not simply generate sentences. They generate them *after* thinking about purposes, content, and so forth. Evidence from Matsuhashi (1981) suggests that sentences may be initially laid out in semantic chunks, with syntactic relationships planned but without specific lexical content. Finally, Bereiter, Fine, and Gartshore (1979) found slight differences between orally forecast words and words actually written, indicating a kind of last-minute editing process which attends to "correctness" and minor stylistic matters, and suggesting that language held in memory for transcription is not fully formed. The point is that if the study of grammar and mechanics is brought to bear on the composing process at all, it is likely to influence only the most concrete levels, the planning and editing of specific sentences. But such study would have no effect on the higher-level processes of deciding on intentions and generating and organizing ideas. Yet, clearly these higher-level processes give rise to the content, organization, and flavor of individual sentences.

Nor does grammar study facilitate higher-level planning by reducing mechanical demands. If the need to attend to "correctness" in writing—a need thought by some to be addressed by grammar study—interfered significantly with higher-level planning, then we would expect the quality ratings for written work to be significantly lower than for oral. However, Scardamalia and Bereiter (1979) and Gould (1980), who compared quality ratings for oral and written work, concluded that mechanical demands had no significant impact on quality.

Studies by Loban (1976) and others before him indicate that by the time children enter school they already use most of the syntactic constructions available in English. Further, the study of traditional school grammar is not designed to help children generate sentences but only to parse already-generated sentences. Thus, the study of grammar is unlikely to be helpful even in the planning of specific sentences. The study of mechanics and usage (what might be called "conventional correctness") is likely to have effect only in the last-minute editing done during transcription or in the editing process following it. In short, the findings of research on the composing process give us no reason to expect the study of grammar or mechanics to have any substantial effect on the writing process or on writing ability as reflected in the quality of written products. Experimental studies show that they have little or none. These findings have been consistent for many years.

Models

A second mainstay in traditional approaches to teaching writing has been the use of exemplary pieces of writing (models), sometimes selected to illustrate effective rhetorical strategies and sometimes selected simply to illustrate "good" writing. One assumption underlying this approach is that knowledge of the characteristics of good writing will enable students to produce effective writing on their own. A second assumption is that simply reading and analyzing the examples will provide such knowledge. Generally speaking, the programs and texts which make these assumptions tend to devote major time allotments to analyses of the pieces of writing before making assignments which require students to use similar techniques. As we have seen, however, the controlled model treatments display an aggregate experimental/control effect size smaller than the experimental/control effect size for all treatments.

Both Hayes and Flower (1980) and Bereiter and Scardamalia (1982) suggest that writers may be guided by schemata of various kinds in developing a given piece of writing. This idea might lead us to expect that the study of models would have a greater effect than it does. That it does not, however, may be explained by several considerations. First, studying a complex literary model is not the same as learning a schema. Schemata are skeletal frameworks, the elements of which can be carefully defined and shown to exist in every instance of the type represented by a given schema, e.g., goal-oriented stories. The complex models studied in composition programs are often so fully elaborated that whatever schemata may underlie them are obscured. Beyond that, the work on schemata has begun fairly recently and most of the research has focused on goal-oriented stories (Stein and Glenn 1979). It may be that useful schemata have not been or cannot be abstracted from the types of works assigned to students in schools and colleges.

Second, research by Graves (1981f) and his colleagues and particularly by Bereiter and Scardamalia (1982) and by Hayes and Flower (1980) has clearly shown that generating ideas is an important part of the composing process. Further, as Flower and Hayes (1981b) suggest, a writer starts with a body of knowledge and acts on it by "drawing inferences, creating relationships, or abstracting large bodies of ideas" (p. 45). Generating data and making inferences about them appear to be necessary antecedents, or at least concomitants, of making decisions about form. Programs which emphasize the study of models, however, ignore those necessary processes, expecting students to generate the data and make the necessary operations on them by themselves. It is one thing to know what the forms and rhetorical devices are (e.g., to list the parts of an argument) and quite another to generate the ideas and operate upon them so that they may be used in a new example of the form.

A final consideration is the finding by Flower and Hayes (1981b) that some of their subjects based their plans "on the features of the final written product" (p. 49). But when they did, such "product-based" plans were "peculiarly ineffective," because they "appeared to interfere with the normal generating process that occurs during writing." For example, some writers using such plans assumed that they should generate sentences "with close logical and syntactic links" (p. 51) from the beginning. Others, because a formal paper often begins with an overview of the major ideas to be treated, attempted to write such an introduction, thus short-circuiting their idea-generating processes, which so much research has shown to be important. The erratic bobbing up and down from high-level plans to specific sentences, typical of the composing process, is diminished.

Perhaps the persistent study of models leads some students to the notion that they must sit down and produce a finished essay without the necessary intervening processes. On the other hand, such instruction may not affect process at all. At this writing we know very little about how various kinds of instruction affect composing processes. But it is fairly clear that the available research into process would not lead us to expect the study of models to have much impact on improvement in writing.

Sentence Combining

As the narrative review in Chapter 5 reveals, many studies have been devoted to sentence combining (SC) or syntactic manipulation of a related kind, most of which have shown significant gains of some kind over their controls. The majority of SC treatments examining effects on writing quality have shown significant gains over their controls. The meta-analysis indicates a significantly greater effect size for SC studies than for a focus on grammar or free writing, but not so great an effect as for inquiry.

SC studies typically ask students to generate new sentences from already-formed sentences. Unlike grammar studies, SC treatments are not concerned with parsing sentences but with creating new ones from existing ones. In addition, with the exception of studies like Faigley's (1979c), they are not concerned with higher-level planning. However, the process studies by Bereiter and Scardamalia (1982), Bracewell and Scardamalia (1979), and Bracewell (1980) suggest reasons for the effectiveness of sentence combining. These studies indicate that overhauling an existing sentence or syntactic structure (as opposed to the process used in sentence combining) is a very difficult task. In their samples the students avoided it altogether or made only very minor changes. When they made more thorough revisions successfully, they retained the basic sentence plan already present. Attempts to change the existing structure entirely but to retain the same content often resulted in flawed structures. Bereiter and Scardamalia (1982) argue that when children encounter sentences already formulated, the stimulus provided by the existing sentence is of such strength that it overwhelms attempts to create a new one making use of the same content. They argue that writers may need to have knowledge of syntactic options organized hierarchically so that they can systematically survey and evaluate what is available, instead of relying on intuition to somehow think of a superior alternative structure. Most SC exercises, of course, provide just such knowledge organized around various syntactic concepts, such as the relative clause, and provide ample practice in constructing sentences using a variety of devices. Bereiter and Scardamalia believe that such practice helps young writers to consider alternative structures more readily.

The effects on quality of writing achieved in sentence combining studies are what we might expect, given the hypothesis about levels of composing suggested earlier. SC exercises can influence syntactic planning more than grammar study can. But SC exercises alone cannot influence higher-level plans dealing with content, audience, voice, and so forth. Interestingly, the Faigley study (1979c) included in the meta-analysis with the SC studies does more. Each lesson asked students to observe some phenomenon—perhaps as simple as a student walking across campus—and then develop a sentence using particular syntactic structures. This method involves somewhat higher levels of planning, deciding what details to include and what effect is intended, as well as syntactic planning. We might expect the method to have a more powerful effect than ordinary SC exercises. And it does have the greatest effect size (.51, compared to .35 for the mean effect over five SC studies).

Scales

The experimental treatment studies included in this group were those which presented students with a set of criteria in the form of questions to answer about pieces of writing or in the form of actual scales. Further, the scales and question sets had to be used by students in judging their own or others' writing. Most also required more than simple judgments. Students had to make concrete suggestions for improvement. The scales turned students' attention to matters well beyond the level of syntax: to evaluating information, organization, and the effect of the whole. Such techniques appear to provide a set of criteria which may very well serve to guide the generation of subsequent initial texts. That seems to have been the effect, for the students were tested not on their ability to rate or revise compositions but on their ability to generate new ones.

The research of Bereiter, Scardamalia, and their colleagues might very well lead us to expect such a result. The criteria learned in the application of scales or questions to pieces of writing should lead students to use "means-ends" strategies instead of "what-next" strategies. That is, the criteria should help them write for some overall effect, rather than simply writing what comes to mind as the result of an associative chain. And means-ends strategies are implicit in the higher-level planning which Flower and Hayes, in their studies, find to be important in competent composing.

Studies whose experimental treatments focus on the study of models have a similar goal: to learn criteria which identify good writing. Students examining models are supposed to learn the criteria from examples. However, they tend to be passive recipients of information, rather than users of it. Students working with scales, on the other hand, learn the criteria through actively applying them to various pieces of writing. They are engaged in the process of *using* what they are to learn.

Inquiry

The treatments categorized as inquiry also focus on higher-level planning, particularly on structuring data and on what Flower and Hayes (1981b) call creating a focus "by such complex actions as drawing inferences, creating relationships, or abstracting large bodies of ideas" (p. 45). Inquiry treatments typically help students decide what to use and how to use it—what Flower and Hayes call "forming for use" (p. 47). They appear to contribute to Bereiter and Scardamalia's (1982) means-ends strategies. In addition they may also help students internalize criteria for guiding and/or revising their own texts. Thus, students in an "observing and writing" treatment (Hillocks 1979) are likely to become aware of the need for detail as they generate texts. Similarly, college students having learned to examine ethical situations (McCleary 1979b) are likely to recognize the needs to identify central ethical issues, to eliminate irrelevant information, and so forth. In general, the research on process suggests that treatments which help students learn how to generate information, analyze it, and plan how to use it, and which provide practice in using higher-level criteria for guiding and rethinking the results, should bring about better writing. Such treatments have done so.

Free Writing and Natural Process

The research on the composing process provides little evidence to suggest that free writing as a main focus in the natural process mode of instruction will be effective. While Graves and his colleagues argue in favor of letting children choose their own topics, write what they want, submit it to peer review, and then revise, some of the actual evidence presented is negative, and some suggests that their subjects' writing is not so free as it might be. Kamler (1980) reports, for example, that the subject Jill chose two of her own topics, which proved infelicitous, before she finally found one in conference with her teacher that would "work" for her. Then she wrote fifty-seven words and after a half-hour's guidance from her teacher she added eighty-eight words. And while the subject Andrea (Calkins 1979 and 1981) appeared to become more sophisticated simply by writing what she wished, it is at least arguable that she learned a new form through hints from the teacher.

The research of Bereiter and Scardamalia (1982) is far less supportive of free writing than that of Graves and his colleagues. Bereiter and Scardamalia describe a "what next" strategy which is very common to young writers, who write a sentence, think of something else to write, write it, then think of another idea—all without any overriding plan governing the statements, holding them together, and giving them focus. As a result, successive ideas have less and less to do with earlier ideas. The researchers see this strategy as deriving from conversational patterns in which each speaker relies on his or her respondent to prompt what comes next and to maintain a meaningful context.

Flower and Hayes (1981b) describe a college writer who appeared to use a "what next" strategy, a writer whom they dubbed "Freewrite." This writer appeared to have no plan other than to write whatever came to mind. The result is a transcript of free-flowing associations without focus or purpose. Yet the writer himself saw no problems with the written product.

The descriptions of free writing available suggest that it may reinforce the "what next" strategy. That is, free writing may allow students to write whatever comes to mind, ignoring the need to build a meaningful verbal context, attend to a purpose, and so on. While free writing may be useful as a means of generating ideas, it may not, in itself, go much beyond that. Indeed, even with the other features of the natural process mode, the meta-analysis indicates that free writing has only minimal effect on the quality of writing.

The results of research into process, then—especially that which deals with planning as part of process—seem highly compatible with the findings of experimental treatment studies. Indeed, the former help to explain the results of the latter. Although the findings of neither set of research studies can be regarded as definitive, their mutual support provides evidence of their validity and a basis for action in research and practice.

Implications and Recommendations for Research

This review has identified a large number of factors important to instructors in writing. These factors fall into four major groups: the writer's repertoire, the writing process, the focus of instruction, and the design of instruction. While we have gained considerable knowledge of variables in these categories, there is far more to be learned not only about the variables themselves but also about their interactions.

The Writer's Repertoire

The concept of the writer's repertoire is an ancient one. The *Beowulf* poet spoke of the *scōp* reaching into his word hoard to pull forth the words and lines to make songs in the mead hall. In a similar way a writer calls upon lexical, syntactic, and generic forms to generate a discourse. In addition, as various studies suggest, writers have to call upon strategies which enable them to process the raw data which is to be the substance of the discourse. It is useful to think of the repertoire as including two types of knowledge—what several writers have called declarative and procedural knowledge—or, to put it more simply, knowledge of what and knowledge of how (Glaser 1984, Mandler 1983, Stein 1983). Traditional approaches to teaching composition have concentrated on declarative knowledge of grammar (the naming of parts of speech and sentences), various forms of discourse, and certain principles of rhetoric. Research examined in this review indicates clearly that approaches which focus on procedural knowledge (e.g., sentence combining, scales, inquiry) are more successful than those which focus on declarative knowledge.

We need more information about the schemata, if any, which guide writers in producing various types of discourse and about the strategies requisite to the production of those types. Psychologists have been examining story schemata to determine (1) the essential elements of the schemata, (2) what children at various ages know about them, and (3) how these elements may be taught (Stein and Trabasso 1982). Primary trait scoring (Lloyd-Jones 1977b) provides a method for the examination of the essential elements of other types of discourse. A primary trait analysis asks what characteristics of a type of discourse are most necessary in a successful piece of that type. It can be the first step in a task analysis which would also examine what strategies are necessary to producing an example of the type. In writing extended definitions, for example, the writer must produce criteria which indicate how the definiendum differs from related concepts. To generate such criteria, writers must compare instances of the definiendum with noninstances and identify as precisely as possible the characteristics which make the difference.

Research of this kind into discourse types has only begun. We need more information about the essential elements of the types and about the strategies used to generate them. Such research can be pursued through analyses of the forms, through case studies of writers, and through various experimental studies. In addition we need to know the extent to which declarative and procedural knowledge interact.

The Writing Process

As we have seen, many researchers over the past decade have concerned themselves with the process of writing, particularly with the general phases of prewriting, writing, and revision. Other researchers have begun to identify some of the specific subprocesses involved, for example, searching memory for appropriate information and applying criteria to make revisions. Knowledge of these subprocesses should prove extremely valuable to planning more effective instruction. But there is still a great deal to be learned about them. In the matter of revision, to take one example, it would be useful to know more about what Bereiter and Scardamalia (1982) call the "executive" tasks of shifting from generating text to evaluation, more about the specific nature of criteria available to writers as they evaluate, and more about the role of repertoire as writers generate new structures to replace old ones.

We also need to know how knowledge affects process. To what extent, for example, is the discourse type selected for a given task dependent on knowledge available to the writer? Some who theorize about composing argue that formal knowledge of structure is inhibitive. Researchers who have studied story forms, however, believe that story schemata are learned, that they guide the production of stories, and that without them stories are likely to be ill-formed. If the story grammarians are right, then the writing processes of those with appropriate knowledge are likely to be quite different from the processes of those without such knowledge. Similarly, in writing definitions, those who know the strategies for devising criteria are likely to display writing processes different from those of writers who do not. Knowing what these differences are and how they affect the actual texts produced should be very useful.

Only a very few studies have dealt with how awareness of the needs of particular audiences affects writing. We need to know whether such knowledge is best learned intuitively or through direct instruction and whether audience knowledge can be expected to affect the quality of writing, the substance of writing, or both. Several researchers have found that specifying the audience and other rhetorical aspects of writing assignments does not result in better pieces of writing. Specifications of audience, purpose, and so forth in assignments may make the task too complex for some writers. If that is the case, perhaps direct instruction would be useful to them. How would such instruction affect responses to specified assignments and the processes involved? Questions of this type are clearly related to the third category of variables: focus of instruction.

Focus of Instruction

Although the meta-analysis has indicated some foci of instruction which are more effective in improving writing than others, it does not claim to be comprehensive. It is necessarily constrained by the studies available and by the sometimes limited descriptions of the treatments. Consideration of the writer's repertoire and of the writing process suggests foci of instruction which are not represented (e.g., specific instruction about varying discourse for different audiences), as well as foci which might be examined in greater detail (e.g., applying sets of criteria or scales relevant to particular types of discourse such as argument). Many questions remain about the foci examined. It would be interesting to determine, for example, whether students with instruction in sentence combining would be better able to identify and rectify ill-formed sentences than those without, as Bereiter and Scardamalia (1982) suggest. Similarly, although instruction in grammar has little or no effect on the quality of writing, perhaps some minimal grammatical knowledge is necessary to achieve a satisfactory level of accuracy in adhering to the conventions of punctuation. In addition, many questions remain about the strategies required to develop various types of discourse effectively. How do writers generalize from specifics? How do they order supporting detail? How do they predict opposing arguments or points of view? How do they collect data and organize it? Case and experimental studies might develop and explore hypotheses related to questions of this kind. Once these strategies are better understood, instructional materials and procedures will have to be designed and tested.

Design of Instruction

The studies of instructional design reviewed here reveal a large number of instructional variables, including (1) the nature of objectives, and who sets the objectives, (2) the nature and frequency of learning tasks, (3) the presence or absence of models, (4) the types and frequency of writing assignments and (5) the nature, source, and occurrence of feedback. A number of rather complex problems are associated with each of these aspects of design.

Objectives

As we have seen in some treatments examined above, the objectives are quite general, e.g., to increase the quality of writing or to learn the "stages" of the composing process. In others, the objectives are more specific, e.g., to use comparison and contrast effectively. General objectives are typical of the natural process mode. Specific objectives are typical of the presentational and environmental modes. The free writing focus of instruction involves general objectives, but the other foci tend to have specific objectives. Among treatments with specific objectives is another useful distinction. Objectives may be specific *and* operationally clear to students. Or they may be specific but not operationally clear. For example, the objectives in McCleary's study (1979b) are specific: to identify principles, obligations, consequences, exceptions, and conflicts appearing in ethical problems. And because students were engaged in the actual analysis of a number of problems in which they made those identifications, the objectives may also be considered operationally clear. Similarly, in sentence combining activities, when students are asked to combine sentences using some specific syntactic structures and are given examples of how to do it and a set of problems of that type, we can assume that the objectives of the lessons are not only specific but operationally clear. In both cases, students spend classroom time working through the kinds of problems they will be expected to solve in their independent work later on.

In other treatments, although objectives may be specific, they tend *not* to be operationally clear. In treatments with an instructional focus on models, for example, objectives may be specific (e.g., to organize according to some particular kind of plan) but not operationally clear, because students must themselves make inferences about how to put the kind of plan into action in relation to some new set of data. Were the instructional materials to include sets of data for practice in organizing, we might assume that the objectives would become operationally clear. Or were the instructional materials to include poorly organized compositions for students to reorganize according to plans exemplified by the models, we might assume that the objectives were operationally clear. Research on the use of objectives of these types should be useful to instructional planning.

Learning Tasks

As suggested above, whether objectives are operationally clear is partly dependent upon the nature of learning tasks. Generally speaking, the learning tasks in studies reviewed here fall into two general groups: those in which students are primarily passive recipients and those in which they are primarily active agents. Some learning tasks involve writing (e.g., free writing about something of interest) and some do not (e.g., reading and analyzing a model composition). Other tasks are combinations of writing and nonwriting activities (e.g., observing an animal and writing a list of its characteristics). We do not know the optimal distribution, if there is one, of writing and nonwriting tasks.

Learning tasks may also be classified in terms of the character and quality of the learning cues they involve. Learning cues are indications of what students are to learn or procedures they are to follow. These cues may be judged along dimensions of negative to positive, concrete to abstract, and simple to complex. When the little girl Andrea is told to begin her writing in a different way (Calkins 1979 and 1981), the cue is negative because it tells Andrea what to avoid (what she has already done). The cue is abstract because though the specific action of writing something new is apparently clear, the principles involved remain unstated. And the cue is complex because Andrea will have to make many inferences, some right and some wrong, before she finds the *in medias res* opening that the teacher wishes. The fact that several months elapsed before Andrea regained her former fluency suggests an interesting problem for research. If learning cues are instead positive, concrete, and simple, will youngsters learn what Andrea did, but faster, without her loss in fluency?

The typical study of a model in college rhetoric programs involves cues which are positive (because they present models that the student is to imitate) but abstract (because the rules for imitation indicate what the final result should be but not how to produce it) and complex (because the models imply many rules simultaneously). As we have seen, the study of models is less effective than the average experimental treatment. If learning cues were concrete and simple, would the learning be greater than it is under ordinary conditions with abstract and complex cues? Useful experiments might contrast the traditional use of whole-discourse models with treatments using discourse parts. For example, one treatment might present several models of argumentative writing with practice in writing full-fledged arguments comparable to those in the models. The second treatment might begin with a single model of argument before proceeding to models that illustrate, variously, the following: generalization and support; assertions, evidence, and warrant; the ordering of several related generalizations, as in a syllogism; and the prediction and analysis of opposing points of view. In this second treatment students might practice the parts before attempting to develop a whole argument.

Learning tasks may also be contrasted on the basis of whether they are undertaken (1) by individuals simultaneously in whole-class instruction, (2) by individuals in tutorial situations, or (3) by small groups of peers working together. The results of the meta-analysis suggest that the latter is most effective when the tasks are carefully structured (i.e., when the cues are clear, as in environmental instruction) but not so effective when the tasks are largely unstructured (i.e., when the learning cues are covert or left to the learner to discover, as in natural process instruction). It may be, however, that when whole-class presentational instruction is carefully cued, it will be as effective as environmental instruction. The question is empirical, and might be examined, in part, by extending experiments such as the one outlined for argument above so that whole-discourse treatments would include both presentational and environmental versions, as would the treatments that examine not only whole arguments but parts.

Learning tasks may also be contrasted for the feedback they afford. The conventional focus on models in the presentational mode appears to provide little opportunity for feedback except after the students have written their major compositions. Experiments on mastery learning (none of which deals with composition) indicate that what Benjamin Bloom (1976) calls "formative evaluation" (intermediate evaluation which allows for corrective instruction) is far more effective than final evaluation alone. Common sense suggests that the same would be true for composition. If, for example, students have opportunities to practice specific strategies in argument (e.g., devising and supporting generalizations) *and* receive feedback and further instruction as needed, it seems likely that they will be more successful than students who receive feedback only after writing whole arguments. In the latter case, the feedback serves only as evaluation and cannot influence immediate performance. And it probably has little effect on learning at all, except affectively.

Models

The use of models may be thought of as an attempt to teach declarative knowledge about discourse. Such knowledge may be contrasted with the procedural knowledge necessary to the production of structures inherent in a type of discourse. While the study of models alone has a relatively weak effect on the quality of writing, and while treatments emphasizing procedural knowledge have very strong effects, we know little about the combination of the two, even though the latter usually include some reference to models. It would be useful to know whether procedures for generating parts of discourse can be taught without reference to models, or whether, in learning procedures, (e.g., how to generate specific detail) students generate their own forms. Researchers might profitably ask what proportion of variance in performance procedural and declarative knowledge of discourse types account for and to what extent that proportion varies by type.

Writing Assignments

A strong tradition in American education is that the key to the effective teaching of writing is the carefully selected assignment.

While assignment condition studies (see Chapter 7) seem not to bear this out, lists of topics (up to several thousand) remain very popular with teachers. At the other extreme, many natural process advocates recommend no assigned topics. Graves (1981a), for example, compares assignments to welfare, arguing that they make youngsters dependent on the system, unable to invent their own topics. Useful research might examine change in writing over a period of time with no assigned topics in one condition, randomly assigned topics in another, and topics selected according to some sequence in a third. All of these might be examined against other conditions with explicit instruction planned to help students deal with assignments of a given type, e.g., personal narrative or argument.

Considerable ambiguity exists about what an assignment is. When teachers ask students to write but do not stipulate content, type of discourse, or audience, we have what must be regarded as a minimal assignment. When students may write or not as they please, with no penalties or rewards, we have no assignment. Beyond these types, assignments vary in terms of whether they stipulate discourse type, content, audience, or some combination of these. In addition they vary in terms of the detail in which any of the three factors is designated. Exploration of such assignment variables both as they occur in single instances and in sequences should be quite valuable.

Finally, although Graves (1981a) does not qualify his recommendation that no topics be assigned, his illustrations of the recommendation are largely confined to children in grades 1–4. The meta-analysis reported above deals largely with students in grades 6 to 13 and suggests that specific assignments are effective when accompanied by effective instruction. Perhaps for beginning writers assignments are inhibiting under any circumstance. The same is clearly not true of older writers. Perhaps the various characteristics of assignments interact with the accompanying instruction and the age of the students. The question is empirical and could have considerable import for practice.

Feedback

Traditions in the teaching of English hold that compositions must be marked and commented upon—the more thoroughly, the better. But research reported in this review suggests that such feedback has very little effect on enhancing the quality of student writing—regardless of frequency or thoroughness. Unfortunately, however, the treatments in this review have not examined all of the possible variables systematically. Variables associated with feedback include the character of the feedback, its source (teacher, peer, or combination), its appearance in the instructional sequence, and its combination with other features of instruction.

Feedback has been characterized as negative or positive, intensive or partial, frequent or infrequent, and even as marginal or terminal. Except for positive and negative, these distinctions appear to make little or no difference. Given the time that teachers spend in making their marginal or terminal comments, this is a discouraging finding. However, other characterizations of feedback are possible. Teacher comments may be diffuse or focused, abstract or concrete. They may provide the actual changes necessary or they may pose questions which help the student make the necessary changes.

A few studies have printed sample comments from teachers. In most cases these comments are diffuse, commenting on a fairly wide variety of problems from organization and content to usage and style. Such comments also tend to be abstract, e.g., "Your first paragraph is too general. Be more specific." (Teachers who write such comments seem unaware of the irony.) On the other hand, comments might be focused, dealing with one or two related problems (e.g., focus and specificity) over several pieces of writing. In addition, comments might be even more specific (e.g., "Your first paragraph talks about the 'war effort.' Include a sentence or two that give some examples of the specific *efforts* that make up the 'war effort.' "). One study (Hillocks 1982) indicates that focused, specific comments probably have a positive effect on quality. However, the study does not contrast such comments with diffuse and abstract comments or with no comments.

Some teacher comments provide substantive changes for students on the assumption that the students will see what to do the next time. Others ask questions or make suggestions which help the student writer to make or think through the necessary changes. This distinction is similar to the difference between what Bereiter and Scardamalia (1982) call substantive facilitation and procedural facilitation. Substantive changes may deprive students of the chance to work through the problem, while questions or suggestions may facilitate their working them through.

The source of feedback may be the teacher (or teacher surrogate), peers, or a combination. The meta-analysis of pretest to posttest effect sizes indicates that the combination of peer and teacher feedback is consistently somewhat stronger than only teacher feedback when objectives are not operationally clear. Unfortunately, these are not controlled effect sizes and a number of questions remain unanswered. The main question is this: if other features of instruction were the same, would there be a difference among conditions of no feedback, teacher feedback, peer feedback, and combinations of teacher and peer feedback?

The preceding comments on feedback have been largely in terms of the traditional English-teaching notion of feedback as teacher comment (written or oral) on a composition after its completion. Natural process advocates have argued that students should receive feedback from teachers and peers at various points during the "drafting" of a piece, both while drafts are in progress and on early drafts prior to working on later ones. No studies have isolated such feedback for examination, as it has been incorporated into the natural process studies. Only Beach (1979) has shown significant changes as the result of between-draft comments.

It is common for students to receive feedback at points in the instructional process other than during or after writing. During sentence combining activities, as students use scales, or as they engage in inquiry, they undoubtedly receive feedback from peers and teachers as they work. Stein (1984) has suggested that a major reason for the success of the environmental approach may be its increased opportunities for feedback. In addition, feedback during sentence combining, scales, and inquiry treatments may be more concrete and focused because the objectives tend to be operationally clearer to both students and teachers. At any rate, nothing is known about the effects of feedback during prewriting activities. Observational and experimental studies should be extremely useful in adding to knowledge about the nature and effects of feedback of this kind.

Interaction of Variables

This review could not examine the interaction of mode of instruction and focus of instruction because too few studies were available, but the interaction of such variables appears to be a promising area. For example, while we know that the environmental mode appears significantly more effective than other modes, we do not know how it interacts with the various foci of instruction. We *do* know that the focus on models for the purpose of learning the characteristics of good writing is less effective than three other foci (sentence combining, scales, and inquiry). If the mode of instruction were systematically varied with the focus on models, what would be the results? By definition, the natural process mode could not be used for teaching models because it excludes the imposition of forms from sources external to the learner. However, models might be used with the presentational, individualized, or environmental modes. If models were studied in the presentational mode of instruction, which is the case in some of the studies included here, the teacher would ask students to read the model and would then explain the parts, qualities, or rhetorical strategies which it exemplifies. Eventually, students would write one or more compositions reflecting those same characteristics. If models were studied in the individualized mode, teachers would work with one student at a time, examining a model with the student and explaining its qualities and characteristics.

If models were the focus of instruction in the environmental mode, students might examine one model under the direction of the teacher but would proceed to the examination of others in small groups, assisted perhaps by a set of questions to guide their analysis. They might then report their ideas to the whole class. Disagreements would be examined and would prompt further explanations and analysis by the students, with the teacher acting as a moderator. This review encountered only one such treatment of models.

In the same way, other foci of instruction might be varied across modes of instruction. Thus, researchers might ask whether sentence combining or sentence construction is more effective when the mode of instruction is primarily presentational or when it is environmental, with students working in small groups to determine the most effective constructions, given certain substantive and rhetorical constraints. Similarly, one might ask whether inquiry is as effective when the teacher leads analysis of all data sets by explaining and asking questions or when the students themselves, working collaboratively in small groups, examine data and develop their own analyses, making use of specific strategies.

Such experimental work should eventually provide clearer information on the effects of the interaction of mode of instruction and focus of instruction. Careful case-study research could reveal interesting data on how mode and focus of instruction affect writing processes.

Another promising area for research appears to be the interaction of variables *within* the dimension of instructional focus. Models and scales, for example, are both used to teach criteria which presumably aid not only in evaluating texts but in generating them. Successful revision must require that the reviser bring criteria to bear on the product to be revised. In the Sager (1973a) study, sixth-grade students were provided with prompts implying criteria to use as guides in revising. A useful study might systematically examine the relative effects of these three approaches to teaching criteria (models, scales, and revision) and then proceed to examine their interactions.

Similarly, the problem of feedback may be examined most profitably in terms of its interactions with other aspects of instruction. Case studies might examine how students react to diffuse and abstract feedback as opposed to how they react to focused and specific feedback, and whether those conditions have different effects for different age groups. But perhaps more important is to examine the nature of feedback in relation to the focus and mode of instruction. If prewriting instruction is ineffective, one would not expect feedback to be effective. On the other hand, if some focus of instruction is known to be effective, one might expect feedback with a related focus to be effective when the two are used in conjunction. For example, if prewriting instruction involves inquiry, specifically the development and support of generalizations, feedback might then focus on the adequacy of the generalizations and support produced by students. Initially, these hypotheses might be examined through case studies, and later through experimental studies.

Proceeding with Research

Even the above brief discussion of variables indicates an enormous amount of research to be done. One hopes that the research effort in teaching composition will continue to expand. At the same time, one hopes that the quality of both experimental and case-study research will improve. It would be possible to make a long list of recommendations about sample size, the use of statistical methods, and other technical matters. But those are available elsewhere. I would like, instead, to discuss a few less technical but recurrent problems: the selection or development of research problems, the use and description of controls, the reporting of data, the need for programs of research, and the use of different modes of research.

Research Problems

Such a great abundance of questions for research exists that it may be difficult to know where to begin. Not all questions are significant. Some of the research problems examined for this review appear to have been selected almost at random, or at least without much reflection. Unfortunately, the costs of doing research do not vary with the significance of the question. A good research design will be just as costly for a trivial problem as for a significant one. While no one can predict which questions will be most significant, researchers would be well-advised to develop a rationale for posing the problems they wish to address. Such a rationale would include a careful examination of existing evidence and theoretical statements, the development of related hypotheses, and the conducting of preliminary field tests of various kinds—including observation, case studies, and small-scale experiments. Field tests might have revealed to one researcher that two days of instruction on using certain criteria would not be likely to affect the quality of student writing, to another that two days of reading lists of words would not affect comprehension or composition abilities, and to a third that the size of writing paper would have no effect on the quality of writing. This is not to say that findings of no significant differences are inconsequential. They are not. It is simply a plea for carefully thought-out hypotheses within at least the beginnings of a theoretical framework.

Controls

Many of the studies examined for this review paid scant attention to controls. In qualitative research studies, control groups were almost universally absent. While this is understandable, it severely limits the assertions which can be made, especially when those assertions have to do with conditions thought to be responsible for the way students write or learn to write. When the concern is with conditions affecting writing, it is a relatively simple matter to vary the conditions and observe the effects of the change.

Perhaps the most important problem in case-study research is what might be called "observer controls." Most case studies examined for this review made no attempt to document the validity or reliability of the categories used. Several did not use categories but relied on narrative descriptions, which included a mixture of what appears to be fact and value judgment. For the research to be convincing we need evidence that two or more observers watching the same phenomena recorded the same facts. And because behavior such as writing is quite complex, some clearly elucidated system of categories may be required to make sense of the bits of behavior that are recorded. The interpretation of the behavior presents an even greater problem. As we have seen, for example, Emig (1971) offers an interpretation of the comments her subjects made as they turned in their pieces of writing. Emig interprets comments such as, "Well, I guess that's it," and "Here it is," to indicate that her subjects care nothing about what they have written. This interpretation is used later to support other contentions. But as suggested in Chapter 1 of this review, other interpretations of the student comments are possible, perhaps even likely.

If one were interested in the attitudes of students toward their writing for researchers, it would be useful to (1) contrast those attitudes with attitudes toward writing under other conditions (e.g., school or personal), (2) determine which behavior expressed attitudes toward writing, (3) establish guidelines for and reliability in recording such behavior, and (4) provide checks on the validity of interpretation of the behaviors recorded.

Some of the same problems obtain in experimental studies. Often the problems are with the adequacy and description of controls. As indicated earlier, control treatments often do not meet even modest standards. In some studies the experimenter teaches all treatment groups. In others, there are no control treatments. In some, the experimenter teaches all experimental treatments, while others teach the control groups. Even when studies incorporate reasonably adequate controls, they frequently say little or nothing about what happens in the control treatments, often dismissing them as "traditional" or "usual."

Careful description of controls will enhance the value of the research results. First, it allows greater precision in examining specific variables within a particular study. Second, it may allow, in the future, comparison of treatments across studies without respect to control or experimental status. Future integrative reviews of research may be better able to examine pretest to posttest effect sizes if studies provide detailed descriptions of the control treatments.

Reporting Data

A surprisingly large number of studies report data inadequately. Many fail to report reliabilities on the scoring of compositions. Others fail to report means and standard deviations for pretest and posttests, instead reporting only probabilities. Some report only parts of the results for analysis of covariance. Some appear to hide results, perhaps because null hypotheses were borne out. With the advent of integrative review methods, adequate reporting of data coupled with adequate descriptions of treatments can provide valuable information, whether the results of a specific study indicate significant differences or nonsignificant differences.

Programs of Research

Few researchers in composition have developed programs of research which set out to explore a range of related variables. Most notable of those who *have* done so, at this writing, are Bereiter, Scardamalia, and their colleagues and Flower, Hayes, and their colleagues. More often, researchers conduct one or two studies which may or may not be related. The value of conducting a series of studies, with subsequent studies exploring the implications of previous ones, should be obvious. Such systematic programs of research are far more likely to provide valuable insight than are scattered studies, even if those studies are related to previous research.

Research Modes

Finally, there has been an unfortunate tendency for researchers working in one mode of research to reject even the possibility of value in the competing mode. Emig (1982) and Graves (1980), for example, have condemned all experimental research as positivistic and scientistic. As this review demonstrates, the results of experimental research can be instructive. Some experimental research is badly flawed, but then the same is true of case-study research. We cannot afford to reject one mode of research in favor of another. Rather, if we wish to understand the processes of composing and to improve the teaching of composition, we need to use whatever modes of research are useful to learn as much as we can.

Implications and Recommendations for Practice

Although we have much to learn from future research, the findings of this review provide some clear directions for practice and policymaking, particularly for grades 6–13, and particularly in two areas: mode of instruction and focus of instruction.

Mode of Instruction

The findings indicate that the dimensions of effective instruction are quite different, on the one hand, from what is commonly practiced in schools and colleges (the presentational mode) and, on the other hand, from what has been recommended by adherents of the natural process mode. In the most common and widespread mode (presentational), the instructor dominates all activity, with students acting as the passive recipients of rules, advice, and examples of good writing.

This is the least effective mode examined—only about half as effective as the average experimental treatment.

In the natural process mode, the instructor encourages students to write for other students, to receive comments from them, and to revise their drafts in light of comments from both students and the instructor. But the instructor does not plan activities to help develop specific strategies of composing. This instructional mode is about 25 percent less effective than the average experimental treatment, but about 50 percent more effective than the presentational mode. In treatments which examine the effects of individualized work with students, the results are essentially the same.

I have labeled the most effective mode of instruction *environmental*, because it brings teacher, student, and materials more nearly into balance and, in effect, takes advantage of all resources of the classroom. In this mode, the instructor plans and uses activities which result in high levels of student interaction concerning particular problems parallel to those they encounter in certain kinds of writing, e.g., generating criteria and examples to develop extended definitions of concepts or generating arguable assertions from appropriate data and predicting and countering opposing arguments. In contrast to the presentational mode, this mode places priority on high levels of student involvement. In contrast to natural process, the environmental mode places priority on structured problem-solving activities, with clear objectives, planned to enable students to deal with similar problems in composing. On pre-to-post measures, the environmental mode is over four times more effective than the traditional presentational mode and three times more effective than the natural process mode.

To some extent, these three modes of instruction represent an historical progression. The presentational mode is undoubtedly the oldest and certainly the most widespread, dominating not only composition instruction (A. Applebee 1981) but instruction in other areas as well (Goodlad 1984). The natural process mode has intellectual antecedents in Rousseau's *Emile* and in some interpretations of Dewey's work. As it affects writing instruction in the United States, its more recent roots can be traced to the Dartmouth Conference (see, for example, John Dixon 1967) and to the work of Emig (1971), which emphasize the need to attend to the process of writing as part of instruction. In a very real sense, what I have called the natural process movement, dating from the 1960s, was and is a reaction against the dominant presentational mode with its often arbitrary assignments given with no preparation; with its structures to be learned from rigid models, such as the "five-paragraph theme"; and with its emphasis on the "correctness" of products. Certainly, there is a need for young writers to learn that writing involves more than imitating models "correctly."

Environmental instruction has intellectual antecedents in the work of Herbart and Dewey. In composition, however, it appears to be relatively recent. Even though some studies date to the 1960s, its strategies have not received the attention accorded natural process approaches to teaching writing. Environmental instruction moves beyond process without abandoning it. Exponents of such instruction, for instance, recognize the need for prewriting. However, in instructional situations they focus on prewriting activities which help develop skills to be used in ensuing writing. They assume that something more than discussing general ideas and jotting notes is necessary, especially if students are to learn dimensions of writing which are new to them.

At the same time, environmental instruction may incorporate certain elements common to presentational instruction. For example, it may recognize the need for students to be aware of form and may use model pieces of writing. But it differs from the presentational in emphasizing activities which help students learn the procedures for instantiating the forms.

Environmental instruction, then, incorporates elements of both the presentational and the natural process modes, but moves beyond both to suggest more powerful approaches to teaching composition.

Focus of Instruction

Like modes of instruction, the foci of instruction examined have important ramifications for instructional practice.

The study of traditional school grammar (i.e., the definition of parts of speech, the parsing of sentences, etc.) has no effect on raising the quality of student writing. Every other focus of instruction examined in this review is stronger. Taught in certain ways, grammar and mechanics instruction has a deleterious effect on student writing. In some studies a heavy emphasis on mechanics and usage (e.g., marking every error) resulted in significant losses in overall quality. School boards, administrators, and teachers who impose the systematic study of traditional school grammar on their students over lengthy periods of time in the name of teaching writing do them a gross disservice which should not be tolerated by anyone concerned with the effective teaching of good writing. We need to learn how to teach standard usage and mechanics after careful task analysis and with minimal grammar.

What I have referred to as teaching from models undoubtedly has a place in the English program. This research indicates that emphasis on the presentation of good pieces of writing as models is significantly more useful than the study of grammar. At the same time, treatments which use the study of models almost exclusively are less effective than other available techniques.

The focus of free writing asks students to write freely about whatever interests or concerns them. As a major instructional technique, free writing is more effective than teaching grammar in raising the quality of student writing. However, it is less effective than any other focus of instruction examined. Even when examined in conjunction with other features of the "process" model of teaching writing (writing for peers, feedback from peers, revision, and so forth), these treatments are only about two-thirds as effective as the average experimental treatment.

The practice of building more complex sentences from simpler ones has been shown to be effective in a large number of experimental studies. This research shows sentence combining, on the average, to be more than twice as effective as free writing as a means of enhancing the quality of student writing.

Scales, criteria, and specific questions which students apply to their own or others' writing also have a powerful effect on enhancing quality. Through using the criteria systematically, students appear to internalize them and bring them to bear in generating new material even when they do not have the criteria in front of them. These treatments are two times more effective than free writing techniques.

Inquiry focuses the attention of students on strategies for dealing with sets of data, strategies which will be used in writing. For example, treatments categorized as inquiry might involve students in the following: finding and stating specific details which convey personal experience vividly, examining sets of data to develop and support explanatory generalizations, or analyzing situations which present problems of various kinds and developing arguments about those situations. On the average, these treatments are nearly four times more effective than free writing and over two-and-a-half times more powerful than the traditional study of model pieces of writing.

While the results for the various treatments differ greatly from each other, this does not imply that the less-effective techniques have no place in the writing curriculum. Indeed, sentence combining, scales, and inquiry all make occasional use of models, but they certainly do not emphasize the study of models exclusively. And structured free writing, in which writers jot down all of their ideas on a particular topic, can be successfully integrated with other techniques as a means of both memory search and invention.

Ramifications for Policymakers

The above results have important ramifications for those in positions to make and recommend policy at local, state, and national levels. Unfortunately, recommendations at the state and national levels are likely to have little effect on classroom practice without funds designated for training teachers how to use the more effective teaching strategies. Surveys of instructional practices indicate clearly that the vast majority of teachers do not have the most effective teaching strategies in their repertoires. Nor will hearing about them help much. To learn the strategies, teachers will have to learn the theories underlying them, discuss the strategies, develop their own materials for use in their own classrooms, try those strategies and materials, discuss the results with others, try them again, and cycle through the process again.

Mandates by local boards of education on curricular matters can have greater impact. Boards, for example, which require that large amounts of time be spent on the study of traditional grammar can expect lower achievement in actual writing than those which do not. Boards which mandate the more effective methods *and* which make funds available to teach teachers how to use them can expect higher levels of achievement in writing.

Further, without effective in-service and pre-service training, recommendations are likely to have little or no effect. To provide for such training, funding will be required for efforts such as the following:

1. The National Writing Project and its affiliated agencies already have demonstrated their ability to change the behaviors of teachers of composition. Several writing projects, such as the Bay Area, Colorado, and New Jersey Projects, have provided evidence of gains in the writing of students taught by teachers attending summer workshops. The National Writing Project has over 120 affiliates in at least forty-four states and could well be the most effective agent for change.

   The Writing Project at the University of California at Irvine has engaged teachers in developing materials which use inquiry and environmental instruction—the most effective focus and mode of instruction identified by this research. Given appropriate funding, participants in projects like the one at Irvine can provide leadership in moving others toward increasingly effective instruction.

2. We need national institutes for college and university faculty who are responsible for teaching others the most effective methods of teaching writing. Without effective training at this level, new practitioners entering the field are likely to rely on such relatively ineffective foci of instruction as grammar and free writing—neither of which requires much understanding of the dynamics of composing.

3. Local in-service training programs can involve teachers in learning about more effective techniques, collaborative planning for the use of those techniques across the writing curriculum, systematic observation and evaluation of their use and results, and continued revision. Such in-service obviously requires more than the one or two days available in most school systems. It may require summer workshops, released time during the school day for planning and observing, and time for follow-up evaluations and revisions. Without such a serious commitment, change in teachers' behavior and, therefore, in students' writing is likely to be negligible.

4. Although this review provides directions for improving instruction, it also indicates necessary research efforts. Funding is required to support and coordinate those efforts by teams working on different parts of the problem. Without coordination, research may continue to be an atheoretical, hit-and-miss affair.

The research of the past two decades indicates clear directions. If we wish our schools and colleges to teach writing effectively, we cannot retreat to the grammar book or rely on the presentation of rules and advice, or expect students to teach themselves how to write effectively simply by writing whatever they wish for varied groups of their peers. We must make systematic use of instructional techniques which are demonstrably more effective. We must also continue our efforts to evaluate and understand those techniques, and to develop new instructional procedures.

Bibliography

The entries in this bibliography are placed in two categories: references for the present study and additional bibliographic resources. An asterisk after a dissertation entry indicates that the dissertation itself was examined rather than just the abstract from *DA* or *DAI*. ED numbers refer to documents in the ERIC system (see p. 355 for ordering information). The following abbreviations for journals and organizations are used:

ABCA—American Business Communication Association
AERA—American Educational Research Association
AERJ—American Educational Research Journal
BJEP—British Journal of Educational Psychology
BJER—British Journal of Educational Research
CCC—College Composition and Communication
CCCC—Conference on College Composition and Communication
CE—College English
DA—Dissertation Abstracts
DAI—Dissertation Abstracts International
EJ—English Journal
JEM—Journal of Educational Measurement
JEP—Journal of Educational Psychology
JER—Journal of Educational Research
LA—Language Arts
MLA—Modern Language Association
NCTE—National Council of Teachers of English
RTE—Research in the Teaching of English

References for the Present Study

Abartis, C., and C. Collins. "The Effect of Writing Instruction and Reading Methodology upon College Students' Reading Skills." *Journal of Reading* 23 (1980): 408–13.

Abraham, G. R. "A Comparison of Freshman Composition Grading Standards between Public Two-Year and Four-Year Institutions of Higher Education in the Southern Association of Colleges and Schools." *DAI* 37 (1976): 1420-A.

Abrahamson, R. F. *The Effects of Formal Grammar Instruction vs. the Effects of Sentence Combining Instruction on Student Writing: A Collection of Evaluative Abstracts of Pertinent Research Documents.* 1977. ED 145 450.

Ackerman, P. G., Jr. "The Effect of Size of Writing Paper on College Freshman Composition Course Writing." *DAI* 36 (1976): 5266-A.

Adams, F. B. "A Study of Writing as a Counseling Technique." *DAI* 41 (1981): 3878-A.

Adams, R. R., and L. Brody. *An Evaluation of the Written Composition of High School Students in Five College Discovery Centers in New York City. Research Report.* New York: City University of New York, Division of Teacher Education, 1968. ED 035 704.

Adams, V. A. "A Study of the Effects of Two Methods of Teaching Composition to Twelfth Graders." Diss., University of Illinois at Champaign-Urbana, 1971.*

Adamson, H. K. "Competence Demonstrated by English Majors and Majors in Other Areas in Selected Factors of Written Communication." *DA* 24 (1964): 5212.

Adkins, B. "An Analysis of Business Communications Skills and Knowledges as Perceived by Selected Businesspersons, Teachers, and Students in Kentucky." *DAI* 41 (1981): 3545-A.

Adler, A. "Content-Free Analysis of Composition Content." *DAI* 42 (1982): 3893-A.

Adler, R. "An Investigation of the Factors Which Affect the Quality of Essays by Advanced Placement Students." *DAI* 32 (1972): 5645-A.

Agler, L. S. "Evaluation of Teaching English by Open-Circuit Television in a Community College." *DAI* 38 (1978): 5859-A.

Ajay, H. B. "Strategies for Content Analysis of Essays by Computer." *DAI* 34 (1973): 2375-A.

Akeju, S. A. "The Reliability of General Certificate of Education Examination English Composition Papers in West Africa." *JEM* 9, no. 2 (Summer 1972): 175–80.

Aleamoni, L. M., and S. B. Eitelbach. "Comparison of Six Examinations Given in Rhetoric 101, at the University of Illinois, Fall 1965." *Research in Higher Education* 4 (1976): 347–54.

Allen, A. E. "Frequency and Control of Selected Syntactic Structures as Related to Quality Rating of Written Expression." *DAI* 32 (1972): 4477-A.

Allen, C. L. "A Study of the Effect of Selected Mechanical Errors on Teachers' Evaluation of the Non-mechanical Aspects of Students' Writing." *DAI* 37 (1977): 5554-A. ED 147 812.*

Allen, F. A., Jr. "A Comparison of the Effectiveness of the Intensive and Concurrent Scheduling Plans for Teaching First-Semester English Composition in the Community College." *DAI* 35 (1975): 5766-A.

Allen, R. H. *A Comparison of the Reading and Language Skills Performances of Boys and Girls.* Bulletin No. 9341. Madison, Wisconsin: Wisconsin State Department of Public Instruction, 1977. ED 155 614.

Alloway, E., J. Carroll, J. Emig, B. King, I. Marcotrigiano, J. Smith, and W. Spicer. *The New Jersey Writing Project.* New Brunswick, New Jersey: Rutgers University, The Educational Testing Program Service, and Nineteen New Jersey Public School Districts, 1979. ED 178 943.

Alpren, P. F. "Can Children Be Helped to Increase the Originality of Their Story Writing." *RTE* 7 (1973): 372–86.

———. "An Investigation of Whether Feedback about 'Originality' of Story Writing Is Associated with Increased Originality in Subsequent Writings of Fifth-Grade Students." *DAI* 33 (1972): 1579-A.*

Altschull, J. H., and E. Einsiedel. "Study Shows Newswriting Difficult to Judge Objectively." *Journalism Educator* 30, no. 1 (1975): 43–47.

Anderson, H. E., Jr., and W. L. Bashaw. "An Experimental Study of First Grade Theme Writing." *AERJ* 5 (1968): 239–47. ED 027 290.

Anderson, J. E. "An Evaluation of Various Indices of Linguistic Development." *Child Development* 8 (1937): 62–68.

Anderson, R. B. "A Study of the Relationship between Set Induction and Originality in the Creative Writings of Elementary School Children." *DAI* 34 (1974): 6490-A.

Anderson, V., C. Bereiter, and D. Smart. "Activation of Semantic Networks in Writing: Teaching Students How To Do It Themselves." Paper, Annual Meeting of AERA, 1980.

Andreach, J. R. "The Use of Models to Improve Organizational Techniques in Writing." *DAI* 36 (1976): 4980-A.

Andrich, D. "Latent Trait Psychometric Theory in the Measurement and Evaluation of Essay Writing Ability." Diss., University of Chicago, 1973.*

Andrich, D., and R. Hake. "The Application of a Discourse Theory and a Rasch Model for Measuring in the Evaluation of Written Expression." *Education Research and Perspectives* (Australia) 1, no. 2 (December 1974): 51–61.

Annese, C. "An Examination of English Skills Programs in New Jersey Public Two-Year Colleges." *DAI* 40 (1980): 3722-A.

Antico, J. "An Experiment in the Cooperative Grading of the Research Paper." *CCC* 19 (1968): 145–48.

Antista, J. A. "A Comparative Study of Computer-Assisted and Non Computer-Assisted Instruction in Senior High School English Classes." *DAI* 35 (1975): 7600-A.

Apple, N. C., and P. O. Tierney. *Two Studies of Composition and Literature Objectives for Gifted and Academically Talented Pupils.* Pittsburgh, Pennsylvania: University of Pittsburgh, 1979. ED 189 633.

Applebee, A. N. *The Child's Concept of Story: Ages Two to Seventeen.* Chicago: University of Chicago Press, 1978a.

———. *A Survey of Teaching Conditions in English, 1977.* Urbana, Illinois: ERIC/RCS and NCTE, 1978. ED 151 796.

———. "Teaching Conditions in Secondary School English: Highlights of a Survey." *EJ* 67, no. 3 (March 1978b): 57–65.

———. "Teaching High-Achieving Students: A Survey of the Winners of the 1977 NCTE Achievement Awards in Writing." *RTE* 12 (1978c): 339–48, 338.

———. *Writing in the Secondary School: English and the Content Areas.* NCTE Research Report #21. Urbana, Illinois: NCTE, 1981.

Applebee, A. N., F. Lehr, and A. Auten. "Learning to Write in the Secondary School: How and Where." *EJ* 70, no. 5 (September 1981): 78–82.

———. *A Study of Writing in the Secondary School. Final Report.* Urbana, Illinois: NCTE, 1980. ED 197 347.

Applebee, R. K. "National Study of High School English Programs: A Record of English Teaching Today." *EJ* 55 (1966): 273–81.

Applebee, R., D. Applequist, R. W. Johannsen, R. A. Jones, R. E. Kallio, H. S. Maclay, and J. J. Scanlon. *Report on the Status of Student Writing in the College.* Urbana, Illinois: University of Illinois, College of Liberal Arts and Sciences, 1976. ED 133 772.

Ardell, V. "A Study of the Effects of Two Methods of Teaching Composition to Twelfth Graders." Ph.D. diss., University of Illinois at Urbana-Champaign, 1973.

Armbrecht, B. G. "The Effects of Sentence-Combining Practice on the Syntactic Maturity, Quality of Writing, and Reading Comprehension of a Select Group of College Students in Remedial English in Southeast Georgia." *DAI* 42 (1981): 1071-A.

Armstrong, A. C. "A Comparison of the Garrison Method and the Traditional Method of Teaching Composition in a Community College." *DAI* 40 (1980): 6127-A.

Armstrong, R. D. "An Objective Measure of the Quality of the Written Composition of Fifth-Grade Pupils." *DA* 26 (1966): 7174.

Arnold, L. V. "Effects of Frequency of Writing and Intensity of Teacher Evaluation upon Performance in Written Composition of Tenth Grade Students." *DA* 24 (1963): 1021-A.

———. "Writer's Cramp and Eyestrain—Are They Paying Off?" *EJ* 53 (1964): 10–15.

Arthur, S. V. "The Effects of Two Writing Treatments on the Reading and Writing of Third Graders." *DAI* 41 (1981): 4278-A.

Ashe, M. R. B. "A Study of Change Measured Personality Adjustment and Release of Creativity through Freedom of Expression in Writing." *DA* 26 (1963): 860.

Ashida, M. E. "Form, Syntax and Statistics: A Quantitative Approach to Written Composition." Diss., University of Nebraska, 1967.*

———. "Something for Everyone: A Standard Corpus of Contemporary American Expository Essays." *RTE* 2 (1968): 14–23.

Ashida, M. E., and L. T. Whipp. "A Slide-Rule Composition Course." *CE* 25 (1963): 18–22.

Atlas, M. A. *Addressing an Audience: A Study of Expert-Novice Differences in Writing. Technical Report No. 3.* New York: Siegel & Gale, Inc., 1979. ED 192 338.

———. "Expert-Novice Differences in the Writing Process." Paper, Annual Meeting of AERA, 1979. ED 170 769.

———. "Writer Insensitivity to Audience—Causes and Cures." Paper, Annual Meeting of AERA, 1980. ED 185 568.

Atwell, M. A. "The Evolution of Text: The Interrelationship of Reading and Writing in the Composing Process." *DAI* 42 (1981): 116-A.

Aubrey, G. O. "Oral and Written Expression—The Early Stages." *Opinion* (Australia) 11, no. 3 (December 1967): 5–13. ED 029 863.

Auguste, J. A., and F. B. Nalven. "ITA and TO Training in the Development of Children's Creative Writing." *RTE* 3 (1969): 178–80.

Aven, S. D., and M. Chrisp. "English Proficiency of Males and Females—Is There a Difference?" 1967. ED 015 213.

Avery, L. A. Y. "A Comparative Analysis of the Professional Background of

Secondary English Teachers in Harris County, Texas, in the Southwest, and in the Nation." *DAI* 32 (1971): 2293-A.

Ayscue, V. G. "A Descriptive Study of the Teaching of Composition in North Carolina Public High Schools: 1964–1969." *DAI* 33 (1972): 1557-A.

Badaczewski, D. S. "Seventeen Elements of Prose Style and Their Relationship to Superior, Average and Poor Student Compositions." *DAI* 32 (1972): 5528-A.

Baden, M. J. P. "A Comparison of Composition Scores of Third-Grade Children with Reading Skills, Pre-Kindergarten Verbal Ability, Self-Concept, and Sex." *DAI* 42 (1981): 1517-A.

Baden, R. C. "College Freshman Can't(?) Write." *CCC* 25 (1974a): 430–33.

———. "Freshman English: An Action Analysis of Two Models." *DAI* 35 (1974b): 392-A.

Baggett, R. C. "A Transformational Analysis of Syntax in Tenth-Grade Writing." *DAI* 39 (1978): 846-A.*

Bailey, P. L. "The Adolescent Writer's Developing Sense of Audience: Implications for Teaching." *DAI* 40 (1979): 3276-A.

Bailey, R. W., R. T. Brengle, and E. L. Smith, Jr. "Measuring Student Writing Ability." Paper, Annual Meeting of the Canadian Council of Teachers of English, 1979. ED 175 009.

Baird, R. C. "Survey of Errors in English Compositions." *JER* 56 (1963): 228–35.

Baker, G. A. P. "The Efficiency of Diagnostic, Readiness, and Achievement Instruments as Predictors of Language Arts Achievement: A Longitudinal Study from Kindergarten through Second Grade." *DAI* 30 (1970): 3624-A.

Baker, P. "Sabbatical Report: A Study of College Freshman English Courses." 1980. ED 199 712.

Baker, W. H. "A Study to Determine the Effectiveness of Letter Evaluation as a Learning Device in Business Correspondence Courses." *DAI* 36 (1976): 6431-A.*

Ballard, K. D., and T. Glynn. "Behavioral Self-Management in Story Writing with Elementary School Children." *Journal of Applied Behavior Analysis* 8 (1975): 387–98.

Bamberg, B. J. "Composition Basics for College Prep Students." Paper, Annual Meeting of the California Association of Teachers of English, 1977. ED 149 351.

———. "Composition in the Secondary English Curriculum: Some Current Trends and Directions for the Eighties." *RTE* 15 (1981): 257–66.

———. "Composition Instruction Does Make a Difference: A Comparison of the High School Preparation of College Freshmen in Regular and Remedial English Classes." *RTE* 12 (1978): 47–59. ED 140 342.

———. "Relationships among Attitudes toward Language Activities, Composition Instruction, and Composition Achievement." *DAI* 37 (1976): 107-A.

Barbig, E. V. "An Exploration of Growth in Written Composition to Determine the Relationship of Selected Variables to Poor Writing in Grades Nine and Twelve." *DA* 29 (1969): 2140-A.

Barkman, P. R. "The Role of the Planning Board in the Writing of College Freshmen." *DAI* 42 (1981): 2112-A.

Barksdale, M. *A Program to Discover an Effective Method of Teaching Communication Skills to College Freshmen Who Have One or More Deficiencies in the Ability to Communicate in Writing.* Ft. Worth, Texas: Tarrant County Junior College, 1971. ED 056 029.

Barrett, C. J. "The Influence of High School Senior English Teachers and the Senior Courses in High School English on Students' Performance in Freshman Composition at the University of Arkansas." *DAI* 31 (1970): 919-A.

Bata, E. J. "A Study of the Relative Effectiveness of Marking Techniques on Junior College Freshman English Composition." *DAI* 34 (1973): 62-A.*

Bateman, D. R. "More Mature Writing through a Better Understanding of Language Structure." *EJ* 50 (1961): 457–60, 468.

Bateman, D. R., and F. J. Zidonis. *The Effect of a Knowledge of Generative Grammar upon the Growth of Language Complexity.* Columbus, Ohio: Ohio State University Research Foundation, 1964. ED 001 241.

———. *The Effect of a Study of Transformational Grammar on the Writing of Ninth and Tenth Graders.* Champaign, Illinois: NCTE, 1966. ED 018 424.

Bator, P. G. "The Impact of Cognitive Development upon Audience Awareness in the Writing Process." *DAI* 41 (1980): 653-A.

Battista, J. R. "The Effects of a Triad Method of Teaching on the Attitudes of Twelfth Graders toward a Business English Course." *DAI* 42 (1982): 3124-A.

Battle, M. V. "Error Reduction by Freshman Writers and Its Relationship to Grouping." Paper, Annual Meeting of CCCC, 1980. ED 188 170.

Bavery, E. A. "A Study of Selected Aspects of Oral and Written Language of Fifth Grade Pupils." *DA* 29 (1968), 397-A.

Bay Area Writing Project. *Bay Area Writing Project/California Writing Project/National Writing Project: An Overview.* Berkeley, California: University of California, School of Education, 1979. ED 184 123.

Bay, L., and E. McCulloch. "Towards Uniformity in Grading Standards." Paper, Annual Meeting of the New York State English Council, 1976. ED 137 782.

Beach, R. "The Effects of Between-Draft Teacher Evaluation Versus Student Self-Evaluation on High School Students' Revising of Rough Drafts." *RTE* 13 (1979): 111–119.

———. "Self-Evaluation Strategies of Extensive Revisers and Nonrevisers." *CCC* 27 (1976): 160–64.

Bean, A. S. "A Descriptive Study of Creative Writing at the Junior High School Level." *DAI* 35 (1974): 3288-A. ED 101 347.

Beard, J. D. "Toward a Rationale for Analyzing Writing in Peer Groups." *DAI* 40 (1980): 5299-A.

Bebensee, E. L. "The Relationship between Inner-City Fifth-Graders' Reading Comprehension and Writing Achievement." *DAI* 39 (1978): 166-A.

Bechtel, J. "Videotape Analysis of the Composing Processes of Six Male College Freshmen Writers." Paper, Annual Meeting of the Midwest Regional Conference on English in the Two-Year College, 1979. ED 177 558.

Beckstrand, P. E. "The Adaptation of Transactional Analysis as a Means to the Teaching of Written Expression in High School." *DAI* 33 (1972): 1409-A.

Beeker, R. A. "The Effects of Oral Planning on Fifth-Grade Composition." *DAI* 30 (1970): 4870-A.

Beidler, A. E. "The Effects of the Peabody Language Development Kits on the Intelligence, Reading, Listening, and Writing of Disadvantaged Children in the Primary Grades." *DA* 29 (1969): 3760-A.

Belanger, J. F. "Calculating the Syntactic Density Score: A Mathematical Problem." *RTE* 12 (1978a): 149–53.

———. "Reading Skill as an Influence on Writing Skill." Diss., University of Alberta, 1978b. ED 163 409.*

Bell, E., and A. Price. "Some Effects of Induced Grade Anxiety on Motivation and Performance in Composition Sections." Paper, Annual Meeting of the Pennsylvania Council of Teachers of English, 1980. ED 197 379.

Bell, E. S. "Training the Tutor: A Comparison of Attitudes toward Writing." Paper, Spring Conference of the South Carolina Council of Teachers of English, 1981. ED 199 766.

Bell, J. B. "A Study of the Written Composition Interests of Senior High School Students." *DAI* 32 (1971): 1257-A.

Bell, J. E. "An Investigation of Narrative Blend in the Expository Writing of Students Enrolled in Introductory College Composition Courses." *DAI* 42 (1981): 1518-A.

Bell, K. B. A. "A Report of Practices, Procedures, and Materials Used by Teachers to Develop Pupil Competencies in Original Written Composition, Grades Three through Six in the Houston, Texas, Public Schools." *DA* 24 (1963): 2380.

Bennett, B. "The Process of Writing and the Development of Writing Abilities, 15 to 18: Australian Research in Progress." Paper, Annual Meeting of the Canadian Council of Teachers of English, 1979. ED 174 984.

Bennett, B., and A. Walker. "The Development of Writing Abilities, 15 to 17: Research in Progress." *English in Australia* no. 44 (June 1978): 5–15.

Bennett, J. C. "Using the Typewriter for Learning: Composing." *Balance Sheet* 58 (1977): 244–46, 248–49.

Bennett, J. R., B. Brigham, S. Carson, J. Fleischauer, T. Kobler, F. Park, and A. Thies. "The Paragraph: An Annotated Bibliography." *Style* 11 (1977): 107–18.

Bennett, M. F. "A Comparison of Two Methods for Teaching Structure in Writing to Remedial Students in an Urban Community College." *DAI* 33 (1972): 2728-A.

Bennett, M. K. "The Relationship between Composition Teachers' Ability to Write and the Writing Achievement of Their Students." *DAI* 42 (1981): 2058-A.

Bennett, N. *Teaching Styles and Pupil Progress.* Cambridge, Massachusetts: Harvard University Press, 1976.

Bennett, R. A. "A Comparison of the Effects of Programmed Instruction and Lecture-Textbook Instruction on English Language Learning of Eleventh Grade Students." *DA* 26 (1966): 7109.

Benson, B. A. "A Quantitative Analysis of Language Structures in Compositions Written by First and Second Language Learners." *DAI* 41 (1980): 1984-A.

Benson, N. L. "The Effects of Peer Feedback During the Writing Process on Writing Performance, Revision Behavior, and Attitude toward Writing." *DAI* 40 (1979): 1987-A.*

Bereiter, C. "Development in Writing." In *Cognitive Processes In Writing.* Edited by L. W. Gregg and E. R. Steinberg, 73–93. Hillsdale, New Jersey: Lawrence Erlbaum Associates, Publishers, 1980.

Bereiter, C., J. Fine, and S. Gartshore. "An Exploratory Study of Microplanning in Writing." Paper, Annual Meeting of AERA, 1979.

Bereiter, C., and M. Scardamalia. "Cognitive Demands of Writing as Related to Discourse Type." Paper, Annual Meeting of AERA, 1978.

———. "From Conversation to Composition: The Role of Instruction in a Developmental Process." In *Advances in Instructional Psychology*, Vol. 2. Edited by R. Glaser, 1–64. Hillsdale, New Jersey: Lawrence Erlbaum Associates, Publishers, 1982.

Bereiter, C., M. Scardamalia, V. Anderson, and D. Smart. "An Experiment in Teaching Abstract Planning in Writing." Paper, Annual Meeting of AERA, 1980.

Bereiter, C., M. Scardamalia, and L. Turkish. "The Child as Discourse Grammarian." Paper, Annual Meeting of AERA, 1980.

Berger, G. "The Effect of Structure and Topic on Dialect Usage in Written English." *DA* 29 (1968): 1862-A.

Berghoff, P. J. "The Effects of an Instructor's Written Reactions on Student Logs upon Certain Student Perceptions, Attitudes, Values, and Behaviors." *DAI* 32 (1972): 3773-A.

Bergman, F. L. "The Construction and Analysis of an Objective Test Measuring the Ability of High School Students to Write Assigned Compositions." *DA* 27 (1967): 2266-A.

Bergmann, P. J. "An Analysis of Television Commercials as a Vehicle to Improved Comprehension and Performance of Writing: An Alternative Means of Teaching Freshman Composition." *DAI* 38 (1977): 1913-A.

Berkenkotter, C. "Understanding a Writer's Awareness of Audience." *CCC* 32 (1981): 388–99.

Bernard, M. E. "Does Sex Role Behavior Influence the Way Teachers Evaluate Students?" *JEP* 71 (1979): 553–62.

Bernhardt, N. W. "Trends in the Teaching of English Written Composition in the Secondary Schools of the United States: 1900–1960." *DA* 24 (1964): 3192.

Berse, P. "Criteria for the Assessment of Pupils' Compositions." *Educational Research* 17 (1974): 54–61.

Bevis, H. A., R. E. Carpenter, D. J. Faricy, D. L. Kelly, C. Morris, K. Ritch, J. Webb, and W. Hellstrom. "Report of the Taskforce on Composition." 1978. ED 177 570.

Biberstine, R. D. "Fourth Graders Do Write about Their Problems." *Elementary English* 45 (1968): 731–35. ED 035 655.

———. "Response to Personal Writing." *LA* 54 (1977): 791–93.

———. "A Study of Selected Areas of Teacher Influence upon the Written Composition of Fourth Graders." *DA* 27 (1967): 3604-A. ED 030 648.

Biesbrock, E. F. "The Development and Use of a Standardized Instrument for Measuring Composition Ability in Young Children (Grades Two and Three)." *DA* 29 (1969): 4175-A.

———. "A Study of Composition Ability as Assessed with a Standardized Instrument for Second and Third Grade Children." 1969. ED 029 696.

Biesbrock, E. F., and L. R. Veal. "A Study Comparing Global Quality and

Syntactic Maturity in the Written Composition of Second and Third Grade Students." Paper, Annual Meeting of AERA, 1969. ED 029 697.

Biola, H. R. "Performance Variables in Essay Testing." *DAI* 40 (1980): 5410-A.

Bippus, A. C. M. "The Relationship of the Quality of Students' Written Language, Productivity of Writing, and Reading Comprehension in Grades Four and Six." *DAI* 38 (1978): 3993-A.

Birnbaum, J. C. "A Study of Reading and Writing Behaviors of Selected Fourth Grade and Seventh Grade Students." *DAI* 42 (1981): 152-A.

Bissex, G. L. "Patterns of Development in Writing: Case Study of a Child from Five to Ten Years Old." Paper, Annual Meeting of the National Conference on Language Arts in the Elementary School, 1979. ED 188 232.

Bivens, W. P., III, and A. B. Edwards. "Transformational Grammar and Writing Improvement." Paper, Annual Meeting of CCCC, 1974. ED 101 361.

Blades, S. "Poetry and Linguistic Awareness." 1980. ED 188 194.

Blake, B. W. "The Composing Process of Adult Basic Writing Students." *DAI* 41 (1981): 4388-A.

Blake, H., and N. A. Spennato. "The Directed Writing Activity: A Process with Structure." *LA* 57 (1980): 317–18.

Blass, T., and A. W. Siegman. "A Psycholinguistic Comparison of Speech, Dictation and Writing." *Language and Speech* 18 (1975): 20–34.

Bloom, B. S. *Human Characteristics and School Learning.* New York: McGraw Hill, 1976.

Bloom, B. S., and L. A. Sosniak. "Talent Development vs. Schooling." *Educational Leadership* 39, no. 2 (November 1981): 86–94.

Bloom, L. Z. "The Composing Processes of Anxious and Non-Anxious Writers: A Naturalistic Study." Paper, Annual Meeting of CCCC, 1980. ED 185 559.

Bloom, L. Z., and M. Bloom. "Stereotypes Examined: The Relation between Learning Grammar and Mechanics and the Ability to Write College Compositions." Paper, Annual Meeting of CCCC, 1977. ED 141 830.

Blount, N. S., W. C. Fredrick, and S. L. Johnson. *The Effect of a Study of Grammar on the Writing of Eighth-Grade Students. Technical Report No. 69.* Madison, Wisconsin: Wisconsin Research and Development Center for Cognitive Learning, The University of Wisconsin, 1968. ED 036 515.

Blount, N. S., S. L. Johnson, and W. C. Fredrick. *A Comparison of the Writing of Eighth- and Twelfth-Grade Students. Technical Report No. 78.* Madison, Wisconsin: Wisconsin Research and Development Center for Cognitive Learning, University of Wisconsin, 1968. ED 035 652.

Blount, N. S., W. C. Fredrick, and S. L. Johnson. *Measures of Writing Maturity from Two 500-Word Writing Samples. Technical Report No. 97.* Madison, Wisconsin: University of Wisconsin, Wisconsin Research and Development Center for Cognitive Learning, 1969. ED 036 522.

Blount, N. S., H. J. Klausmeier, S. L. Johnson, W. C. Fredrick, and J. G. Ramsay. *The Effectiveness of Programed Materials in English Syntax and the Relationship of Selected Variables to the Learning of Concepts. Technical Report No. 17.* Madison, Wisconsin: University of Wisconsin, 1967. ED 013 256.

Bodkin, A. Z. "Children's Writing: Selected Differences by Sex, Grade Level, and Socioeconomic Status." *DAI* 39 (1978): 1317-A.

―――. "Observed Differences in the Written Expression of Boys and Girls." In *The Writing Processes of Students*. Edited by W. Petty and P. Finn, 71–75. Report of the Annual Conference on Language Arts, State University of New York at Buffalo, 1975.

Boettcher, K. D. *An Experimental Program Offering Junior College Remedial English Instruction Simultaneously to High School Students and Junior College Freshmen via Open Circuit Television. Final Report*. Sacramento, California: American River Junior College, 1968. ED 021 559.

Boggs, S. T., and K. A. Watson-Gegeo. "Interweaving Routines: Strategies for Encompassing a Social Situation." *Language in Society* 7 (1978): 375–92.

Bond, C. A. "A New Approach to Freshman Composition: A Trial of the Christensen Method." *CE* 33 (1972): 623–27.

―――. "The Relationship between Advocated Practices, as Found in Selected Literature and Relevant Research, and the Method and Content Used in the Teaching of Composition in Six Public Senior High Schools, Judged as Having Innovative Curricula, in Three Southeast Michigan Counties." *DAI* 31 (1970): 1503-A.

Bonds, L., and C. Bonds. "The Effects of Positive and Negative Comments on Children's Creative Writing." 1980. ED 200 959.

Book, V. "Some Effects of Apprehension on Writing Performance." Paper, Annual Meeting of ABCA, 1976. ED 132 595.

Borodkin, T. "Teaching Writing through Consciousness-Raising About Language." *DAI* 38 (1978): 3949-A.

Bortz, D. R. "The Written Language Patterns of Intermediate Grade Children When Writing Compositions in Three Forms: Descriptive, Expository, and Narrative." *DAI* 30 (1970): 5332-A.

Bosco, J. A. "Sector Analysis: An Approach to Teaching Fourth Grade Students Certain Aspects of English Sentence Structure." *DA* 28 (1968): 3544-A.*

Bossone, R. M. *The Writing Problems of Remedial English Students in Community Colleges of the City University of New York*. New York: City University of New York Research and Evaluation Unit for Special Programs, 1969. ED 028 778.

Bossone, R. M., and R. L. Larson. *Needed Research in the Teaching of Writing*. New York: Center for Advanced Study in Education, The Graduate School and University Center of the City University of New York, 1980. ED 184 136.

Bossone, R. M., and L. Q. Troyka. *A Strategy for Coping with High School and College Remedial English Problems*. New York: City University of New York, Graduate School and University Center, 1976. ED 130 268.

Bossone, R. M., and M. Weiner. *Three Modes of Teaching Remedial English: A Comparative Analysis; A Pilot Study*. New York: City University of New York, New York Graduate School and University Center, 1973. ED 074 514.

Botel, M., and A. Granowsky. "A Formula for Measuring Syntactic Complexity: A Directional Effort." *EE* 49 (1972): 513–16.

Bouton, K., and G. Tutty. "The Effect of Peer-Evaluated Student Compositions on Writing Improvement." *The English Record* 26, no. 4 (Fall 1975): 64–69.

Bova, R. J. "The Entry Skills, Methods, and Attitudes of the Intermediate Composition Student in a Post-Secondary Composition Program." *DAI* 40 (1980): 5342-A.

Bowden, S. P. "The Effects of Formal, Traditional Grammar Study on the Writing Ability of Secondary School Students." *DAI* 40 (1979), 1389-A.*

Bowes, J. E., and K. R. Stamm. "Science Writing Techniques and Methods: What the Research Tells Us." Paper, Annual Meeting of the Association for Education in Journalism, 1978. ED 166 702.

Bowles, C. E. R. "A Case Study of the Impact of Teacher-Student Interaction on the Remediation of Writing Deficiencies in the Community College." *DAI* 40 (1979): 2496-A.

Boyd, C. A. "Field-Dependence-Independence and Writing and Revision in the Referential, Expressive, and Persuasive Aims." *DAI* 40 (1980): 6196-A.

Boze, N. S. "A Content Analysis of the Methods Course for the Teaching of English in Secondary Schools." *DA* 28 (1967): 137-A.

Bracewell, R. J. "The Ability of Primary School Students to Manipulate Language Form When Writing." Paper, Annual Meeting of AERA, 1980.

Bracewell, R. J., C. Bereiter, and M. Scardamalia. "A Test of Two Myths about Revision." Paper, Annual Meeting of AERA, 1979.

Bracewell, R. J., J. Fine, and L. Ezergaile. "Cohesion as a Guide to Writing Processes." Paper, Annual Meeting of AERA, 1980.

Bracewell, R. J., and M. Scardamalia. "Children's Ability to Integrate Information When They Write." Paper, Annual Meeting of AERA, 1979.

Bracewell, R. J., M. Scardamalia, and C. Bereiter. "The Development of Audience Awareness in Writing." Paper, Annual Meeting of AERA, 1978. ED 154 433.

Braddock, R. "English Composition." In *Encyclopedia of Educational Research*. 4th ed. Edited by R. I. Ebel, 443–61. London: The Macmillan Company, Collier-Macmillan Ltd., 1969. ED 030 662.

———. "Evaluation of Writing Tests." In *Reviews of Selected Published Tests in English*. Edited by A. H. Grommon, 118–26. Urbana, Illinois: NCTE, 1976.

———. "The Frequency and Placement of Topic Sentences in Expository Prose." *RTE* 8 (1974): 287–302.

Braddock, R., and C. R. Statler. *Evaluation of College Level Instruction in Freshman Composition, Part II*. Iowa City, Iowa: University of Iowa, 1968. ED 021 878.

Braddock, R., R. Lloyd-Jones, and L. Schoer. *Research in Written Composition*. Champaign, Illinois: NCTE, 1963. ED 003 374.

Bradshaw, J. R. "An Experimental Study Comparing a Traditional Teacher-Lecture Method with an Individualized Method of Instructing Business Report Writing." *DAI* 35 (1975): 3382-A.*

Braine, M. D. S. "Children's First Word Combinations." *Monographs of the Society for Research in Child Development* 41, no. 1 (1976): entire issue.

Brand, A. G. "The Therapeutic Benefits of Free or Informal Writing among Selected Eighth Graders." 1977. ED 173 853.

Brannan, D. M. "A Comparison of the Errors Made by Grammar and Technical School Students in Alternative Papers in G.C.E. English Language." *BJEP* 36 (1966): 121–23.

Braun, C., and B. Klassen. "A Transformational Analysis of Written Syntactic Structures of Children Representing Varying Ethno-Linguistic Communities." *RTE* 7 (1973): 312–23.

Brazil, J. M. "On Teaching Composition at the Community College." *DAI* 36 (1975): 3431-A.

Breland, H. M. "Multiple-Choice Test Assesses Writing Ability." *Findings* 4, no. 1 (1977): 1–4.

———. *A Study of College English Placement and the Test of Standard Written English* (CEEB RDR 76–77, No. 4, ETS PR-77-1). Princeton, New Jersey: Educational Testing Service, 1976.

Breland, H. M., and J. L. Gaynor. "A Comparison of Direct and Indirect Assessments of Writing Skill." *JEM* 16 (1979): 119–28.

Breneman, B. "Reaction: The Cloze and the Composition Process." Paper, Annual Meeting of NCTE, 1975. ED 117 699.

Bridges, J. B. "An Honors Course in Freshman Composition for the Two-Year College." *DAI* 42 (1981): 980-A.

Bridwell, L. S. "Revising Processes in Twelfth Grade Students' Transactional Writing." *DAI* 40 (1980a): 5765-A.

———. "Revising Strategies in Twelfth Grade Students' Transactional Writing." *RTE* 14 (1980b): 197–222.

Briggs, J., J. Kraft, and G. Venne. "Survey: Writing in the Content Area." Paper, Annual Meeting of Wisconsin Council of Teachers of English, 1981. ED 207 062.

Britton, J. N. "The Composing Processes and the Functions of Writing." In *Research on Composing: Points of Departure.* Edited by C. R. Cooper and L. Odell, 13–28. Urbana, Illinois: NCTE, 1978.

———. *Language and Learning.* Baltimore, Maryland: Penguin Books, 1970.

Britton, J. N., T. Burgess, N. Martin, A. McLeod, and H. Rosen. *The Development of Writing Abilities (11–18).* London: Macmillan Education Ltd., 1975.

Britton, J. N., N. C. Martin, and H. Kasen. *Multiple Marking of Compositions.* London: Her Majesty's Stationery Office, 1966.

Broadhead, G. J., and J. A. Berlin. "Teaching and Measuring Sentence Skills: The Importance of Length, Variability, Variety, and Punctuation." Paper, Annual Meeting of CCCC, 1978. ED 208 409.

Broderick, J. P. "Usage Varieties and Writing Competence: A Study of Formal and Informal Written English Elicited from Selected Groups of American College Freshmen." *DAI* 32 (1972): 5211-A.

Brodkey, L. C. "Toward a Theory of College Composition and Academic Prose: The Role of Deixis." *DAI* 41 (1980): 2581-A.

Brooks, L. Y. "The Effect of a Study of Generative Rhetoric on the Syntactic Fluency of Seventh-Graders." *DAI* 36 (1976): 7148-A.*

Brooks, N. R. "The Growth and Development of the Observing Ego: Letter Writing as a Mediation Process between Private and Public Ways of Knowing." *DAI* 40 (1980): 4481-A.

Brosnahan, I., and J. Neulieb. "Sentence Combining as a Composition Technique." *Illinois English Bulletin* 66, no. 1 (1978): entire issue.

Brossell, G. "Rhetorical Specification in Essay Examination Topics." *CE* 45 (1983): 165–173.

Brothers, E. S. "The Effect of Three Types of Teacher Evaluation on the Compositions of College Freshmen." *DAI* 40 (1979): 1390-A.

Brown, G. H. "Observing Children Writing: The Activity and the Product." 1977. ED 162 302.

Brown, R. W. *How the French Boy Learns to Write: A Study in the Teaching of the Mother Tongue.* Champaign, Illinois: NCTE, 1963. ED 039 216.

Brown, W. A. "A Study of Communications I Classes at the University of Northern Colorado to Determine Their Effectiveness in Improving Student Performance in Writing." *DAI* 31 (1970): 2784-A.

Brown, W. C., Jr. "An Investigation of the Effects of a Literary Training on the Composition Skills of Fourth Grade Students." *DAI* 42 (1982): 3430-A.

Brozick, J. R. "The Inter-Relationships among Personality, Audience, Purpose, and Cognitive Functioning in Composing." 1976. ED 139 018.

———. "An Investigation into the Composing Process of Four Twelfth-Grade Students: Case Studies Based on Jung's Personality Types, Freudian Psychoanalytic Ego Psychology and Cognitive Functioning." *DAI* 38 (1977): 31-A.

Bruce, B., A. Collins, A. D. Rubin, and D. Gentner. *A Cognitive Science Approach to Writing. Technical Report No. 89.* Cambridge, Massachusetts: Bolt, Beranek and Newman, Inc.; Champaign, Illinois: University of Illinois, Center for the Study of Reading, 1978. ED 157 039.

Bruner, J. S., R. R. Oliver, P. M. Greenfield, and others. *Studies in Cognitive Growth: A Collaboration at the Center for Cognitive Studies.* New York: John Wiley & Sons, Inc., 1966.

Bruno, B. J. "The Effect of Sentence Combining on the Writing of Ninth Graders." *DAI* 41 (1981): 4352-A.

Brusling, C. "Composition Training in the Primary School. Effects of Vocabulary-building Conversation." *Scandinavian Journal of Educational Research* 17, no. 1 (1973): 11–22.

Bryant, A. J. G. "An Analysis of Selected Instructional Approaches Used in the Teaching of Freshman Composition Classes to Determine the Effectiveness in Improving Students' Writing." *DAI* 37 (1977): 6236-A. ED 147 811.

Bryant, Y. L. L. "Language Achievement of Fifth, Eighth, and Eleventh-Grade Students as Determined by an Analysis of Written Compositions." *DAI* 31 (1971): 5024-A.

Buchholz, W. J. "Behavioral Evaluation: The Checkmark Grading System." *CCC* 30 (1979): 302–05.

Buckley, M. H., and O. Boyle. "Mapping and Composing." In *Theory and Practice in the Teaching of Composition: Processing, Distancing, and Modeling.* Edited by M. Myers and J. Gray, 59–66. Urbana, Illinois: NCTE, 1983.

Buckley-Byrne, T. A. "A Survey of the Attitudes of the Teaching Faculty at a State College toward Students in the Basic Skills Programs: A Preliminary Investigation." 1981. ED 205 905.

Buckner, S. B. "Practices and Products: The Composing of Skilled and Less Skilled First-Year College Students." *DAI* 42 (1981): 581-A.

Budd, W. C. "An Experimental Comparison of Writing Achievement in English Composition and Humanities Classes." *RTE* 3 (1969): 209–21.

———. "Research Designs of Potential Value in Investigating Problems in English." *RTE* 1 (1967): 1–9.

Budz, J., and T. Grabar. "Tutorial versus Classroom in Freshman English." *CE* 37 (1976): 654–56.

Bullock, A. L. C. *A Language for Life: Report of the Committee of Inquiry appointed by the Secretary of State for Education and Science under the Chairmanship of Sir Alan Bullock.* London: Her Majesty's Stationery Office, 1975.

Burge, G. *A Survey of Training, Assignments, and Attitudes of English Teachers in Iowa Public Schools—Grades 9–12.* Des Moines, Iowa: Iowa State Department of Public Instruction, 1967. ED 015 176.

Burne, K. *Evaluation of an Innovative Approach to English Composition Instruction: Phases Two and Three.* Long Beach, California: Long Beach City College, 1973. ED 073 748.

Burns, H. L., Jr. "Stimulating Rhetorical Invention in English Composition through Computer-Assisted Instruction." *DAI* 40 (1980): 3734-A. ED 188 245.

Burrows, A. T. "Composition: Prospect and Retrospect." In *Reading and Writing Instruction in the United States: Historical Trends.* Edited by H. A. Robinson, 17–43. Urbana, Illinois: International Reading Association and ERIC, 1977. ED 142 995.

———. *Teaching Composition: What Research Says to the Teacher. No. 18.* Washington, D.C.: National Education Association, 1966. ED 017 482.

Burrows, A. T., M. B. Parke, N. R. Edmund, J. J. DeBoer, T. D. Horn, V. E. Herrick, and R. G. Strickland. *Children's Writing: Research in Composition and Related Skills.* Champaign, Illinois: NCTE, 1961.

Burrus, D. J. "A Three Year Comparative Study of the Functional Approach to Teaching the Mechanics of Language." *DAI* 31 (1971): 5243-A.

Burt, R. M. "Effects of an Individualized, Humanistic Program of Confluent Literature and Composition Instruction on the Writing Performance of Low Ability Suburban Eleventh Grade High School Students." *DAI* 41 (1980): 1984-A.

Burton, D. L. "Research in the Teaching of English: The Troubled Dream." *RTE* 7 (1973): 160–89.

Burton, D. L., and L. Arnold. *Effects of Frequency of Writing and Intensity of Teacher Evaluation upon High School Students' Performance in Written Composition.* Washington, D. C.: U. S. Office of Education, Cooperative Research Project #1523, 1964. ED 003 281.

Bushman, J. R. "Teacher Observation Systems: Some Implications for English Education." *RTE* 6 (1972): 69–85.

Bushner, D. E. "The Relationship between the Reading Comprehension Ability of Seventh and Eighth Grade Subjects and the Syntactic Complexity of Their Written Language." *DAI* 40 (1980): 4978-A.

Butler, D. A. "A Descriptive Analysis of the Relationships between Writing Apprehension and the Composing Processes of Selected Secondary Students." *DAI* 41 (1981): 3854-A.

Butler, M. S. "A Study of Credit Remedial Courses in the Two-Year Colleges in the United States." *DAI* 41 (1980): 1043-A.

Butterworth, P., J. A. Klein, and C. G. Galloway. "The Modification of

Syntactic Style Through Modelling." *Alberta Journal of Educational Research* 16 (1970): 95–101.

Bynum, H. S. D. "A Study of the Perceived Need for Emphasis on Writing Skills among Faculty and Graduate Students and of the Effectiveness of a Model for Individualized Instruction in Writing Improvement at the Graduate Level." *DAI* 40 (1979): 1298-A.

Cain, B. "Discourse Competence in Nonsense Paralogs." *CCC* 24 (1973): 171–81.

Calderonello, A. H., K. A. Hart, and D. P. Quinn. *A Study to Determine the Efficacy of an Individualized-Modularized Writing Course.* 1981. ED 199 740.

Caldwell, J. M. "The Effects of a Generative Rhetoric Program on Writing Performance of Eleventh Grade Students." *DAI* 39 (1978): 1391-A.*

Calhoun, J. L. "The Effect of Analysis of Essays in College Composition Classes on Reading and Writing Skills." *DAI* 32 (1971): 1971-A.*

California Association of Teachers of English. *You've Made the Assignment. Now What? An Annotated Bibliography on the Process of Teaching Composition.* Redlands, California: California Association of Teachers of English, 1977. ED 145 467.

California State Department of Education. *An Assessment of the Writing Performance of California High School Seniors.* Sacramento, California: California State Department of Education, Office of Program Evaluation and Research, 1977. ED 139 036.

Calkins, L. M. "Andrea Learns to Make Writing Hard." *LA* 56 (1979): 569–76.

———. "Case Study of a Nine Year Old Writer." In *A Case Study Observing the Development of Primary Children's Composing, Spelling, and Motor Behaviors during the Writing Process, Final Report.* NIE Grant No. G-78-0174. Edited by D. H. Graves, 239–62. Durham, New Hampshire: University of New Hampshire, 1981.

———. "Children Learn the Writer's Craft." *LA* 57 (1980a): 207–13.

———. "Children's Rewriting Strategies." *RTE* 14 (1980b): 331–41.

———. "When Children Want to Punctuate: Basic Skills Belong in Context." *LA* 57 (1980c): 567–73. ED 170 766.

Callaghan, T. F. "The Effects of Sentence-Combining Exercises on the Syntactic Maturity, Quality of Writing, Reading Ability, and Attitudes of Ninth Grade Students." *DAI* 39 (1978): 637-A.*

Campana, J. M. "Effects of Implementing Affective Objectives in Teaching a Literature-Composition Course." *DAI* 33 (1973): 6051-A.

Campbell, D. B. "A Study of Two Methods of Teaching in a Community College Setting." *DAI* 37 (1977): 4808-A.

Campbell, M. "Assessment or Processing?" *English Quarterly* 3, no. 1 (Spring 1970): 81–86.

Campbell, M. L. M. "An Investigation of the Relationship between Secondary Generative and Receptive Communication Skills at the College Freshman Level." *DAI* 37 (1977): 5655-A.

Cannon, W. W. "Terrors and Affectations: Students' Perceptions of the Writing Process." Paper, Annual Meeting of CCCC, 1981. ED 199 720.

Caplan, R., and C. Keech. *Showing-Writing: A Training Program to Help Students Be Specific.* Berkeley, California: University of California, Bay Area Writing Project, 1980. ED 198 539.

Capps, B. H. "Composition Instruction in Elementary Teacher Training Programs, 1886–1926." *DAI* 34 (1973): 4812-A.

Carey, J. E. "The Relationship between Creative Thinking Ability, Intellectual Ability, Educational Achievement, and Writing Ability of Sixth Grade Children." *DA* 27 (1967): 2095-A.

Carey, S. F. "Exploration of Prospective English Teachers' Values and Attitudes as They Relate to the Process and Product of Composition." *DAI* 37 (1977): 6415-A.

Carkeet, D. "Understanding Syntactic Errors in Remedial Writing." *CE* 38 (1977): 682–86, 695.

Carlsmith, J. M., B. E. Collins, and R. L. Helmreich. "Studies in Forced Compliance: I. The Effect of Pressure for Compliance on Attitude Change Produced by Face-to-Face Role Playing and Anonymous Essay Writing." In *Role Playing, Reward, and Attitude Change: An Enduring Problem in Psychology.* Edited by A. C. Elms, 113–33. New York: Van Nostrand Reinhold Company, 1969.

Carlson, C. H. *Development of Writing Skills at the Secondary and College Levels. Final Report.* Washington, D. C.: Office of Education (Dept. of Health, Education, and Welfare), Bureau of Research, 1968. ED 027 327.

Carlson, E. C. "Language Arts Curriculum Planning and Execution in the Middle Schools of a Florida District." *DAI* 39 (1978): 37-A.

Carner, R. L. "The Relative Effectiveness of the Initial Teaching Alphabet and Traditional Orthography on Reading, Spelling and Writing Achievement of First and Second Grade Children." *DAI* 32 (1972): 5466-A.

Caroselli, M. "The Effect of Parental Involvement on the Writing Skills and Attitudes of Secondary Students." *DAI* 41 (1980): 1915-A.*

Carr, J. A. E. "The Interrelatedness of Present Course Offerings and Teacher Preparation in English Education in the Public High Schools of Nebraska." *DAI* 36 (1975): 808-A.

Carroll, J. A. "Process into Product: Awareness of the Composing Process Affects the Written Product." *DAI* 40 (1980): 3964-A.

Carroll, J. B. "Language Development." In *Encyclopedia of Educational Research.* Edited by C. W. Harris, 744–52. New York: The Macmillan Company, 1960.

Carter, W. S., III. "The Effect of Two Diagnostic-Prescriptive Methods of Instruction on Seventh Grade Language Arts Achievement Scores in the Senatobia, Ms., Municipal Separate School District." *DAI* 39 (1978): 1209-A.

Cartwright, P. J. "Writing Behaviour of Selected Fifth Grade Students in an Open Classroom." *DAI* 40 (1979): 3165-A.

Casey, B. M. "Teachers' Assessments of the Aims of Teaching English in Secondary Schools." *BJEP* 36 (1966): 106–09.

Cash, M. V. "Selected Factors for Individualizing the Instruction of English in Secondary Schools in the State of Alabama." *DAI* 36 (1976): 5763-A.

Cayer, R. L., and R. K. Sacks. "Oral and Written Discourse of Basic Writers: Similarities and Differences." *RTE* 13 (1979): 121–28.

Cazden, C. B. *Child Language and Education.* New York: Holt, Rinehart, and Winston, 1972.

Ceniza, R. E. "An Application of Achievement Motivation Principles and Strategies to the Teaching-Learning of Nine English Sentence Patterns by Some Disadvantaged Students of Project Opportunity at University College, Syracuse University." *DAI* 38 (1977): 2516-A.

Chamberlain, J. D. K. "An Assessment by Selected Secondary English Teachers of Their Undergraduate Preparation and Present Needs in Teaching Composition." *DAI* 40 (1979): 716-A.

Champagne, M., M. Scardamalia, C. Bereiter, and J. Fine. "Children's Problems with Focus and Cohesion in Revising." Paper, Annual Meeting of AERA, 1980. ED 186 901.

Chappel, J. H. "Increasing Linguistic Self-Respect through Sentence Combining." Paper, Annual Meeting of CCCC, 1977. ED 144 076.

Chew, C. R. "A Study to Determine Skills of Written Composition Present in Resources Available to Teachers." *DAI* 36 (1975): 3347-A.

———. "A Study to Determine the Relationship between Indexes of Maturity and a Quality Grade in a Written Examination." 1978. ED 178 914.

Childers, N. M. "An Investigation into the Composing Processes and Graphic Linguistic Awareness of Three Very Young Children." *DAI* 42 (1981): 2482-A.

Childers, P. R., and V. J. Haas. "Effect of Detailed Guidance on the Writing Efficiency of College Freshmen." *Journal of Experimental Education* 39, no. 1 (Fall 1970): 20–23.

Chinn, J. A. "Verb Choice and Its Relationship to a Composition's Effectiveness as Measured by Holistic Evaluation." 1979. ED 198 545.

Chisholm, W. "Degrees of Syntactic and Rhetorical Fluency-Competency in Freshman Writing: A Computer-Assisted Study." Paper, Annual Meeting of the Midwest Modern Language Association, 1976. ED 132 568.

Chlebicki, A. N. "An Investigative Study of the Degree of Implementation and Efficacy of Project Literacy." *DAI* 41 (1981): 3398-A.

Christen-Edwards, J. M. "Effects of a Question Strategy upon Sixth-Grade Sentence Production." *DAI* 40 (1980): 3978-A.

Christensen, F. "A Generative Rhetoric of the Paragraph." *CCC* 16 (1965): 144–56.

———. "A Generative Rhetoric of the Sentence." *CCC* 14 (1963): 155–61.

———. *Notes Toward a New Rhetoric: Six Essays for Teachers.* New York: Harper & Row, 1967.

———. "The Problem of Defining a Mature Style." *EJ* 57 (1968): 572–79.

Christensen, G. N. "Theme-A-Day: An Evaluation of the Effectiveness of Daily Practice in a College Composition Course." *DAI* 36 (1975): 6438-A.

Christensen, J. K. "A Comparison of an Individually Prescribed Method of Instruction and a Conventional Large Group Method of Instruction When Assessing English Competence and Writing Skills in a Collegiate Business Report Writing Course." *DAI* 40 (1980): 5696-A.*

Christensen, M. "The College-Level Examination Program's Freshman English Equivalency Examinations." *RTE* 11 (1977): 186–92.

Christiansen, M. A. "The Relative Effectiveness of Two Methods of Teaching Composition in Freshman English at Metropolitan Junior College-Kansas City." *DA* 26 (1965): 900.

———. "Tripling Writing and Omitting Readings in Freshman English: An Experiment." *CCC* 16 (1965): 122–24.

Christie, T., and P. Kline. "The Effects of Studying Classics to 'A' Level on the Writing of English." *Educational Research* (Britain) 9 (1966): 67–70.

Ciani, A. J. "Syntactic Maturity and Vocabulary Diversity in the Oral Language of First, Second, and Third Grade Students." *RTE* 10 (1976): 150–56.

Clark, P. M., and H. L. Mirels. "Fluency as a Pervasive Element in the Measurement of Creativity." *JEM* 7 (1970): 83–86.

Clark, W. G. *An Evaluation of Two Techniques of Teaching Freshman Composition. Final Report.* Colorado Springs, Colorado: Air Force Academy, 1968. ED 053 142.

Clarke, A. L. P. "A Study of the Adequacy of Education of Louisiana English Teachers in Terms of Certain Established Guidelines." *DA* 29 (1968): 1463-A.

Clarke, G. A. "Interpreting the Penciled Scrawl: A Problem in Teacher Theme Evaluation." 1969. ED 039 241.

Clemmons, S. M. "Identification of Writing Competencies Needed by Secondary Students to Perform Assignments in Science and Social Studies Classes." *DAI* 41 (1980): 3037-A.

Clifford, J. P. "Composing in Stages: The Effects of a Collaborative Pedagogy." *RTE* 15 (1981): 37–53.

———. "An Experimental Inquiry into the Effectiveness of Collaborative Learning as a Method for Improving the Experiential Writing Performance of College Freshmen in a Remedial Writing Class." *DAI* 38 (1978): 7289-A.*

Clinton, J. K. H. "A Study of Maryland Public Community College English Teachers' Attitudes towards Composition and their Professional, Academic and Personal Backgrounds." *DAI* 38 (1978): 3895-A.

Clipner, R. B. "Enhancing Syntactic Fluency in the Written Expression of Junior High Students: A Project Report." Diss., Harvard University, 1970.

Clopper, R. R. "A Study of Contract Correcting as a Means of Significantly Increasing Writing and English Skills." *DA* 27 (1967): 3769-A.*

Coe, R. M. "Closed System Composition." *ETC.* 32 (1975): 403–12.

Coffman, W. E. "On the Reliability of Ratings of Essay Examinations in English." *RTE* 5 (1971): 24–36.

Cohen, A. M. "Assessing College Students' Ability to Write Compositions." *RTE* 7 (1973): 356–71.

Cohen, E., and M. Scardamalia. "The Effects of Instructional Intervention in the Revision of Essays by Grade Six Children." Downsview, Ontario: York University, n.d.

Coleman, C. J. "The Evaluation of a Hierarchy of Composition Skills." *DAI* 35 (1974): 3387-A.

Coleman, D. R. "The Effects of Pupil Use of a Creative Writing Scale as an Evaluative and Instructional Tool by Primary Gifted Students." *DAI* 42 (1982): 3409-A.

Coleman, V. B. "A Comparison between the Relative Effectiveness of Marginal-Interlinear-Terminal Commentary and of Audiotaped Commentary in Responding to English Compositions." *DAI* 33 (1973): 3945-A.*

Collingwood, L. "Some Questions for Composition Teachers." *Freshman English News* 4, no. 1 (Spring 1975): 13–15.

Collins, C. D. "The Effect of Expressive Writing upon College Freshmen's Cognitive and Affective Development." 1978. ED 173 801.

———. "The Effect of Writing Experiences in the Expressive Mode upon the Reading, Self-Esteem, Attitudes, and Academic Achievement of Freshmen in a College Reading Course." *DAI* 40 (1980): 3804-A.

Collins, G. A. "A Comparative Study of the Effects of Different Methods of Teaching Writing Skills to Students in a Community College." *DAI* 36 (1976): 7230-A.

Collins, J. L. "Teaching Writing: An Interactionist Approach to Abbreviated and Idiosyncratic Language in the Writing of Secondary School Students." *DAI* 40 (1979): 1425-A.

Collins, J. L., and M. M. Williamson. "Spoken Language and Semantic Abbreviations in Writing." *RTE* 15 (1981): 23–35.

Collins, J. T. "The Effects of Written Communication Skills Training upon the Communication of Empathy." *DAI* 37 (1976): 704-A.

Collins, T. P. "A Study of the Freshman Composition Program at the University of Kentucky and Six of Its Affiliated Community Colleges." *DAI* 30 (1969): 1770-A.

Combs, W. E. "Further Effects of Sentence-Combining Practice on Writing Ability." *RTE* 10 (1976a): 137–49.

———. "Notes and Comments [A Response to Christine San Jose]." *RTE* 12 (1978): 282–84.

———. "Sentence-Combining Mythinformation." *EJ* 65, no. 9 (December 1976b): 20–21.

———. "Sentence-Combining Practice: Do Gains in Judgments of Writing 'Quality' Persist?" *JER* 70 (1977): 318–21.

———. "Some Further Effects and Implications of Sentence-Combining Exercises for the Secondary Language Arts Curriculum." *DAI* 36 (1975): 1266-A.

———. *Structural Variation in Five Persuasive Writings of Mature Writers. Studies in Language Education, Report No. 38.* Athens, Georgia: University of Georgia, Department of Language Education, 1980. ED 191 044.

Combs, W. E., and B. Sitko. "See for Yourself: A Rationale for In-Class Research." *EJ* 70, no. 4 (April 1981): 80–81.

Conry, J. J. *Validity of the Rearrangement Exercise as a Predictor of Essay Writing Ability.* Madison, Wisconsin: University of Wisconsin, Research and Development Center for Cognitive Learning, 1967. ED 016 646.

Conte, M. J., and L. W. Ferguson. "Rated Effectiveness of Antidrug Letters by Drug Users and Nonusers." *Journal of Psychology* 86 (1974): 335–39.

Cook, D. L. L. "A Comparison of the Content of English Methods Courses with the Needs of Beginning Secondary School English Teachers." *DAI* 37 (1977): 4816-A.

Cook, D. L., and J. King. "A Study of the Hawthorne Effect in Educational Research." *RTE* 2 (1968): 93–98.

Coomber, J. E. "Perceiving the Structure of Written Materials." *RTE* 9 (1975): 263–66.

Cooper, C. R. "Holistic Evaluation of Writing." In *Evaluating Writing: Describing, Measuring, Judging.* Edited by C. R. Cooper and L. Odell, 3–31. Urbana, Illinois: NCTE, 1977.

———. "Research Roundup." *EJ* 65, no. 6 (September 1976): 84–86.

———. "Research Roundup: General English Curriculum and Methods." *EJ* 64, no. 5 (May 1975a): 94–96.

————. "Research Roundup: Measuring Growth in Writing." *EJ* 64, no. 3 (March 1975b): 111–20.

————. "Research Roundup: Oral and Written Composition." *EJ* 62 (1973): 1201–03.

————. "Research Roundup: Oral and Written Composition." *EJ* 63, no. 6 (September 1974): 102–04.

————. "Research Roundup: Oral and Written Composition." *EJ* 64, no. 9 (December 1975c): 72–74.

————. "Summary of Investigations Relating to the English Language Arts in Secondary Education: 1971." *EJ* 61 (1972): 728–739, 747.

Cooper, C. R., R. Cherry, R. Gerber, S. Fleischer, B. Copley, and M. Sartisky. *Writing Abilities of Regularly Admitted Freshmen at SUNY/Buffalo.* Buffalo, New York: University Learning Center and Graduate Program in English Education and English Department, 1979.

Cooper, C. R., and L. Odell. "Considerations of Sound in the Composing Process of Published Writers." *RTE* 10 (1976): 103–15.

————, eds. *Evaluating Writing: Describing, Measuring, Judging.* Urbana, Illinois: NCTE, 1977.

————, eds. *Research on Composing: Points of Departure.* Urbana, Illinois: NCTE, 1978.

Cooper, D. "An Investigation into Two Methods of Teaching English in Modern Schools." *BJEP* 36 (1966): 105–06.

Cooper, G. C. W. "The Relationship between Errors in Standard Usage in Written Compositions of College Students and the Students' Cognitive Styles." *DAI* 40 (1980): 6257-A.

Cope, J. A. "Writing Apprehension." Paper, Annual Meeting of the Western College Reading Association, 1978. ED 154 425.

Copland, J. B. "A Twelve Week Study on the Effects of Peer Evaluation for Improving Narrative Writing Performance at the Eighth Grade Level." *DAI* 41 (1980): 1014-A.

Cost, D. L. "The Importance of Written Communication in Business as Viewed by Executives in a Metropolitan Area." *DAI* 42 (1982): 3398-A.

Couture, B. A. Z. "Reading to Write: An Exploration of the Uses of Analytic Reading to Teach Composition." *DAI* 41 (1981): 4021-A.

Covino, W. A., N. Johnson, and M. Feehan. "Graduate Education in Rhetoric: Attitudes and Implications." *CE* 42 (1980): 390–98.

Cowardin, J. H. "Modifying the Syntactical Maturity of Compositional Writing by Academically Handicapped Secondary Students." *DAI* 39 (1979): 6060-A.

Cox, V. E. L. "Reciprocal Oracy/Literacy Recognition Skills in the Language Production of Language Experience Approach Students." *DAI* 32 (1971): 2905-A.

Craig, B. J. "Oral Response Groups before and after Rough Drafts: Effects on Writing Achievement and Apprehension. *DAI* 42 (1982): 3476-A.

Craig, W. E. "Investigation of Syntactic-Semantic Relationships in the Selected Writing of Students in Grades 4–12." *DAI* 32 (1971): 1258-A.

Cramer, R. L., and B. B. Cramer. "Writing by Imitating Language Models." *LA* 52 (1975): 1011–14, 1018.

Crew, L. "What Should We Tell Student Writers?" Paper, Annual Meeting of CCCC, 1979. ED 179 968.

Crews, R. *The Influence of Linguistically-Oriented Techniques on the English*

Sentence Structure and Reading Comprehension of Fourth Grade Students. Washington, D. C.: Office of Education (Dept. of Health, Education, and Welfare), Bureau of Research, 1968. ED 024 692.

————. "A Linguistic Versus a Traditional Grammar Program—The Effects on Written Sentence Structure and Comprehension." *Educational Leadership* 5 (November 1971): 145–49.

————. "A Study in the Use of Sector Analysis as an Approach to Teaching Fifth-Grade Students Certain Aspects of English Sentence Structure." *DA* 27 (1966): 698-A.*

Crick, R. C. "A Technical Communication Procedure to Produce Attitude Change through the Use of Scientifically Designed Messages." *DAI* 42 (1982): 4972-A.

Crisp, R. D. *Current Research in English Teacher Preparation: A First Report.* Urbana, Illinois: Illinois State-Wide Curriculum Study Center in the Preparation of Secondary School English Teachers, University of Illinois, 1968. ED 016 661.

Cronnell, B. *The Scoring of Writing Samples: A Study.* Los Alamitos, California: Southwest Regional Laboratory for Educational Research and Development, 1980. ED 199 758.

Cross, D. P. "The Effects of a Systematic Group Language Development Program with Low-Achieving and Regular Class Third Grade Subjects." *DA* 29 (1968): 1819-A.

Crow, H. J. "Public Perceptions of Student Writing Ability: Abstractions and Realities." *DAI* 41 (1980): 1368-A.

Crowhurst, M. "Cohesion in Argumentative Prose Written by Sixth-, Tenth- and Twelfth-Graders." Paper, Annual Meeting of AERA, 1981. ED 202 023.

————. "The Effect of Audience and Mode of Discourse on the Syntactic Complexity of the Writing of Sixth and Tenth-Graders." *DAI* 38 (1978): 7300-A.

————. "On the Misinterpretation of Syntactic Complexity Data." *English Education* 11 (1979): 91–97.

————. "Syntactic Complexity and Teachers' Quality Ratings of Narrations and Arguments." *RTE* 14 (1980): 223–31.

————. "Syntactic Complexity in Two Modes of Discourse at Grades 6, 10 and 12." 1978. ED 168 037.

————. "The Writing Process: A Developmental Perspective on Persuasive Writing." Paper, Annual Meeting of CCCC, 1983.

Crowhurst, M., and G. L. Piché. "Audience and Mode of Discourse Effects on Syntactic Complexity in Writing at Two Grade Levels." *RTE* 13 (1979): 101–09.

Crowley, S. "Components of the Composing Process." Paper, Annual Meeting of CCCC, 1976. ED 126 514.

Crump, W. D., and N. T. Morris. "An Application of Belanger's Correction to Golub and Kidder's Syntactic Density Score." *RTE* 14 (1980): 342–44.

Crymes, R. "The Relation of Study about Language to Language Performance: With Special Reference to Nominalization." *TESOL Quarterly* 5 (1971): 217–30.

Culbert, T. "Teaching Grammar and Mechanics in Freshman Composition." *JER* 58 (1965): 291–92.

Cummings, B. J. "Prewriting, Writing, Rewriting: Teaching the Composing Process to Basic Writers at the College Level." *DAI* 42 (1981): 2465-A.

Curran, B. N. "The Comparative Effectiveness of Two Audiotutorial Learning Methods." *DAI* 38 (1978): 3904-A.

Daiker, D., A. Kerek, and M. Morenberg. "Sentence-Combining and Syntactic Maturity in Freshman English." *CCC* 29 (1978): 36–41.

——, eds. *Sentence Combining and the Teaching of Writing.* Conway, Arkansas: University of Akron and University of Central Arkansas, 1979.

Daiute, C. A. "Psycholinguistic Foundations of the Writing Process." *RTE* 15 (1981): 5–22.

Daker, L. P. "The Comparative Effects of Two Composition Methodologies on the Syntactic Maturity, Writing Apprehension, and Overall Writing Ability of Ninth and Tenth Grade Students." *DAI* 41 (1981): 4954-A.

Daly, J. A. "The Effects of Writing Apprehension on Message Encoding." *Journalism Quarterly* 54 (1977): 566–72.

——. "Writing Apprehension and Writing Competency." *JER* 72 (1978): 10–14.

——. "Writing Apprehension in the Classroom: Teacher Role Expectencies of the Apprehensive Writer." *RTE* 13 (1979): 37–44.

Daly, J. A., and M. D. Miller. "Apprehension of Writing as a Predictor of Message Intensity." *Journal of Psychology* 89 (1975a): 175–77.

——. "The Empirical Development of an Instrument to Measure Writing Apprehension." *RTE* 9 (1975b): 242–49.

——. "Further Studies on Writing Apprehension: SAT Scores, Success Expectations, Willingness to Take Advanced Courses, and Sex Differences." *RTE* 9 (1975c): 250–56.

Daly, J. A., and W. Shamo. "Academic Decisions as a Function of Writing Apprehension." *RTE* 12 (1978): 119–26.

D'Angelo, F. J. *A Conceptual Theory of Rhetoric.* Cambridge, Massachusetts: Winthrop Publishers, Inc., 1975.

——. "A Generative Rhetoric of the Essay." *CCC* 25 (1974): 388–96.

——. "Modes of Discourse." In *Teaching Composition: Ten Bibliographical Essays.* Edited by G. Tate, 111–35. Fort Worth, Texas: Texas Christian University Press, 1976.

Danis, M. F. "Peer-Response Groups in a College Writing Workshop: Students' Suggestions for Revising Compositions." *DAI* 41 (1981): 5008-A.

Darnell, D. "Effects of Three Different Methods of Evaluating Writing on Creativity in Writing." *DA* 23 (1963): 3683.

Darrell, B. "A Faculty Survey of Undergraduate Reading and Writing Needs." *Peabody Journal of Education* 57 (1980): 85–93.

Dauterman, F. P. "Syntactic Maturity Test for Narrative Writing." 1969. ED 091 757.

——. "The Syntactic Structures Employed in Samples of Narrative Writing by Secondary School Students." *DAI* 30 (1970):4434-A.*

Davenport, H. D. "The Effects of Instruction in Generative Grammar on the Writing Ability of Students in the Ninth Grade." *DAI* 31 (1971): 4594-A.

Davis, D., ed. "Search and Research." *English in Australia* no. 29 (November 1974): 46–50.

Davis, D. M. "The Development and Testing of a Program of Systematic Desensitization for the Treatment of Writing Apprehension." *DAI* 40 (1980): 4797-A.

Davis, K. "Significant Improvement in Freshman Composition as Measured by Impromptu Essays: A Large-Scale Experiment." *RTE* 13 (1979): 45–48.

Davis, M. T. "Evaluating Remedial and Compensatory English/Writing Programs: Procedures and Effects." *DAI* 40 (1980): 3931-A.

Davis, M. W. "A Comparative Analysis of Sentences Written by Eighth Grade Students Instructed in Transformational-Generative Grammar and Traditional Grammar." *DA* 28 (1967): 213-A.

Davis, O. L., Jr., H. C. Smith, Jr., and N. D. Bowers. "High School Students' Awareness of Structural Relationships in English." *JER* 58 (1964): 69–71.

Davis, R. J. "Student-to-Student Tutoring in Selected English Language Skills at the Island Trees Junior High School, Levittown, New York." *DA* 28 (1968): 4404-A.

Davis, R. M. "Experimental Research in the Effectiveness of Technical Writing." In *The Teaching of Technical Writing.* Edited by D. H. Cunningham and H. A. Estrin, 109–22. Urbana, Illinois: NCTE, 1975.

———. "A Modest Proposal." *The Technical Writing Teacher* 2, no. 2 (Winter 1975): 1–8.

———. *Technical Writing: Its Importance in the Engineering Profession and Its Place in Engineering Curricula—A Survey of the Experience and Opinions of Prominent Engineers. Technical Report No. 75–5.* Wright-Patterson AFB, Ohio: Air Force Institute of Technology, 1975. ED 116 224.

Davis, W. J. "The Mastery Learning and Conventional Modes of Instructing College-Level Composition: A Comparative Study Based upon Selected Student Characteristics." *DAI* 36 (1976): 6502-A.

Dawson, J. H. "The English Program in a Changing Culture: An Assessment of the Impact of the Changing Technological Culture on English Programs and Instructional Practices of Selected Secondary Schools in the Rockville Centre Diocese, Long Island, New York." *DAI* 36 (1975): 2587-A.

De Beaugrande, R. "Psychology and Composition." *CCC* 30 (1979): 50–57.

DeHaven, E. R. P. "The Effect of Typewriting on Seventh Grade Students' Ability to Recognize Composition Errors." *DAI* 30 (1970): 4871-A.

Delaney, M. C. "A Comparison of a Student-Centered, Free Writing Program with a Teacher-Centered Rhetorical Approach to Teaching College Composition." *DAI* 41 (1980): 1985-A.*

De la Rosa, M. C. "The Effects on Reading Achievement of Students Engaged in Creative Writing and Students Engaged in Sustained Silent Reading and Creative Writing." *DAI* 40 (1979): 663-A.

Denby, R. V. "NCTE/ERIC Report—Composition Evaluation." *EJ* 57 (1968): 1215–21.

Denman, M. E. "The Measure of Success in Writing." *CCC* 29 (1978): 42–46.

———. "Personality Changes Concomitant with Learning Writing." *RTE* 15 (1981): 170–71.

DeStefano, J. S. *Language, the Learner, and the School.* New York: John Wiley & Sons, Inc., 1978.

———. "Productive Language Differences in Fifth Grade Black Students' Syntactic Forms." *Elementary English* 49 (1972): 552–58.

DeStefano, J. S., H. B. Pepinsky, and T. S. Sanders. *Transition into Literacy: An Analysis of Language Behavior during Reading and Writing Instruction in a First Grade Classroom.* Paper, Annual Meeting of the International Reading Association, 1980. ED 186 865.

Detore, E. A. "An Investigation of the Resolution of Anaphora in Written Discourse." *DAI* 39 (1979): 5289-A.

DeVries, T. D. "An Analysis of Selected English Teaching Practices in Thirteen Indiana Public School Systems as Related to Research." *DA* 28 (1968): 3882-A.

———. "Reading, Writing Frequency and Expository Writing." *Reading Improvement* 7, no. 1 (Spring 1970): 14–15, 19.

DeWine, S. "Student Journals in the Communication Classroom: A Reassessment through Grounded Theory Development." Paper, Annual Meeting of the American Psychological Association, 1978. ED 172 218.

Dial, R. L. "Multivariate Analysis in Sentence-Combining Research." In *Sentence Combining and the Teaching of Writing.* Edited by D. Daiker, A. Kerek, and M. Morenberg, 116–22. Conway, Arkansas: University of Akron and University of Central Arkansas, 1979.

Diamond, C. T. P. "The Headwaters: English Teachers' Constructs of Teaching Writing." Paper, International Conference "Learning to Write," 1979. ED 198 519.

———. "A Note on Measuring Teachers' Constructs." *RTE* 14 (1980): 161–64.

———. "On a Different Level: Two Pedagogies of Written Expression." Paper, Annual Fall Conference of Illinois Association of Teachers of English, 1980. ED 197 369.

———. " 'They Won't Let Me!': Administrative Constraints in Teaching English." Paper, Annual International Conference on the Teaching of English, 1980. ED 194 911.

Diederich, P. B. "Cooperative Preparation and Rating of Essay Tests." *EJ* 56 (1967): 573–84, 590. ED 091 750.

———. "Definitions of Ratings on the ETS Composition Scale." 1977. ED 145 454.

———. "The Development of a National Assessment Program in English." *RTE* 3 (1969): 5–14.

———. "How to Measure Growth in Writing Ability." *EJ* 55 (1966): 435–49.

———. "Problems and Possibilities of Research in the Teaching of Written Composition." In *Research Design and the Teaching of English: Proceedings of the San Francisco Conference,* 52–73. Champaign, Ill.: NCTE, 1964.

———, ed. *Measuring Growth in English.* Urbana, Illinois: NCTE, 1974.

Dieterich, D. J. "Composition Evaluation: Options and Advice." *EJ* 61 (1972): 1264–71.

———. "Teaching High School Composition." *EJ* 62 (1973): 1291–93.

Dillinger, E. L. "Composition in the Secondary School: A Survey in the Light of a Theoretical Paradigm." *DA* 29 (1968): 1358-A. ED 037 441.

Dilworth, C. B., Jr. "Predilection in the Assessment of Writing." Paper, Annual Meeting of CCCC, 1981. ED 200 987.

Dilworth, C. B., Jr., and R. W. Reising. "Validity in Composition Evaluation: Practicing What You Preach." *Clearing House* 53 (1979): 43–46.

Dilworth, C. B., Jr., R. W. Reising, and D. T. Wolfe. "Language Structure and Thought in Written Composition: Certain Relationships." *RTE* 12 (1978): 97–106.

Di Russo, L., and S. D. Aven. "Does Remedial English Help for College Freshmen." *California Journal of Educational Research* 22 (1971): 5–8.

DiStefano, P., and S. Howie. "Sentence Weights: An Alternative to the T-Unit." *English Education* 11 (1979): 98–101.

District of Columbia Public Schools. *Success in Reading and Writing: Pilot Project, Second Semester, School Year 1978–79. Final Report.* Washington, D.C.: District of Columbia Public Schools, Department of Research and Evaluation, 1980. ED 186 841.

Dittmer, A. E. "A Comparison of the Grammatical Structures of Professional, Senior High and Junior High Expository Writing." *DAI* 32 (1971): 2399-A.*

Dixon, E. "Indexes of Syntactic Maturity (Dixon-Hunt-Christensen)." 1970a. ED 091 748.

———. "Syntactic Indexes and Student Writing Performance." Diss., The University of Chicago, 1970b.*

Dixon, J., ed. *Growth through English: A Report Based on the Dartmouth Seminar.* Reading, England: National Association for the Teaching of English, 1967.

Dixon, J., and L. Stratta. *Achievements in Writing at 16 +. Paper 1. Staging Points Reached in Narratives Based on Personal Experience.* 1980. ED 208 389.

Donelson, K. L. "Variables Distinguishing between Effective and Ineffective Writers in the Tenth Grade." *Journal of Experimental Education* 35, no. 4 (Summer 1967): 37–41. ED 038 384.

Donlan, D. M. "Dilemma of Choice: Revolution in English Curricula, 1958–1968." *DAI* 32 (1972): 6740-A.

Donlan, D. "The Effect of Four Types of Music On Spontaneous Writings of High School Students." *RTE* 10 (1976a): 116–26.

———. "Mathematics Textbooks and the Teaching of Assigned Writing." 1976b. ED 122 306.

———. "Science Textbooks and the Teaching of Assigned Writing." 1976c. ED 122 305.

———. "Social Studies Textbooks and the Teaching of Assigned Writing." 1976d. ED 122 303.

———. "Teaching Models, Experience, and Locus of Control: Analysis of a Summer Inservice Program for Composition Teachers." *RTE* 14 (1980): 319–30.

———. "Teaching Writing in the Content Areas: Eleven Hypotheses from a Teacher Survey." *RTE* 8 (1974): 250–62.

———. "Textbook Writing Assignments in Three Content Areas." 1976e. ED 123 635.

Donnelly, C., and G. Stevens. "Streams and Puddles: A Comparison of Two Young Writers." *LA* 57 (1980): 735–41.

Dow, R. H. "The Student-Writer's Laboratory: An Approach to Composition." *DAI* 34 (1973): 2435-A.

Downey, C. M. "An Evaluation of a Program of Teaching Independent Writing in Grade III." *DA* 25 (1963): 2880.*

Downing, J., T. Fyfe, and M. Lyon. "The Effects of the Initial Teaching Alphabet (i.t.a.) on Young Children's Written Composition." *Educational Research* 9 (1967): 137–44. ED 032 295.

Downing, J., L. Ollila, and P. Oliver. "Cultural Differences in Children's Concepts of Reading and Writing." *BJEP* 45 (1975): 312–16.

Dreussi, R. M. E. "A Study of the Effects of Expressive Writing on Student Attitudes and Exposition." *DAI* 37 (1976): 2806-A.*

Driver, B. *Children's Negotiation of Answers to Questions, Working Papers in Sociolinguistics, No. 51.* Austin, Texas: Southwest Educational Development Laboratory, 1978. ED 165 491.

Dudenhefer, J. P. "An Experiment in Grading Papers." *CCC* 27 (1976): 406–07.

———. "An Experimental Study of Two Techniques of Composition Revision in a Developmental English Course for Technical Students." *DAI* 36 (1976): 7230-A.

Duke, C. R. *Basic Writing Skills Assessment Project: An Interpretative Report.* Plymouth, New Hampshire: Plymouth State College, 1978. ED 153 245.

Dumas, W. W. "Strengths and Weaknesses of Student Teachers in English." *Journal of Experimental Education* 35, no. 1 (Fall 1966): 19–27.

Duncan, P. H. "Developing Children's Composition Following Targeted Discussions of a Literature Selection." Paper, Annual Meeting of Eastern Educational Research Association, 1981. ED 203 345.

Duncan, P.H., and A. M. McLeod. "The Development of Children's Composition Following Targeted Discussions of a Distinctive Literature Selection." Paper, Annual Meeting of the American Reading Conference, 1980. ED 194 882.

Dunham, M. G. "An Assessment by Selected English Teachers in Pennsylvania High Schools of Their Undergraduate Education in Composition." *DAI* 35 (1975): 7767-A.

Dupuis, M. M. "Transformational Analysis of Compositions." 1972. ED 091 747.

Duszynski, T. J. "Writing Skills in Community College Vocational-Technical Programs: A Modified Delphi Application." *DAI* 42 (1981): 2003-A.

Dutch, W. L. "A Comparison of the Use of Student-Generated Heuristics with the Use of Larson-Generated Heuristics in a College Classroom." *DAI* 40 (1980): 6177-A.

Dye, J. M. "An Experimental Study in Selected Sectioning of Freshman English Composition Students." *DA* 26 (1966): 6466.

Dye, J. M., and J. C. Bledsoe. "An Experiment With Grouping of Freshman English Composition Students." *Journal of Experimental Education* 35, no. 3 (Spring 1967): 71–74.

Dyer, D. "When Kids Are Free to Write." *EJ* 65, no. 5 (May 1976): 34–41.

Dyro, R. T. "The Effect of Sentence Development Exercises on Junior High School Students' Writing: An Exploratory Study." *DAI* 40 (1980): 5343-A.*

Dyson, A. H., and C. Genishi. " 'Whatta Ya Tryin' to Write?': Writing as an Interactive Process." *LA* 59 (1982): 126–32.

Eachus, H. T. "The Effects of Token Reinforcement and Verbal Remediation on the Rate, Accuracy, and Length of Sentence Composition by Deaf Children." *DAI* 30 (1970): 4825-A.

Eagleton, C. J. "Reciprocal Effects of Eleventh-Graders and Twelfth-Graders as Tutors to Sixth-Graders in Reading, Written Expression, and Attitude Modification." *DAI* 34 (1974): 7513-A.*

Early, M. "Important Research in Reading and Writing." *Phi Delta Kappan* 57 (1976): 298–301.

Ebbert, G. M. "A Comparison of Three Instructional Approaches for Teaching Written Composition: Pentadic, Tagmemic, and Control Treatment." *DAI* 41 (1980): 1985-A.*

Eckhardt, C. D., and D. H. Stewart. "Towards a Functional Taxonomy of Composition." *CCC* 30 (1979): 338–42.

Edelsberg, C. M. "A Collaborative Study of Student Writers' Uses of Teacher Evaluation." *DAI* 41 (1981): 4373-A.

———. "Evaluation and Revision: A Field Study into Student Writers' Uses of Teacher Evaluation." Paper, Annual Meeting of CCCC, 1981. ED 202 042.

Edmiaston, R. K. "An Investigation of the Interrelationships of Selected Aspects of Oral and Written Language." *DAI* 41 (1981): 3046-A.

Edmonds, G. F. "An Evaluation of the Effectiveness of the Writing Component in a Freshman Remedial Program at a Community College." 1979. ED 178 946.

Effingham (Illinois) School District. *The Effingham Program for the Improvement of Pre-College English. Final Evaluation Report*. Springfield, Illinois: Illinois State Office of the Superintendent of Public Instruction, Gifted Children Section, 1972. ED 072 573.

Effros, C. *An Experimental Study of the Effects of Guided Revision and Delayed Grades on Writing Proficiency of College Freshmen. Final Report*. West Haven, Connecticut: New Haven University, 1973. ED 079 764.

Einhorn, L. "Oral Style and Written Style: An Examination of Differences." *Southern Speech Communication Journal* 43 (1978): 302–11.

Eldredge, C. C. "A Study of the Relationship between the Oral and Written Composition of Third Grade Children." *DA* 28 (1967): 875-A.

Elias, K. M. "A Comparison between Teacher-Centered and Peer-Centered Methods for Creating Voice in Writing." *DAI* 42 (1982): 3537-A.

Elkins, D. "An Experimental Investigation of Intensive Reading and Intensive Writing to Improve Composition at the Eighth Grade Level." *DA* 29 (1968): 1162-A.

Elley, W. B., I. H. Barham, H. Lamb, and M. Wyllie. "The Role of Grammar in a Secondary School English Curriculum." *New Zealand Journal of Educational Studies* 10, no. 1 (May 1975): 26–42. Reprinted in *RTE* 10 (1976): 5–21. ED 112 410.

Ellis, W. G., Jr. "The Use in Writing of Currently Taught Methods of Paragraph Development." *DA* 28 (1967): 3360-A.

Ellis, W. M. P. "A Comparison of Changes in Performance on Selected Factor-Referenced Tests in Conjunction with an Intensive Creative Writing Curriculum." *DAI* 42 (1981): 1459-A.

Emig, J. *The Composing Process of Twelfth Graders*. Urbana, Illinois: NCTE, 1971. ED 058 205.

———. "Inquiry Paradigms and Writing." *CCC* 33 (1982): 64–75.

———. "On Teaching Composition: Some Hypotheses as Definitions." *RTE* 1 (1967): 127–35.

Endicott, A. L. "A Proposed Scale for Syntactic Density." *RTE* 7 (1973): 5–12.

England, R. D. "The Ideal Characteristics of Foxfire-Type Projects as Perceived by Teacher-Advisors." *DAI* 41 (1980): 190-A.

Epes, M., C. Kirkpatrick, and M. Southwell. *An Evaluation of the Comp-Lab Project. Final Report.* Jamaica, New York: City University of New York, 1980. ED 194 909.

Ervin-Tripp, S. M. *From Conversation to Syntax. Papers and Reports on Child Language Development, No. 13.* Stanford, California: Stanford University, Department of Linguistics, 1977. ED 163 771.

Esau, H., and C. Yost. "Measuring Writing Ability with the Cloze Test Is Not Closed." Paper, Meeting of the Linguistic Society of America, 1978. ED 166 974.

Essary, W. H. "A Comparative Investigation of Several Methods of Aiding College Freshmen to Achieve Grammatical Accuracy in Written Composition." *DAI* 31 (1970): 2611-A.*

Estrin, H. A., and M. Adelstein. *The Teaching of College English to the Scientific and Technical Student: Final Report of the Committee on College English for the Scientific and Technical Student.* Champaign, Illinois: NCTE, 1963. ED 020 197.

Eulert, D. "The Relationship of Personality Factors to Learning in College Composition." *CCC* 18 (1967): 62–66.

Euster, S. D. "Utilization of the Cloze Procedure as a Measure of Writing Skill of College Students." *DAI* 39 (1979): 5900-A.

Evanechko, P., L. Ollila, and R. Armstrong. "An Investigation of the Relationships Between Children's Performance In Written Language and Their Reading Ability." *RTE* 8 (1975): 315–26.

Evans, P. J. A. *Evaluation of Writing in Ontario: Grades 8, 12 and 13.* Toronto: The Ontario Institute for Studies in Education. *Review and Evaluation Bulletins* 1, no. 2 (1979). ED 179 959.

Evans, R. V. "The Relationship between the Reading and Writing of Syntactic Structures." *RTE* 13 (1979): 129–35.

———. "The Relationship of Reading Comprehension to Written Production of Transformationally Lengthened Prose." *Journal of Reading Behavior* 9 (1977): 295–300.

Evertts, E., N. Thompson, V. Hansen, and D. ˙Nemanich. *The Nebraska Study of the Syntax of Children's Writing, 1964–1965. Vol. I.* Lincoln, Nebraska: University of Nebraska, Curriculum Development Center, 1967. ED 013 814.

Ewing, J. B. "A Study of the Influence of Various Stimuli on the Written Composition of Selected Third Grade Children." *DA* 28 (1968): 4525-A.

Ezor, E. L., and T. Lane. "Applied Linguistics: A Discovery Approach to the Teaching of Writing, K–12." Paper, Annual Meeting of NCTE, 1972.

Fadala, S. N. "Development of Composition Skills in the University of Arizona Model Freshman Composition Program." *DAI* 35 (1975): 5156-A.

Fagan, W. T., C. R. Cooper, and J. Jensen, eds. "Measures: Writing." In *Measures for Research and Evaluation in the English Language Arts*, 185–206. Urbana, Illinois: NCTE, 1975. ED 099 835.

Faigley, L. L. "Another Look at Sentences." *Freshman English News* 7, no. 3 (1979a): 18–21.

———. "Generative Rhetoric as a Way of Increasing Syntactic Fluency." *CCC* 30 (1979b): 176–81.

———. "The Influence of Generative Rhetoric on the Syntactic Maturity and Writing Effectiveness of College Freshmen." *RTE* 13 (1979c): 197–206.

———. "Measuring Growth in College Writing." Paper, Annual Meeting of CCCC, 1977. ED 143 028.

———. "Problems in Analyzing Maturity in College and Adult Writing." In *Sentence Combining and the Teaching of Writing.* Edited by D. Daiker, A. Kerek, and M. Morenburg, 94–100. Conway, Arkansas: University of Akron and University of Central Arkansas, 1979d.

———. "Using Text Structure Models for Analyzing Revision." Paper, Annual Meeting of CCCC, 1981. ED 200 978.

Faigley, L. L., J. A. Daly, and S. P. Witte. "The Role of Writing Apprehension in Writing Performance and Competence." *JER* 75 (1981): 16–21.

———. "The Role of Writing Apprehension in Writing Performance and Competence." Paper, Annual Meeting of AERA, 1981. ED 200 984.

Faigley, L. L., T. P. Miller, P. R. Meyer, and S. P. Witte. *Writing after College: A Stratified Survey of the Writing of College Trained People. Technical Report No. 1.* Austin, Texas: University of Texas, 1981. ED 210 708.

Faigley, L. L., and others. "The Role of Writing Apprehension in Writing Performance and Competence." *JER* 75 (1981): 16–21.

Faigley, L. L., and S. P. Witte. "Analyzing Revision." *CCC* 32 (1981): 400–414.

Fairbanks, M. M., and M. K. Elliott. "Reading and Writing: Relationships and Functional Reading Component in a Freshman Composition Course for Underprepared Students." 1979. ED 195 939.

Falk, J. S. "Language Acquisition and the Teaching and Learning of Writing." *CE* 41 (1979): 436–47.

Farmer, M. N. "Concerns and Issues in the Professional Education of English Teachers, 1963–1973." *DAI* 36 (1975): 3581-A.

Farmer, W. L. "Individualized Evaluation as a Method of Instruction to Improve Writing Ability in Freshman College Composition." *DAI* 37 (1976): 3472-A.*

Farrell, K. J. "A Comparison of Three Instructional Approaches for Teaching Written Composition to High School Juniors: Teacher Lecture, Peer Evaluation, and Group Tutoring." *DAI* 38 (1977): 1849-A.*

Fay, R. S. "The Revolution in English Teaching, 1910–1917." *Journal of Education* (Boston) 151, no. 3 (1969): 22–26.

Feider, H. "A Comparative Syntactic Description of Spoken and Written English." *DAI* 30 (1969): 1545-A.

Feld, M., D. J. Dieterich, and H. Smith, eds. *ERIC Documents on the Teaching of English, Volume Six: January–June 1971.* Urbana, Illinois: NCTE and ERIC Clearinghouse on the Teaching of English, 1972.

Feldstein, C. R. "The Relationship between the Writing of Practiced and Unpracticed Freshman University Writers to a Multisystemic Perspective of Paragraphing." *DAI* 41 (1981): 4317-A.

Felland, N. A. "A National Study of the Level of Composition Achievement (Superior/Average) of Twelfth-Grade Composition Students and Selected Personal Characteristics/Environmental Factors." *DAI* 41 (1981): 3037-A.

Ferrill, J. O. "Self-Exploration through Creative Writing: An Experiment in College Composition." *DAI* 38 (1977): 1196-A.

Ferry, R. E. "An Investigation of Differences in Language Arts Achievement Caused by a Planned Program in Personal Writing." *DAI* 30 (1969): 203-A.

Fichtenau, R. L. "The Effect of Teaching Rhetorical Concepts of Invention, Arrangement and Style on the Written Composition of Selected Elementary School Children in Grades Three through Six." *DAI* 30 (1969): 1465-A.

———. *Teaching Rhetorical Concepts to Elementary Children: A Research Report.* Pontiac, Michigan: Oakland County Schools, 1968. ED 026 383.

Fillman, T. W. "The Effects of Teaching Study Skills and Reading, Writing, and Listening Skills as a Specific Course of Study for Ninth Grade Students." *DAI* 30 (1970): 2416-A.*

Fils, K. A. "Changes in Self-Concept and Locus of Control as a Result of Using Structured versus Unstructured Journal Writing." *DAI* 41 (1981): 3950-A.

Findlay, K. R. "Teaching Invention by Heuristic Procedures: A Model for High School Composition." *DAI* 35 (1974): 400-A.

Findlen, G. L., III. "A Course on Teaching College English Based upon a Job Analysis and a Content Analysis." *DAI* 38 (1978): 6067-A.

Finn, P. J. "Computer-Aided Description of Mature Word Choices in Writing." In *Evaluating Writing: Describing, Measuring, Judging.* Edited by C. R. Cooper and L. Odell, 69–89. Urbana, Illinois: NCTE, 1977.

Fischer, C. A., Jr. "The Relationship between the Reflection-Impulsivity Dimension of Cognitive Style and Selected Temporal Aspects of Time Bound, First Draft, Expository Transcribing." *DAI* 42 (1981): 583-A.

Fishco, D. T. "A Study of the Relationship between Creativity in Writing and Comprehension in Reading of Selected Seventh Grade Students." *DA* 27 (1967): 3220-A.

Fisher, K. D. "An Investigation to Determine if Selected Exercises in Sentence-Combining Can Improve Reading and Writing." *DAI* 34 (1973): 4556-A.*

Florio, S., and C. M. Clark. "The Functions of Writing in an Elementary Classroom." *RTE* 16 (1982): 115–130.

Flower, L. S. "Writer-Based Prose: A Cognitive Basis for Problems in Writing." *CE* 41 (1979): 19–37.

Flower, L. S., and J. R. Hayes. "The Cognition of Discovery: Defining a Rhetorical Problem." *CCC* 31 (1980a): 21–32.

———. "A Cognitive Process Theory of Writing." *CCC* 32 (1981a): 365–387.

———. "The Dynamics of Composing: Making Plans and Juggling Constraints." In *Cognitive Processes in Writing.* Edited by L. W. Gregg and E. R. Steinberg, 31–50. Hillsdale, New Jersey: Lawrence Erlbaum Associates, Publishers, 1980b.

———. "Plans That Guide the Composing Process." In *Writing: The Nature, Development, and Teaching of Written Communication.* Vol. 2. Edited by C. H. Frederiksen and J. F. Dominic, 39–58. Hillsdale, New Jersey: Lawrence Erlbaum Associates, Publishers, 1981b.

———. "The Pregnant Pause: An Inquiry into the Nature of Planning." *RTE* 15 (1981c): 229–43.

———. "Problem-Solving Strategies and the Writing Process." *CE* 39 (1977): 449–61.

———. "Process-Based Evaluation of Writing: Changing the Performance, Not the Product." Paper, Annual Meeting of AERA, 1981d. ED 204 795.

Follman, J. C., and J. A. Anderson. "An Investigation of the Reliability of Five Procedures for Grading English Themes." *RTE* 1 (1967): 190–200.

Follman, J. C., A. J. Lowe, P. Pfost, S. Silverman, and E. Uprichard. "Descriptive Vs. Evaluative Grading of Themes." *Perceptual and Motor Skills* 35 (1972): 986.*

Follman, J. C., W. G. Miller, A. J. Lowe, and D. W. Stefurak. "Effects of Time and Typeface on Level and Reliability of Theme Grades." *RTE* 14 (1970): 51–58.

Folsom, J. *Montana English Teacher Preparation and Needs: Survey and Action, 1973–1977.* Bozeman, Montana: Montana State University, 1976. ED 136 293.

Ford, B. W. "The Effects of Peer Editing/Grading on the Grammar-Usage and Theme-Composition Ability of College Freshmen." *DAI* 33 (1973): 6687-A.

Ford, N. A. *Improving Reading and Writing Skills of Disadvantaged College Freshmen.* Champaign, Illinois: NCTE, 1967. ED 018 447.

Ford, P. M. "Lay Readers in the High School Composition Program: Some Statistics." *EJ* 50 (1961): 522–28.

Foss, D. J. "Decision Processes during Sentence Comprehension: Effects of Lexical Item Difficulty and Position upon Decision Times." *Journal of Verbal Learning and Verbal Behavior* 8 (1969): 457–62.

Fostvedt, D. R. "Criteria for the Evaluation of High School English Composition." Diss., Montana State University, 1964.

Fowler, L. M. "Descriptive and Persuasive Writing Skills of Children." *DAI* 42 (1982): 4362-A.

Fowler, R. J. "An Analysis of the Composing Processes of Three Black Adolescents." *DAI* 40 (1980): 4934-A.

Fox, R. F. "Treatment of Writing Apprehension and Its Effects on Composition." *DAI* 40 (1979): 81-A.

———. "Treatment of Writing Apprehension and Its Effects on Composition." *RTE* 14 (1980): 39–49.

Franke, T. L. "Effects of Transformational Grammar Study and Sentence Combining Practice on the Use of Syntactic Strategies in the Writing and Reading of College Freshmen." *DAI* 41 (1980): 1970-A.*

Frederiksen, C. H., and J. F. Dominic, eds. *Writing: The Nature, Development, and Teaching of Written Communication.* Vol. 2. Hillsdale, New Jersey: Lawrence Erlbaum Associates, Publishers, 1981.

Fredrick, V. *Writing Assessment Research Report: A National Survey.* Madison, Wisconsin: Wisconsin State Department of Public Instruction, Division for Management and Planning Services, 1979. ED 200 988.

Fredrick, W. C. "Reliability of Measures from 500 Written Words." *Psychological Reports* 27 (1970): 126.

Freedman, A., and I. Pringle. "Writing in the College Years: Some Indices of Growth." *CCC* 31 (1980): 311–24. See also Paper, Annual Meeting of NCTE, 1979. ED 194 894.

Freedman, S. W. "College Students Reveal Their Learning Processes." Paper, Annual Meeting of MLA, 1979. ED 181 452.

———. "A Comparative Evaluation of Student and Professional Prose." Paper, Annual Meeting of AERA, 1979. ED 172 217.

———. "The Evaluators of Student Writing." 1978. ED 157 079.

———. "How Characteristics of Student Essays Influence Teachers' Evaluations." *JEP* 71 (1979): 328–38.

———. "Influences on Evaluators of Expository Essays: Beyond the Text." *RTE* 15 (1981): 245–55.

———. "Influences on the Evaluators of Student Writing." *DAI* 38 (1978): 5306-A.

———. "Teaching and Learning in the Writing Conference." Paper, Annual Meeting of CCCC, 1980. ED 185 599.

———. "Why Do Teachers Give the Grades They Do?" *CCC* 30 (1979): 161–64.

Friedman, M., and E. Fowler. "Assessing Elementary Students' Writing Skills." Paper, Annual Meeting of AERA, 1979. ED 172 201.

Friesen, H. "The Effect That Decision Making Instruction Has on the Simple Expository Writing of Grade Six Students: A Study of Incidental Learning Transfer." *DAI* 42 (1981): 70-A.

Friesen, W. S. "A Descriptive Study of Freshman Performance in English Composition I at Kansas State University, 1961, in Relation to Fifty-Two Variables." *DA* 25 (1964): 290.

Fritts, M. F. H. "The Effects of Individual Teacher Conferences on the Writing Achievement and Self-Concept of Developmental Junior College Students." *DAI* 37 (1977): 4185-A. ED 138 988.

Fritze, D. E. "The Relationship between Expenditure per Pupil and Achievement in English." *DAI* 30 (1970): 4180-A.

Frogner, E. A. *Using the "Language Inquiry" as a Teaching Device.* Urbana, Illinois: Illinois State-Wide Curriculum Study Center in the Preparation of Secondary School English Teachers, 1969. ED 034 778.

Fry, D. J. W. "The Effects of Transformational Grammar upon the Writing Performance of Students of Low Socio-economic Backgrounds." *DAI* 32 (1972): 4835-A.

Frye, E. T. "The Effect of a Performance-Based Writing Program on the Writing Ability of Fifth and Sixth-Grade Children." *DAI* 37 (1976): 3374-A.

Frye, T. F. and G. Ligon. *ESAA Pilot: Written Composition Program. Final Technical Report.* Austin, Texas: Austin Independent School Districts, Office of Research and Evaluation, 1979. ED 176 312.

Furbee, J. W. "Writing Complexity of College Freshmen." *DAI* 31 (1971): 6275-A.

Gades, R. E., and B. Dougal. "What Are the Effects of a Composition Emphasis During Two Semesters of Typewriting?" *Business Education Forum* 34, no. 2 (November 1979): 18–20.

Gaer, E. P. "Children's Understanding and Production of Sentences." *Journal of Verbal Learning and Verbal Behavior* 8 (1969): 289–94.

Gaies, S. J. "College Freshman Writing Ability in 1963 and 1977: A Pilot Study Comparison." Paper, Annual Meeting of Midwest MLA, 1980. ED 197 387.

Gajadharsingh, J. L. "A Study of the Effects of Instruction in the Rhetoric of the Sentence on the Written Composition of Junior High School Students." Diss., University of Alberta, 1971.

Gale, I. F. "An Experimental Study of Two Fifth-Grade Language-Arts Programs: An Analysis of the Writing of Children Taught Linguistic

Grammars Compared to Those Taught Traditional Grammar." *DA* 28 (1968): 4156-A.

Gale, I. F., and L. Boisvert. "The Negative 'Aspects' of Children's Writing." 1971. ED 062 341.

Ganong, F. L. "Teaching Writing through the Use of a Program Based on the Work of Donald M. Murray." *DAI* 35 (1975): 4125-A.*

Ganter, K. K. "A Comprehensive Survey of the Status of the English Methods Course in New England Colleges and Universities." *DAI* 39 (1978): 2876-A.

Garner, R. A. "Differential Semantic Feature Emphasis across Sentence Contexts: An Investigation of Fifth-Graders' Learning and Application of the Principle for Nouns." *DAI* 38 (1978): 4681-A.

Garrett-Petts, W. "Re: Revision—An Analysis of the Revision Strategies of College Writers." Paper, Annual Meeting of CCCC, 1981. ED 199 760.

Gatschet, P. A. "Representative Guidelines for Teaching Composition: Grades 7–13." *DAI* 34 (1974): 5909-A.

Gauntlett, J. F. "Project WRITE and Its Effect on the Writing of High School Students." *DAI* 38 (1978): 7189-A.*

Geach, P. "Should Traditional Grammar Be Ended or Mended? II" *Educational Review* 22, no. 1 (November 1969): 18–25.

Gebhard, A. O. "The Relationship of Writing Quality to Syntax: A Transformational Analysis of Three Prose Samples." *DAI* 37 (1977): 6852-A.

———. "Writing Quality and Syntax: A Transformational Analysis of Three Prose Samples." *RTE* 12 (1978): 211–31.

Gee, T. C. "The Effects of Written Comment on Expository Composition." *DAI* 31 (1971): 3412-A.

———. "Students' Responses to Teacher Comments." *RTE* 6 (1972): 212–21.

Gentry, L. A. *Capitalization Instruction in Elementary School Textbooks.* Los Alamitos, California: Southwest Regional Laboratory for Educational Research and Development, 1980. ED 199 756.

———. *Punctuation Instruction in Elementary School Textbooks.* Los Alamitos, California: Southwest Regional Laboratory for Educational Research and Development, 1981. ED 199 757.

Georgiades, C. J. "An Evaluation of an English Team-Teaching Design." *DAI* 33 (1972): 1562-A.

Georgiades, W., and J. Bjelke. "Evaluation of English Achievement in a Ninth Grade, Three-Period, Team Teaching Class." *California Journal of Educational Research* 17 (1966): 100–12.

Gere, A. R. "writing and WRITING." *EJ* 66, no. 8 (November 1977): 60–64.

Gere, A. R., and others. "Measuring Teacher Attitudes toward Instruction in Writing." 1980. ED 199 717.

German, L. B. "The Teaching of Lyric Poetry Writing as Part of the Freshman English Program." *DAI* 39 (1978): 2228-A.

Geuder, P. A. "A Writing Seminar for Speakers of Black English." *DAI* 33 (1973): 3256-A.

Giaconia, R. M., and L. V. Hedges. "Identifying Features of Effective Open Education." *Review of Educational Research* 52 (1982): 579–602.

Giannasi, J. M. "Dialects and Composition." In *Teaching Composition: Ten Bibliographical Essays.* Edited by G. Tate, 275–304. Fort Worth, Texas: Texas Christian University Press, 1976.

Gilbert, J. P. "A Comparison of the Effectiveness of Two Grouping Plans for Teaching Community College First-Semester Freshman English Composition." *DAI* 32 (1972): 3719-A.*

Gillespie, B. O. W. "An Investigation of the Level of Teacher Competence Needed to Teach Writing in Selected Subject Areas of the Secondary School. " *DAI* 41 (1981): 4956-A.

Gillet, J. W. "Pedagogical Implications of Concept of Word Research." Paper, Annual Meeting of National Reading Conference, 1979. ED 186 838.

Gillis, C. "A Methodology for Examining the Relative Emphases on Four Components of English in Secondary English Elective Programs." *DAI* 36 (1976): 5765-A.

Giovanninni, M. E. "Teaching Business Communications by the Traditional Writing and the Word Processing Methods—A Comparison." *DAI* 42 (1981): 513-A.

Glaser, R. "Education and Thinking: The Role of Knowledge." *American Psychologist* 39 (1984): 93–104.

Glass, G. V. "Integrating Findings: The Meta-analysis of Research." In *Review of Research in Education, Volume 5*. Edited by L. S. Shulman. Itasca, Illinois: F. E. Peacock, 1978.

Glassner, B. M. "Preliminary Report: Hemispheric Relationships in Composing." *Journal of Education* (Boston) 162, no. 2 (1980): 74–95.

Glazer, J. I. "The Development of the Glazer Narrative Composition Scale." *DAI* 32 (1972): 3556-A.

———. *The Effect of Literature Study on the Ability of Fourth and Sixth Grade Pupils to Create Written Stories. Final Report*. Providence, Rhode Island: Rhode Island College, 1973. ED 095 538.

Glynn, S. M., B. K. Britton, K. D. Muth, and N. Dogan. "Writing and Revising Persuasive Documents: Cognitive Demands." *JEP* 74 (1982): 557–67.

Goddin, M. A. P. "A Comparison of the Effect on Student Achievement of a Generative Approach and a Traditional Approach to the Teaching of English Grammar at Grades Three and Seven." *DAI* 29 (1969): 3522-A.

Godshalk, F. I. "A Survey of the Teaching of English in Secondary Schools." Berkeley, California: Educational Testing Service, 1969. ED 033 113.

Godshalk, F. I., F. Swineford, and W. E. Coffman. *The Measurement of Writing Ability*. New York: College Entrance Examination Board, 1966. ED 029 028.

Goldstein, E. O. "The Relationship between Written Coherence and Thinking." Paper, Annual Meeting of New York College English Association, 1980. ED 193 691.

Goldstein, E. O., and C. Perfetti. "Connections, Coherence, and Cognition in Composition." Paper, Annual Meeting of CCCC, 1980. ED 185 598.

Golub, L. S. "Linguistic Structurers in Students' Oral and Written Discourse." *RTE* 3 (1969): 70–85.

———. "Syntactic and Lexical Deviations in Children's Written Sentences." 1972. ED 073 475.

———. "Syntactic and Semantic Elements of Students' Oral and Written Discourse: Implications for Teaching Composition." *DAI* 28 (1967): 2664-A.

———. "Syntactic Density Score (SDS) with Some Aids for Tabulating." 1973. ED 091 741.

Golub, L. S., and W. C. Fredrick. "An Analysis of Childrens' Writing under Different Stimulus Conditions." *RTE* 4 (1970a): 168–80.
——. "Written Language." Papers, Annual Meeting of AERA, 1970b. ED 042 750.
Golub, L. S., and C. Kidder. "Syntactic Density and the Computer." *Elementary English* 51 (1974): 1128–31.
Goodin, G., and K. Perkins. "Discourse Analysis and the Art of Coherence." *CE* 44 (1982): 57–63.
Goodlad, J. I. *A Place Called School: Prospects for the Future.* New York: McGraw-Hill Book Co., 1984.
Goodman, A. D. J. "Utilization of Positive Feedback in a Classroom Environment of Acceptance to Promote Enhanced Learner Self-Concept and Improved Written Performance." *DAI* 36 (1976): 6550-A.
Gorrell, D. K. "Controlled Composition for Teaching Basic Writing to College Freshmen: A Comparison with Grammar Lessons." *DAI* 41 (1981): 3460-A.
——. "Defining the Basic Writing Student by Count." Paper, Annual Meeting of CCCC, 1981. ED 199 725.
Goswami, D., and L. Odell. "Naturalistic Studies of Nonacademic Writing." Paper, Annual Meeting of CCCC, 1980. ED 188 247.
Gottschalk, J. P. "Two Instructional Methods for Teaching Composition: Product-Oriented and Process-Oriented." *DAI* 42 (1982): 5046-A.
Gough, J. P. "An Inquiry into Children's Understanding of the Time Concept with Implications for Written Compositions." *DA* 26 (1966): 6551. See also ED 026 368.
Gould, J. D. "An Experimental Study of Writing, Dictating, and Speaking." In *Attention and Performance VII*. Edited by J. Requin, 299–319. Hillsdale, New Jersey: Lawrence Erlbaum Associates, Publishers, 1978a.
——. "Experiments on Composing Letters: Some Facts, Some Myths, and Some Observations." In *Cognitive Process in Writing*. Edited by L. W. Gregg and E. R. Steinberg, 97–127. Hillsdale, New Jersey: Lawrence Erlbaum Associates, Publishers, 1980.
——. "How Experts Dictate." *Journal of Experimental Psychology: Human Perception and Performance* 4 (1978b): 648–61.
Gould, J. D., and S. J. Boies. "How Authors Think about Their Writing, Dictating, and Speaking." *Human Factors* 20 (1978a): 495–505.
——. "Writing, Dictating, and Speaking Letters." *Science* 201 (1978b): 1145–47.
Gozemba, P. A. "The Effect of Rhetorical Training in Visual Literacy on the Writing Skills of College Freshmen." *DAI* 36 (1975): 1269-A.
Graham, M. R. "A Study of the Comparative Influence of Learning Writing Conventions upon the Expressive Literacy of Average Ability Blue and White Collar Children." *DAI* 32 (1971): 3153-A.*
Graves, D. H. "Break the Welfare Cycle: Let Writers Choose Their Topics." In *A Case Study Observing the Development of Primary Children's Composing, Spelling, and Motor Behaviors during the Writing Process. Final Report.* NIE Grant No. G-78-0174. Edited by D. H. Graves, 388–94. Durham, New Hampshire: University of New Hampshire, 1981a. ED 218 653.
——. "An Examination of the Writing Process of Seven Year Old Children." *RTE* 9 (1975): 227–241.

———. "The Growth and Development of First Grade Writers." In *A Case Study Observing the Development of Primary Children's Composing, Spelling, and Motor Behaviors during the Writing Process. Final Report.* NIE Grant No. G-78-0174. Edited by D. H. Graves, 219–38. Durham, New Hampshire: University of New Hampshire, 1981b. ED 218 653.

———. "Let Children Show Us How to Help Them Write." *Visible Language* 13 (1979a): 16–28.

———. "Patterns of Child Control of the Writing Process." In *A Case Study Observing the Development of Primary Children's Composing, Spelling, and Motor Behaviors during the Writing Process. Final Report.* NIE Grant No. G-78-0174. Edited by D. H. Graves, 177-88. Durham, New Hampshire: University of New Hampshire, 1981c. ED 218 653.

———. "Research Update: How Do Writers Develop?" *LA* 59 (1982): 173–179.

———. "Research Update: A New Look at Writing Research." *LA* 57 (1980): 913–19.

———. "Research Update: Research Doesn't Have to Be Boring." *LA* 56 (1979b): 76–80.

———. "Research Update: Research for the Classroom: Promising Research Studies." *LA* 54 (1977): 453–58.

———. "Research Update: A Six-Year-Old's Writing Process: The First Half of First Grade." *LA* 56 (1979d): 829–35.

———. "Research Update: We Won't Let Them Write." *LA* 55 (1978): 635–40.

———. "Research Update: What Children Show Us about Revision." *LA* 56 (1979e): 312–19.

———. "Research Update: Writing Research for the Eighties: What Is Needed." *LA* 58 (1981d): 197–206.

———. "Sex Differences in Children's Writing." *Elementary English* 50 (1973): 1101–06.

———. "Where Have All the Teachers Gone?" *LA* 58 (1981e): 492–97.

———, ed. *A Case Study Observing the Development of Primary Children's Composing, Spelling, and Motor Behaviors during the Writing Process. Final Report,* NIE Grant No. G-78-0174. Durham, New Hampshire: University of New Hampshire, 1981f. ED 218 653.

Graves, D. H., and M. E. Giacobbe. "Research Update: Questions for Teachers Who Wonder If Their Writers Change." *LA* 59 (1982): 495–503.

Graves, D. H., and D. M. Murray. "Revision: In the Writer's Workshop and in the Classroom." *Journal of Education* (Boston) 162, no. 2 (1980): 38–56.

Graves, R. L. "Levels of Skills in the Composing Process." *CCC* 29 (1978): 227–32.

Gray, S., and C. Keech. *Writing from Given Information. Collaborative Research Study No. 3.* Berkeley, California: University of California, 1980. ED 198 533.

Greathouse, L. J. "Relationships between Language Development and Verbal Associative Learning of Third and Fifth-Grade Pupils." *DA* 29 (1969): 3912-A.

Green, E. A. "An Experimental Study of Sentence-Combining to Improve Written Syntactic Fluency in Fifth-Grade Children." *DAI* 33 (1973): 4057-A.*

Green, R. F. "An Investigation to Determine Whether the Relationship between Syntactic Maturity and Socio-Economic Status Can Be Measured by a Process of Clause Consolidation." Diss., Indiana University, 1969.

Greenbaum, S., and J. Taylor. "The Recognition of Usage Errors by Instructors of Freshman Composition." *CCC* 32 (1981): 169–74.

Greenberg, K. L. "The Effects of Variations in Essay Questions on the Writing Performance of College Freshmen." *DAI* 42 (1981): 685-A.

Gregg, L. W., and E. R. Steinberg, eds. *Cognitive Processes in Writing.* Hillsdale, New Jersey: Lawrence Erlbaum Associates, Publishers, 1980.

Griffin, J. "Remedial Composition at an Open-Door College." *CCC* 20 (1969): 360–63.

Griffin, W. J. "Children's Development of Syntactic Control." In *Developments in Applied Psycholinguistics Research.* Edited by S. Rosenberg and J. H. Koplin, 19–65. New York: Macmillan, 1968.

———. "Developing Syntactic Control in Seventh Grade Writing through Audio-Lingual Drill on Transformations." Paper, Annual Meeting of AERA, 1967. ED 012 437.

Grimmer, F. L. "The Effects of an Experimental Program in Written Composition on the Writing of Second-Grade Children." *DAI* 31 (1971): 5666-A.*

Grise, R. N. "The English Teacher in Kentucky: A Study of the Academic and Professional Preparation of Public High School Teachers of English in Kentucky." *DAI* 31 (1970): 1663-A.

Grobe, C. "Syntactic Maturity, Mechanics, and Vocabulary as Predictors of Quality Ratings." *RTE* 15 (1981): 75–85.

Groff, P. "Children's Oral Language and Their Written Composition." *Elementary School Journal* 78 (1978): 180–91.

———. "Does Negative Criticism Discourage Children's Compositions?" *LA* 52 (1975): 1032–34.

———. "The Effects of Talking on Writing." *English in Education* 13, no. 3 (1979): 33–37.

———. "U.S. Office of Education: Report on Cooperative Research Projects." *EJ* 56 (1967): 617–21.

Gunderson, D. V. "Flaws in Research Design." *RTE* 1 (1967): 10–16.

———. "Report on Research Projects." *EJ* 59 (1970): 304–07.

Gundlach, R. A. "The Composing Process and the Teaching of Writing: A Study of an Idea and Its Uses." *DAI* 38 (1978): 6497-A.

Gunter, G. O., and H. McNitt. *Effectiveness of an Interest-Motivated Approach to Junior College Remedial English Instruction.* York, Pennsylvania: York Junior College, 1966. ED 010 121.

Gurley, J. "The Comparative Effects of Using Alternative Modes of Instruction in Developmental Writing on the Achievement of Selected Groups of College Students." *DAI* 36 (1976): 5766-A.

Guthrie, J. T., and T. L. Baldwin. "Effects of Discrimination, Grammatical Rules, and Application of Rules on the Acquisition of Grammatical Concepts." *JEP* 61 (1970): 358–64.

Haas, V. J., P. R. Childers, E. Babbitt, and S. M. Dylla. "English Composition by Workshop." *Journal of Experimental Education* 40, no. 3 (Spring 1972): 33–37.

Hache, M. D. "Can Creative Writing Be Taught?" 1974. ED 166 717.

———. "High School Writing Programs and Their Effect on College Composition." 1977. ED 181 468.

Hackman, J. D., and P. Johnson. *Yale College Freshmen: How Well Do They Write?* New Haven, Connecticut: Yale University, 1976. ED 140 753.

Hagen, L. B. "An Analysis of Transitional Devices in Student Writing." *RTE* 5 (1971): 190–201.

Hagstrum, J. H. "Research in Written Composition." *CE* 26 (1964): 53–56.

Hairston, M. "Not All Errors Are Created Equal: Nonacademic Readers in the Professions Respond to Lapses in Usage." *CE* 43 (1981): 794–806.

Hairston, M. C., and C. L. Selfe, eds. *Selected Papers from the 1981 Texas Writing Research Conference.* Austin, Texas: University of Texas, Texas Writing Research Group, 1981. ED 208 417.

Hake, R. L. "Composition Theory in Identifying and Evaluating Essay Writing Ability." Diss., University of Chicago, 1973.

Hake, R. L., and J. M. Williams. "Sentence Expanding: Not Can, or How, but When." In *Sentence Combining and the Teaching of Writing.* Edited by D. Daiker, A. Kerek, and M. Morenberg, 134–46. Conway, Arkansas: University of Akron and University of Central Arkansas, 1979.

———. "Style and Its Consequences: Do as I Do, Not as I Say." *CE* 43 (1981): 433–51.

Hall, M., S. A. Moretz, and J. Statom. "Writing Before Grade One—A Study of Early Writers." *LA* 53 (1976): 582–85.

Halliday, M. A. K. "Language Structure and Language Functions." In *New Horizons in Linguistics.* Edited by J. Lyons, 140–65. Middlesex: Penguin, 1970.

Halliday, M. A. K., and R. Hasan. *Cohesion in English.* London: Longman Group, 1976.

Halpern, S., E. Spreitzer, and S. Givens. "Who Can Evaluate Writing?" *CCC* 29 (1978): 396–97.

Hammond, E. R. "Professional Writing Programs: Lessons for Freshman Composition." Paper, Annual Meeting of CCCC, 1979. ED 176 325.

Hammond, W. D. "Certain Differences in the Syntactic Structure of Creative Writing at Four Elementary Grade Levels." *DAI* 30 (1970): 3188-A.

Hancock, R. J. "An Analytical Study of The Written Verb Tense Usage of Selected Sixth-Grade Pupils." *DA* 27 (1967): 3773-A.

Hansen, B. "The Effect of Teacher-Guided Theme-Revision on Composition Performance of University Freshmen." *DAI* 32 (1971): 1473-A.*

———. "Rewriting Is a Waste of Time." *CE* 39 (1978): 956–60.

Hansen, H. R. "Instructor's Cognitive Style or Psychological Type and the Teaching of Freshman Composition." *DAI* 41 (1981): 3444-A.

Hanson, R. A., and others. *SWRL Communicaiton Skills Programs: Quality Assurance Information for the 1973–74 Academic Year.* Los Alamitos, California: Southwest Regional Laboratory for Educational Research and Development, 1975. ED 124 951.

Hardaway, J. M. "Generative Rhetoric: An Analysis of Its Influence on the Writing of College Freshmen." *DAI* 30 (1969): 2418-A.*

Hardy, P. S. "Process, Product and Concepts about Writing: A Study of Sixteen Children Ages Three through Six." *DAI* 42 (1982): 3504-A.

Harris, M[ary M[cDonnell]]. "Oral and Written Syntax Attainment of Second Graders." *RTE* 11 (1977): 117–32.

Harris, M[averick] M[arvin]. "The Effectiveness of Programmed Instruction for Teaching Expository Writing to College Freshmen and High School Juniors." *DAI* 33 (1973): 5036-A.*

Harris, R. "Some Thoughts on Research and the Teaching of English." *RTE* 2 (1968): 5–13.

Harris, R. J. "An Experimental Inquiry into the Functions and Value of Formal Grammar in the Teaching of English, with Special Reference to the Teaching of Correct Written English to Children Aged Twelve to Fourteen." Diss., University of London, 1962.

Harris, W. J. H. "Teacher Response to Student Writing: A Study of the Response Patterns of High School English Teachers to Determine the Basis for Teacher Judgment in Evaluating Student Writing." *DAI* 35 (1974): 1352-A.

———. "Teacher Response to Student Writing: A Study of the Response Patterns of High School English Teachers to Determine the Basis for Teacher Judgment of Student Writing." *RTE* 11 (1977): 175–85.

Harrison, A. E. "A Study of Current Content, Practices, and Philosophy of Terminal English in the Community Junior Colleges of Kansas." *DAI* 33 (1973): 3321-A.

Hart, E. J. "The Effect of a Knowledge of Selected Reading Skills on the Acquisition and Retention of These Skills in Written Composition." *DAI* 41 (1980): 1510-A.

Hart, M. M. S. "An Assessment of the Ability to Manipulate Syntactic Structures As Described by Transformational Grammar Theory." 1971. ED 080 995.

Harter, M. T. "A Study of the Effects of Transformational Grammar on the Writing Skills of Seventh Graders." *DAI* 39 (1978): 2794-A.

Hartig, H. "Needed Research in Grammar Teaching." *Reading Improvement* 7, no. 1 (Spring 1970): 9–13.

———. "A Study of the Relation between Certain Attitudes toward Major Composition Tasks and Expository Writing Proficiency of College Freshmen." *DA* 27 (1966): 52-A.

Hartnett, C. G. "Cohesion as a Teachable Measure of Writing Competence." *DAI* 41 (1980): 2086-A.

Hartvigsen, M. K. "A Comparative Study of Quality and Syntactic Maturity between In-Class and Out-of-Class Writing Samples of Freshmen at Washington State University." *DAI* 42 (1981): 2111-A.

Hartwell, P. "Dialect Interference in Writing: A Critical View." *RTE* 14 (1980): 101–18.

———. "Writers as Readers." Paper, Annual Meeting of CCCC, 1981. ED 199 701.

Hass, W. A. "On the Heterogeneity of Psychological Processes in Syntactic Development." 1970. ED 040 764. Also published as a chapter in *Language Training in Early Childhood Education*. Edited by C. Lavatelli, 49–59. Urbana, Illinois: Published for the ERIC Clearinghouse on Early Childhood Education by the University of Illinois Press, 1971.

Haswell, R. H. "Within-Group Distribution of Syntactic Gain Through Practice in Sentence-Combining." *RTE* 15 (1981): 87–96.

Hatch, E. R. "Four Experimental Studies in the Syntax of Young Children." *DAI* 30 (1970): 2990-A.

Haugh, O. M., and E. F. Condon. "Studies of the Language Arts in Grades 7–13 at the University of Kansas." *Kansas Studies in Education* 16, no. 1 (1966): 1–48.

Hausner, R. M. "Interaction of Selected Student Personality Factors and Teachers' Comments in a Sequentially-Developed Composition Curriculum." *DAI* 36 (1976): 5768-A.*

Hawkins, T. "Intimacy and Audience: The Relationship between Revision and the Social Dimension of Peer Tutoring." Paper, Annual Meeting of MLA, 1979. ED 179 996.

Haworth, L. H. "Figuratively Speaking." *LA* 55 (1978): 837–40.

———. "Using Poetry to Stimulate the Writing of Descriptive Prose at the Grade Five Level." *DAI* 36 (1976): 6377-A.

Hayes, C. G. "Exploring Apprehension: Composing Processes of Apprehensive and Non-Apprehensive Intermediate Freshmen Writers." Paper, Annual Meeting of CCCC, 1981. ED 210 678.

Hayes, J. R., and L. S. Flower. "Identifying the Organization of Writing Processes." In *Cognitive Processes in Writing*. Edited by L. W. Gregg and E. R. Steinberg, 3–30. Hillsdale, New Jersey: Lawrence Erlbaum Associates, Publishers, 1980.

———. "Writing as Problem Solving." In *A Process Model of Composition*, *Technical Report No. 1.* Edited by L. S. Flower and J. R. Hayes, 84–103. Pittsburgh, Pennsylvania: Carnegie-Mellon University, 1979.

Hayes, L. H. "Evaluating the Impact and Efficacy of Classroom Learning by the Use of Daily Logs." *DAI* 37 (1976): 2667-A.

Hayhurst, H. "Some Errors of Young Children in Producing Passive Sentences." *Journal of Verbal Learning and Verbal Behavior* 6 (1967): 634–39.

Hays, J. N. "The Effect of Audience Considerations upon the Revisions of a Group of Basic Writers and More Competent Junior and Senior Writers." Paper, Annual Meeting of CCCC, 1981. ED 204 802.

Hazen, C. L. "The Relative Effectiveness of Two Methodologies in the Development of Composition Skills in College Freshman English." *DAI* 33 (1973): 4243-A.*

Hazen, D. W. "The Biasing Effects of Curriculum and Academic Status Labels upon Community College English Instructors' Evaluations of Written Compositions." *DAI* 35 (1975): 7611-A.

Head, R. B., and P. T. Wilson. "A Study of Freshman Composition Curricula." 1976. ED 151 852.

Heard, G. C. "The Relationship of Psychocultural Factors to Standard English Use in the Writing of Selected Black College Freshman." *DAI* 36 (1976): 6444-A.

Heard, G. C., and L. D. Stokes. *Psycho-Cultural Considerations in Black Students' Written Language Use: A Case Study.* New Brunswick, New Jersey: Rutgers—The State University, 1975. ED 137 815.

Heaton, H. F. "A Study of Writing Anxiety among High School Students Including Case Histories of Three High and Three Low Anxiety Students." *DAI* 41 (1980): 2068-A.

Hedges, L. V. "Distribution Theory for Glass's Estimator of Effect Size and Related Estimators." *Journal of Educational Statistics* 6 (1981): 107–28.

———. "Estimating Effect Size from a Series of Independent Experiments." *Psychological Bulletin* 92 (1982a): 490–99.

———. "Fitting Categorical Models to Effect Sizes from a Series of Experiments." *Journal of Educational Statistics* 7 (1982b): 119–37.

Heider, F. K., and G. M., Heider. "A Comparison of Sentence Structure of Deaf and Hearing Children." *Psychological Monographs* 52, no. 1 (1940): 42–103.

Heil, H. F. "The Development of Selected Language Variables in Two Modes of Writing and Their Relationship to Reading Comprehension in the Primary Grades." *DAI* 38 (1977): 137-A.

Hekman, B. A. "A Study of English Programs and Inservice Teacher-Training Opportunities in Selected, Private, Church-Related High Schools." *DAI* 32 (1972): 5652-A.

Held, J. R. "Teaching Punctuation in the Ninth Grade by Means of Intonation Cues." *RTE* 3 (1969): 196–208.

Heller, M. F. "The Reading-Writing Connection: An Analysis of the Written Language of University Freshmen at Two Reading Levels." *DAI* 40 (1980): 4452-A.

Helpin, J. "An Experimental Investigation of Eliminating Technical Errors in Writing through the Use of Learning Activity Packages." *Master's Abstracts* 11 (1973): 432.*

Hemphill, J. M. "The Effects of Different Models of Language Arts Instruction on the Writing of Second and Third Graders." *DAI* 42 (1982): 4290-A.

Henderson, C. A. "A Study of the Relationship between Awareness of Basic Structural Relationships in English and Increased Ability in Written Composition." *DA* 29 (1968): 184-A.

Henderson, H. K. "A Comparison of the Effects of Practice with Signaled or Open Sentence-Combining Exercises within Varying Instructional Time Frames." *DAI* 41 (1981): 5009-A.

Henderson, J. E. T. "An Investigation of Practitioner Evaluation and Agreement Regarding Effective Language Arts Instruction." *DA* 29 (1968): 1806-A.

Henderson, M. E. "The Composing Process of Prospective Elementary Teachers: Implications for a Treatment Program for the Poor Writers." *DAI* 41 (1980): 2424-A.

Henderson, M. M. "A Study of the Structure of the Writing Laboratory Programs in Two-Year Community Colleges." *DAI* 41 (1981): 3924-A.

Hendrickson, C. A. "The Effect of Sentence-Combining Techniques upon the Development of Syntactic Complexity and Composition Quality in High-School Students." *DAI* 41 (1981): 4957-A.

Hennig, K. R., Jr. "Composition Writing and the Functions of Language." *DAI* 41 (1980): 2424-A.

Henning, G. H. "Measurement of Psychological Differentiation and Linguistic Variation: A Study of the Relationship between Field-Dependence-Independence, Locus-of-Control, Hemispheric Localization,and Variations in the Occurrence of Syntactic Classes in Written Language." *DAI* 38 (1978): 6620-A.

Herman, J. *The Tutor and the Writing Student: A Case Study. Curriculum Publication No. 6.* Berkeley, California: University of California, School of Education, 1979. ED 192 324.

Herring, G. A. "Improving Preparation of Teachers through Self-Study: An Experiment with Sound Film Recordings in an English Methods Class." *DAI* 30 (1969): 1895-A.

Herrmann, R. W. "Expressive Writing: Psychological Development and Education Setting in a New Language Curriculum." *DAI* 35 (1975): 5215-A.

Hertz, V. L. "Cognitive-Field Implications for the Teaching of Technical Writing to Non-Traditional Students." *DAI* 41 (1981): 4306-A.

Heward, W. L., and H. T. Eachus. "Acquisition of Adjectives and Adverbs in Sentences Written by Hearing Impaired and Aphasic Children." *Journal of Applied Behavioral Analysis* 12 (1979): 391–400.

Heyda, J. F. "Captive Audiences: Composition Pedagogy, the Liberal Arts Curriculum, and the Rise of Mass Higher Education." *DAI* 40 (1979): 2642-A.

Heys, F. Jr. "The Theme-a-Week Assumption: A Report of an Experiment." *EJ* 51 (1962): 320–22.

Hiatt, M. P. *Artful Balance: The Parallel Structures of Style.* New York: Teachers College Press, 1975.

Hidi, S., and A. Hildyard. "The Comparison of Oral and Written Productions of Two Discourse Types." *Discourse Processes* 6 (1983): 91–105.

Higgins, E. T. G. "A Social and Developmental Comparison of Oral and Written Communication Skills." *DAI* 34 (1974): 4081-B.

Higgins, J. A. "Remedial Students' Needs vs. Emphases in Text-Work-books." *CCC* 24 (1973): 188–92.

Hildyard, A., and S. Hidi. "Resolving Conflict in Narratives." Paper, Annual Meeting of AERA, 1980.

Hilfman, T. "Can Second Grade Children Write More Complex Sentences?" *Elementary English* 47 (1970): 209–14.

Hilgers, T. L. "Training College Composition Students in the Use of Free-writing and Problem-Solving Heuristics for Rhetorical Invention." *RTE* 14 (1980): 293–307. See also *DAI* 41 (1981): 2977-A.

Hill, J[ames] D. "A Study of the Professional Preparation of English Teachers in Certain Alabama Secondary Schools." *DAI* 30 (1970): 2881-A.

Hill, J[ohn] D. "An Analysis of the Writing on Elementary Children, Grades Two Through Six, to Determine the Presence, Frequency of Use and Development by Grade Level of Specified Literary Devices." *DAI* 33 (1973): 5970-A.

Hiller, J. H., D. R. Marcotte, and T. Martin. "Opinionation, Vagueness, and Specificity-Distinctions: Essay Traits Measured by Computer." *AERJ* 6 (1969): 271–86.

Hillerich, R. L. "Evaluation of Written Language." Paper, Annual Meeting of AERA, 1970. ED 041 944.

———. "Evaluation of Written Language." *Elementary English* 48 (1971): 839–42.

Hillocks, G., Jr. *Alternatives in English: A Critical Appraisal of Elective Programs. ERIC/RCS Information Analysis Series: Group 1.* Urbana, Illinois: ERIC Clearinghouse on Reading and Communication Skills, 1972. ED 068 951.

———. "An Analysis of Some Syntactic Patterns in Ninth Grade Themes." *JER* 57 (1964): 417–20.

———. "The Effects of Observational Activities on Student Writing." *RTE* 13 (1979): 23–35.

———. "The Interaction of Instruction, Teacher Comment, and Revision in Teaching the Composing Process." *RTE* 16 (1982): 261–78.

———. "The Responses of College Freshmen to Three Modes of Instruction." *American Journal of Education* 89 (1981): 373–95.

———. "What Works in Teaching Composition: A Meta-analysis of Experimental Treatment Studies." *American Journal of Education* 93, no. 1 (1984): 133–70.

Hillocks, G., Jr., E. A. Kahn, and L. R. Johannessen. "Teaching Defining Strategies as a Mode of Inquiry: Some Effects on Student Writing." *RTE* 17 (1983): 275–84.

Hirsch, E. D., Jr. *The Philosophy of Composition.* Chicago: The University of Chicago Press, 1977. ED 145 468.

Hirsch, E. D., Jr., and D. P. Harrington. "Measuring the Communicative Effectiveness of Prose." In *Writing: The Nature, Development, and Teaching of Written Communication.* Vol. 2. Edited by C. Frederiksen and J. Dominic, 189–207. Hillsdale, New Jersey: Lawrence Erlbaum Associates, Publishers, 1981.

Hobbs, J. H. "The Poetry-Composing Processes of Proficient Twelfth-Grade Writers." *DAI* 42 (1982): 3477-A.

Hodgkinson, H., W. Walter, and R. Coover. *Bard Corrects Freshmen Themes on Tape.* Washington, D.C.: American Association for Higher Education, 1968. ED 017 531.

Hoetker, J. "Essay Examination Topics and Students' Writing." *CCC* 33 (1982): 377–92.

Hoetker, J., and G. Brossell. "An *EJ* Readership Survey Report." *EJ* 69, no. 5 (May 1980): 13–19.

———. "An *EJ* Readership Survey: Who (If Anyone) Is Teaching Them Writing and How?" *EJ* 68, no. 7 (October 1979): 19–25.

Hoffman, R. A., and D. L. Smith. "Use of the Test of Everyday Writing Skills in a College Screening Program." *JER* 73 (1980): 668–71.

Hoffman, W. E. "A Study of the Effectiveness of Programmed Instruction in English Grammar and Usage in the High School English Classroom." *DA* 29 (1968): 1040-A.

Hoffmann, R. J. "The Relationship of Reading Comprehension to Syntactic Maturity and Writing Effectiveness." In *Sentence Combining and the Teaching of Writing.* Edited by D. Daiker, A. Kerek, and M. Morenberg, 109–15. Conway, Arkansas: University of Akron and University of Central Arkansas, 1979.

Hogan, C. "Let's Not Scrap the Impromptu Test Essay Yet." *RTE* 11 (1977): 219–25.

Hogan, M. "A System Approach Design for Freshman Composition." *DAI* 41 (1981): 3555-A.

Hogan, M. P. "On the Need for Organizational Identity-Advanced Composition: A Survey." Paper, Annual Meeting of the CCCC, 1979. ED 181 492.

Hogan, R. C. "The Rationale, Design, Implementation, and Evaluation of a Composition Program Employing Backward Sequence." *DAI* 36 (1976): 5770-A.

———. "Self-Instructional Units Based on the Christensen Method." *CCC* 28 (1977): 275–77.

Hogan, T. P. "Students' Interests in Writing Activities." *RTE* 14 (1980): 119–25.

Hohmann, C. F. "Assessing the Episodic Structure, Information Structure and Cohesion of Children's Written Narratives as Indices of Their Sophistication in Writing." *DAI* 39 (1978): 3533-A.

Hollman, M. J. "Good School Writing: An Exploration of the Opinions of Thirty-Two Professionals." *DAI* 41 (1980): 2424-A.

Hook, J. N., and others. *Illinois State-Wide Curriculum Study Center in the Preparation of Secondary School English Teachers. Final Report.* Urbana, Illinois: Illinois State-Wide Curriculum Study Center in the Preparation of Secondary School English Teachers, 1969. ED 033 135.

Hooks, J. "An Analysis of Writing Skills as Described by Selected Professional Writers." *DAI* 33 (1973): 5004-A.

Hopkins, K. H. "The Relative Effectiveness of Two Methodologies in High School Senior English in the Development of Composition Skills." *DAI* 28 (1968): 3558-A.

Horgan, D. "How to Answer Questions When You've Got Nothing to Say." *Journal of Child Language* 5 (1978): 159–65.

Horne, R. N. "A Study of the Use of Figurative Language by Sixth Grade Children." *DAI* 27 (1967): 3367-A. See also ED 026 368.

Houck, D. W. "A Descriptive Study of Selected Elementary and Secondary Act Title I Language Arts Programs." *DAI* 30 (1970): 3191-A.

House, E. B. and W. J. House. "Some Similarities and Differences between Compositions Written by Remedial and Non-Remedial College Freshmen." Paper, Annual Meeting of the CCCC, 1980. ED 186 931.

Houston, R. S. "Exemption from College Freshman Composition: The College Level Examination Program (CLEP) General Examination in English Composition and the American College Testing Program (ACT) English Usage Test." *DAI* 41 (1980): 1971-A.

Houston, S. H. "An *EJ* Readership Survey: Language Attitudes and Information Study." *EJ* 67, no. 3 (March 1978): 33–38.

Howie, S. M. H. "A Study: The Effects of Sentence Combining Practice on the Writing Ability and Reading Level of Ninth Grade Students." *DAI* 40 (1979): 1980-A.*

Huber, P. J. *Robust Statistical Procedures.* Philadelphia, Pennsylvania: Society for Industrial and Applied Mathematics, 1977.

Huck, S. W., and W. G. Bounds. "Essay Grades: An Interaction Between Graders' Handwriting Clarity and the Neatness of Examination Papers." *AERJ* 9 (1972): 279–83.

Hudson, S. A., and L. R. Veal. *An Empirical Investigation of Direct and Indirect Measures of Writing. Report of the 1980–1981 Georgia Competency Based Education Writing Assessment Project.* Atlanta, Georgia: Georgia State Department of Education, 1981. ED 205 993.

Huebner, C., and G. Jasso. "Communication Skills Survey." Paper, Annual Meeting of the California Association of Teachers of English, 1977. ED 145 431.

Huffman, H. A. "The Identification of Critical Components in a Staff Development Program Based on the 1976 Recommendations of the National Council of Teachers of English." *DAI* 39 (1979): 1490-A.

Hughes, D. C., and others. "Essay Marking and the Context Problem." *Educational Research* 22, no. 2 (1980): 147–48.

———. "Influence of Context Position and Scoring Method on Essay Scoring." *JEM* 17 (1980): 131–35.

Hughes, T. "What the British Tell the U.S. about Writing and Reading." Paper, Annual Great Lakes Regional Conference of the International Reading Association, 1978. ED 175 020.

Hulewicz, R. R. "A Prototype for Objectively Measuring Composition Ability." *DAI* 35 (1975): 7167-A.

Hull, G. A. "Effects of Self-Management Strategies on Journal Writing by College Freshmen." *RTE* 15 (1981): 135–48.

Hulteng, J. L. *How Basic Newswriting Courses Are Taught at the Schools and Departments of Journalism.* Eugene, Oregon: University of Oregon, School of Journalism, 1973. ED 083 590.

Hunt, B. J. "Establishing and Implementing a Writing Center on the College Level." *DAI* 41 (1980): 2083-A.

Hunt, K. W. *Differences in Grammatical Structures Written at Three Grade Levels. Cooperative Research Project No. 1998.* Tallahassee, Florida: Florida State University, 1964.

———. "Early Blooming and Late Blooming Syntactic Structures." In *Evaluating Writing.* Edited by C. R. Cooper and L. Odell, 91–104. Urbana, Illinois: NCTE, 1977.

———. *Grammatical Structures Written at Three Grade Levels. NCTE Research Report No. 3.* Champaign, Illinois: NCTE, 1965a. ED 113 735.

———. "Recent Measures in Syntactic Development." *Elementary English* 43 (1966): 732–39.

———. "Response to 'How Not to Analyze the Syntax of Children,' by Roger McCaig." *Elementary English* 47 (1970): 619–23.

———. "A Synopsis of Clause-to-Sentence Length Factors." *EJ* 54 (1965b): 300, 305–09.

———. "Syntactic Maturity in School Children and Adults." *Monographs of the Society for Research in Child Development* 35, no. 1 (1970): entire issue.

———. "Syntax, Science, and Style." In *The Language Arts in the Elementary School: A Forum for Focus.* Edited by M. L. King, R. Emans, and P. J. Cianciolo, 111–125. Urbana, Illinois: NCTE, 1973.

Hunt, K. W., and R. C. O'Donnell. *An Elementary School Curriculum to Develop Better Writing Skills.* Tallahassee, Florida: Florida State University, 1970. ED 050 108.

Hunt, K. W., and others. *An Instrument to Measure Syntactic Maturity (Preliminary Version).* Tallahassee, Florida: Florida State University, 1968. ED 020 926.

Huntington, J. R. "Effects of Instructional Variables on Syntactic Complexity and Clarity in Children's Written Composition." *DA* 29 (1969): 2149-A.*

———. "Pre-Writing Activities: Effects on Syntactic Complexity and Clarity in Children's Written Composition." *Elementary English* 49 (1972): 730–34.

Hurlow, M. L. "Linguistic Insecurity and Linguistic Complexity." Paper, Annual Meeting of CCCC, 1981. ED 203 314.

Hurst, D. W. "A Comparative Study of Two Dissimilar Writing Programs as an Influence on Syntactical Fluency: The Moffett Sequence and the Traditional Rhetorical Modes." *DAI* 40 (1980): 3841-A.*

Hutkin, R. M., comp. *A Vocational Approach to Written Communications. Final Report.* Columbus, Nebraska: Platte Technical Community College, 1975. ED 113 601.

Hyatt, S. J. "The Syntactic Density of the Written Discourse of Selected Economically Disadvantaged Secondary Students: The Relationship between Language Performance and Linguistic Ability." *DAI* 37 (1976): 2694-A.

Hyndman, R. "Some Factors Related to the Writing Performance of Tenth-Grade Students." *DA* 30 (1969): 1468-A.

Illo, J. "From Senior to Freshman: A Study of Performance in English Composition in High School and College." *RTE* 10 (1976): 127–36.

Inman, T. H. "A Study to Determine the Effect of Varying the Frequency of Writing upon Student Achievement in Business Correspondence." *DAI* 31 (1971): 3106-A.

"*The Instructor* Reports on the First National Survey on the Status of Language Arts." *The Instructor* 75, no. 7 (March 1966): 31–35.

Irvine, J. T. *Formality and Informality in Speech Events. Working Papers in Sociolinguistics, No. 52.* Austin, Texas: Southwest Educational Development Lab, 1978. ED 165 492.

Ivarie, T. W., Jr. "An Experiment to Determine the Effectiveness of Teaching Grammar, Punctuation, and Capitalization by Programmed Instruction to Collegiate Business Communications Students." *DA* 29 (1968): 512-A.

Jackson, G. L. "The Relationship between the Observed Classroom Behavior of High School Teachers of English and the Growth of Pupils in Knowledge of Grammar Skills." *DA* 28 (1967): 1656-A.

Jackson, K. D. D. "The Effect of Sentence Combining Practice on the Reduction of Syntactic Errors in Basic Writing." *DAI* 42 (1982): 5046-A.

Jackson, L. M. "Preference Scaling of Titles in English Composition." *JER* 61 (1968): 395–97.

Jackson, W. S., Jr. "Creativity Training's Effect on Poetry Writing." *DAI* 42 (1981): 2047-A.

Jacobs, S. E. "Student Writing in the Academic Context: A Linguistic Study of Well-Shaped vs. Poorly-Shaped Essays with Implications for Learning and Teaching." 1979. ED 191 074.

———. "A Study of Coherence: Implications for Teaching Writing in an Academic Context." *DAI* 40 (1980): 4383-A.

Jacobson, T. "Sentence Combining in the College Remedial Classroom: A Real Basic." Conference on Sentence Combining and the Teaching of Writing, Miami University, 1978.

Janzen, H. L., and H. J. Hallworth. "Demographic and Biographic Predictors of Writing Ability." *Journal of Experimental Education* 41, no. 4 (Summer 1973): 43–53.

Jeffery, C. "Teachers' and Students' Perceptions of the Writing Process." *RTE* 15 (1981): 215–28.

Jenks, E. C. "An Experimental Method to Develop Creativity in the Writing of Tenth Grade Students." *DA* 26 (1966): 4501.

Jennings, K. A. E. "A Study of the Remedial English Course at Ball State University and a Proposal for a More Effective Method of Teaching Remedial Composition." *DAI* 39 (1979): 5372-A.

Jennings, M. S. "A Comparison of Middle Managerial Written Business Communications Practices and Problems and Collegiate Written Business Communications Instruction." *DAI* 35 (1975): 4861-A.

Jewell, R. M., J. Cowley, and G. Bisbey. *Instruction in College Freshman Composition. Final Report.* Cedar Falls, Iowa: Northern Iowa University, 1970. ED 054 176.

Jobe, R. A. "Factors That Influence Children's Free Choice of Topics for Creative Writing." *DAI* 35 (1975): 7529-A.

Johnson, C. M. "The Creative Thinking, Verbal Intelligence, and Creative Writing Ability of Young Gifted Children." *DA* 29 (1969): 4187-A.

Johnson, L. G. "Teaching Punctuation with Dictated Lessons." *DA* 25 (1965): 5125.

Johnson, M. "Assessment Results for Student Writing Samples." Paper, Annual Meeting of NCTE, 1979. ED 191 057.

Johnson, N. R. "A Comparison of Syntactic Writing Maturity with Reading Achievement." *DAI* 41 (1981): 4346-A.

Johnson, N. W. "The Uses of Grammatical and Rhetorical Norms, Pedagogical Strategies, and Statistical Methods in Designing and Validating a Composition Placement Instrument." *DAI* 37 (1977): 7111-A.

Johnson, R. S. "A Comparison of English Teachers' Own Usage with Their Attitudes Towards Usage." *DAI* 31 (1970): 377-A.

Johnson, S. T. "Some Tentative Strictures on Generative Rhetoric." *CE* 31 (1969): 155–65.

Johnson, W. S. "Cognitive Tempo and Verbal Abilities in the Composing Process of College Writers." *DAI* 41 (1981): 2978-A.

Johnston, L. T. "Using Story Starters and General Topics as Motivation for Improving Writing on the Fifth and Sixth-Grade Levels." *DAI* 38 (1978): 3933-A.*

Jolley, N. E. "Techniques for Improving the Teaching of Written Composition in the Self-Contained Classroom." Thesis, Ohio State University, 1961.

Jolly, T. "ERIC/RCS Report: Reading, Writing, Listening, Speaking." *LA* 57 (1980): 664–68.

Jones, B. E. W. "Marking of Student Writing by High School English Teachers in Virginia during 1976." *DAI* 38 (1978): 3911-A.

Jones, B. F., and J. W. Hall. "Effects of Cross-Classification Strategies for Recalling Prose and for Writing Compare-and-Contrast Essays." Revision of a paper presented at the Annual Meeting of AERA, 1979. ED 182 712.

Jones, C. K. "Curricular Issues and Trends in High School English Instruction as Reflected in *English Journal*—1959–1976." *DAI* 39 (1978): 2796-A.

Jones, E. A. "A Study of the Relationship between Objective Tests and Written Essays as Measures of the Writing Ability of Grade Ten Students." Diss., University of Alberta, 1969.

Jones, M. A. C. "An Investigation to Determine the Rate of Syntactic Growth as a Result of Sentence-Combining Practice in Freshman English." *DAI* 41 (1981): 4321-A.

———. "Sentence-Combining: Measuring the Rate of Syntactic Growth in Freshman Composition." 1979. ED 208 391.

Jones, T. L. "An Exploratory Study of the Impact on Student Writing of Peer Evaluation." *DAI* 39 (1978): 95-A.

Joos, M. *The Five Clocks—A Linguistic Excursion into the Five Styles of English Usage.* New York: Harcourt, Brace and World, 1961. ED 016 684.

Judd, K. E. "The Effectiveness of Tape Recorded Evaluations of Compositions Written by Seventh-Grade and Eighth-Grade Students." *DAI* 34 (1973): 1770-A.*

Judy, S. N. "The Teaching of English Composition in American Secondary Schools, 1850–1893." *DA* 28 (1967): 2210-A.

Jurgens, J. M., and W. J. Griffin. *Relationships between Overall Quality and Seven Language Features in Compositions Written in Grades Seven, Nine, and Eleven.* Nashville, Tennessee: George Peabody College for Teachers, Institute on School Learning and Individual Differences, 1970. ED 046 932.

Kafka, T. T. "A Study of the Effectiveness of Four Motivational Stimuli on the Quality of Compositions of Intermediate Students in One School District." *DAI* 32 (1971): 2549-A.

Kagan, D. M. "Run-on and Fragment Sentences: An Error Analysis." *RTE* 14 (1980): 127–38.

Kahler, A. D., Jr. "The Effects of Programmed Grammar and Journal Writing on Student Writing Ability: An Exploratory Study." *DA* 27 (1966): 74-A.

Kahn, E. A., and L. R. Johannessen. "Does the Assignment Make a Difference? Four Variations of a Writing Task and Their Effects on Student Performance." University of Chicago: Unpublished manuscript, 1982.

Kamler, B. "One Child, One Teacher, One Classroom: The Story of One Piece of Writing." *LA* 57 (1980): 680–93.

Kantor, K. J. "Creative Expression in the English Curriculum: An Historical Perspective." *RTE* 9 (1975): 5–29.

Karegianes, M. L., E. T. Pascarella, and S. W. Pflaum. "The Effects of Peer Editing on the Writing Proficiency of Low-Achieving Tenth Grade Students." *JER* 73 (1980): 203–07.

Katchen, L. C. "A Study in the Effects of Paradigmatic Language Training and Its Transfer to the Reading and Writing Performance of Adult Illiterates." *DAI* 41 (1980): 2404-A.

Kates, J. *The Santa Barbara County Experiment on Individualizing Ninth Grade English Composition: The Kates Method.* Cypress, California: Santa Barbara County Schools, Writing Teachers In-Service Program, 1977. ED 141 834.

Kauchak, D. P. "Attitude Change as a Function of Essay Writing." *DAI* 34 (1974): 4988-A.

Kaufman, S. D. S. "Cognitive Style and Writing: An Inquiry." *DAI* 42 (1981): 1519-A.

Kearns, P. K. "The Effect of Relaxation and Guided Imagery on the Creative Thinking and Writing of Fourth, Fifth, and Sixth Grade Students Identified as Gifted." *DAI* 40 (1979): 83-A.*

Keech, C. *Evaluation of the Bay Area Writing Project, Report on the Writing Assessment.* Berkeley, California: Bay Area Writing Project, 1979.

Keenan, E. O., and others. *Propositions across Utterances and Speakers. Papers and Reports on Child Language Development, No. 12.* Stanford, California: Stanford University, Committee on Linguistics, 1976. ED 161 298.

Keeney, M. L. "An Investigation of What Intermediate-Grade Children Say about the Writing of Stories." *DAI* 36 (1976): 5802-A.

Kegler, S. B., and others. *Preparation and Evaluation of Curricular Materials and Guides for English Language Study in Grades 7 to 12. Final Report.* Minneapolis: University of Minneapolis, Center for Curriculum Development in English, 1968. ED 027 316.

Keil, E. C. "An Investigation into the Relationship between Students' and Instructors' Goals and Learnings in Freshman English as Related to Course Grades and Achievement." *DAI* 31 (1970): 71-A.

Kelley, M. E. "Effects of Two Types of Teacher Response to Essays upon Twelfth-Grade Students' Growth in Writing Performance." *DAI* 34 (1974): 5801-A.

Kelly, H. F. "Systematic Description of Procedures Used in Teaching Two College Freshman Composition Courses." *DAI* 33 (1972): 1080-A.

Kelly, M. K. "A Study to Determine the Effects of Structured Reflective Writing on the Professional and Personal Development of Teachers." *DAI* 40 (1980): 6237-A.

Kemp, J. H. "A Comparison of Two Procedures for Improving the Writing of Developmental Writers." *DAI* 40 (1979): 1928-A.*

Kennedy, L. D., and A. D. Larson. "The Influence of Structural and of Traditional Grammatical Instruction upon Language Perception and Writing Ability." *Illinois School Research* 5, no. 2 (1969): 31–36.

Kennison, J. H. "Case Studies Showing Similarities and Differences among Ten Selected Students of Varying Proficiency in English Composition." *DAI* 42 (1982): 5046-A.

Kent, T. H. "A Study of the English Instructors in the Junior and Community Colleges." *DAI* 32 (1971): 200-A.

Kerek, A. "Measuring and Evaluating Syntactic Maturity: Some Questions of Methodology." 1979. ED 173 783.

Kerek, A., D. A. Daiker, and M. Morenberg. "The Effects of Intensive Sentence Combining on the Writing Ability of College Freshmen." In *Linguistics, Stylistics and the Teaching of Composition*. Edited by D. McQuade, 81–90. Akron, Ohio: University of Akron, 1979a.

———. "Experimental Study in Transformational Sentence Combining as a Means to Increase Syntactic Maturity, Writing Effectiveness, and Reading Comprehension among Students in Introductory College Composition Courses." Unpublished Final Report to the Exxon Education Foundation and Miami University of Ohio, 1979b.

———. "Sentence Combining and College Composition." *Perceptual and Motor Skills* 51 (1980): 1059–1157.

Kernan, M. N. "The Effects of a Human Development Program on Performance in College Freshman Writing Classes." *DAI* 34 (1973): 3237-A.*

Kidder, C. L. "Using the Computer to Measure Syntactic Density and Vocabulary Intensity in the Writing of Elementary School Children." *DAI* 35 (1974): 3524-A.

Kinchen, G. M. "An Oral-Aural-Visual Approach to Written Communicative Ability of Selected Third Grade Students." *DAI* 39 (1978): 166-A.*

King, B. J. M. "Peer and Teacher Evaluation: A Comparison of Evaluation Methods for Written Composition of Eleventh-Grade Students." *DAI* 42 (1982): 2998-A.

King, B. L. "Measuring Attitudes toward Writing: The King Construct Scale." Paper, Annual Meeting of CCCC, 1979. ED 172 258.

———. "Two Modes of Analyzing Teacher and Student Attitudes Toward Writing: The Emig Attitude Scale and the King Construct Scale." *DAI* 40 (1980): 3934-A.

King, C. P. " 'TOPOI' and the Generation of Discourse: A Critical Analysis." Paper, Annual Meeting of the Speech Communication Association, 1975. ED 116 246.

King, D. B., and E. Cotter. "An Experiment in Writing Instruction." *English Quarterly* 3, no. 2 (Summer 1970): 51–56.

King, H[arriet] L[owry]. "Teacher Verification of Improvement in Student Writing Generated through the Addition of Free Modifiers." *DAI* 40 (1979): 84-A.

King, H[elen] L[amar]. "Story Tellers, Story Writers: A Research Report." *INSIGHTS into Open Education* 11, no. 8 (1979): entire issue. ED 169 561.

King, J. A. "Teachers' Comments on Students' Writing: A Conceptual Analysis and Empirical Study." *DAI* 40 (1980): 4872-A.

King, M. L. "Research in Composition: A Need for Theory." *RTE* 12 (1978): 193–202.

King, M. L., and V. M. Rentel. *How Children Learn to Write: A Longitudinal Study. Final Report.* Columbus, Ohio: The Ohio State University, Research Foundation, 1981. ED 213 050.

———. "Toward a Theory of Early Writing Development." *RTE* 13 (1979): 243–53.

King, R. P. "Sensory Approach to Creative Writing: A Study of the Effect of Increasing the Number of Types of Sensory Stimuli Intended to Motivate Children to Write Creatively." *DAI* 35 (1974): 302-A.

Kinghorn, N. D., and others. *A Syntactic Approach to College Writing: An Analysis of Theory and Effect.* Grand Forks, North Dakota: North Dakota Study Group on Evaluation, 1981. ED 208 407.

Kinneavy, J. L. "Sentence Combining in a Comprehensive Language Framework." In *Sentence Combining and the Teaching of Writing.* Edited by D. Daiker, A. Kerek, and M. Morenberg, 60–76. Conway, Arkansas: University of Akron and University of Central Arkansas, 1979.

———, "Theories of Composition and Actual Writing." *Kansas English* 59 (1973): 3–17.

———. *A Theory of Discourse: The Aims of Discourse.* Englewood Cliffs, New Jersey: Prentice-Hall, 1971.

Kinneavy, J. L., and C. R. Kline, Jr. "Composition and Related Fields." In *Teaching Composition: Ten Bibliographical Essays.* Edited by G. Tate, 241–73. Fort Worth, Texas: Texas Christian University Press, 1976.

Kinney, J. "Classifying Heuristics." *CCC* 30 (1979): 351–56.

Kintsch, W., and T. A. van Dijk. "Toward a Model of Text Comprehension and Production." *Psychological Review* 85 (1978): 363–94.

Kirkton, C. M. "NCTE/ERIC Report: Learning to Write: Steps in the Process." *Elementary English* 48 (April 1971): 303–11.

Kirschner, S., and G. H. Poteet. "Non-Standard English Usage in the Writing of Black, White, and Hispanic Remedial English Students in an Urban Community College." *RTE* 7 (1973): 351–55.

Kita, M. J. "Children's Concepts of Reading and Writing." Paper, Annual Meeting of the National Reading Conference, 1979. ED 182 722. See also *DAI* 41 (1981): 3967-A.

Kitterman, R. W. "A Comparison of the Effectiveness on Student Writing of Two Methods of Teaching Freshman Composition." *DAI* 33 (1973): 5038-A.

Kivits, V. M. "An Experiment in Teaching English Composition Using an Oral Laboratory Approach." *The General College Studies* (University of Minnesota) 5, no. 6 (1968–69): 1–12. ED 032 871.

———. "Using Undergraduate Teaching Assistants in an Experiment in Theme Correction." *CCC* 19 (1968): 148–52.

Klaus, C. H. "Research on Writing Courses: A Cautionary Essay." *Freshman English News* 11, no. 1 (Spring 1982): 1–4, 13–14.

Kleen, J. M. S. "Sentence-Combining and Developmental Psycholinguistics: A Critique of Seven Sentence-Combining Textbooks." *DAI* 41 (1981): 3461-A.

Klein, M. *Teaching Sentence Structure and Sentence Combining in the Middle Grades.* Madison, Wisconsin: Department of Public Instruction, 1976. ED 126 510.

Klein, M. L., and B. L. Grover. *An Assessment of the Effectiveness of Symbolic Logic in the Teaching of Composition. Final Report.* Plymouth, Wisconsin: Cooperative Educational Service Agency 10. 1970. ED 059 209.

Klein, S. P., and F. M. Hart. "Chance and Systematic Factors Affecting Essay Grades." *JEM* 5 (1968): 197–206.

Kline, C. R., Jr., and W. D. Memering. "Formal Fragments: The English Minor Sentence." *RTE* 11 (1977): 97–110.

Klinger, G. C. "A Campus View of College Writing." *CCC* 28 (1977): 343–47.

Kluwin, T. N. "The Effect of Experience on the Discourse Structure of Beginning English Teachers." Paper, Annual Meeting of AERA, 1978. ED 153 248.

Knapp, J. V., and H. B. Slotnick. *Writing: Group Results A and B for Objectively-Scored Exercises; 1969–1970 Assessment, National Results by Region, Sex, Color, Size and Type of Community, and Parental Education.* Denver, Colorado: Education Commission of the States, National Assessment of Educational Progress. 1973. ED 077 029.

Koch, C. J. "Small Groups in the Composition Class: A Case Study of Developing Linguistic Security and Written Fluency." *DAI* 36 (1975): 3629-A.

Koch, S. J. "The Interests and Concerns of Adolescents, Grades Seven through Twelve, as Expressed in Their Written Composition." *DAI* 37 (1977): 7729-A.

Kock, R. A. "A Study of Free Association as a Technique to Improve Student Writing." *DAI* 32 (1972): 6292-A.

Koen, F., A. Becker, and R. Young. "The Psychological Reality of the Paragraph." *Journal of Verbal Learning and Behavior* 8 (1969): 49–53. ED 021 236.

Kohr, R. L. "Correlates of Reading and Writing Achievement." Paper, Annual Meeting of AERA, 1981. ED 199 642.

Konek, C. W. "The Effect of Compensatory Composition Tracking on High-Risk Students in an Open Admissions University." *DAI* 38 (1978): 5276-A.

Koops, J. B. "Recent Practices in Teaching Writing: A Critical Examination of Junior and Senior High School Composition Textbooks." *DAI* 36 (1975): 3547-A.

———. "Warmed Up Leftovers and Hot Apple Pie: A Report on Widely Used Secondary School Writing Textbooks." *English Education* 10 (1978): 17–24.

Kramer, H. W. "The Relationship between Personality Type and Achievement in Expository and Creative Writing." *DAI* 38 (1977): 3384-A.

Kroll, B. "Learning and Acquisition: Two Paths to Writing." *English Education* 11 (1979): 83–90.

Kroll, B. M. "Cognitive Egocentrism and the Problem of Audience Awareness in Written Discourse." *RTE* 12 (1978): 269–81.

———. "Cognitive Egocentrism and Written Discourse." *DAI* 38 (1977): 3439-A.

———. "Developmental Perspectives and the Teaching of Composition." *CE* 41 (1980): 741–52.

Krupka, J. B. *Is Anyone Learning to Write at NCACC?* Bethlehem, Pennsylvania: Northampton County Area Community College, 1970. ED 040 703.

Kuntz, E. M. "Developing Elaborating Skills in Writing Based on Theories of Language and Learning." *DAI* 38 (1978): 7116-A.

Kuntz, M. H. "The Relationship between Written Syntactic Attainment and Reading Ability in Seventh-Grade." *DAI* 36 (1975): 2159-A.

Kyhos, R. M. "An Analysis of the Attitudes of Senior High School Students toward Student-Evaluated Composition." *DAI* 40 (1980): 4934-A.

Labov, W. "The Evaluation of Writing: How Linguistics Can Help Us." Paper, Conference on Writing Evaluation, Beaver College, 1978. ED 157 358.

La Brant, L. L. "The Changing Sentence Structure of Children." *The Elementary English Review* 11 (1934): 59–65, 86.

––––––. "A Study of Certain Language Developments of Children in Grades 4–12 Inclusive." *Genetic Psychology Monographs* 14, no. 4 (1933): 387–491.

Lacampagne, R. J. "A National Study of Selected Attitudes and Approaches to Writing of Twelfth Grade Students with Superior Writing Performance versus Those with Average Writing Performance." *DAI* 30 (1969): 212-A.

Lackey, G. H., Jr. "Written Communicative Ability: An Analysis and Treatment." *DAI* 28 (1968): 3562-A. ED 031 470.

Ladenburg, M. "A Curriculum to Stimulate Psychological Development and Writing Maturity in College Freshmen." *DAI* 42 (1981): 2574-A.

Lagana, J. R. "The Development, Implementation, and Evaluation of a Model for Teaching Composition which Utilizes Individualized Learning and Peer Grouping." *DAI* 33 (1973): 4063-A.

Lamberg, W. J. "Design and Validation of Instruction in Question-Directed Narrative Writing, Developed through Discrimination Programming." *DAI* 35 (1974): 2839-A. ED 097 689.

––––––. "Major Problems in Doing Academic Writing." *CCC* 28 (1977): 26–29.

––––––. "Practices and Attitudes in Providing Information on Writing Performance." 1977. ED 158 276.

––––––. "Self-provided and Peer-provided Feedback." *CCC* 31 (1980): 63–69.

Lange, B. "ERIC/RCS Report: Writing Instruction for the Writing Teacher." *English Education* 11 (1979): 121–25.

Lareau, E. H., Jr. "Comparison of Two Methods of Teaching Expository Composition and Evaluation of a Testing Instrument." *DAI* (1971): 2437-A.*

LaRocque, G. E. "The Effectiveness of the Inductive and Deductive Methods of Teaching Figurative Language to Eighth Grade Students." *DA* 26 (1966): 6555.

Larson, R. L., ed. *Children and Writing in the Elementary School: Theories and Techniques.* New York: Oxford University Press, 1975.

––––––. "Discovery through Questioning: A Plan for Teaching Rhetorical Invention." *CE* 30 (1968): 126–34.

––––––. "Invention Once More: A Role for Rhetorical Analysis." *CE* 32 (1971): 665–72.

––––––. "Structure and Form in Non-Fiction Prose." In *Teaching Composition: Ten Bibliographical Essays.* Edited by G. Tate, 45–71. Fort Worth, Texas: Texas Christian University Press, 1976.

Larson, S. A. "A Curriculum Unit Designed to Enhance Seventh-Grade Students' Competency in Developing Expository Paragraphs through Time Order." *DAI* 41 (1980): 87-A.

Lash, H. J. "The Effect of Instruction in Transformational Grammar on Basic Writing Skills." *DAI* 31 (1971): 5383-A.

Laubner, G. F. "The Effect of a Series of Lessons on Proofreading Abilities in Capitalization and Punctuation." *DA* 26 (1965): 3174.

Lawler, R. W. *One Child's Learning: Introducing Writing with a Computer.* A. I. Memo No. 575. Cambridge, Massachusetts: Massachusetts Institute of Technology, Artificial Intelligence Laboratory, 1980. ED 208 415.

Lazdowski, W. P. "Determining Reading Grade Levels from Analysis of Written Compositions." *DAI* 37 (1976): 1504-A.

Ledesma, L. G. "Sentence-Combining: Its Role in Comprehension at Literal, Reasoning, and Evaluative Levels and at Three Syntactic Complexities. *DAI* 41 (1981): 3027-A.

Lee, L. L., and S. M. Canter. "Developmental Sentence Scoring: A Clinical Procedure for Estimating Syntactic Development in Children's Spontaneous Speech." *Journal of Speech and Hearing Disorders* 36 (1971): 315–40.

Lees, E. O. "Evaluating Student Writing." *CCC* 30 (1979): 370–74.

Leffert, B. G. "Synchronic and Diachronic Analysis of Linguistic Factors in the Written Composition of High School Students." *DAI* 39 (1978): 3503-A. ED 173 857.

Leonard, B. E. D. "Stylistic Discriminates of Good and Poor Writing at Tenth-Grade Level." *DAI* 38 (1977): 3345-A.

Leone, A. H. "A Study of the Interrelationships of Writing Ability, Writing Interest, Reading Readiness and Reading Performance of a Given Kindergarten Population." *DAI* 41 (1980): 525-A.

Levine, S. S. "The Effect of Transformational Sentence-Combining Exercises on the Reading Comprehension and Written Composition of Third-Grade Children." *DAI* 37 (1977): 6431-A.*

Lewis, H. P., and E. R. Lewis. "Written Language Performance of Sixth-Grade Children of Low Socio-Economic Status from Bilingual and from Mono-lingual Backgrounds." *Journal of Experimental Education* 33 (1965): 237–42.

Lewis, J. R. "Nonsimulation Academic Games and the Teaching of Language Usage Skills." 1975. ED 136 267.

Ley, T. C. "Student Self-Assessment of Language Ability." *DAI* 35 (1974): 2052-A.

Lilja, L. D. "A Study of the Written Poetry Responses of Fifth Graders Given Selected Methods of Instruction." *DAI* 31 (1970): 2258-A.

Lim, C. C. C. "The Analysis of Teachers' Attitudes toward Students' Writing." *DAI* 35 (1974): 3301-A. ED 101 348.

Lindell, E. *Composition in the Intermediate Stage of the Comprehensive School (FRIS).* Stockholm, Sweden: Stockholm School of Education, Institute of Educational Psychology, 1971. ED 060 039.

———. *Six Reports on Free Writing: A Summary of the FRIS Project.* "Didakometry" No. 61. Malmo, Sweden: School of Education, Department of Educational and Psychological Research, 1980. ED 207 083.

Lindsley, J. R. "Producing Simple Utterances. How Far Ahead Do We Plan?" *Cognitive Psychology* 7 (1975): 1–19.

Linn, B. "Psychological Variants of Success: Four In-Depth Case Studies of Freshmen in a Composition Course." *CE* 39 (1978): 903–17.

Litowitz, B. "Learning to Make Definitions." *Journal of Child Language* 4 (1977): 289–304.

Little, G. "Form and Function in the Written Language of Sixteen Year Olds." Thesis, University of New South Wales, 1975.

Llabre, M. M. "An Application of Generalizability Theory to the Assessment of Writing Ability." *DAI* 39 (1979): 6085-A.

Lloyd-Jones, R. "The Politics of Research into the Teaching of Composition." *CCC* 28 (1977a): 218–22.

————. "Primary Trait Scoring." In *Evaluating Writing*. Edited by C. R. Cooper and L. Odell, 33–66. Urbana, Illinois: NCTE, 1977b.

Loban, W. D. *Language Development: Kindergarten through Grade Twelve*. NCTE Research Report No. 18. Urbana, Illinois: NCTE, 1976. ED 128 818.

————. *The Language of Elementary School Children*. Champaign, Illinois: NCTE, 1963.

————. "The Limitless Possibilities for Increasing Knowledge About Language." *Elementary English* 47 (1970): 624–30.

————. *Stages, Velocity, and Prediction of Language Development: Kindergarten through Grade Twelve. Final Report*. Berkeley, California: University of California, 1970. ED 040 198.

Loewenthal, K., and B. Kostrevski. "The Effects of Training in Written Communication on Verbal Skills." *BJEP* 43 (1973): 82–86.

Logan, R. L. "The Effects of Structured Language Programs on Linguistic Skills of Culturally Different Children." *DAI* 38 (1978): 4096-A.

London Association for the Teaching of English. *Assessing Compositions: A Discussion Pamphlet*. London: Blackie & Son Ltd., 1965. ED 091 758.

Long, K. L. "Measurement of Language Skills in Primary Grades." *DAI* 31 (1971): 4553-A. ED 056 033.

Long, R. C. "Common Features of Writing and Oral Reading: Implications and Applications." 1980. ED 196 012.

Loritsch, R. H. "A Comparative Study of Traditional and Self-Paced Methods of Teaching Freshman English Composition at the Northern Virginia Community College." *DAI* 37 (1977): 5634-A.*

Lotto, E., and B. Smith. "Making Grading Work." *CE* 41 (1979): 423–31.

Love, J. M., and C. Parker-Robinson. "Children's Imitation of Grammatical and Ungrammatical Sentences." *Child Development* 43 (1972): 309–19.

Lowery, A. M. "A Study of the Adequacy of Undergraduate Teacher Preparation in Composition in the State of Florida." *DAI* 31 (1970): 269-A. ED 060 011.

Ludlow, L. H. "HSTAT: A Fortran Program for Computing the Homogeneity of a Quantitative Research Synthesis." Boston College: Unpublished manuscript, 1983.

Lundsteen, S. W. "Manipulating Abstract Thinking as a Subability to Problem Solving in the Context of an English Curriculum." *AERJ* 7 (1970): 373–96.

————. "A Model of the Teaching-Learning Process for Assisting Development of Children's Thinking During Communication." *Journal of Communication* 18 (1968): 412–35.

————, ed. *Help for the Teacher of Written Composition: New Directions in Research*. Urbana, Illinois: ERIC Clearinghouse on Reading and Communication Skills and the National Conference on Research in English, 1976. ED 120 731.

Lunsford, A. A. "An Historical, Descriptive, and Evaluative Study of Remedial English in American Colleges and Universities." *DAI* 38 (1977): 2743-
A.

―――. "Measurable Improvement in the Writing of Remedial College Students." 1978. ED 155 725.

―――. "What We Know—and Don't Know—About Remedial Writing." *CCC*
29 (1978): 47–52.

Lynch, C., and P. Klemans. "Evaluating Our Evaluations." *CE* 40 (1978):
166–80.

Lynch, J. J. "The Conference as a Method in the Teaching of English
Composition in the Junior-Senior High School." *DA* 22 (1961): 503.

Lynch, M. D., and L. May. "Some Effects of Heightening Anxiety Levels on
Writing Performance of Students with Different Levels of Creativity and
Prior Anxiety." Paper, Annual Meeting of AERA, 1977. ED 141 814.

Lynch, R. M. "An Analysis of Freshman English in Illinois Public Junior
Colleges." *DAI* 37 (1976): 276-A.

―――. "Reliving the Past." *CE* 39 (1977): 42–44.

Lyng, J. E. "An Analysis of the Language Structures Present in the Written
Compositions of Selected Junior High School Pupils." *DAI* 33 (1972): 2820-
A.

Lyons, W. D. "The Effects of Teacher-Peer Response and Teacher-Only
Response upon Attitudes toward Writing, and upon Writing Performance."
DAI 38 (1977): 615-A.

Maat. D. W. "An Inquiry into Empirical Relationships between the Reading
and Writing of Exposition and Argument." *DAI* 38 (1978): 4631-A.

McAfee, D. C. "Effect of Sentence-Combining Instruction on the Reading
and Writing Achievement of Fifth-Grade Children in a Suburban School
District." *DAI* 42 (1981): 156-A.

McCabe, B. J. "The Composing Process: A Theory." In Hillocks, G., Jr.,
B. J. McCabe, and J. McCampbell. *The Dynamics of English Instruction:
Grades 7–12*. New York: Random House, Inc., 1971.

McCaig, R. A. "How Not to Analyze the Syntax of Children: A Critique and
a Proposal." *Elementary English* 47 (1970): 612–18.

―――. "A Model for the Evaluation of Student Writing." *DAI* 42 (1981): 583-
A.

―――. "What Your Director of Instruction Needs to Know about Standardized English Tests." *:A* 54 (19077): 491–95.

McCaleb, J. L. "Effects of Selected Variables in an English Education
Program upon the Language Attitudes of Preservice Teachers." *DAI* 37
(1976): 2798-A.

McCarthy, D. A."Language Development in Children." In *Manual of Child
Psychology*. Edited by L. Carmichael, 492–630. New York: John Wiley &
Sons, Inc., 1954.

McCartney, W. A. "The Development of an Objective Instrument for Measuring the Writing Ability of College Freshmen." *DA* 23 (1963): 2375.

McClanahan-Devet, R. L. "The Professional Opinions, Instructional Prac-
tices, and Attitudes of South Carolina Public High School Teachers of
English Concerning the Teaching of Composition." *DAI* 39 (1978): 6052-
A.

McClarty, W. K. D. "A Comparison of Academic Performances of Remedial
English Students and Freshman Composition Students at the University

of Montana, and a Study of the Attitudes of These Remedial English Students toward Remedial English." *DA* 29 (1968): 1047-A.

McCleary, W. J. "A Note on Reliability and Validity Problems in Composition Research." *RTE* 13 (1979a): 274–77. See also R. F. Thompson's and M. G. Southwell's comments on McCleary in *RTE* 14 (1980): 154–58.

————. "Teaching Deductive Logic: A Test of the Toulmin and Aristotelian Models for Critical Thinking and College Composition." *DAI* 40 (1979b): 1247-A.*

McColley, J. *Effects of a Method of Teaching Sentence Structure upon Sentence Structure Used in Writing.* Cooperative Research Project No. S-092. Pittsburg, Kansas: Kansas State College, Department of Language and Literature, 1965.

McColly, W. *The Dimensions of Composition Annotation.* Oswego, New York: State University of New York at Oswego, 1965.

————. "What Does Educational Research Say About the Judging of Writing Ability?" *JER* 64 (1970): 148–56.

McCrory, N. R. "An Analysis of the Teaching of Composition in Selected Secondary Schools of Alabama." *DAI* 33 (1972): 2803-A.

McCurdy, S. H. "A Study of Relationships between Goals for the Teaching of Literature and Teachers' Attitudes towards the Major Categories of Written Student Responses to Literature." *DAI* 36 (1976): 4995-A.

McDaniel, E., and T. Pietras. "Conventional Test Scores and Creative Writing among Disadvantaged Pupils." *RTE* 6 (1972): 181–86.

McDonald, A. A. "A Multimodal Remedial Program for Teaching Skills of Written Expression to Intermediate Grade Students." *DAI* 37 (1976): 1976-A.

McDonald, M. P. "Supervisory Influences of State Curriculum Bulletins on the Teaching of Written Expression in the Fourth Grade." *DA* 26 (1965): 4387.

McDonald, S. P. "Interpreting Growth in Writing." *CCC* 31 (1980): 301–10.

McDonnell, G. M., and E. B. Osburn. "Beginning Writing: Watching It Develop." *LA* 57 (1980): 310–14.

McElwee, G. W. "Systematic Instruction in Proofreading for Spelling and Its Effects on Fourth and Sixth Grade Composition." *DAI* 35 (1975): 7031-A.

McGee, N. R. "Writing in the Content Areas: A Survey of the Instructional Uses of Writing in Selected Central Florida High Schools." *DAI* 38 (1978): 6505-A.

McGrew, J. B. *An Experiment to Assess the Effectiveness of the Dictation Machine as an Aid to Teachers in Evaluation and Improvement of Student Composition. Final Report.* Lincoln, Nebraska: Lincoln Public Schools, 1969. ED 034 776.

McGuiness, T. P., and W. H. Heiner. "Individualization of Composition Instruction through the Use of Dictation Equipment and Transformational Sentence-Combining." Paper, Annual Meeting of AERA, 1972. ED 067 662.

McIntyre, F. H. "Reform in Freshman English in Black Virginia Colleges, 1954–1974." *DAI* 36 (1976): 6450-A.

McIvor, A. K. "The Language of Vocational Students." Paper, Annual Meeting of the Canadian Council of Teachers of English, 1979. ED 177 565.

McKeag, R. A. "How Do Employers View Writing Skills?" 1978. ED 198 526.

McKee, B. "Types of Outlines Used by Technical Writers." *Journal of English Teaching Techniques* 7, no. 4 (Winter 1974/1975): 30–36.

McKeown, L. F. "A Survey of Opinions About English Usage Held by Secondary Language Arts Teachers." *DAI* 30 (1969): 1053-A. ED 041 889.

Mackie, B. C. "The Effects of a Sentence-Combining Program on the Reading Comprehension and Written Composition of Fourth-Grade Students." *DAI* 42 (1982): 4779-A.

McLean, H. W. "A Comparison of Selected Aspects of the Oral and Written Language of Fourth, Fifth, and Sixth Grade Pupils." *DA* 25 (1964): 943.

MacLennan, T. G. "A Descriptive Survey of the Prewriting Planning Practices of Selected North Carolina Post-Secondary Composition Instructors." *DAI* 42 (1981): 528-A.

McLeod, A. M., and J. S. Oehler. "Can We Improve Attitudes toward Writing and Evaluating Writing?" *Clearing House* 53 (1980): 357–59.

McNeill, J. L., Jr. "A Study of Six Methods of Teaching Formal English Writing." *DAI* 38 (1978): 7257-A.

McNulty, D. M. "An Examination of the Quality of Fourth Grade Children's Creative Writing Resulting from Three Approaches of Motivation Involving Stimulus, Questioning, and Verbal Interaction." *DAI* 42 (1981): 82-A.

McTeague, F., and others. *An Investigation of Secondary Student Writing Across the Curriculum and Some Suggestions for School Language Policies.* Toronto, Ontario: York Borough Board of Education, 1980. ED 182 770.

Madaus, G. F., and R. M. Rippey. "Zeroing in on the STEP Writing Test: What Does It Tell a Teacher?" *JEM* 3 (1966): 19–25. ED 022 751.

Maddox, R. M. "The One-to-One Student Writing Conference: An Evaluation Study of Its Effectiveness in Improving Writing Skills." *DAI* 42 (1982): 3479-A.

Madigan, C. "A Response to Sharon Pianko's 'A Description of the Composing Processes of College Freshman Writers.'" *RTE* 14 (1980): 158–60.

Maertens, R. E. "The Teaching of Written Composition in Representative Public High Schools Accredited by the North Central Association." *DAI* 29 (1969): 3777-A. ED 040 183.

Magee, M. "A Study of the Relationship between Written Syntactic Fluency and Silent Reading Comprehension in Mature Readers." *DAI* 39 (1978): 6598-A.

Magnuson, R. W. "The Effects of an Alphabet Having a High Sound-Letter Correspondence upon Children's Ability to Express Themselves in Written Form." *DAI* 30 (1969): 1076-A.*

Maguire, M. H. "A Psycholinguistic Descriptive Analysis of Six Selected Secondary IV Students' Perceptions of the Reading and Writing Processes and Their Language Performance: Case Studies of Above Average, Average and Poor Readers." 1978. ED 207 002.

Mahoney, M. A. J. "Hemispheric Dominance and Imagaic Writing." *DAI* 42 (1982): 2999-A.

Maimon, E. P., and B. F. Nodine. "Measuring Behavior and Attitude in the Teaching of Writing among Faculties in Various Disciplines." Paper, Annual Meeting of MLA, 1978a. ED 167 999.

———. "Measuring Syntactic Growth: Errors and Expectations in Sentence-Combining Practice with College Freshmen." *RTE* 12 (1978b): 233–44.

———. "Words Enough and Time: Syntax and Error One Year After." In *Sentence Combining and the Teaching of Writing.* Edited by D. Daiker, A.

Kerek, and M. Morenberg, 101–08. Conway, Arkansas: University of Akron and University of Central Arkansas, 1979.

Mair, D., and N. Roundy. "The Composing Process of Technical Writers. A Preliminary Study." Paper, Annual Meeting of CCCC, 1981. ED 200 994.

Makino, S. "Paragraph, Is It a Legitimate Linguistic Unit?—A Case Study from English and Japanese." 1978. ED 155 950.

Malgady, R. G., and P. R. Barcher. "Psychological Scaling of Essay Creativity: Effects of Productivity and Novelty." *JEP* 69 (1977): 512–18.

Malmquist, E., and H. Grundin. *Reading, Writing and Other Communication Skills among Adults*. Stockholm: National Swedish Board of Education, 1976. ED 128 828.

Maloney, H. B. "An Identification of Excellence in Expository Composition Performance in a Selected 9A Population with an Analysis of Reasons for Superior Performance." *DA* 28 (1968): 3564-A.

Maloney, K. B., and B. L. Hopkins. "The Modification of Sentence Structure and Its Relationship to Subjective Judgments of Creativity in Writing." *Journal of Applied Behavior Analysis* 6 (1973): 425–33.

Mandler, J. M. "Representation." In *Handbook of Child Psychology*. Vol. 3. Edited by P. Mussen (Series Editor), J. H. Flavell and E. M. Markman (Volume Editors), 420–94. New York: John Wiley & Sons, Inc. 1983.

Manitoba Department of Education. *Manitoba Writing Assessment Program. Summary Report*. Winnipeg, Manitoba: Manitoba Department of Education, 1979. ED 194 902.

Manship, D. W. "A Study of the Effect of Three Different Methods of Presenting a Review of Writing Principles and Grammar to Business Communication Students." *DAI* 35 (1975): 4968-A.*

Marchak, N., and others. *Assessing Communication Skills: A Review of the Literature*. Edmonton, Alberta: Alberta Department of Education, Minister's Advisory Committee on Student Achievement, 1979. ED 179 573.

Marckworth, M. L., and L. M. Bell. "Sentence-Length Distribution in the Corpus." In *Computational Analysis of Present-day American English*. Edited by H. Kučera and W. Francis, 368–405. Providence, Rhode Island: Brown University Press, 1967.

Marcotte, D. R. "A Computerized Contingency Analysis of Content Graded Essays." *DAI* 30 (1970): 2854-A.

Marsh, H. U. "A Task-Oriented Learning Group Approach to Teaching Descriptive-Narrative-Expository Writing to Eleventh-Grade Students." *DAI* 36 (1976): 7259-A.

Marshall, B. R. "A Survey and Analysis of Teachers' Markings on Selected Compositions of Average Students in Grades 10 and 12." *DAI* 32 (1971): 2553-A.

Marshall, F. K. "Comparison of Elective English Courses with Assigned English Courses in Relation to Achievement Scores in English Usage of High School Seniors." *DAI* 36 (1975): 1998-A.

Marshall, J. C. "The Effect of Selected Composition Errors on Grades Assigned to an Essay Examination by High School Teachers." *DA* 27 (1966): 1662-A.

———. "A Note on the Characteristics of Students Using the Writing Lab at an Urban University." *RTE* 15 (1981): 280–81.

———. "Writing Neatness, Composition Errors, and Essay Grades Reexamined." *JER* 65 (1972): 213–15.

Marshall, J. C., and J. M. Powers. "Writing Neatness, Composition Errors, and Essay Grades." *JEM* 6 (1969): 97–101.

Marshall, W. J. A., and S. P. Quigley. *Quantitative and Qualitative Analysis of Syntactic Structure in the Written Language of Hearing Impaired Students.* Urbana, Illinois: University of Illinois, Institute of Research for Exceptional Children, 1970. ED 046 207.

Martellock, H. A. "A Psycholinguistic Description of the Oral and Written Language of a Selected Group of Middle School Children." *DAI* 32 (1972): 6107-A.

Martin, C. A. "Syntax and Success: Stylistic Features of Superior Freshman Essays." *DAI* 40 (1980): 4010-A.

Martin, E. M. "An Analytical Study of Essays Written by Nominees in the Communicative Arts for the Governor's Honors Program in Georgia." *DAI* 38 (1978): 6582-A.

Martin, H. C. "Writing and Thinking." In *Essays on the Teaching of English: Reports of the Yale Conferences on the Teaching of English.* Edited by E. J. Gordon and E. S. Noyes, 161–74. New York: Appleton-Century-Crofts, Inc., 1960.

Martin, J. B. "A Study to Determine the Predictability of an Individual Student's Improvement in Writing Ability from His Performance on His First Writing Assignment." *DAI* 34 (1974): 3701-A.

Martin, J. J. "The Development of Sentence-Writing Skills at Grades Three, Four, and Five." *DAI* 30 (1969): 1077-A.*

Martin, R. G. "A Prediction Formula for a Sample of 'Good' Writing." *DA* 29 (1968): 1221-A.

Martin, W[alter] D[on]. "Applying and Exploring the Diederich Method for Measuring Growth in Writing Ability in a High School." *DAI* 31 (1970): 2616-A.

———. "The Sex Factor in Grading Composition." *RTE* 6 (1972): 36–47.

Martin, W[illiam] D[ennis]. "The Effects of a Program of Models-Imitation on the Writing of Seventh Grade Students." *DAI* 41 (1981): 3067-A.

Martínez San José, C. P. "Grammatical Structures in Four Modes of Writing at Fourth-Grade Level." *DAI* 33 (1973): 5411-A.*

Marwit, S. J., K. L. Marwit, and J. J. Boswell. "Negro Children's Use of Nonstandard Grammar." *JEP* 63 (1972): 218–24.

Marzano, R. J. "Basic Skills in Composition: Measurement, Competency Testing, Instructional Technique." 1978a. ED 179 954.

———. "On the Validity of Analytic Ratings." 1975. ED 112 412.

———. "The Sentence Combining Myth." *EJ* 65, no. 2 (February 1976): 57–59.

Marzano, R. J., and S. Arthur. "Teacher Comments on Student Essays: It Doesn't Matter What You Say." 1977 ED 147 864.

Marzano, R. J., and P. DiStefano. "Five Empirically Based Composition Skills." 1978b. ED 162 337.

Mason, J. L. "Syntactic Maturity in Young Children's Compositions." *Masters Abstracts* 16 (1978): 89.

Massad, C. E. "A Comparative Study of Creativity, Language Aptitude, and Intelligence in Sixth-Grade Children from Low-Socioeconomic and Middle-Socioeconomic Levels." *DAI* 29 (1969): 4331-A.

Mathews, M. "The Relationship between Listening and Writing Abilities of Selected Sixth Grade Children." *DAI* 30 (1970): 5347-A.

Matsuhashi, A. "Explorations in the Real-Time Production of Written Discourse." In *What Writers Know: The Language, Process, and Structure of Written Discourse.* Edited by M. Nystrand, 269–90. New York: Academic Press, 1982.

———. "Pausing and Planning: The Tempo of Written Discourse Production." *RTE* 15 (1981): 113–34.

———. "Producing Written Discourse: A Theory-Based Description of the Temporal Characteristics of Three Discourse Types from Four Competent Grade 12 Writers." *DAI* 40 (1980): 5035-A.

Matsuhashi, A., and C. Cooper. "A Video Time-Monitored Observational Study: The Transcribing Behavior and Composing Processes of a Competent High School Writer." Paper, Annual Meeting of AERA, 1978. ED 155 701.

May, A. M. "Syntactic Punctuation and Syntactic Complexity in the Writing of Certain Students in Grades Eight, Ten, and Twelve." *DAI* 38 (1977): 1944-A.

Mayo, N. B. "The Effects of Discussion and Assignment Questions on the Quality of Descriptive Writing of Tenth-Grade Students." *DAI* 36 (1976): 7839-A.*

———. "Tenth Grade Students' Perceptions of the Writing Process." Paper, Annual Meeting of the Southwest Educational Research Association, 1981. ED 202 036.

Mazur, C. *Young Writers' Error Tendency.* New Paltz, New York: State University College of New York, 1976. ED 134 987.

Mead, M. S. "An Examination of Attitudes toward Current Secondary School English Programs in Greater Boston." *DAI* 37 (1977): 4828-A.

Meade, R. A., and W. G. Ellis. "The Use in Writing of Textbook Methods of Paragraph Development." *JER* 65 (1971): 74–76.

Means, B., and others. "Organization and Content in Writing and Speech." 1980. ED 208 403.

Means, H. J. "An Analysis of the Content, Proportion of Time Spent on Content, and Course Structure of Secondary English Methods Courses in Iowa." *DAI* 35 (1975): 7774-A.

Meckel, H. "Research on Teaching Composition and Literature." In *Handbook of Research on Teaching.* Edited by N. L. Gage, 966–1006. Chicago: Rand McNally, 1963.

Mehaffie, S., T. C. Gee, and W. G. Larmer. "English Teachers' Use of Student-Centered Approaches in Teaching." *English Education* 9 (1978): 111–16.

Mehaffie, S[hamus]. "Composition Evaluation: Historical Background and an Applied Theory." *DAI* 32 (1972): 6294-A.

Mehta, M. P. "A Study of Preparation Programs for Secondary School English Teachers at the Universities and Colleges of Montana." *DAI* 31 (1971): 4603-A. ED 056 027.

Meier, T. R., and C. B. Cazden. "A Focus on Oral Language and Writing from a Multicultural Perspective." *LA* 59 (1982): 504–12.

Melas, D. D. "Difference of Themes in Assigned and Unassigned Creative Writing of Elementary School Children." *DAI* 35 (1975): 6577-A.

Melder, E. M. "A Study of the Effect of Sentence-Combining on the Writing of Selected Black Students and Graduates of Small High Schools in University Freshman English Classes." *DAI* 41 (1981): 4270-A. See also ED 203 324.

Mellon, J. C. "Issues in the Theory and Practice of Sentence Combining: A

Twenty-Year Perspective." In *Sentence Combining and the Teaching of Writing*. Edited by D. Daiker, A. Kerek, and M. Morenberg, 1–38. Conway, Arkansas: University of Akron and University of Central Arkansas, 1979.

————. *National Assessment and the Teaching of English: Results of the First National Assessment of Educational Progress in Writing, Reading, and Literature—Implications for Teaching and Measurement in the English Language Arts*. Urbana, Illinois: NCTE, 1975a. ED 112 427.

————. *Sentence-Combining Skills: Results of Sentence-Combining Exercises in the 1978–79 National Writing Assessment*. Denver, Colorado: Education Commission of the States, National Assessment of Educational Progress, 1981. ED 210 696.

————. "A Taxonomy of Compositional Competencies." Paper, Minnesota Perspectives on Literacy Conference, 1977. ED 157 058.

————. *Transformational Sentence-Combining: A Method for Enhancing the Development of Syntactic Fluency in English Composition. NCTE Research Report No. 10*. Champaign, Illinois: NCTE, 1969.

————. "The Writing Assessment." In *National Assessment and the Teaching of English*, 14–38. Urbana, Illinois: NCTE, 1975b.

Melrose, J. E. "The Effectiveness of Direction Practice on the Letter-Writing Performance of University Students Enrolled in Business Communication Courses." *DAI* 35 (1975): 4988-A.

Melvin, M. P. "The Effects of Sentence Combining Instruction on Syntactic Maturity, Reading Achievement, and Language Arts Skills Achievement." 1980. ED 191 007.

Meredith, C. V. "Multiple-Elective Programs in English in the State of New Jersey." *DAI* 36 (1975): 686-A.

Mersand, J. *Attitudes toward English Teaching*. Philadelphia, Pennsylvania: Chilton Company, Book Division, 1961.

————. "What Has Happened to Written Composition?" *EJ* 50 (1961): 231–37.

Merz, M. A. "A Comparative Analysis of Planning Considerations in the Composing Process: Seven Case Studies." *DAI* 42 (1982): 4803-A.

Metviner, E. S. "Rhetorically Based and Rhetorically Deficient Writing: The Effects of Purpose and Audience on the Quality of Ninth Grade Students' Compositions." *DAI* 41 (1981): 3977-A.

Metzger, E. A. "Causes of Failure to Learn to Write: Exploratory Case Studies at Grade Seven, Grade Ten, and College Level." *DAI* 38 (1977): 3346-A.

————. "The Composing Process of Students in Grade 7, Grade 10, and College." Paper, Annual Meeting of the New York State English Council, 1976. ED 132 589.

————. "An Instrument for Describing Written Products." 1976. ED 133 749.

Meyers, G. D. "The Influence of Using Speaking as a Pre-Writing Activity on Community College Freshmen Composition Pupils' Performance in Writing," 1979. ED 203 316.

————. "The Influence of Using Speaking as a Pre-Writing Activity on Community College Freshman Composition Pupils' Performance in and Attitudes toward Writing." *DAI* 41 (1980): 2482-A.*

————. "Speaking as a Pre-Writing Activity: Its Application to Teaching Community College Freshman Composition Pupils." Paper, Annual Meeting of the CCCC. 1980. ED 185 585.

Michael, W. B., T. Cooper, P. Shaffer, and E. Wallis. "A Comparison of the Reliabilty and Validity of Ratings of Student Performance on Essay Examinations by Professors of English and by Professors in Other Disciplines." *Educational and Psychological Measurement* 40 (1980): 183–95.

Michlin, M. L. "The Effects of Social, Perceptual and Causal Attributional Variables on Teachers' Perceptions and Ratings of Students' Written Composition." *DAI* 41 (1981): 4628-A.

Mikulecky, L., and W. Diehl. *Literacy Requirements in Business and Industry.* Bloomington, Indiana: Indiana University, School of Education, 1979. ED 186 867.

Miles, J. *Working Out Ideas: Predication and Other Uses of Language. Curriculum Publication No. 5.* Berkeley, California: Bay Area Writing Project, 1979. ED 184 117.

Milic, L. T., T. W. Wilcox, A. M. Tibbetts, and W. E. Britton. *Theories of Style and Their Implications for the Teaching of Composition—and Other Essays.* Edited by W. F. Irmscher. Champaign, Illinois: NCTE, 1965. ED 038 391.

Millar, B., and M. Nystrand. "The Language Trap." *EJ* 68, no. 3 (March 1979): 36–41. See also ED 154 385.

Miller, B. D., and J. W. Ney. "The Effect of Systematic Oral Exercises on the Writing of Fourth-Grade Students." *RTE* 2 (1968): 44–61.

———. "Oral Drills and Writing Improvement in the Fourth Grade." *Journal of Experimental Education* 36, no. 1 (Fall 1967): 93–99. ED 015 179.

Miller, D. W. "Attitude Change in Three Populations Undergoing College Training in Methods of Teaching English." *DAI* 38 (1977): 2061-A.

Miller, F. "Sequential Patterns of Structures in the English Language Compatible with Written Expressions of Junior High Students." *JER* 59 (1966): 201–03.

Miller, J. D. "An Examination of Language Arts—Social Studies Programs in Grades Seven, Eight, and Nine of Oregon Public Schools." *DAI* 32 (1971): 1261-A.

Miller, M. A. "A Comparative Study of Two Approaches to Teaching Freshman Remedial Composition in a Comprehensive Community College." *DAI* 35 (1975): 7083-A.

Miller, O. V. "The Effects and Relationships of a Unit of Instruction in Self-Evaluation on Student Skill in Self-Evaluating Written Compositions." *DAI* 33 (1972): 116-A.*

Miller, R. L. "An Evaluation of an Experimental Written Composition Program for Second Grade." *DAI* 28 (1968): 3374-A.*

Miller, S. "How Writers Evaluate Their Own Writing." *CCC* 33 (1982): 176–83.

Miller, T. E. "A Comparison of the Effects of Oral and Written Teacher Feedback with Written Teacher Feedback Only on Specific Writing Behaviors of Fourth-Grade Children." *DAI* 38 (1978): 5912-A.

Miller, T. J. "A Quantitative Study of the 'Free Modifiers' in Narrative-Descriptive Compositions Written by Black College Freshmen after Leaving the Influence of The Christensen Rhetoric Program and a Study of Their Attitudes toward Written Composition." *DAI* 33 (1973): 3483-A.*

Mills, E. B. "An Experimental Study in the Use of Literary Models in Written Composition." *DAI* 28 (1968): 3900-A. ED 030 642. See also ED 026 368.*

Minars, E. J. "The Effects of Individually Prescribed Instruction on Achievement, Self-Concept and Study Orientation among Engineering Students Enrolled in English Composition at Oklahoma State University." *DAI* 33 (1973): 6693-A.*

Mindell, P., and D. Stracher. "Assessing Reading and Writing of the Gifted: The Warp and Woof of the Language Program." *Gifted Child Quarterly* 24 (1980): 72–80.

Minnis, M. "An Analysis of Effective Expository Prose: Instruction and Self-Assessment for Writers." *DAI* 41 (1980): 962-A.

Mischel, T. "A Case Study of a Twelfth-Grade Writer." *RTE* 8 (1974): 303–14.

Modu, C. C., and E. Wimmers. "The Validity of the Advanced Placement English Language and Composition Examination." *CE* 43 (1981): 609–20.

Moffett, J. W. *Teaching the Universe of Discourse*. Boston, Massachusetts: Houghton Mifflin, 1968.

Monkowski, P. G., and M. E. Kelly. "The Lincoln Writing Laboratory: A Systems-Based Model for Individual Instruction." Paper, Annual Meeting of the Association for Supervision and Curriculum Development, 1979. ED 175 007.

Montag, G. E., and others. *An Oral-Audio-Visual Approach to Remedial Writing. Final Report*. Hillsboro, Missouri: Jefferson College, 1969. ED 033 123.

Morenberg, M. "Sentence Combining Over a Three-Year Period: A Case Study." Paper, Annual Meeting of the CCCC, 1980. ED 186 921.

Morenberg, M., D. Daiker, and A. Kerek. "Sentence Combining at the College Level: An Experimental Study." *RTE* 12 (1978): 245–56.

Morgan, B. "A Case Study of a Seventh Grade Writer." *The English Record* 26, no. 4 (Fall 1975): 28–39.

Morgan, G. D. "A Study of the Writing Maturity of Students in a Linguistically-Based Composition Program at the Intermediate Level." *DAI* 31 (1971): 3178-A.

Moriarty, D. J. "An Investigation of the Effect of Instruction in Five Components of the Writing Process on the Quality and Syntactic Complexity of Student Writing." *DAI* 39 (1978): 2727-A. ED 172 259.

Morris, B. S. "Videotape and Writing in the University of Michigan Assessment." Paper, Annual Meeting of CCCC, 1979. ED 174 992.

Morris, E. C. "Critique of a Short Story: An Application of the Elements of Writing about a Literary Work." *RTE* 10 (1976): 157–75.

Morris, N. T. "Syntactic and Vocabulary Development in the Written Discourse of Learning Disabled and Normal Children and Adolescents." *DAI* 41 (1979): 140-A.

Morrissey, T. J., and B. M. Maid. "The Real and Perceived Writing Needs of Students and Graduate Professionals: A Mimetic Approach to Helping Student Writers." Paper, Annual Meeting of the New York State English Council, 1980. ED 198 551.

Morrow, L. M. "Analysis of Syntax of Six-, Seven-, and Eight-Year-Old Children. *RTE* 12 (1978): 143–48.

Mortimer, J. R. "A Student-Centered Language Arts Curriculum and Its Effect on Pupils' Attitudes and Achievements." *DAI* 32 (1972): 5110-A.*

Moscovici, S., and C. Humbert. *Studies of Verbal Behavior in Oral and Written Language. Professional Paper 68–14*. Nashville, Tennessee: George Peabody College, Institute on School Learning and Individual Differences, 1968. ED 031 469.

Mosenthal, P., R. Davidson-Mosenthal, and V. Krieger. "How Fourth Graders Develop Points of View in Classroom Writing." *RTE* 15 (1981): 197–214.

Mosenthal, P., and T. J. Na. "Classroom Competence and Childrens' Individual Differences in Writing." *JEP* 73 (1981): 106–21.

Moslemi, M. H. "The Effects of an Intensive Unit of Instruction in Creative Writing on the Creative Compositions of Secondary School Students." *DAI* 34 (1973): 1775-A.*

———. "The Grading of Creative Writing Essays." *RTE* 9 (1975): 154–61.

Moss, A. I. "Toward a Rhetoric of Inquiry: A Study of the Theory, Application, and Evaluation of the Interdisciplinary Writing Course." *DAI* 37 (1976): 2153-A.

Moss, P. "A Study of the Effect of Selected Methods of Instruction Designed to Increase Originality in Written Expression." *DA* 28 (1967): 881-A.

Mulcahy, G. J. "A Comparison of the Traditional Methods Approach and the Linguistic Methods Approach to the Teaching of English Grammar and Composition to College Freshmen." *DAI* 34 (1974): 5487-A.

Mulder, J. E. M., C. Braun, and W. G. Holliday. "Effects of Sentence-Combining Practice on Linguistic Maturity Level of Adult Students." *Adult Education* 28 (1978): 111–20.

Mulligan, E. A. "A Survey of Grammatical Errors in Creative Writings of Children." *DAI* 26 (1966): 3704.

Mullis, I. V. S. *The Primary Trait System for Scoring Writing Tasks.* Denver, Colorado: Education Commission of the States, National Assessment of Educational Progress, 1976. ED 124 942.

Munday, R. G. "The Effects of the Use of 'English 3200,' a Programed Textbook, on Achievement in English Grammar at the Twelfth-Grade Level in a Large Metropolitan High School." *DA* 26 (1966): 3928.

Murdock, M. L. "Independent Study Versus Lecture-Discussion in Teaching Freshman Composition." *DAI* 34 (1974): 6951-A.*

Murphy, D. K. "A Study of the Effectiveness of a Linguistic Approach in Teaching Composition to Secondary School English Students." *DA* 28 (1967): 1735-A.

Murray, D. M. "Internal Revision: A Process of Discovery." In *Research on Composing: Points of Departure.* Edited by C. R. Cooper and L. Odell, 85–103. Urbana, Illinois: NCTE, 1978.

Myers, A. E., C. B. McConville, and W. E. Coffman. "Simplex Structure in the Grading of Essay Tests." *Educational and Psychological Measurement* 26 (1966): 41–54.

Myers, C. F. "Teacher and Peer Evaluative Feedback in the Development of Two Composition Skills: Punctuation and Paragraph Unity." *DAI* 40 (1979): 1318-A.

Myers, M. "Approaches to the Teaching of Composition." In *Theory and Practice in the Teaching of Composition: Processing, Distancing, and Modeling.* Edited by M. Myers and J. Gray, 3–43. Urbana, Illinois: NCTE, 1983.

Myers, M. S. "Written Communication at the Managerial and Professional/ Technical Levels: A Case Study." *DAI* 42 (1981): 775-A. ED 199 749.

Naccarato, R. W. "A Generalizability Analysis of a Rhetorical Rating Experiment." 1972. ED 204 791.

Nagle, J. E. "The Effects of a Directed Writing Activity in Eighth Grade Social Studies Instruction on General Reading Achievement and Social Studies Reading Achievement." *DAI* 33 (1972): 1523-A.

Nail, P., R. Fitch, J. Halverson, P. Grant, and N. F. Winn. *A Scale for Evaluation of High School Student Essays.* Urbana, Illinois: NCTE, 1960.

Najjar, M. M. "The Relationship between Syntactic Development and Performance by Freshman Students on Selected Competencies in English Composition." *DAI* 39 (1979): 5374-A.

Nalven, F. B., and J. Auguste. "How Lasting Are the Effects of ITA vs. TO Training in the Development of Children's Creative Writing?" *RTE* 6 (1972): 17–19.

National Assessment of Educational Progress. *Explanatory and Persuasive Letter Writing: Selected Results from the Second National Assessment of Writing.* Denver, Colorado: Education Commission of the States, 1977a. ED 135 006.

―――. *Expressive Writing: Selected Results from the Second National Assessment of Writing.* Denver, Colorado: Education Commission of the States, 1976. ED 130 312.

―――. *National Assessment Report 5: 1969–1970 Writing: Group Results for Sex, Region and Size of Community.* Denver, Colorado: Education Commission of the States, 1971. ED 051 246.

―――. *Procedural Handbook, 1978–79 Writing Assessment.* Denver, Colorado: Educational Commission of the States, 1980. ED 199 263.

―――. *Report 3: 1969–1970 Writing: National Results.* Denver, Colorado: Education Commission of the States, 1970. ED 051 245.

―――. *The Second National Assessment of Writing: New and Reassessed Exercises with Technical Information and Data.* Denver, Colorado: Education Commission of the States, 1978. ED 155 728.

―――. *Selected Essays and Letters: A Selection of Papers Collected During the 1969–70 Assessment of Writing. Report No. 10.* Denver, Colorado: Education Commission of the States, 1972. ED 075 822.

―――. *Write/Rewrite: An Assessment of Revision Skills; Selected Results from the Second National Assessment of Writing.* Denver, Colorado: Education Commission of the States, 1977b. ED 141 826.

―――. *Writing: Group Results A and B for Objectively-Scored Exercises; 1969–70 Assessment, National Results by Region, Sex, Color, Size and Type of Community, and Parental Education.* Denver, Colorado: Education Commission of the States, 1973. ED 077 029.

―――. *Writing Achievement, 1969–79: Results from the Third National Writing Assessment, Volume I—17-Year-Olds.* Denver, Colorado: Education Commission of the States, 1980. ED 196 042.

―――. *Writing Achievement, 1969–79: Results from the Third National Writing Assessment, Volume II—13-Year-Olds.* Denver, Colorado: Education Commission of the States, 1980. ED 196 043.

―――. *Writing Achievement, 1969–79: Results from the Third National Writing Assessment, Volume III—9-Year-Olds.* Denver, Colorado: Education Commission of the States, 1980. ED 196 044.

―――. *Writing Mechanics, 1969–1974: A Capsule Description of Changes in Writing Mechanics.* Denver, Colorado: Education Commission of the States, 1975. ED 113 736.

―――. *Writing Objectives for the 1973–74 Assessment.* Denver, Colorado: Education Commission of the States, 1972. ED 072 460.

Nawarat, P. "Differences between Teaching Methods and Materials Used by English Teachers with Vocational and Non-Vocational Students." *DAI* 41 (1981): 3518-A.

NCTE. "Composition Opinionnaire: The Student's Right to Write." Urbana, Illinois: NCTE, Commission on Composition, 1972. ED 068 938.

NCTE Committee on National Interest. *The National Interest and the Teaching of English: A Report on the Status of the Profession.* Champaign, Illinois: NCTE, 1961. ED 027 289.

Neel, J. "Comparing Various Approaches to Theme Grading." *Education* 95 (1974): 92–93.

Neidig, M., and S. P. Bowden. "A Study of the Relationships between College English Grades and Writing Ability of Education Majors." 1976. ED 202 038.

Neilsen, L., and G. L. Piché. "The Influence of Headed Nominal Complexity and Lexical Choice on Teachers' Evaluation of Writing." *RTE* 15 (1981): 65–73.

Nelson, M. W. "Writers Who Teach: A Naturalistic Investigation." *DAI* 42 (1982): 3480-A.

Nemanich, D. D. "Passive Verbs in Children's Writing." *Elementary English* 49 (1972): 1064–66.

———. "The Verb System in the Writing of Children." *DA* 29 (1969): 4475-A.

Neuleib, J. "The Relation of Formal Grammar to Composition." *CCC* 28 (1977): 247–50.

Neville, M. M., and A. L. Papillon. *Advanced Composition in the Preparation of Secondary School English Teachers Interim Report.* Urbana, Illinois: Illinois State-Wide Curriculum Study Center in the Preparation of Secondary English Teachers, 1969. ED 031 499.

Newbery, R. A. "Objective Indices in the Assessment of Essays." *BJEP* 37 (1967): 403–05.

Newcomb, J. S. "The Influence of Readers on the Holistic Grading of Essays." *DAI* 38 (1977): 1133-A.

Newcomb, M. J. "An Experimental Study of Freshman English in the Small Community Junior College Using Disparate Methods of Instruction." *DAI* 31 (1971): 3180-A.

Newkirk, T. R. "Grammar Instruction and Writing: What Does the Research Really Prove?" 1977. ED 153 218.

———. "James Britton and the Teaching of Writing in Selected British Middle and Secondary Schools." *DAI* 38 (1977), 2622-A.

Newkirk, T. R., T. D. Cameron, and C. L. Selfe. "What Johnny Can't Write: A University View of Freshman Writing Ability." *EJ* 66, no. 8 (November 1977): 65–69.

Ney, J. W. "Applied Linguistics in the Seventh Grade." *EJ* 55 (1966): 895–97, 902.

———. "Cognitive Styles and Miscue Analysis of Reading and Writing." Paper, Annual International Conference on the Teaching of English, 1980a. ED 194 886.

———. "A Comparison of Reading Miscues and Writing Miscues." Tempe, Arizona: Arizona State University, 1975a. ED 161 009.

———. "Counterstatement [Response to Donald A. Daiker, Andrew Kerek, and Max Morenberg, 'Sentence-Combining and Syntactic Maturity in Freshman English,' *CCC*, 29 (February, 1978), 36–41.]" *CCC* 29 (1978): 303–04.

———. "The Hazards of the Course: Sentence-Combining in Freshman English." *The English Record* 27, no. 3 (Summer-Autumn 1976a): 70–77.

———. *Linguistics, Language Teaching, and Composition in the Grades.* The Hague and Paris: Mouton, 1975b.

———. *Miscue Analysis: The Writing of Three Hispanic American Students in a Class of Twenty Fourth Graders.* Tempe, Arizona: Arizona State University, 1977. ED 161 077.

———. "Myths and Mythology: The Pro's and Con's of Sentence Combining." *EJ* 65, no. 9 (1976b): 20.

———. "Notes Towards a Psycholinguistic Model of the Writing Process." *RTE* 8 (1974): 157–69.

———. "On Not Practicing Errors." *CCC* 14 (1963): 102–06.

———. "A Short History of Sentence Combining: Its Limitations and Use." *English Education* 11 (1980b): 169–77.

Niedermeyer, F. C., and others. *Functions of Status Testing in the Development of an Instructional Program.* Los Alamitos, California: Southwest Regional Laboratory for Educational Research and Development, 1972. ED 106 871.

Nielsen, B. F. "Effects of Reading on Childrens' Narrative Writing." *DAI* 41 (1980): 99-A.

Nietz, J. A. "Old Secondary School Grammar Textbooks." *EJ* 54 (1965): 541–46.

Nietzke, D. A. "The Influence of Composition Assignment upon Grammatical Structure." *DAI* 32 (1972): 5476-A.*

Nikas, G. B. "Initial Teaching Alphabet and Traditional Orthography—Their Impact on Spelling and Writing." *Elementary School Journal* 70 (1970): 321–30.

Nikoloff, S. E. B. "The Relationship of Teacher Standards to the Written Expression of Fifth and Sixth Grade Children." *DA* 26 (1966): 6560-A.

Nolan, F. "The Birth of a Story." *LA* 56 (1979): 763–68.

Nold, E. W. "The Basics of Research: Evaluation of Writing." Paper, Annual Meeting of MLA, 1978. ED 166 713.

———. "Revising." In *Writing: The Nature, Development and Teaching of Written Communication.* Edited by E. H. Frederiksen, M. F. Whiteman, and J. F. Dominic, 67–79. Hillsdale, New Jersey: Lawrence Erlbaum Associates, Publishers, 1981.

———. "Revising: Toward a Theory." Paper, Annual Meeting of CCCC, 1979. ED 172 212.

Nold, E. W., and S. W. Freedman. "An Analysis of Readers' Responses to Essays." *RTE* 11 (1977): 164–74.

Noonan-Wagner, D. "Black Writers in the Classroom: A Question of Language Experience, Not Grammar." Paper, Annual Meeting of CCCC, 1980. ED 189 599.

Noreen, R. G. "Placement Procedures for Freshman Composition: A Survey." *CCC* 28 (1977): 141–44.

Norwood, M. C. D. "Achievement as Related to the Ethnic Origin of the Student in an Experience-Centered Approach to the Teaching of Freshman Composition." *DAI* 35 (1974): 806-A.

Nugent, H. E. "The Role of Audience Awareness in the Writing of College Freshmen." *DAI* 40 (1979): 3279-A.

Nugent, S. M. "A Comparative Analysis of Two Methods of Invention." *DAI* 41 (1981): 4018-A.

Nurss, J. R., and D. E. Day. "Imitation, Comprehension, and Production of

Grammatical Structures." *Journal of Verbal Learning and Verbal Behavior* 10 (1971): 68–74.

Nymann, J. R. "A Study of the Relationship of Third-Grade Children's Originality in Narrative Writing, IQ, and MA to Their Locus of Evaluation and Control." *DA* 26 (1965): 3176.

Nystrand, M. "Using Readability Research to Investigate Writing." *RTE* 13 (1979): 231–42.

————, ed. *What Writers Know: The Language, Process, and Structure of Written Discourse*. New York: Academic Press, 1981.

Obenchain, A. "Developing Paragraph Power through Sentence Combining." In *Sentence Combining and the Teaching of Writing*. Edited by D. Daiker, A. Kerek, and M. Morenberg, 123–33. Conway, Arkansas: University of Akron and University of Central Arkansas, 1979.

Odegaard, J. M. "The Effects of Instruction in Creative Grammar on the Creativity of Stories and the Usage of Sentence Patterns and Transformations of a Selected Group of Third Grade Students." *DAI* 32 (1972): 4332-A.

Odell, L. "Discovery Procedures for Contemporary Rhetoric: A Study of the Usefulness of the Tagmemic Heuristic Model in Teaching Composition." *DAI* 31 (1971): 6476-A.

————. "Measuring Changes in Intellectual Processes as One Dimension of Growth in Writing." In *Evaluating Writing: Describing, Measuring, Judging*. Edited by C. R. Cooper and L. Odell, 107–132. Urbana, Illinois: NCTE, 1977.

————. "Measuring the Effect of Instruction in Pre-Writing." *RTE* 8 (1974): 228–40.

————. "Piaget, Problem-Solving, and Freshman Composition." *CCC* 24 (1973): 36–42.

Odell, L., and J. Cohick. "You Mean, Write It Over in Ink?" *EJ* 64, no. 9 (1975): 48–53.

Odell, L., and C. R. Cooper. "Describing Responses to Works of Fiction." *RTE* 10 (1976): 203–25.

Odell, L., and S. Sage. "Written Products and the Writing Process." Paper, Annual Meeting of AERA, 1978. ED 157 059.

Odom, R. D., R. M. Liebert, and J. E. Hill. "The Effects of Modeling Cues, Reward, and Attentional Set on the Production of Grammatical and Ungrammatical Syntactic Constructions." *Journal of Experimental Child Psychology* 6 (1968): 131–40.

O'Donnell, B. "NCTE/ERIC Summaries and Sources: Priority Projects for the Teaching of English: 1970." *EJ* 59 (1970): 868–74; also appeared in *Elementary English* 47 (1970): 769–76.

O'Donnell, H. "ERIC/RCS Report: Writing Problems of the Learning Disabled Student." *LA* 57 (1980): 802–05.

————. ERIC/RCS Report: Children Writing: Process and Development." *LA* 56 (1979): 839–43.

O'Donnell, J. F. "An Experimental Study of the Effects of the Supplemental Use of a Psycho-Linguistic Remedial Tutorial Program on the Reading and Writing Behaviors of Black High-Risk College Freshmen and on Their Attitudes toward Reading, Writing, and Other College-Related Stimuli."*DAI* 35 (1974): 1552-A.

O'Donnell, R. C. "The Correlation of Awareness of Structural Relationships in English and Ability in Written Composition." *JER* 57 (1964): 464–67.
————. "A Critique of Some Indices of Syntactic Maturity." *RTE* 10 (1976a): 31–38.
————. "Research in the Teaching of Secondary English: Actuality and Potential." Paper, Annual Meeting of the Secondary School English Conference, 1976b. ED 120 799.
————. *Semantic Roles, Relations, and Constructs: Theory and Applications. Studies in Language Education, Report No. 18.* Athens, Georgia: University of Georgia, Department of Language Education, 1975. ED 108 248.
————. *A Survey of "Research in the Teaching of English," Volumes 1–10. Report No. 31.* Athens, Georgia: University of Georgia, Department of Language Education, 1977. ED 143 031.
————. "A Survey of *Research in the Teaching of English*, Volumes 1–10." *RTE* 14 (1980): 82–88.
O'Donnell, R. C., W. J. Griffin, and R. C. Norris. *Syntax of Kindergarten and Elementary School Children: A Transformational Analysis. NCTE Research Report No. 8.* Champaign, Illinois: NCTE, 1967a. ED 017 508.
————. "A Transformational Analysis of Oral and Written Grammatical Structures in the Language of Children in Grades Three, Five, and Seven." *JER* 61 (1967b): 35–39.
O'Donnell, R. C., and W. L. Smith. "Increasing Ninth-Grade Students' Awareness of Syntactic Structure through Direct Instruction." *RTE* 9 (1975): 257–62.
————. *Use of an Instructional Module to Heighten Awareness of Syntactic Structure. Studies in Language Education, Report No. 3.* Athens, Georgia: University of Georgia, Department of Language Education, 1973. ED 077 026.
Oehlkers, W. J. "The Contribution of Creative Writing to Reading Achievement in the Language Experience Approach." *DAI* 32 (1972): 6689-A.
Ofsa, W. J. "An Experiment in Using Research in Composition in the Training of Teachers of E glish." *DAI* 35 (1975): 7174-A.*
O'Hare, F. "The Effect of Sentence-Combining Practice Not Dependent on Formal Knowledge of a Grammar on the Writing of Seventh Graders." *DAI* 32 (1972): 6387-A.
————. *Sentence Combining: Improving Student Writing without Formal Grammar Instruction. NCTE Committee on Research Report Series, No. 15.* Urbana, Illinois: NCTE, 1973. ED 073 483.
Ohmann, R. M., and W. Douglas. "English 101 and the Military-Industrial Complex." In *English in America: A Radical View of the Profession.* Edited by R. M. Ohmann, 93–206. New York: Oxford University Press, 1976.
Olson, D. R. "From Utterance to Text: The Bias of Language in Speech and Writing." *Harvard Education Review* 47 (1977): 257–81.
Olson, M. C., and P. DiStefano. "Describing and Testing the Effectiveness of a Contemporary Model for In-Service Education in Teaching Composition." *English Education* 12 (1980): 69–76.
Ong, W. J. "The Writer's Audience Is Always a Fiction." *Publications of the Modern Language Association* 90 (1975): 9–21.
Orchard, D. T. "A Primary Teacher's Inservice Support System for Writing."

Based on a paper presented at the Annual Meeting of National Conference on Language Arts in the Elementary School, 1981. ED 202 033.

Osborn, A. F. *Applied Imagination: Principles and Procedures of Creative Problem-Solving.* New York: Charles Scribner's Sons, 1963.

Osburn, C. R. "A Study of Selected Usage Errors in the Written Expression of Boys and Girls in Grades Three through Six." *DAI* 27 (1966): 1295-A.

Osterlind, S. J. "Attitudes and Cognitive Achievements of Secondary School Students within Selected Language Arts Elective Courses." *DAI* 38 (1977): 1203-A.

Overton, B. J. "An Analysis of the Effects of Two Methods of Teaching Remedial Composition." *DAI* 42 (1981): 118-A.

Owens, F. L. "A Study of Creative Writing Ability of Third-Grade Students in a Communication Skills through Authorship Program." *DAI* 33 (1973): 3485-A.

Owens, L. "Syntax in Children's Written Composition, Socioeconomic Status, and Cognitive Development." *Australian Journal of Education* 20 (1976): 202–22.

Ozier, P. W. "The Concurrent Validity of CLEP Composition Scores in Relation to Writing Performance." *DAI* 40 (1980): 5017-A.

Page, E. B. "The Use of the Computer in Analyzing Student Essays." *International Review of Education* 14 (1968): 210–25.

Palmer, O. "Seven Classic Ways of Grading Dishonestly." *EJ* 51 (1962): 464–67.

Palmer, W. S. "The Free Modifier: A Fresh Mode of Teaching Composition." *DAI* 31 (1971): 6477-A.

———. "Measuring Written Expression: Quality Scales and the Sentence." *High School Journal* 60, no. 1 (1976): 32–40.

Pappas, C. C. "The Development of Narrative Capabilities within a Synergistic, Variable Perspective of Language Development: An Examination of Cohesive Harmony of Stories Produced in Three Contexts—Retelling, Dictating and Writing." *DAI* 42 (1981): 584-A.

Paris, P., M. Scardamalia, and C. Bereiter. "Discourse Schemata as Knowledge and as Regulators of Text Production." Paper, Annual Meeting of AERA, 1980.

Parker, R. P., Jr. "From Sputnik to Dartmouth: Trends in the Teaching of Composition." *EJ* 68, no. 6 (1979): 32–37.

Parker, R. P., Jr., and L. Meskin. "Who Says Johnny Can't Write?" *EJ* 65, no. 8 (1976): 42–46.

Pascale, M. A. "The Effect of a Visual-Motor Integration Training Program on Beginning Writing Skills of Kindergarten Children." *DAI* 31 (1970): 270-A.

Patty, A. H. "A Comparison of the Relative Effectiveness of Teaching Composition by Closed-Circuit Television and by Conventional Classroom Procedures." *DA* 27 (1967): 4173-A. ED 029 881.*

Peaster, M. Y. "A Descriptive Analysis of Beginning Reading Combining Language Experiences, Children's Story Writing and Linguistic Principles Tested after the Second Year and the Third Year." *DAI* 31 (1971): 5913-A.

Pechar, G. M. "An Evaluation of an Oral Proofreading Technique Used to Teach Grammar and Composition." *DAI* 38 (1977): 677-A.*

Peck, M. P. "An Investigation of Tenth-Grade Students' Writing." *DAI* 41 (1981): 3926-A.

Pedersen, E. L. "Improving Syntactic and Semantic Fluency in Writing of

Language Arts Students through Extended Practice in Sentence-Combining." *DAI* 38 (1978): 5892-A.*

Peitzman, F. C. "The Composing Processes of Three College Freshmen: Focus on Revision." *DAI* 42 (1982): 5047-A.

Percival, E. "The Dimensions of Ability in English Composition." *Educational Review* 18 (1966): 205–12.

Perfetti, C. A., and S. R. Goldman. *Discourse Functions of Thematization and Topicalization.* Pittsburgh, Pennsylvania: University of Pittsburgh, Learning Research and Development Center, 1975. ED 112 670.

Perkins, K. "Using Objective Methods of Attained Writing Proficiency to Discriminate Among Holistic Evaluations." *TESOL Quarterly* 14 (1980): 61–69.

Perkins, R. L. "A Study of the Effects of a Humanistic, Student-Controlled Method of Teaching Expository Composition on the Writing Performance of a Selected Group of Disadvantaged College Freshmen." *DAI* 35 (1974): 1644-A.*

Perl, S. "The Composing Processes of Unskilled College Writers." *RTE* 13 (1979): 317–36.

Perrin, C. R. "Discovery, Structure and Voice: An Approach to Teaching Composition." *DAI* 34 (1973): 737-A. See also ED 103 862.

Perrin, J. K. "An Analysis of Selected Syntactic Practices of Seventh-Grade Students in Oral and Written Discourse." *DAI* 32 (1972): 3961-A.*

Perron, J. D. "An Exploratory Approach to Extending the Syntactic Development of Fourth-Grade Students through the Use of Sentence-Combining Methods." *DAI* 35 (1975): 4316-A.*

———. "Composition and Cognition." *English Education* 10 (1979): 144–54.

———. "D. K.: Half a Case Study of Writing." Paper, Annual Meeting of the NCTE, 1977a. ED 149 375.

———. *The Impact of Mode on Written Syntactic Complexity: Part I—Third Grade. Report No. 24.* Athens, Georgia: University of Georgia, Department of Language Education, 1976a. ED 126 531.

———. *The Impact of Mode on Written Syntactic Complexity: Part II—Fourth Grade. Report No. 25.* Athens, Georgia: University of Georgia, Department of Language Education, 1976b. ED 126 511.

———. *The Impact of Mode on Written Syntactic Complexity: Part III—Fifth Grade. Report No. 27.* Athens, Georgia: University of Georgia, Department of Language Education, 1976c. ED 128 827.

———. *The Impact of Mode on Written Syntactic Complexity: Part IV—Across-the-Grades Differences and General Summary.* Athens, Georgia: University of Georgia, Department of Language Education, 1976d. ED 147 831.

———. "Written Syntactic Complexity and the Modes of Discourse." Paper, Annual Meeting of AERA, 1977b. ED 139 009.

Perry, M. L. "A Study of the Effects of a Literary Models Approach to Composition on Writing and Reading Achievement." *DAI* 40 (1980): 6137-A. See also ED 191 078.*

Peters, W. H., and A. G. Blues. "Teacher Intellectual Disposition as It Relates to Student Openness in Written Response to Literature." *RTE* 12 (1978): 127–36.

Peterson, E. R. "Achievement Effect of Theme and Paragraph Writing in Senior High School through Use of Lay-Theme Readers." *DA* 22 (1962): 2254.

Peterson, E. W. "A Comparison of Three Methods of Teaching Composition to Seventh and Ninth Graders." *DAI* 30 (1970): 2267-A. ED 046 930.*

Petrick, J. F. "Psychotherapy: Implications for Composition." Paper, Annual Meeting of CCCC, 1981. ED 200 961.

Petrosky, A. R. "Research Roundup: Apprehension, Attitudes, and Writing." *EJ* 65, no. 9 (1976): 74–77.

———. "Research Roundup: Grammar Instruction: What We Know." *EJ* 66, no. 9 (1977): 86–88.

Pettersson, A., and E. Lindell. *Writing Practice in Upper Secondary School (STIG)*. Stockholm: National Swedish Board of Education, 1976. ED 128 825.

Pettigrew, J., R. A. Shaw, and A. D. Van Nostrand. "Collaborative Analysis of Writing Instruction." *RTE* 15 (1981): 329–41.

Pfeifer, J. K. "The Effects of Peer Evaluation and Personality on Writing Anxiety and Writing Performance in College Freshmen." *DAI* 42 (1981): 1513-A.

Pfeiffer, S. I. "The Relationship between Cognitive Style and Creative Writing in Children." *DAI* 39 (1978): 201-A.

Phelps, S. F. "The Effects of Integrating Sentence-Combining Activities and Guided Reading Procedures on the Reading and Writing Performance of Eighth-Grade Students." *DAI* 40 (1979): 179-A.*

Phelps, T. O. "An Experiment Comparing Traditional Instruction in College Freshmen Composition with Instruction Employing Learning Cycles Based on Piagetian Theories." *DAI* 42 (1982): 3045-A.

Phillips, C. S. "An Evaluation of a Humanities-Oriented, Cognitive Stimulation Model to Improve Descriptive Writing Development of Underprepared College Freshmen." *DAI* 42 (1981): 1027-A.

Phillips, L. A. "An Assessment of the Preparatory Value of a College Course in Freshman Composition." *DAI* 39 (1979): 4030-A.

Phillips, W. W. "Some Educational Implications Derived from a Comparison of Adult Spoken and Written Vocabularies." *DA* 290 (1969): 4387-A. ED 041 913.

Pianko, S. H. "The Composing Acts of College Freshman Writers: A Description." *DAI* 38 (1978): 3983-A.*

———. "A Description of the Composing Processes of College Freshman Writers." *RTE* 13 (1979): 5–22.

Piché, G. L. "Revision and Reform in the Secondary School English Curriculum." *DA* 28 (1968): 2997-A.

Piché, G. L., D. L. Rubin, and L. J. Turner. "Training for Referential Communication Accuracy in Writing." *RTE* 14 (1980): 309–18.

Piché, G. L., D. L. Rubin, L. J. Turner, and M. L. Michlin. "Teachers' Subjective Evaluations of Standard and Black Nonstandard English Compositions: A Study of Written Language Attitudes." *RTE* 12 (1978): 107–118.

Pickard, K. L. "An Experimental Study of the Effect of Remedial Instruction in English Usage on the Achievement of College Students in Business Letter Writing." *DAI* 33 (1972): 503-A.

Pierson, H. "Peer and Teacher Correction: A Comparison of the Effects of Two Methods of Teaching Composition in Grade Nine English Classes." *DA* 28 (1967): 1350-A.*

Pigott, M. B. "Sexist Roadblocks in Inventing, Focusing, and Writing." *CE* 40 (1979): 922–27.

Pike, K. L. "A Linguistic Contribution to Composition: A Hypothesis." *CCC* 15 (1964): 82–88.

Pinkham, R. G. "The Effect on the Written Expression of Fifth Grade Pupils of a Series of Lessons Emphasizing the Characteristics of Good Writing as Exemplified in Selected Works from the Area of Children's Literature." *DA* 29 (1969): 2613-A.*

Pisano, R. C. "The Effectiveness of an Intervention Study in Critical Thinking Skills Designed to Improve Written Composition in Eleventh and Twelfth Graders." *DAI* 41 (1980): 192-A.*

Pitts, B. J. M. "The Newswriting Process: A Protocol Analysis Case Study of Three Practicing Journalists." *DAI* 42 (1982): 3332-A.

Pitts, M. R. "The Relationship of Classroom Instructional Characteristics and Writing Performance in Required Composition Classrooms."*DAI* 40 (1979): 86-A.

Plagens, D. J. "A Pilot Study Concerning the Measurement of the Typewriter Composition Skills of Selected Postsecondary Students." *DAI* 39 (1978): 3315-A.

Plasse, L. A. "The Influence of Audience on the Assessment of Student Writing." *DAI* 42 (1982): 3940-A.*

Platt, P. "Grapho-Linguistics: Children's Drawings in Relation to Reading and Writing Skills. *Reading Teacher* 31 (1977): 262–68.

Plowden Report. *Children and Their Primary Schools; A Report of the Central Advisory Council for Education.* London: Her Majesty's Stationery Office, 1967.

Polanyi, L. *Not So False Starts. Working Papers in Sociolinguistics, No. 41.* Austin, Texas: Southwest Educational Development Lab, 1977. ED 155 915.

Pollio, H. R. *Figurative Language: A Neglected Aspect of the Elementary School Language Arts Curriculum. Final Report.* Knoxville, Tennessee: University of Tennessee, Department of Psychology, 1973. ED 079 747.

Pollio, M. R. D. "The Development and Augmentation of Figurative Language." *DAI* 34 (1974): 4712-A.

Pope, M. "The Syntax of Fourth Graders' Narrative and Explanatory Speech." *RTE* 8 (1974): 219–27.

Porter, E. J. "Research Report: 'Applied Linguistics: A Discovery Approach to the Teaching of Writing, Grades K–12' [E. L. Ezor and T. Lane]." *LA* 52 (1975): 1019–21.

———. "Research Report: Martin, James J., 'The Development of Sentence-Writing Skills at Grades Three, Four, and Five'." *Elementary English* 49 (1972): 867–70.

———. "Research Report: 'The Grading of Original Stories—A Survey' [P. F. Alpren]." *Elementary English* 50 (1973): 1237–40.

Porter, P. T. "Teacher Expectancy: The Effect of Race, Sex, Direction of Writing Performance and Trials on the Grading of Essays." *DAI* 40 (1979): 1251-A.

Potter, R. R. "An Exploratory Study of the Relationship between Certain Aspects of Sentence Structure and the Overall Quality of Tenth-Grade Writing." *DAI* 27 (1967a): 2745-A.

————. "Sentence Structure and Prose Quality: An Exploratory Study." *RTE* 1 (1967b): 17–28.

Powell, W. R., and E. J. Bolduc. "Indicators for Learning and Teacher Competencies in the Basic Skills: Speaking, Writing, Spelling, Handwriting." *Research Bulletin* 13, no. 2 (1979). ED 198 521.

Powers, W. G., J. A. Cook, and R. Meyer. "The Effect of Compulsory Writing on Writing Apprehension." *RTE* 13 (1979): 225–30.

Prater, D. L. "The Construction and Validation of a Criterion-Referenced Test in Basic Writing Skills." *DAI* 39 (1978): 99-A.

Prentice, W. C. "The Effects of Intended Audience and Feedback on the Writings of Middle Grade Pupils." *DAI* 41 (1980): 934-A.

Presland, J. L. "In Search of an 'Early Teaching Grammar'." *Educational Research* 16, no. 2 (1974): 112–120.

Press, H. B. "Basic Motivation for Basic Skills: The Interdependent Approach to Interdisciplinary Writing." *CE* 41 (1979): 310–13.

Price, G. B., and R. L. Graves. "Sex Differences in Syntax and Usage in Oral and Written Language." *RTE* 14 (1980): 147–53.

Pritchard, R. J. "A Study of the Cohesion Devices in the Good and Poor Compositions of Eleventh Graders." *DAI* 42 (1981): 688-A.

Propp, V. *Morphology of the Folktale.* Translated by L. Scott. Austin, Texas: University of Texas Press, 1968.

Purves, A., ed. *Cognition and Written Language: A Symposium.* Papers presented at the Symposium on Cognition and Written Language, 1979. ED 178 918.

Putty, E. R. "Predictors of Success in a Selected Community College Freshman English Writing Program." *DAI* 40 (1980): 5018-A.

Putz, J. M. "The Effectiveness of Non-Directive Teaching as a Method of Improving the Writing Ability of College Freshmen." *DAI* 31 (1970): 1252-A.

Quinn, A. V. "Some Effects of Experience-Related Reading Instruction on the Written Language Development of First-Grade Children." *DAI* 38 (1977): 1946-A.

Rabianski, N. E. M. "An Exploratory Study of Individual Differences in the Use of Free Writing and the Tagmemic Heuristic Procedure, Two Modes of Invention in the Composing Process." *DAI* 40 (1980): 4876-A.

————. *Systematic or Unsystematic Invention Instruction: Which Is More Effective for a Student Writer?* 1980. ED 192 326.

Rachal, J. R. "Grading Consistency among Teachers of Freshman English Composition at Selected North Carolina Post-Secondary Institutions." *DAI* 41 (1980): 900-A.

Radcliffe, T. "Talk-Write Composition: A Theoretical Model Proposing the Use of Speech to Improve Writing." *RTE* 6 (1972): 187–99.

Raiser, V. L. "Syntactic Maturity, Vocabulary Diversity, Mode of Discourse and Theme Selection in the Free Writing of Learning Disabled Adolescents." *DAI* 42 (1981): 2544-A.

Raisman, N. A. "Teaching Composition and Neurolinguistics: An Investigation of Transient Dysfunctions and Teaching Freshman Composition." *DAI* 40 (1980): 4454-A.

Rakauskas, W. V. "A Comparative Study of a Laboratory Approach versus a Conventional Approach to Teaching Developmental Freshman Composition at the University of Scranton." *DAI* 34 (1973): 1657-A.*

Raub, D. K. "The Audio-Lingual Drill Technique: An Approach to Teaching Composition." Thesis, George Peabody College for Teachers, 1966.

Raybern, J. A. "An Investigation of Selected Syntactic Differences Present in the Oral and Written Language of Lower Socioeconomic Status Black Third-Grade and Fifth-Grade Students." *DAI* 35 (1975): 6122-A.

Redd, V. P. "A Comparison of Two Methods of Language Arts Instruction for Low-Achieving Eighth-Grade Urban and Suburban Students." *DAI* 36 (1975): 810-A.

Redish, J. C., and K. Racette. *Teaching College Students How to Write: Training Opportunities for Document Designers.* New York: Siegel & Gale, Inc., 1979. ED 192 333.

Redman, G. W., Jr. "The Philosophy of Teaching Composition Held by Selected Teachers and Students at the University of Northern Colorado, Winter Quarter, 1973." *DAI* 35 (1974): 932-A.

Reed, C. E. *The Learning of Language.* New York: Appleton-Century-Crofts, 1971.

Reedy, J. B. "An Investigation of the Effect of a Whole-Brain Learning/ Teaching Model, Bi-Modal Development and Synthesis, on Tenth Grade Student Writers." *DAI* 42 (1981): 2544-A.

Reedy, J. E., Jr. "A Comparative Study of Two Methods of Teaching the Organization of Expository Writing to Ninth-Grade Pupils." *DA* 26 (1966): 5923.*

Rees, R. L. "A Comparison of Three Teaching Procedures to Develop Creativity in Written Expression." *DAI* 26 (1966): 4345.

Reesink, G. P., S. B. Holleman-van der Sleen, K. Stevens, and G. A. Kohnstum. "Development of Syntax among School Children and Adults: A Replication-Investigation." *Psychological Abstracts* 47, Abstract No. 10536 (1972): 1186–87.

Reff, M. S. "The Effect of Discussion on Freshman Composition." *DAI* 27 (1966): 1036-A.

Reigstad, T. J. "Conferencing Practices of Professional Writers: Ten Case Studies." *DAI* 41 (1981): 3406-A.

Remondino, C. "A Factorial Analysis of the Evaluation of Scholastic Compositions in the Mother Tongue." *BJEP* 29 (1959): 242–51.

Renehan, W. *Seven-Year-Olds: Talking and Writing.* Hawthorn, Victoria: Australian Council of Educational Research, 1977.

Reynolds, H. M. "The Design and Testing of a Focused and Sequenced Free Writing Approach to a First Course in Composition for Two Year College Students." *DAI* 42 (1981): 989-A.

Rhoads, P. A. "Relationship between Teacher Comments and the Performance of Slow Learners." *DAI* 28 (1968): 2498-A.

Rhodes, B. "Who's Learning?" *College Press Review* 18, nos. 1–2 (Fall-Winter 1978–79): 30–32.

Richardson, E. M. "The Quality of Essays Written for Distant and Intimate Audiences by High and Low Apprehensive Two-Year College Freshmen." *DAI* 41 (1980): 971-A.

Richardson, K., M. Calnan, J. Essen, and L. Lambert. "The Linguistic Maturity of 11-Year-Olds: Some Analysis of the Written Compositions of Children in the National Child Development Study." *Journal of Child Language* 3 (1976): 99–115.

Rider, D., and E. H. Rusk. *Preparing English Teachers for the Secondary School. Unified, Academic and Professional Experiences in Language and Writing for the Preparation of Secondary School Teachers of English. Final Report.* East Lansing, Michigan: Michigan State University, College of Education, 1967. ED 016 674.

Rietz, S. A. "A Comparison of Certain Structural Characteristics of Language Selections Representing Both Oral and Written Thought and Purpose." *DAI* 37 (1977): 4925-A.

Rippey, R. "An Experiment in the Teaching of English Composition." *Irish Journal of Education* 2, no. 2 (1968): 112–26. ED 040 179.

Rippey, R. M. "Analysis of Written Language about Problems and Pressures." *School Review* 76, no. 4 (1968): 379–95.

Robards, S. J. N. "An Analysis of Selected Textbooks to Identify Scope and Sequence in Elementary School Composition." *DAI* 33 (1978): 6599-A.

Roberts, R. S. "A Comparison of the Written Language Performance of Pupils in Four Fifth-Grades in Schools Varying in Racial Composition." *DAI* 36 (1975): 3569-A.

Robinson, C. F. "An Investigation of New Rhetoric Lessons for Improved Written Composition on the Secondary School Level." 1978. ED 188 196.

Robinson, E. H., III. "Students' Perceptions of Teachers' Abilities to Provide Certain Facilitative Conditions and Their Relationship to Language Arts Achievement Gains." *DAI* 37 (1977): 4144-A.

Robinson, H. A., ed. *Reading and Writing Instruction in the United States: Historical Trends.* Newark, Delaware: International Reading Association, 1977. ED 142 995.

Robinson, R. L. H. "The Effects of an Oral Language Task as Opposed to a Written Language Task on the Production of Figurative Language in Sixth-Grade Students." *DAI* 38 (1977): 2545-A.

Rodd, L. J., and M. D. S. Braine. "Children's Imitations of Syntactic Constructions as a Measure of Linguistic Competence." *Journal of Verbal Learning and Verbal Behavior* 10 (1971): 430–33.

Rodrigues, R. J. "A Comparison of the Written and Oral English Syntax of Mexican-American Bilingual and Anglo-American Monolingual Fourth-Grade and Ninth-Grade Students." *DAI* 35 (1975): 6123-A.

Rodriguez, O. "Egocentrism in the Language of Six to Seven-Year-Old Mexican Children." Paper, International Symposium on Language Acquisition, 1976. ED 140 676.

Rogers, L. "The Composing Acts of College Freshman Writers: A Description with Two Case Studies." *DAI* 39 (1978): 101-A.

Rohman, D. G. "Pre-Writing: The Stage of Discovery in the Writing Process." *CCC* 16 (1965): 106–12.

Rohman, D. G., and A. Wlecke. *Prewriting: The Construction and Application of Models to Concept Formation in Writing.* East Lansing, Michigan: Michigan State University, 1964. ED 001 273.

Roos, M. E. "Syntactic Maturity and Grading: A Correlational Study." Paper, Annual Meeting of the Wyoming Conference on Freshman and Sophomore English, 1981. ED 207 071.

Rose, M. A. "The Cognitive Dimension of Writer's Block: An Examination of University Students." *DAI* 42 (1981): 1520-A.

Rose, R. C. "The Design, Implementation, and Evaluation of an Exportable

Personalized System of Instruction for Teaching Applied Sentence Writing Skills to High School Students." *DAI* 41 (1981): 3519-A.

Rosen, H. "An Investigation of the Effects of Differentiated Writing Assignments on the Performance in English Composition of a Selected Group of 15–16 Year Old Pupils." Diss., University of London, 1969.

———. "Written Language and the Sense of Audience." *Educational Research* 15, no. 3 (1973): 177–87.

Rosen, L. S. "A Study of an Inservice Program for College Teachers of Freshman English." *DAI* 33 (1972): 149-A.

Rosen, M. "A Structured Classroom Writing Method: An Experiment in Teaching Rhetoric to Remedial English College Students." *DAI* 34 (1974): 7524-A.*

Ross, J. "A Transformational Approach to Teaching Composition." *CCC* 22 (1971): 179–84.

Ross, S. B. "A Syntactic Analysis of the Written Language of Selected Black Elementary School Children with Reference to Sociological Variables." *DAI* 33 (1973): 5710-A.

Rothstein, R. N. "A Comparison of the Teaching of Composition Using Literature as a Model with a Program for the Writing of an Informal Essay." *DAI* 31 (1970): 2622-A.*

Rubin, D. L., and G. L. Piché. "Development in Syntactic and Strategic Aspects of Audience Adaptation Skills in Written Persuasive Communication." *RTE* 13 (1979): 293–316.

Rubin, J. B. "A Descriptive Study of Teachers' Conceptions of Language as Affecting the Decision-Making in Planning and Evaluating Students' Writing in Grades Four, Five, and Six." *DAI* 40 (1979): 1427-A.

Rubin, R., and N. Buium. "Language Parameters in Written Compositions of Nine-Year-Old Children." Paper, Annual Meeting of the American Psychological Association, 1974. ED 097 718.

Rucker, G. H. "The Composing Processes of Gifted and Average Sixth Grade Students: A Case Study." *DAI* 42 (1982): 3481-A.

Ruddell, R. B. "An Investigation of the Effect of the Similarity of Oral and Written Patterns of Language Structure on Reading Comprehension." *DAI* 24 (1964): 5207.

Ruffner, M. R. "Psychological and Stylistic Correlates of Written Encoding Behavior." *DAI* 38 (1977): 534-A.

Rule, L. B. "Composition Problems Encountered by Upward Bound Graduates in Freshman Composition." *DAI* 35 (1974): 2660-A.

Rule, R. "Concept Descriptions." In *A Case Study Observing the Development of Primary Children's Composing, Spelling, and Motor Behaviors during the Writing Process, Final Report.* Edited by D. H. Graves, 421–26. NIE Grant No. G-78-0174. Durham, New Hampshire: University of New Hampshire, 1981a.

———. "The Spelling Process: A Look at Strategies." In *A Case Study Observing the Development of Primary Children's Composing, Spelling, and Motor Behaviors during the Writing Process, Final Report.* Edited by D. H. Graves, 207-17. NIE Grant No. G-78-0174. Durham, New Hampshire: University of New Hampshire, 1981b.

Rumelhart, D. E. "Schemata: The Building Blocks of Cognition." In *Theoretical Issues in Reading Comprehension.* Edited by R. Spiro, B. Bruce,

and W. Brewer, 33–58. Hillsdale, New Jersey: Lawrence Erlbaum Associates, Publishers, 1980.

Rupley, W. H., and D. E. Norton. "ERIC/RCS Report: Preservice and
Inservice Education of Language Arts Teachers." *LA* 55 (1978): 641–47.

Rushton, J., and G. Young "Elements of Elaboration in Working Class
Writing." *Educational Research* 16, no. 3 (1974): 181–88.

Russell, L. A. "The Influence of Linguistic Grammar on the Grammar
Curriculum in the Secondary School as Measured by Textbook Analysis."
DAI 42 (1981): 79-A.

Sage, S. F. "Intellectual Strategies Used in Composing: An Analysis of
Intellectual Processes Reflected in Fictional Biography Written by High
and Low Achievers of Grades IX and XII." *DAI* 41 (1980): 927-A.

Sager, C. "Improving the Quality of Written Composition through Pupil Use
of Rating Scale." Paper, Annual Meeting of NCTE, 1973a. ED 089 304.

―――. "Improving the Quality of Written Composition through Pupil Use
of Rating Scale." *DAI* 34 (1973b): 1496-A. See also "Sager Writing Scale."
ED 091 723.*

St. Amant, M. M. "Objective Evaluation of English Composition." *DAI* 37
(1976): 3475-A.

St. Romain, M. D. "A Study of Differences in Creative Writing of Children
under Varying Stimuli." *DAI* 36 (1975): 244-A.

Saltzman, I. A. "Journal Keeping: A Self-Study Approach to Behavior
Change." *DAI* 41 (1981): 4660-A.

Salvner, G. M. "Using Collaboration to Teach English Composition: Theory,
Model, and Research." *DAI* 38 (1978): 4634-A.

Sanborn, J. M. "Writing: A Bridge to the Whole Being." *DAI* 40 (1980):
6255-A.

Sandel, L. "A Comparison of Oral and Written Language of Third-Grade
Children Instructed in Initial Teaching Alphabet (ITA) or Traditional
Orthography (TO) in First Grade." *DAI* 32 (1971): 313-A.

Sanders, S. E. "A Comparison of 'AIMS' and 'MODES' Approaches to the
Teaching of Junior College Freshman Composition both with and without
an Auxiliary Writing Lab." *DAI* 34 (1974): 5666-A.*

Sanders, S. E., and J. H. Littlefield. "Perhaps Test Essays Can Reflect
Significant Improvement in Freshman Composition: Report on a Successful
Attempt." *RTE* 9 (1975): 145–53.

San José, C. "In the Mind and onto Paper: A Study of Children's Writing."
1974. ED 170 775.

―――. "Notes and Comments [on studies of sentence-combining]." *RTE* 12
(1978): 91–92.

Sarlin, L. "A Study of Teachers' Concerns and Questions Related to the
Teaching of Creative Writing in the Intermediate Grades of the Plainedge
Public Schools; Ascertaining Teachers' Needs as the Basis for Writing a
Teachers' Guide for Helping Children Write Creatively (Parts I and II).
DAI 31 (1970): 1124-A.

Sauer, E. H. *Contract Correcting: The Use of Lay Readers in the High School
Composition Program.* Report to the Cooperative Research Program of
the United States Department of Health, Education, and Welfare, and to
the School and University Program for Research and Development. 1962.

Sauer, L. E. "Fourth Grade Children's Knowledge of Grammatical Structure." *Elementary English* 47 (1970): 807–13.

Sawkins, M. W. "The Oral Responses of Selected Fifth Grade Children to Questions Concerning Their Written Expression." *DAI* 31 (1971): 6287-A.

———. "What Children Say about Their Writing." In *The Writing Processes of Students.* Edited by W. Petty and P. Finn, 45–58. Buffalo, New York: Report of the Annual Conference on Language Arts, State University of New York at Buffalo, 1975.

Sbaratta, P. A. "Does General Knowledge Affect Writing Skills?" *Community College Review* 6, no. 4 (1979): 4–6.

———. "A Flexible Modular System: An Experiment in Teaching Freshman Composition." *DAI* 36 (1975): 1280-A.*

Scaglione, A. *The Classical Theory of Composition: From Its Origin to the Present: A Historical Survey.* Chapel Hill, North Carolina: The University of North Carolina Press, 1972.

Scannell, D. P., and O. M. Haugh. *Teaching Composition Skills with Weekly Multiple Choice Tests in Lieu of Theme Writing. Final Report.* Washington, D.C.: U. S. Office of Education, Bureau of Research, 1968. ED 021 850.

Scannell, D. P., and J. C. Marshall. "The Effect of Selected Composition Errors on Grades Assigned to Essay Examinations." *AERJ* 3 (1966): 125–30.

Scardamalia, M. "How Children Cope with the Cognitive Demands of Writing." In *Writing: The Nature, Development and Teaching of Written Communication.* Edited by C. H. Frederiksen, M. F. Whiteman, and J. F. Dominic, 81–103. Hillsdale, New Jersey: Lawrence Erlbaum Associates, Publishers, 1981.

Scardamalia, M., and W. Baird. "Children's Strategies for Composing Sentences." Paper, Annual Meeting of AERA, 1980.

Scardamalia, M., and C. Bereiter. "Audience-Adaptedness in Knowledge-Telling and Problem-Solving Strategy." Paper, Conference on Models and Process of Children's Writing, 1980a.

———. "The Development of Evaluative, Diagnostic, and Remedial Capabilities in Children's Composing." In *The Psychology of Written Language: A Developmental Approach.* Edited by M. Martlew, 67–95. London: John Wiley & Sons, 1983.

———. "The Effects of Writing Rate on Children's Composition." Paper, Annual Meeting of AERA, 1979.

———. "Procedural Facilitation as a Way of Helping Children Attain More Complex Levels of Thinking." Paper, NIE-LRDC (Learning Research and Development Center) Conference on Thinking and Learning Skills, 1980b.

Scardamalia, M., C. Bereiter, S. Gartshore, and C. Cattani. "Locating the Source of Children's Revision Difficulties." Paper, Annual Meeting of AERA, 1980.

Scardamalia, M., C. Bereiter, and H. Goelman. "The Role of Production Factors in Writing Ability." In *What Writers Know: The Language, Process, and Structure of Written Discourse.* Edited by Martin Nystrand, 173–210. New York: Academic Press, 1982.

Scardamalia, M., C. Bereiter, and J. D. S. McDonald. "Role-Taking in Written Communication Investigated by Manipulating Anticipatory Knowledge." Paper, Biennial Meeting of the Society for Research in Child Development, 1977. ED 151 792.

Scardamalia, M., C. Bereiter, and E. Woodruff. "The Effects of Content Knowledge on Writing." Paper, Annual Meeting of AERA, 1980.

Scardamalia, M., C. Bereiter, E. Woodruff, J. Burtis, and L. Turkish. "The Effects of Modeling and Cueing on High-Level Planning." Paper, Annual Meeting of AERA, 1981.

Scardamalia, M., and R. J. Bracewell. "Local Planning in Children's Writing." Paper, Annual Meeting of AERA, 1979.

Scardamalia, M., C. Cattani, L. Turkish, and C. Bereiter. "Part-Whole Relationships in Text Planning." Unpublished manuscript, The Ontario Institute for Studies in Education. Presented at Annual Meeting of AERA, 1981.

Schank, R. C., and R. P. Abelson. *Scripts, Plans, Goals, and Understanding.* Hillsdale, New Jersey: Lawrence Erlbaum Associates, Publishers, 1977.

Scheib, V. V. "The Relationships among the Various Language Abilities: Oral Reading, Written Language, Oral Language and Verbal Language in Grades One through Eight." *DAI* 39 (1978): 3337-A.

Scheiber, H. J. *New Mexico Writing: A Statewide Sample.* Sante Fe, New Mexico: New Mexico State Department of Education, 1981. ED 200 975.

Schiff, P. M. "Problem Solving and the Composition Model: Reorganization, Manipulation, Analysis." *RTE* 12 (1978): 203–10.

Schifsky, J. P. "Toward a Description of Expressive Discourse: A Stylistic Analysis of the Writing of 13 and 17-Year-Olds on a National Assessment Exercise." *DAI* 42 (1982): 3140-A.

Schippers, L. V. "Using the Affton Scale of Acceptable Written Expression to Decrease Disparity in Teachers Assigning a Level to Pupils' Written Expression." *DAI* 36 (1975): 3595-A.

Schlattman, R. D. "The Effectiveness of Programmed English Usage on the Achievement of College Students Enrolled in Business Communications." *DAI* 37 (1976): 1362-A.

Schleicher, J. G. "The Effect of Knowledge of Results on the Maintenance of Writing Skills." *DAI* 40 (1979): 656-A.

Schmeling, H. H. "A Study of the Relationship between Certain Syntactic Features and Overall Quality of College Freshmen Writing." *DAI* 30 (1970): 4970-A.

Schneider, V. L. "A Study of the Effectiveness of Emphasizing the Teaching of Reading Skills to Improve Composition Skills in Remedial English Classes at Kansas City Kansas Community Junior College." *DAI* 31 (1971): 6369-A.

Schroeder, T. S. "The Effects of Positive and Corrective Written Teacher Feedback on Selected Writing Behaviors of Fourth-Grade Children." *DAI* 34 (1973a): 2935-A.*

———. "Schroeder Composition Scale." 1973b. ED 091 760.

Schubert, J. P., Jr. "A Transformational Analysis of the Syntax of Oral and Written Language Modes of College Freshmen." *DAI* 35 (1975): 4488-A.

Schuessler, B. F., A. R. Gere, and R. D. Abbott. "The Development of Scales Measuring Teacher Attitudes Toward Instruction in Written Composition: A Preliminary Investigation." *RTE* 15 (1981): 55–63.

Schultz, L. M., and G. D. Meyers. "Measuring Writing Apprehension in Required Freshman Composition and Upper-Level Writing Courses." Paper, Annual Meeting of CCCC, 1981. ED 203 326.

Schulz, H. J. *A Comparative Study of the Effects of the Rhetorical Approach and the Grammatical Approach in the Teaching of English Composition at*

Woodridge High School. Peninsula, Ohio: Boston-Northampton Language Arts Program, 1967. ED 029 019.

Schuster, E. H. "Forward to Basics Through Sentence-Combining." Paper, Annual Meeting of Pennsylvania Council of Teachers of English, 1976. ED 133 774.

———. "Using Sentence Combining to Teach Writing to Inner-City Students." Paper, Annual Meeting of NCTE, 1977. ED 150 614.

Schwartz, H. J. "Teaching Stylistic Simplicity with a Computerized Readability Formula." Paper, International Meeting of the American Business Communication Association, 1980. ED 196 014.

Schwartz, J. I. "A Study of the Relations among Reading Readiness Achievement, Three Programs of Instruction in Personal Writing, and Achievement in Personal Writing." *DAI* 31 (1970): 2266-A.

Schwartz, M. "Six Journeys through the Writing Process." *DAI* 41 (1980): 1450-A.

Seaman, A. "Exploring Early Stages of Writing Development: A Fourth Grader Writes." *The English Record* 26, no. 4 (Fall 1975): 40–46.

Searle, D., and D. Dillon. "The Message of Marking: Teacher Written Responses to Student Writing at Intermediate Grade Levels." *RTE* 14 (1980): 233–42.

Searles, J. R., and G. R. Carlsen. "English—Language, Grammar, and Composition." In *Encyclopedia of Educational Research.* 3rd ed. Edited by C. W. Harris, 454–66. New York: Macmillan, 1960.

Sears, M. O. "Effects of a Student Centered Procedure on the Self-Concepts and Writing Practice of College Freshmen." *DAI* 31 (1971): 4563-A.*

Sebesta, S., N. Thompson, and D. D. Nemanich. *The Nebraska Study of the Syntax of Children's Writing, 1965–66. Vol. II.* Lincoln, Nebraska: University of Nebraska, Curriculum Development Center, 1967. ED 013 815.

Seegers, J. C. "Form of Discourse and Sentence Structure." *The Elementary English Review* 10 (1933): 51–54.

Seidman, E. "Marking Students' Compositions: Implications of Achievement Motivation Theory." *DA* 28 (1968): 2605-A.

Seiler, W. J., J. P. Garrison, and R. K. Bookar. "Communication Apprehension, Student Assistance outside the Classroom, and Academic Achievement: Some Practical Implications for the Classroom Teacher." Paper, Annual Meeting of the Central States Speech Association, 1978. ED 153 292.

Seits, L. E. "The Grading of Community College English Essays: A Study of the Effects of Student Name Stereotypes." *DAI* 42 (1981): 1618-A.

Self, W. P. "A Description, Analysis, and Evaluation of Composition for Personal Growth: An Approach to Teaching Writing." *DAI* 40 (1979): 2456-A.

Selfe, C. L. "The Composing Processes of Four High and Four Low Writing Apprehensives: A Modified Case Study." *DAI* 42 (1982): 3168-A.

Settles, I. L. "The Effects of Instruction with the Initial Teaching Alphabet on the Written Composition of Primary Students." *DA* 28 (1968): 2459-A.

Shades, C. T. "A Study of Practices Considered Effective by Teachers of Language Arts Methods Courses in the 16 Oklahoma Colleges Accredited for Teacher Education Program." *DA* 28 (1967): 147-A.

Shafer, R. E. "Children's Interactions in Sustaining Writing: Studies in an English Primary School." Paper, Annual Meeting of the Virginia Association of Teachers of English, 1980. ED 193 682.

————. "The Crisis in Knowing about Learning to Write." *ADE Bulletin* 6, no. 6 (1975): 52–57.

Shanahan, T. E. "A Canonical Correlational Analysis of the Reading-Writing Relationship: An Exploratory Investigation." *DAI* 41 (1980): 1007-A. See also Paper, Annual Meeting of the International Reading Association, 1981. ED 205 932.

————. "The Impact of Writing Instruction on Learning to Read." *Reading World* 19 (1980): 357–68.

Shandloff, L. G. "The Relationships of Freshman Composition Curriculum Practices in Florida Public Community Junior Colleges to Research in the Teaching of Written Composition." *DAI* 34 (1973): 589-A.

Shane, H. G., J. Walden, and R. Green. *Interpreting Language Arts Research for the Teacher.* Washington, D.C.: Association for Supervision and Curriculum Development, 1971.

Shapiro, B. J., and P. P. Shapiro. "The Effect of Reading Method on Composition: i.t.a. vs. T.O." *Journal of Reading Behavior* 5 (1973): 82–87.

Sharples, D. "Factors Affecting the Composition Performance of Ten-Year-Old Children." *BJEP* 37 (1967): 137–40.

Shaughnessy, M. P. "Basic Writing." In *Teaching Composition: Ten Bibliographical Essays.* Edited by G. Tate, 136–67. Fort Worth, Texas: Texas Christian University Press, 1976.

————. *Errors and Expectations: A Guide for the Teacher of Basic Writing.* New York: Oxford University Press, 1977a.

————. "Some Needed Research on Writing." *CCC* 28 (1977b): 317–20.

Shaver, J. P. "Tutorial Students Two Years Later: A Report on the Logan-Cache Tutorial Center for Underachieving Readers and Writers." Salt Lake City, Utah: Utah State Department of Public Instruction, 1969. ED 046 961.

Shelton, C. S., Jr. "A Study to Determine the Degree of Agreement between a Selected Group of Educators and Bankers Concerning the Objectives and Content of the Basic Collegiate Business Communication Course." *DAI* 42 (1982): 2986-A.

Sherwood, R. I. "A Survey of Undergraduate Reading and Writing Needs." *CCC* 28 (1977): 145–49.

Shook, J. "The Gateway Writing Project: An Evaluation of Teachers Teaching Teachers to Write." *RTE* 15 (1981): 282–84.

Shook, R. R. "One-to-One: An Examination of a Stage/Process Tutorial Model for Teaching English Composition." *DAI* 42 (1981): 2004-A.

Shostak, R. "Developing a Technique for Discovering the Rater Policies of Essay Graders." *DAI* 30 (1970): 2889-A.

Sides, C. H. "Tutorials and Writing Classes: A Pilot Study." 1977. ED 191 077.

Siedow, M. D. "Relationships between Syntactic Maturity in Oral and Written Language and Reading Comprehension of Materials of Varying Syntactic Complexity." *DAI* 34 (1974): 4890-A.

Siff, D. "Teaching Freshman Composition to New York Cops." *CE* 36 (1975): 540–47.

Silberberg Grossman, C. A. "A Comparison of the Attitudes of Elementary Classroom Teachers in Iowa and Experts in the Field of Language Arts toward Creative Self-Expression in Relation to Other Aspects of the Language Arts Curriculum." *DAI* 38 (1978): 3937-A.

Silva, C. M. "A Comparative Study of the Needs and Concepts of Individual

Students in a Post-Secondary Remedial Writing Program." *DAI* 38 (1977): 2533-A.

Silverman, C., ed. *Research Report: The Productive Language Assessment Tasks.* Ypsilanti, Michigan: High/Scope Educational Research Foundation, 1976. ED 147 837.

Simmons, A. A. "Comparison of Written and Spoken Language from Deaf and Hearing Children at Five Age Levels." *DA* 25 (1964): 302.

Simmons, R. F., and J. Slocum. "Generating English Discourse from Semantic Networks." Austin, Texas: University of Texas, 1970. ED 055 473.

Simmons, R. J. "An Analytical Study of the Relationship of Reading Abilities and Writing Abilities of Tenth-Grade Students." *DAI* 38 (1978): 7127-A.

Simon, P. E. "An Exploratory Study of the Relationship between Reading Response and Syntactic Writing Maturity." *DAI* 41 (1980): 2533-A.

Simpson, G. F. "Measures of Writing Ability of Fourth-Grade, Fifth-Grade, and Sixth-Grade Children." *DAI* 34 (1974): 5497-A. ED 092 948.*

Simpson, H. B. "A Descriptive Analysis of Scientific Writing." *DAI* 27 (1960): 468-A.

Simpson, K. J. "Error Acceptability in Written Business Communication as Perceived by Business Educators and by Business Communicators." *DAI* 38 (1977): 600-A.

Singleton, D. J. "The Reliability of Ratings on the Essay Portion of the Language Skills Examination." *DAI* 37 (1977): 7710-A.

Skelton, T. "Research as Preparation: Determining the Instructional Needs of the Two-Year Student." Paper, Annual Meeting of CCCC, 1978. ED 155 695.

Slay, A. L. "A Comparison of the Effectiveness of Programed, Handbook, and Non-Formalized Grammar Instruction in Remedial College Freshman English Composition." *DAI* 30 (1969): 1536-A.

Sloan, G. "Predilections for Plethoric Prose." *CE* 39 (1978): 860–65.

———. "The Subversive Effects of an Oral Culture on Student Writing." *CCC* 30 (1979): 156–60.

Slobin, D. "A Re-Analysis of Adult Responses to Children's Utterances." In *The Ontogenesis of Grammar: A Theoretical Symposium.* Edited by D. Slobin, 133–51. New York: Academic Press, 1971.

Slotnick, H. B. "Do Thirteen-Year-Olds Write as Well as Seventeen-Year-Olds?" *EJ* 60 (1971): 1109–15.

———. "An Examination of the Computer Grading of Essays." *DAI* 32 (1972): 4431-A.

———. "Toward a Theory of Computer Essay Grading." *JEM* 9 (1972): 253–63.

———, comp. *Selected Essays and Letters: A Selection of Papers Collected During the 1969–70 Assessment of Writing.* Report 10. Denver, Colorado: National Assessment of Educational Progress, 1972. ED 075 822.

Slotnick, H. B., and J. V. Knapp. "Essay Grading by Computer: A Laboratory Phenomenon?" *EJ* 60 (1971): 75–87.

Slotnick, H. B., and W. T. Rogers. "Writing Errors: Implications about Student Writers." *RTE* 7 (1973): 387–98.

Slow, R. "Parental Education of English Composition Students." *CCC* 19 (1968): 22–23.

Smart, W. D., and L. O. Ollila. "The Effect of Sentence-Combining Practice on Written Compositions and Reading Comprehension." *The Alberta Journal of Educational Research* 24 (1978): 113–120.

Smeltzer, L. R. "A Study of the Relationship between Leadership Style and
    Writing Style for Supervisors and the Effects of Supervisory Experience,
    Formal Education and a Management Training Program on this Relation-
    ship." *DAI* 41 (1981): 2898-A.
Smith, C. B. "The Development of a Q-Sort to Measure Self-Concept of
    Writing Competence." *DA* 24 (1963): 149.
Smith, C. C., and T. W. Bean. "The Guided Writing Procedure: Integrating
    Content Reading and Writing Improvement." *Reading World* 19 (1980):
    290–94.
Smith, D. A., D. Kinney, and A. C. Graesser. "The Effect of Narrative
    Analogies on the Acquisition of Passages Describing Scientific Mecha-
    nisms." Paper, Annual Meeting of the Western Psychological Association,
    1980. ED 189 605.
Smith, D. I. "Effects of Class Size and Individualized Instruction on the
    Writing of High School Juniors." *DAI* 35 (1974): 2844-A.*
Smith, E. H. *Teacher Preparation in Composition.* Champaign, Illinois:
    NCTE/ERIC Clearinghouse on the Teaching of English, 1969.
Smith, F. P. "The Effects of an Elective English Program on Student Atti-
    tudes and Achievement in Relation to Aptitude." *DAI* 38 (1977): 1865-A.
Smith, H. "The Effect of Developmental Sequencing on a Sentence Combining
    Program." Conference on Sentence Combining and the Teaching of Writ-
    ing, Miami University, 1978.
Smith, H. L., Jr., and H. J. Sustakowski. *The Application of Descriptive
    Linguistics to the Teaching of English and a Statistically-Measured Com-
    parison of the Relative Effectiveness of the Linguistically-Oriented and
    Traditional Methods of Instruction.* Buffalo, New York: State University
    of New York, 1968. ED 021 216.
Smith, J. A. *Creative Teaching of the Language Arts in the Elementary
    School.* 2d ed. Boston, Massachusetts: Allyn and Bacon, Inc., 1973. ED
    077 012.
Smith, J. P. "Writing in a Remedial Reading Program: A Case Study." *LA*
    59 (1982): 245–53.
Smith, L. S. "An Investigation of Three Domain Referenced Strategies to
    Assess Secondary Students' Expository Writing." *DAI* 39 (1979): 7299-
    A.
Smith, M. L. "Competencies Needed by Teachers of Developmental English
    in Two-Year Colleges." *DAI* 38 (1978): 7101-A.
Smith, M. E. "Peer Tutoring in a Writing Workshop." *DAI* 36 (1976): 6645-
    A.
Smith, M. J., and B. A. Bretcko. "Research on Individual Composition
    Conferences." Paper, Annual Meeting of CCCC, 1974. ED 091 709.
Smith, R[on]. "The Composition Requirement Today: A Report on a Nation-
    wide Survey of Four-Year Colleges and Universities." *CCC* 25 (1974): 138–
    48.
———. "Implications of the Results of a Nationwide Survey for the Teaching
    of Freshman English." Paper, Annual Meeting of the CCCC, 1974. ED
    094 400.
Smith, R. A. "An Analysis of Children's Writing to Determine Developmental
    Patterns." *DAI* 39 (1978): 1306-A.
Smith, R. J. "The Effects of Reading a Short Story for a Creative Purpose
    on Student Attitudes and Writing." *DA* 28 (1968): 3082-A. ED 031 471.

Smith, R. J., and K. M. Jensen. "The Effects of Integrating Reading and Writing on Four Variables." *RTE* 5 (1971): 179–89.

Smith, V. H. "An Investigation of Teacher Judgment in the Evaluation of Written Composition Including the Development of a Test for the Measurement Thereof." *DA* 28 (1967): 1354-A.

———. "Measuring Teacher Judgment in the Evaluation of Written Composition." *RTE* 3 (1969): 181–95. ED 091 721.

Smith, W. L. "Syntactic Recoding of Passages Written at 3 Levels of Complexity." *Journal of Experimental Education* 43, no. 2 (Winter 1974): 66–72. ED 081 018.

Smith, W. L., and W. E. Combs. "The Effects of Overt and Covert Cues on Written Syntax." *RTE* 14 (1980): 19–38.

Smith, W. L., and M. B. Swan. "Adjusting Syntactic Structures to Varied Levels of Audience." *Journal of Experimental Education* 46, no. 4 (Summer 1978): 29–34.

Snyder, C. R. "Effects of Comparison Level Feedback on Classroom-Related Verbal Learning Performance." *JEP* 63 (1972): 493–99.

Soldow, G. F. "An Experiment Testing the Relationship between Cognitive Complexity and Syntactic Complexity." *DAI* 37 (1977): 6145-A.

Sommers, N. I. "Revision in the Composing Process: A Case Study of College Freshmen and Experienced Adult Writers." *DAI* 39 (1979): 5374-A.

Southwell, M. G. "Free Writing in Composition Classes." *CE* 38 (1977): 676–81.

———. "A Note on Specifying the Mode and Aim of Written Discourse for Basic Writing Students." *RTE* 14 (1980): 157–58.

Soven, M. "The Design, Implementation, and Evaluation of a Freshman Composition Curriculum." *DAI* 41 (1981): 4273-A.

Søvik, N. "Developmental Trends of Visual Feedback Control and Learning in Children's Copying and Tracking Skills." *Journal of Experimental Education* 49, no. 2 (Winter 1980/81): 106–19.

Sowers, Susan. "A Six-Year-Old's Writing Process: The First Half of First Grade." *LA* 56 (1979): 829–35.

———. "Young Writers' Preference for Non-Narrative Modes of Composition." In *A Case Study Observing the Development of Primary Children's Composing, Spelling, and Motor Behaviors during the Writing Process, Final Report.* Edited by D. H. Graves, 189–206. NIE Grant No. G-78-0174. Durham, New Hampshire: University of New Hampshire, 1981.

Speidel, J. D. "Using Art to Teach Writing: An Experiment in Perceptual Training." *DAI* 30 (1970): 3370-A.

Spigelmire, L. "The Best Stylists: A Survey of Editors, and Implications for the Teaching of Style in Freshman Composition Courses." Paper, Annual Meeting of CCCC, 1980. ED 186 922.

Sponsler, M. G. C. "The Effectiveness of Literary Models in the Teaching of Written Composition." *DAI* 32 (1971): 2322-A.*

Spooner-Smith, L. "Applying Empirical Needs Assessment Procedures to University-Level Instruction in Composition." Paper, Annual Meeting of AERA, 1976. ED 122 294.

Squire, J. R., and R. K. Applebee. *A Study of English Programs in Selected High Schools Which Consistently Educate Outstanding Students in English.* Cooperative Research Project No. 1994. Urbana, Illlinois: University of Illinois, 1966.

———. *A Study of the Teaching of English in Selected British Secondary Schools. Final Report.* Urbana, Illinois: University of Illinois, 1968. ED 017 517.

Stahl, A. "Structural Analysis of Children's Compositions." *RTE* 8 (1974): 184–205.

———. "The Structure of Children's Compositions: Developmental and Ethnic Differences." *RTE* 11 (1977): 156–63.

Staiger, R. C. "Language Arts Research: 1966." *Elementary English* 44 (1967): 617–38.

Stallard, C. K., Jr. "An Analysis of the Writing Behavior of Good Student Writers." *DAI* 33 (1973): 3408-A.

———. "An Analysis of the Writing Behavior of Good Student Writers." *RTE* 8 (1974): 206–18.

Stallard, L. M., and C. K. Stallard, Jr. "Writing Readiness at the Elementary Level." Paper, Annual Meeting of the Secondary School English Conference and the Conference on English Education, 1980. ED 186 918.

Stalnaker, B. J. "A Study of the Influences of Audience and Purpose on the Composing Processes of Professionals." *DAI* 42 (1982): 2933-A.

Stankowski, W. J. "Patterns of Students' Writing in Relation to Test and Academic Performances." *DAI* 28 (1968): 4453-A.

Stanton, B. E. "A Comparison of Theme Grades Written by Students Possessing Varying Amounts of Cumulative Written Guidance: Checklist, Instruction, and Questions and Feedback." *DAI* 35 (1974): 2662-A.

Staton, J. *Analysis of Dialogue Journal Writing as a Communicative Event, Volume I. Final Report to the National Institute of Education.* Washington, D.C.: Center for Applied Linguistics, 1982. ED 217 327.

Stauffer, D. A. "Using Programmed Materials to Teach Freshman College English." *DAI* 37 (1976): 947-A.

Steele, A. C. "An Evaluation of a Competency-Based English Composition Course at Lehigh University." *DAI* 41 (1981): 4599-A.

Stefl, L. D. "The Effect of a Guided Discovery Approach on the Descriptive Paragraph Writing Skills of Third Grade Pupils." *DAI* 42 (1981): 2493-A.

Steidle, E. F. "An Investigation of Writing Ability as a Function of Student Attitude: General and Specific." Paper, Annual Meeting of AERA, 1977. ED 139 023.

Stein, N. L. "Critical Issues in the Development of Literacy Education: Toward a Theory of Learning and Instruction." *American Journal of Education* 93 (1984): 171–99.

———. "On the Goals, Functions, and Knowledge of Reading and Writing." *Contemporary Educational Psychology* 8 (1983): 261–92.

Stein, N. L., and C. G. Glenn. "An Analysis of Story Comprehension in Elementary School Children." In *New Directions in Discourse Processing.* Vol. 2. Edited by R. O. Freedle, 53–120. Norwood, New Jersey: Ablex Publishing Corporation, 1979.

Stein, N. L., and M. Policastro. "The Concept of Story: A Comparison between Children's and Teachers' Viewpoints." In *Learning and Comprehension of Text.* Eds. H. Mandl, N. L. Stein, and T. Trabasso, 113–55. Hillsdale, New Jersey: Lawrence Erlbaum Associates, Publishers, 1984.

Stein, N. L., and T. Trabasso. "What's in a Story: An Approach to Comprehension and Instruction." In *Advances in Instructional Psychology.* Edited by R. Glaser, 213–67. Hillsdale, New Jersey: Lawrence Erlbaum Associates, Publishers, 1982.

Steinberg, E. R. *Needed Research in the Teaching of English*. U.S. Office of Education Cooperative Research Monograph No. 11, Washington, D.C.: U. S. Department of Health, Education, and Welfare; Office of Education, 1963.

―――. "Research in the Teaching of English: Tactics and Logistics." *Universities Quarterly* 20 (1966): 267–274.

―――. "Research on the Teaching of English under Project English." *Publications of the Modern Language Association*. 79, no. 4, part 2 (1964): 50–76.

Steller, N. A. D. "The Effects of Readers' Fatigue on the Grading of Essays." *DAI* 39 (1978): 3541-A.

Sternglass, M. S. "Dialect Features in the Compositions of Black and White College Students: The Same or Different?" *CCC* 25 (1974): 259–63.

―――. "Similarities and Differences in Nonstandard Syntactic Features in the Compositions of Black and White College Students in Freshman Remedial Writing Classes." *DAI* 34 (1974): 5950-A.

Stevens, A. E. "The Effects of Positive and Negative Evaluation on the Written Composition of Low Performing High School Students." *DAI* 34 (1973): 1778-A.

Stewart, D. C. "Comp. vs. Lit.: Which Is Your Job and Which Is Your Strength?" *CE* 40 (1978): 65–69.

―――. "Composition Textbooks and the Assault on Tradition." *CCC* 29 (1978): 171–76.

―――. "Essays, Analysis, and—Better Writing?" *RTE* 3 (1969): 42–51.

Stewart, M. F. "Freshman Sentence Combining: A Canadian Project." *RTE* 12 (1978a): 257–68.

―――. "Sentence-Combining and Syntactic Maturity in First Year University." 1978b. ED 153 240.

―――. "Syntactic Maturity from High School to University: A First Look." *RTE* 12 (1978c): 37–46.

Stewart, M. F., and C. H. Grobe. "Syntactic Maturity, Mechanics of Writing, and Teachers' Quality Ratings." *RTE* 13 (1979): 207–15.

Stewart, M. F., and H. L. Leaman. "Teachers' Writing Assessments across the High School Curriculum." 1981. ED 204 751.

Stewart, O. J. "The Relationships between Reading Comprehension and the Factors of Syntactic Awareness in Oral Reading, Syntactic Maturity in Writing, and Oral Reading Fluency." *DAI* 39 (1979): 5314-A.

Stewig, J. W. "Great Art Leads to Joyful Writing." Paper, Annual Meeting of National Conference on Language Arts in the Elementary School, 1980. ED 185 597.

Stewig, J. W., and P. Lamb. "Elementary Pupils' Knowledge of the Structure of American English and the Relationship of Such Knowledge to the Ability to Use Language Effectively in Composition." *RTE* 7 (1973): 324–37. See also Purdue Research Foundation Final Report, 1972. ED 071 095.

Stiff, R. "The Effect upon Student Composition of Particular Correction Techniques." *RTE* 1 (1967): 54–75.

Stiggins, R. J. "A Comparison of Direct and Indirect Writing Assessment Methods." *RTE* 16 (1982): 101–14.

Stiles, E. E. R. "A Case Study of Remedial Writers in Selected Two-Year Colleges in East Tennessee." *DAI* 37 (1977): 7004-A.

Stine, E. S. "Structural Analysis of the Written Composition of Intermediate Grade Children." *DA* 26 (1966): 6568.

Stock, R. "The Effect of Teaching Sentence Patterns on the Written Sentence Structure of Grade Two Children." Paper, Annual Meeting of the Plains Regional Conference of the IRA, 1980. ED 208 414.

Stone, L. R. "The Development and Evaluation of a Student Tutoring Program Designed to Improve the Language Skills of Both Tutors and Tutees." *DAI* 36 (1975): 1281-A.

Stone, W. B. "Rewriting in Advanced Composition." Paper, Annual Meeting of CCCC, 1981. ED 199 738.

Stone, W. M. "A Correlational and Descriptive Study of Student Writing in Three Aims of Discourse." *DAI* 42 (1982): 4818-A.

Stoner, D., L. L. Beall, and A. Anderson. "A Systems Approach to the Teaching of the Mechanics of English Expression." *RTE* 6 (1972): 200–11.

Stormzand, M. J., and M. V. O'Shea. *How Much English Grammar?* Baltimore, Maryland: Warwick & York, Inc. 1924.

Stotsky, S. *Evaluation of the Writing Program at the William M. Trotter School, Boston, Massachusetts, September 1978—January 1980.* Milton, Massachusetts: Curry College, 1980. ED 196 011.

Stotsky, S. L. "Sentence-Combining as a Curricular Activity: Its Effect on Written Language Development and Reading Comprehension." *RTE* 9 (1975): 30–71.

Straw, S. B. "An Investigation of the Effect of Sentence-Combining and Sentence-Reduction Instruction on Measures of Syntactic Fluency, Reading Comprehension, and Listening Comprehension in Fourth-Grade Students." *DAI* 40 (1979): 720-A.

Streeter, V. J. "Homogeneity in a Sample of Technical English." *DAI* 30 (1969): 2008-A.

Strickland, R. "The Language of Elementary School Children: Its Relationship to the Language of Reading Textbooks and the Quality of Reading of Selected Children." *Bulletin of the School of Education, Indiana University* 38, no. 4 (1962): entire issue.

———. "Reaction to the Article by Roger A. McCaig." *Elementary English* 47 (1970): 631–32.

Strom, D. M. "Research in Grammar and Usage and Its Implications for Teaching Writing." *Bulletin of the School of Education, Indiana University* 36, no. 5 (1960): entire issue.

Stromberg, L. J. "A Developmental Analysis of Sentence Production Errors in the Writing of Secondary School Students." *DAI* 42 (1982): 4751-A.

Strong, W. "Back to Basics and Beyond." *EJ* 65, no. 2 (February 1976): 56, 60–64.

Stugrin, M. "Sentence Combining, Conceptual Sophistication, and Problems of Precision in Technical Exposition." Conference on Sentence Combining and Teaching of Writing, Miami University, 1978.

Stumpe, D. M. "Study of a Nongraded Supplementary Group Communication Skills Program: Rationale, Pupil Personal-Social Characteristics, and Program Effects." *DAI* 28 (1968): 2921-A.

Suggs, L. R. "Structural Grammar Versus Traditional Grammar in Influencing Writing." *EJ* 50 (1961): 174–78.

Suhor, C. "Sentence Manipulation and Cognitive Operations." Paper, Annual Meeting of the Boston University Conference on Language Development, 1978. ED 166 692.

Sullivan, H. J. *Development of First Graders' Composition Skills.* Inglewood, California: Southwest Regional Educational Laboratory, 1971.

Sullivan, H. J., M. Okado, and F. C. Niedermeyer. "Effects of Systematic Practice on the Composition Skills of First Graders." *Elementary English* 51 (1974): 635–41.

Sullivan, J. L. "A Study of the Relative Merits of Traditional Grammar, Generative-Transformational Grammar, or No Grammar in an Approach to Writing in Communication One at Colorado State College." *DA* 29 (1969): 2686-A.

Sullivan, M. A. "The Effects of Sentence-Combining Exercises on Syntactic Maturity, Quality of Writing, Reading Ability, and Attitudes of Students in Grade Eleven." *DAI* 39 (1978): 1197-A.*

———. "Parallel Sentence-Combining Studies in Grades Nine and Eleven." In *Sentence Combining and the Teaching of Writing.* Edited by D. Daiker, A. Kerek, and M. Morenberg, 79–93. Conway, Arkansas: University of Akron and University of Central Arkansas, 1979.

Sussna, S. "The Development of a Self-Administered Analytic Guide for Use by Graduate Students for the Improvement of Writing and the Evaluation of Its Assistance in Improving Writing Skills in Research Papers." *DAI* 40 (1979): 1253-A.

Sutton, D. G. "Evaluating Teaching Methods in Composition." Paper, Annual Meeting of CCCC, 1975. ED 120 730.

Sutton, D. G., and D. S. Arnold. "The Effects of Two Methods of Compensatory Freshman English." *RTE* 8 (1974): 241–49.

Sutton, J. T., and E. D. Allen. "The Effect of Practice and Evaluation on Improvement in Written Composition." Washington, D.C.: U.S. Department of Health, Education, and Welfare; Office of Education, Cooperative Research Program, 1964. ED 001 274.

Sutton, R. S., and M. J. Tingle. *Developing Competency in Written Composition in Children from Kindergarten through Elementary School by Means of Curriculum Materials. Final Report.* Athens, Georgia: University of Georgia, English Curriculum Study Center, 1968. ED 026 363.

Swan, M. B. "The Effects of Instruction in Transformational Sentence-Combining on the Syntactic Complexity and Quality of College-Level Writing." *DAI* 38 (1978): 5440-A.

———. "Sentence Combining in College Composition: Interim Measures and Patterns." *RTE* 13 (1979): 217–24.

Swaney, J. H., C. J. Janik, S. J. Bond, and J. R. Hayes. *Editing for Comprehension: Improving the Process through Reading Protocols.* New York: Siegel & Gale, Inc., 1981. ED 209 642.

Swanson, C. L. "An Investigation of Content Differences in Oral vs. Written College Freshman Discourse." *DAI* 37 (1976): 155-A. ED 126 520.

Sweeder, J. J. "A Descriptive Study of Six Adult Remedial Writers: Their Composing Processes and Heuristic Strategies." *DAI* 42 (1981): 2004-A.

Sweet, J. A. "An Analysis of the Writing of Elementary Children, Grades Four through Six, to Determine the Relationship between Specified Genre and the Development and Use of Figurative Language." *DAI* 35 (1975): 5697-A. ED 105 457.

Swenson, D. H., C. P. Freeman, R. Supnick, and J. T. Segal. "Reducing the Number of Teacher-Graded Papers in the Teaching of Informational Business Writing." Paper, Annual Meeting of the American Business Communication Association, 1981. ED 209 666.

Tang, M. "A Study of the Relationship between the Reading and Writing Abilities of Underprepared College Students." *DAI* 40 (1979): 3215-A.

Tapp, R. L. "A Delineation of the Philosophy and Historical Development of Programmed Instruction and a Descriptive Content Analysis of Currently Available Programmed Materials Designed for the Language, Composition, and Literature Curricula of Secondary Schools." *DAI* 36 (1975): 690-A.

Taylor, H. W. "Listening Comprehension and Reading Comprehension as Predictors of Achievement in College Composition." *DAI* 42 (1981): 66-A.

Taylor, I. "Content and Structure in Sentence Production." *Journal of Verbal Learning and Verbal Behavior* 8 (1969): 170–75.

Taylor, J. L. "An Assessment of the Value of Certain Measuring Devices for Identifying Creative Writing Performance." *DAI* 30 (1970): 3804-A.

Taylor, J. W. *How to Create New Ideas.* Englewood Cliffs, New Jersey: Prentice-Hall, Inc., 1961.

Taylor, K. K. "If Not Grammar, What?—Taking Remedial Writing Instruction Seriously." *DAI* 39 (1978): 168A. See also ED 159 668.

Taylor, P. H. "The English Composition in the Junior School: Prepared or Unprepared? *Educational Research* 5, no. 1 (1962): 57–62.

Taylor, W. F., and K. C. Hoedt. "The Effect of Praise upon the Quality and Quantity of Creative Writing." *JER* 60 (1966): 80–83.

Telleen, J. A. "Self-Assessing Abilities of Freshman Writers." Paper, Annual Meeting of CCCC, 1980. ED 188 224.

Teplitsky, A. "Differential Effects of a Simulation Unit in Tenth Grade English Classes." *DAI* 33 (1972): 668-A.

Terrebonne, N. G., and R. A. Terrebonne. "The Patterning of Language Variation in Writing." Paper, Annual Meeting of the Midwest MLA, 1976. ED 162 312.

Tesch, R. C., Sr. "Determining the Success of Self-Paced Programmed Material for Learning English Grammar and Usage in a Business Communication Course." Paper, Annual Meeting of the American Business Communication Association, 1981. ED 210 688.

Tetroe, J., C. Bereiter, and M. Scardamalia. "How to Make a Dent in the Writing Process." Paper, Annual Meeting of AERA, 1981.

Thaiss, C. J. "The Writing Required by Professors and Managers: Two Surveys." Paper, Combined Annual Meeting of the Conference on English Education and the Secondary School English Conference, 1979. ED 178 938.

Thibodeau, A. L. "A Study of the Effects of Elaborative Thinking and Vocabulary Enrichment Exercises on Written Composition." *DA* 25 (1964): 2388.*

Thibodeau, A. E. "Improving Composition Writing with Grammar and Organization Exercises Utilizing Differentiated Group Patterns." *DAI* 25 (1964): 2389.*

Thomas, E. W. "A Comparison of Inductive and Deductive Teaching Methods in College Freshman Remedial English." DAI 31 (1970): 2268-A.

Thomas, F. L. "The Extent of the Relationship between Reading Achievement and Writing Achievement among College Freshmen." *DAI* 37 (1977): 6320-A.

Thomas, S., and C. Keech. *Field Studies Report. Evaluation of the Bay Area Writing Project. Technical Report.* Berkeley, California: University of California, School of Education, 1979. ED 191 060.

Thompson, B. M. *A Theory of Teacher Change Developed from Teachers of Writing. 1979.* ED 188 197.

Thompson, C. L., and M. Middleton. "Transformational Grammar and Inductive Teaching as Determinants of Structurally Complex Writing." *California Journal of Educational Research* 24 (1973): 28–41.

Thompson, M. O. "Writing Anxiety and Freshman Composition." Paper, Annual Meeting of the Northeastern Conference on English in the Two Year College, 1979. ED 183 235.

Thompson, N. C. A. "The Syntax of Children's Writing." *DA* 28 (1968): 3660-A.

Thompson, N. C. A., D. D. Nemanich, and A. S. Bala. *The Nebraska Study of the Syntax of Children's Writing, 1966–67. Vol. III.* Lincoln, Nebraska: University of Nebraska, Curriculum Development Center, 1967. ED 013 816.

Thompson, R. F. "Is Test Retest a Suitable Reliability in Most Composition Studies?" *RTE* 14 (1980): 154–56.

———. "Peer Grading: Some Promising Advantages for Composition Research and the Classroom." *RTE* 15 (1981): 172–74.

Tigar,P. "ADE Survey of Freshman English." *ADE Bulletin* no. 43 (November 1974): 13–23.

Tighe, M. A. "A Survey of the Teaching of Composition in the English Classroom and in the Content Areas of Social Studies and Science." *DAI* 40 (1979): 2584-A.

Tillman, M. H. "Level of Abstraction in the Written Compositions of Children Varying in Intelligence and Age." *Psychological Reports* 24 (1969): 419–24. See also ED 016 651.

Tixier, L. "The Development, Implementation, and Evaluation of a Model for Teaching Composition Which Utilizes Gestalt Therapy Techniques." 1977. ED 151 797.

Tollefson, N., and D. B. Tracy. "Test Length and Quality in the Grading of Essay Responses." *Education* 101 (1980): 63–67.

Tomlinson, B. M. "The Influence of Sentence Combining Instruction on the Syntactic Maturity and Writing Quality of Minority College Freshmen in a Summer Preentry Preparation Program." *DAI* 41 (1980): 928-A.

———. "A Study of the Effectiveness of Individualized Writing Lab Instruction for Students in Remedial Freshman Composition." Paper, Annual Meeting of the Western College Reading Association, 1975. ED 108 241.

Tonjes, B. A. "An Analysis of Three Methods of Teaching Sentence Construction to Slow Learning Eighth-Grade Students in a Selected Junior High School." *DAI* 38 (1978): 6513-A.*

Torian, C. L. "An Evaluation of the Development of a More Positive Self-Image in Middle School-Aged Children through a Particular Creative Writing Program." *DAI* 37 (1977): 7593-A.

Tovatt, A. "Oral-Aural-Visual Stimuli for Teaching Composition." *EJ* 54 (1965): 191–95.

Tovatt, A., and E. L. Miller. "The Sound of Writing." *RTE* 1 (1967): 176–89.

Trageser, S. G. "The Student in the Role of Spectator-Observer-Communicator: The Relationship between Visual Perception and Specificity in Writing." *DAI* 40 (1979): 2521-A.

Trammell, R. T. "Senior English in Selected High Schools." *DAI* 30 (1970): 3656-A.

Trost, D. M. "Attitudes, Writing Fluency, Reading Achievement—A Comparison between Initial Teaching Alphabet and Traditional Orthography Trained Children." *DAI* 32 (1972): 6114-A.*

Troyka, L. Q. "A Study of the Effect of Simulation-Gaming on Expository Prose Competence of College Remedial English Composition Students." *DAI* 34 (1974): 4092-A. ED 090 541.*

Troyka, L. Q., and J. Nudelman. *Taking Action: Writing, Reading, Speaking, and Listening through Simulation-Games.* Englewood Cliffs, New Jersey: Prentice-Hall, 1975.

Tucker, E. S. *Effects of Written Language and Metalinguistic Awareness on Language Acquisition from 5 to 12.* 1976. ED 137 800.

Tucker, R. W., and A. G. Smithers. "Cognitive Style and Linguistic Style." *Educational Review* 29 (1977): 325–36.

Turley, J. D. "Attitudes of Rhode Island Secondary School English Teachers toward Certain Objectives in the Teaching of English." *DAI* 31 (1970): 669-A.

Turner, D. G. "A Comparison of the Academic Achievement in Reading and Writing by Students Enrolled in Project English Classes with That of Non-Experimental Students." *DAI* 28 (1967): 2051-A.*

Turner, G. C. *Experiment and Research in the Use of a Writing Laboratory.* St. Petersburg, Florida: Saint Petersburg Junior College, 1970. ED 041 576.

Tuttle, F. B., Jr. "The Effect of Training in Visual Composition on Organization in Written Composition in Grade Three." *DAI* 31 (1971): 5950-A.

Tuttle, F. B., Jr., P. Fullforth, M. Letro, and E. Royer. "Written Composition: Integrated Approach Following the Composing Process, Low/Average Students, Ninth Grade; Research Project: West Irondequoit High School, 1976–1977." 1977. ED 146 587.

Tway, D. E. "Literary Rating Scale." 1969. ED 091 726.

———. "A Study of the Feasibility of Training Teachers to Use the Literary Rating Scale in Evaluating Children's Fiction Writing." *DAI* 31 (1971): 5918-A.

Uehara, B. K. "The Effects of Three Different Stimuli on Third-Grade and Fifth-Grade Written Composition." *DAI* 35 (1974): 3582-A.

Ujlaki, V. E. "The Use of Children's Original Writings as a Basis for Individualized Instruction." *DA* 29 (1968): 191-A. ED 033 960.

Underwood, J. L. "Factors Affecting Differences in Quality and Style of Writing in College Freshman Examinations." *DAI* 30 (1970): 3206-A.

University of Georgia, English Curriculum Study Center. *Research in Cognate Aspects of Written Composition.* Athens, Georgia: University of Georgia, English Curriculum Study Center, 1968. ED 026 368.

Vairo, F. M., Jr. "The Relationship between Story Writing Skills and Achievement in Other Selected Language Skills." *DAI* 37 (1976): 1509-A. ED 128 791.

Van der Geest, T., R. Gerstel, R. Appel, and B. Tervoort. *The Child's Communicative Competence: Language Capacity in Three Groups of Children from Different Social Classes.* The Hague: Mouton, 1973.

Van Dyck, B. "On-The-Job Writing of High-Level Business Executives: Implications for College Teaching." Paper, Annual Meeting of CCCC, 1980. ED 185 584.

Van Houten, R., and C. McKillop. "An Extension of the Effects of the Performance Feedback System with Secondary School Students." *Psychology in the Schools* 14 (1977): 480–84.

Van Nostrand, A. D., J. Pettigrew, and R. A. Shaw. *Writing Instruction in the Elementary Grades: Deriving a Model by Collaborative Research.* Providence, Rhode Island: Center for Research in Writing, 1980. ED 203 378.

Van Schaick, S. "The Composition-Reading Machine." *EJ* 49 (1960): 237–41.

Varon, L. R. "Examination of the Content of Unsolicited Compositions Written by Upper Elementary School Children for Their Teacher's Eyes Alone." *DAI* 32 (1971): 1203-A.

Veal, L. R. *Syntactic Measures and Rated Quality in the Writing of Young Children. Studies in Language Education, Report No. 8.* Athens, Georgia: University of Georgia, Department of Language Education, 1974. ED 090 555.

Veal, L. R., and E. F. Biesbrock. "Primary Essay Tests." *JEM* 8 (1971): 45–46.

Veal, L. R., and M. Tillman. "Mode of Discourse Variation in the Evaluation of Children's Writing." *RTE* 5 (1971): 37–45.

Veix, D. B. "A Study of the Influence of Selected Aesthetic Experiences on the Creative Writing of Tenth Grade Students." *DAI* 32 (1971): 260-A.

Vella, D., and T. Hilgers. *An Experiment in Homogeneous Grouping in Freshman Composition Classes.* 1977. ED 155 729.

Verner, Z. B., and M. B. Bauer. "A Study of Needs for Possible Inservice Education Programs as Expressed by Secondary English Teachers and as Perceived by Their Administrators." 1977. ED 140 351.

Vickers, N. L."An Analysis of Three Methods of Teaching English on the Attitude and Achievement of Educationally Deprived Students." *DAI* 33 (1972): 1425-A.

Vik, G. N. "Developmental Composition in College." *DAI* 36 (1976): 8037-A. ED 124 939.

Vinson, L. L. N. "The Effects of Two Prewriting Activities upon the Overall Quality of Ninth Graders' Descriptive Paragraphs." *DAI* 41 (1980): 927-A.*

Vitale, M. R., F. J. King, D. W. Shontz, and G. M. Huntley. "Effect of Sentence-Combining Exercises upon Several Restricted Written Composition Tasks." *JEP* 62 (1971): 521–25.

Votaw, B. L. "Composition Self-Evaluation Related to Changes in Language Self-Concept Accuracy and in Writing Performance." *DAI* 42 (1982): 3424-A.

Vygotsky, L. S. *Thought and Language.* Edited and translated by E. Hanfmann and G. Vakar. Cambridge, Massachusetts: M.I.T. Press, 1962.

Wade, B. "Responses to Written Work: The Possibilities of Utilizing Pupils' Perceptions." *Educational Review* 30 (1978): 149–58.

Wagner, B. J., S. Zemelman, and A. Malone-Trout. *The Chicago Area Writing Project Assessment.* Elmhurst, Illinois: School District 205, 1981.

Wagner, E. N. "Developmental English: More Harm than Good?" *Teaching English in the Two-Year College* 1 (1975): 147–52.

——. "The Impact of Composition Grading on the Attitudes and Writing Performance of Freshman English Students." *DAI* 36 (1976): 5232-A.

———. "When the Bookkeeping System Takes Over: The Effects of Grading Compositions on Student Attitudes." Paper, Annual Meeting of CCCC, 1976. ED 120 802.

Wagner, J. T. "The Effects of Arts Experience and Group Discussion during Prewriting upon the Composing Processes of Pre-Service Teachers." *DAI* 41 (1980): 141-A.

Wahlberg, W. A. "The Effect of Process Intervention on the Attitudes and Learning in a College Freshman Composition Class." *DAI* 31 (1971): 6355-A.

Waldschmidt, E. C. "Peers Paired for Talk-Writing." *Illinois English Bulletin* 62, no. 8 (1975): 2–8.

———. "Pilot Studies in Composition: Their Effects upon Students and Participating English Teachers." *DAI* 34 (1974): 7634-A.

Walker, B. B. "An Analysis of Six Basic Approaches to Teaching Freshman Composition." *DAI* 35 (1975): 5069-A.

Walker, J. P. "A Study of the Comparative Effectiveness of an Experience-Centered and a Knowledge-Centered Method of Teaching Composition." *DAI* 35 (1974): 3704-A.*

Walker, W. G. "The Application and Evaluation of a Sequential Instructional Development Model as Applied to the Area of Written Composition." *DAI* 41 (1980): 2433-A.

Walmsley, S. A. "What Elementary Teachers Know about Writing." *LA* 57 (1980): 732–34.

Walpole, J. R. "Paragraph Analysis for Teaching Composition." *DAI* 40 (1979): 721-A.

Walshe, R. D. "Report on a Pilot Course on the Christensen Rhetoric Program." *CE* 32 (1971): 783–89.

Wardhaugh, R. "Ability in Written Composition and Transformational Grammar." *JER* 60 (1967): 427–29.

Warner, D. E. "Effect of First-Year High School Shorthand Instruction on Selected English Skills." *DAI* 37 (1976): 3578-A.

Warters, S. "The Writing Process of College Basic Writers." Paper, Annual Meeting of the Canadian Council of Teachers of English, 1979. ED 175 008.

Wasson, R., ed. *Proceedings of the Allerton Park Conference on Research in the Teaching of English. Research Project No. G-1006.* Sponsored by the U.S. Office of Education in cooperation with the University of Illinois. Contract No. OE 3-10-058. Urbana, Illinois: University of Illinois, 1962.

Waterfall, C. M. "An Experimental Study of Sentence-Combining as a Means of Increasing Syntactic Maturity and Writing Quality in the Compositions of College-Age Students Enrolled in Remedial English Classes." *DAI* 38 (1978): 7131-A.*

Waterhouse, J. "Pre-Writing Speech and Experiential Constructs in the Teaching of English Composition." *DAI* 34 (1973): 76-A.

Waters, B. L. "Sex-Based Differences in the Written Composition of Freshman Students at Middle Tennessee State University." *DAI* 37 (1976): 1524-A. See also ED 115 113.

Waters, H. S. " 'Class News': A Single-Subject Longitudinal Study of Prose Production and Schema Formation During Childhood." *Journal of Verbal Learning and Verbal Behavior* 19 (1980): 152–67.

Watson, B. "The Master-Apprentice Approach to Teaching Writing." *EJ* 53 (1964): 41–44.

Watson, C. "The Effects of Maturity and Discourse Type on the Written Syntax of Superior High School Seniors and Upper Level College English Majors." *DAI* 41 (1980): 141-A.

Watts, R. W. "The Effects of Grammar-Free Sentence-Combining Practice on the Syntactic Fluency of the Written and Oral Responses of Seventh Grade Students." *DAI* 41 (1981): 3979-A.

Weaver, F. E. "The Composing Processes of English Teacher Candidates: Responding to Freedom and Constraint." *DAI* 34 (1974): 5810-A.

Weber, B. H. "The Effect of Two Language Arts Curricula upon Standardized Achievement Test Scores in the Inner-City." *DAI* 30 (1970): 3208-A.

Weber, P. S. "The Development and Instructional Facilitation of Whole-Text Planning in Children's Story Writing." *DAI* 42 (1982): 5072-A.

Weener, P. "Note Taking and Student Verbalization as Instrumental Learning Activities." *Instructional Science* 3 (1974): 51–73.

Weiss, R. H. "Research on Writing and Learning: Some Effects of Learning-Centered Writing in Five Subject Areas." Paper, Annual Meeting of NCTE, 1979. ED 191 073.

Weiss, R. H., and M. Peich. "Faculty Attitude Change in a Cross-Disciplinary Writing Workshop." *CCC* 31 (1980): 33–41.

Weiss, R. H., and S. A. Walters. "Writing to Learn." Paper, Annual Meeting of AERA, 1980. ED 191 056.

———. "Writing Apprehension: Implications for Teaching, Writing, and Concept Clarity." Paper, Annual Meeting of CCCC, 1980. ED 189 619.

Werth, T. G. "An Assessment of the Reciprocal Effect of High School Senior Low Achievers Tutoring Freshman Low Achievers in English Classes." *DA* 29 (1968): 1057-A.

Wesdorp, H. *SCO Rapport: De Didactiek van Het Stellen: Een Overzicht van Het Onderzoek naar de Effecten van Diverse Instructie—Variabelen op de Stelvaardigheid.* Amsterdam: University van Amsterdam, 1982.

Wesolowski, R. J. "A Study Comparing a Simulation-Game Curriculum with a Traditional Curriculum in Teaching Composition to Tenth Grade Gifted Students." *DAI* 41 (1980): 1934-A.

West, G. B. "An Investigation of the Effects of Instruction in General Semantics on the Critical Writing and Critical Thinking Achievement of Tenth-Grade Students." *DAI* 31 (1971): 4739-A. ED 057 033.*

West, M. G. "An Experimental Comparison of Three Methods of Correcting Themes to Improve Sentence Structure of Seventh Grade Pupils in Large Classes." *DA* 28 (1968): 3577-A.*

West, W. W. "A Comparison of a 'Composition Equivalencies' Approach and a Traditional Approach to Teaching Writing." *DA* 27 (1967): 4178-A.*

Westendorf, E. E. "An Exploratory Study of Informational Writing: A Description of an Inservice Program with Teachers and of Reports Written by Fourth-Grade Children." *DA* 28 (1967): 1220-A.

Whale, K. B. "The Teaching of Writing in an Elementary School." *DAI* 41 (1980): 2433-A.

Whale, K. B., and S. Robinson. "Modes of Students' Writings: A Descriptive Study." *RTE* 12 (1978): 349–55.

Whalen, T. E. "A Computer Analysis of Mechanical Proficiency and Overall Quality in Seventh Grade English Essays." *DAI* 32 (1971): 261-A.

———. "A Validation of the Smith Test for Measuring Teacher Judgment of Written Composition." *Education* 93 (1972): 172–75.

Whalen, T. H. "Total English Equals Writing Competence." *RTE* 3 (1969): 52–61.

Whitcraft, C. J. "Levels of Generative Syntax and Linguistic Performance of Young Children from Standard and Non-Standard English Language Environments." *DAI* 32 (1972): 5644-A.

White, E. M., and L. L. Thomas. "Racial Minorities and Writing Skills Assessment in the California State University and Colleges." *CE* 43 (1981): 276–83.

White, R. H. "The Effect of Structural Linguistics on Improving English Composition Compared to That of Prescriptive Grammar or the Absence of Grammar Instruction." *DA* 25 (1965): 5032.

Whitehead, C. E., Jr. "The Effect of Grammar-Diagraming on Student Writing Skills." *DA* 26 (1966): 3710.*

Whiteman, M. F., ed. *Writing: The Nature, Development and Teaching of Written Communication.* Vol. 1. Hillsdale, New Jersey: Lawrence Erlbaum Associates, Publishers, 1981.

Whittle, D. H. P. "Success in Freshman English Preceded by Developmental English: Predicting Success through Persistence and Selected Demographic Variables." *DAI* 41 (1980): 1363-A.

Widvey, L. I. H. "A Study of the Use of a Problem-Solving Approach to Composition in High School English." *DAI* 32 (1971): 2563-A. ED 059 989.*

Wienke, J. W. "Strategies for Improving Elementary School Students' Writing Skills." 1981. ED 209 679.

Wiggins, R. F. "A Study of the Influence of Oral Instruction on Students' Ability in Written Sentence Structure." *DA* 29 (1969): 3927-A. ED 040 189.

Wilcox, T. W. "The Study of Undergraduate English Programs: Some Preliminary Findings." *CE* 29 (1968): 440–49.

Wilder, M. R. "An Evaluation of the Pre-Service and Inservice Academic Preparation in English for Teachers of Disadvantaged Students in Selected Colleges in the State of Georgia." *DAI* 31 (1971): 4398-A. ED 056 037.

Wilkinson, A. "Criteria of Language Development." *Educational Review* 30 (1978): 23–34.

Wilkinson, A., and E. Wilkinson. "The Development of Language in the Middle Years." *English in Education* 12, no. 1 (1978): 42–52.

Wilkinson, A., G. Barnsley, P. Hanna, and M. Swan. "Assessing Language Development: The Crediton Project." Paper, Annual Meeting of the Canadian Council of Teachers of English, 1979. ED 178 906.

Willardson, M. L. "A Study of the Writing Ability of Second Grade Students in a Communication Skills through Authorship Program." *DAI* 32 (1972): 3585-A.

Wille, S. C. "The Effects of Pre-Writing Observational Activities on Syntactic Structures." Thesis, University of Chicago, 1982.

Williams, G. M. "An Evaluation of the Writing Performance of Students in Grades Seven through Ten in an Urban Junior and Senior High School

Using the Diederich Method of Cooperative Composition Rating, with Attention to the Performance of Selected Subgroups." *DAI* 33 (1973): 5621-A.

Williams, J. M. "Defining Complexity." *CE* 40 (1979): 595–609.

Williams, L. "The Attitudes of a Group of Second and Third Grade Pupils toward Written Communication." *Masters Abstracts* 11 (1973): 432.

Williamson, J. R. W. "A Study of Three Motivational Techniques for Creative Writing." *DAI* 33 (1973): 3490-A.

Willis, D. M. "A Study of the Patterns of Development in Essays of Three Groups of Ohio State University Freshman Writers." *DAI* 40 (1980): 4567-A.

Willis, P. W. P. "A Study of Current Practices in Freshman English in Oklahoma Colleges." *DAI* 34 (1974): 4806-A.

Willy, T. G. "Oral Aspects in the Primitive Fiction of Newly Literate Children." 1975. ED 112 381.

Wilson, A. "A Survey of College-Level Remedial Writing Programs at Selected State-Supported Institutions Currently Admitting the Underprepared." *DAI* 40 (1980): 4881-A.

Wilson, D. "Sentence Combining and the Revising Process." Conference on Sentence Combining and the Teaching of Writing, Miami University, 1978.

Wilson, J. H. "The Teaching of Composition in State Two-Year Technical Institutions in the United States." *DAI* 40 (1979): 709-A.

Wilson, M. B. "The Evaluation of a Performance Based Curriculum in the Language Arts." *DAI* 31 (1971): 6481-A.

Wilson, R. L. "The Effects of First-and Secondhand Sensory Experiences on Student Perception as Measured in Written Composition." *DAI* 37 (1977): 7526-A.

Winder, B. D. "The Effectiveness of a Freshman Composition Values Curriculum for Developing Competency in the Presentation of Alternative Ideas in Writing." *DAI* 42 (1981): 1037-A.

Wingler, E. F. "The Attitudes and Beliefs of English Educators: Three Perspectives." *DAI* 33 (1972): 2827-A.

Winters, L. "The Effects of Differing Response Criteria on the Assessment of Writing Competence." *DAI* 41 (1980): 217-A.

Witte, S. P. "Toward a Model for Research in Written Composition." *RTE* 14 (1980): 73–81.

Witte, S. P., and A. S. Davis. "The Stability of T-Unit Length: A Preliminary Investigation." *RTE* 14 (1980): 5–17.

———. "The Stability of T-Unit Length in the Written Discourse of College Freshmen: A Second Study." *RTE* 16 (1982): 71–84.

Witte, S. P., and L. L. Faigley. "Coherence, Cohesion, and Writing Quality." *CCC* 32 (1981a): 189–204.

———. *A Comparison of Analytic and Synthetic Approaches to the Teaching of College Writing.* Austin, Texas: University of Texas, Department of English, 1981b. ED 209 677.

Witte, S. P., P. Meyer, T. P. Miller, and L. Faigley. *A National Survey of College and University Writing Program Directors. Technical Report Number 2.* Austin, Texas: University of Texas, 1981. ED 210 709.

Witte, S. P., and R. E. Sodowsky. "Syntactic Maturity in the Writing of College Freshmen." Paper, Annual Meeting of CCCC, 1978. ED 163 460.

Wohlgamuth, W. L. "Evaluation of Structured Interpersonal Communication in the Achievement of Business-Writing Principles." *DAI* 42 (1981): 969-A.

Wolf, M. H. *Effect of Writing Frequency upon Proficiency in a College Freshman English Course.* Amherst, Massachusetts: University of Massachusetts, 1966. ED 003 384.

Wolfe, R. F. "An Examination of the Effects of Teaching a Reading Vocabulary upon Writing Vocabulary in Student Compositions." *DAI* 36 (1975): 3337-A.

Wolff, A. "Recursive Moves: A Study of the Composing Process." *DAI* 42 (1981): 119-A.

Wolk, A. "The Passive Mystique: We've Been Had." *EJ* 58 (1969): 432–35.

———. "The Relative Importance of the Final Free Modifier: A Quantitative Analysis." *RTE* 4 (1970): 59–68.

Wolter, D. R. "Effect of Feedback on Performance of a Creative Writing Task." *DAI* 36 (1976): 6573-A. ED 120 801.

Wolter, D. R., and W. J. Lamberg. "Research on the Effect of Feedback on Writing: Review and Implications." 1976. ED 140 355.

Wood, B. W. "A Structured Program for Teaching Composition in Senior High School English Classes." *DAI* 39 (1978): 2173-A.*

Wood, L. R. "A Study of the Relationship of Performance in Written Composition to Performance in Mathematical Reasoning in Elementary School Children." *DAI* 28 (1968): 3913-A.

Woodfin, M. J. "Correlations among Certain Factors and the Written Expression of Third Grade Children." *Educational and Psychological Measurement* 28 (1968): 1237–42.

———. "The Quality of Written Expression of Third-Grade Children Under Differing Time Limits." *Journal of Experimental Education* 37, no. 3 (1969): 89–91.

Woods, E. E. "Effects of the Duke University Teaching of Writing Institute on Five Classes of Students at Grades Five, Six, Eight, and Nine." *DAI* 40 (1980): 6139-A.*

Woods, W. F. *Teaching Writing: The Major Theories Since 1950.* 1978. ED 168 004.

Woods-Elliott, C. A. "Students, Teachers and Writing: An Ethnography of Interactions in Literacy." *DAI* 42 (1981): 2376-A.

Woodward, J. C. "Profile of the Poor Writer—The Relationship of Selected Characteristics to Poor Writing in College." 1965. ED 018 445.

Woodward, J. C., and A. G. Phillips. "Profile of the Poor Writer." *RTE* 1 (1967): 41–53.

Woodworth, P., and C. Keech. *The Write Occasion. Collaborative Research Study No. 1.* Berkeley, California: University of California, School of Education, 1980. ED 198 534.

Worsham, M. E., and C. M. Everston. *Systems of Student Accountability for Written Work in Junior High School English Classes. R & D Report No. 6105.* Austin, Texas: University of Texas, Research and Development Center for Teacher Education, 1980. ED 196 008.

Wright, N. J. "The Effects of Role-Playing on the Improvement of Freshman Composition." *DAI* 36 (1976): 5009-A.*

Wunsch, D. R. "The Effects of Individualized Written Feedback, Rewriting, and Group Oral Feedback on Business Letter Writing Ability." *DAI* 42 (1981): 64-A.

Wynn, D. F. "Changing Patterns in Goals, Methods, and Grading Theories in the Teaching of Written Composition as Evidenced in Professional Literature 1930–1976." *DAI* 39 (1978): 1309-A.

Wynn, J. H. "Determining the Internal Consistency of English Compositions Using Selected Criteria." *DAI* 38 (1977): 3347-A.

Yarlott, G. "The Language of Emotion." *Educational Review* 28 (1976): 190–205.

Ylvisaker, M. *An Experiment in Encouraging Fluency. Curriculum Publication No. 8.* Berkeley, California: University of California, School of Education, 1979. ED 192 322.

Yoder, H. M. "An Analysis of Characteristics of Language Arts Programs in Selected Iowa Elementary Schools." *DAI* 41 (1980): 2434-A.

Young, E. R. K. "The Differential Influence of Three Methods of Sentence Expansion Instruction on the Written Compositions of Second Grade Boys and Girls." *DAI* 33 (1972): 1032-A.

Young, E. W. "An Experimental Study to Determine the Effects of Individually Prescribed Instruction on Achievement in, and Attitudes toward a Written Communication Course." *DAI* 40 (1979): 3068-A.

Young, R. E. "Invention: A Topographical Survey." In *Teaching Composition: Ten Bibliographical Essays.* Edited by Gary Tate, 1–43. Fort Worth, Texas: Texas Christian University Press, 1976.

Young, R. E., and A. L. Becker. "Toward a Modern Theory of Rhetoric: A Tagmemic Contribution." *Harvard Educational Review* 35 (1965): 450–68.

Young, R. E., A. L. Becker, and K. L. Pike. *Rhetoric: Discovery and Change.* New York: Harcourt Brace Jovanovich, 1970.

Young, R. E., and F. M. Koen. *The Tagmemic Discovery Procedure: An Evaluation of Its Uses in the Teaching of Rhetoric.* Ann Arbor, Michigan: University of Michigan, Department of Humanities, 1973. ED 084 517.

Zanotti, R. J. "A Study of the Use of the Tape Recorder as an Aid to Written Composition at the Sixth-Grade Level." *DAI* 31 (1970): 1520-A.

Zeman, S. S. "Reading Comprehension and Writing of Second and Third Graders." *Reading Teacher* 23 (1969): 144–50.

———. "The Relationship between the Measured Reading Comprehension and the Basic Sentence Types and Sentence Structural Patterns in Compositions Written by Second and Third Grade Children." *DA* 27 (1967): 3243-A.

Zemelman, S. "How College Teachers Encourage Students' Writing." *RTE* 11 (1977): 227–34.

Zidonis, F. J. "Generative Grammar: A Report on Research." *EJ* 54 (1965): 405–09.

Zimmerman, J. W. "An Investigation of the Effect of Students' Self-Concept of Writing Ability on Their Writing Processes and Writing Achievement: Case Studies of Eleven Black College Freshmen." *DAI* 38 (1978): 7132-A.

Zirinsky, H. B. "An Investigation of Student Awareness of Teacher Criteria for Evaluating Writing as an Element in the Composing Process." *DAI* 39 (1978): 168-A.

Ziv, N. D. "The Effect of Teacher Comments on the Writing of Four College Freshmen." *DAI* 42 (1982): 3004-A. See also ED 203 317.

Additional Bibliographic Resources

The following entries include additional bibliographies, along with reviews of or guides to research in composition. See also bibliographies published periodically in the following journals:

College Composition and Communication
English Journal
Language Arts (formerly *Elementary English*)
Publications of the Modern Language Association
Research in the Teaching of English

The ERIC Clearinghouse on Reading and Communication Skills also publishes materials dealing with a variety of research and teaching concerns. For a list of current publications, write ERIC/RCS at NCTE, 1111 Kenyon Road, Urbana, IL 61801.

Abrahamson, R. F. *The Effects of Formal Grammar Instruction vs. the Effects of Sentence Combining Instruction on Student Writing: A Collection of Evaluative Abstracts of Pertinent Research Documents.* 1977. ED 145 450.

Bennett, J. R., and others. "The Paragraph: An Annotated Bibliography." *Style* 11 (Spring 1977): 107–18.

Blount, N. S. "Research on Teaching Literature, Language and Composition." In *Second Handbook of Research on Teaching.* Edited by R. M. W. Travers, 1072–97. Chicago: Rand McNally & Company, 1973.

Bowman, M. A., and J. D. Stamas. *Written Communication in Business: A Selective Bibliography, 1967–1977.* Urbana, Illinois: American Business Communication Association, 1980. ED 192 305.

Braddock, R. "English Composition." In *Encyclopedia of Educational Research.* 4th ed. Edited by R. I. Ebel, 443–61. London: The Macmillan Company, Collier-Macmillan Ltd., 1969. ED 030 662.

Braddock, R., R. Lloyd-Jones, and L. Schoer. *Research in Written Composition.* Urbana, Illinois: NCTE, 1963. ED 003 374.

British Council. *Discourse Analysis and Grammar above the Sentence. Specialised Bibliography A4.* London: British Council, English-Teaching Information Centre, 1973. ED 112 696.

Burrows, A. T. "Composition: Prospect and Retrospect." In *Reading and Writing Instruction in the United States: Historical Trends.* Edited by H. A. Robinson, 17–43. Urbana, Illinois: International Reading Association and ERIC, 1977.

——. *Teaching Composition: What Research Says to the Teacher.* No. 18. Washington, D.C.: National Education Association, 1966. ED 017 482.

Burrows, A. T., and others. *Children's Writing: Research in Composition and Related Skills.* Champaign, Illinois: NCTE, 1961.

Burton, D. L. "Research in the Teaching of English: The Troubled Dream." *RTE* 7 (1973): 160–89.

California Association of Teachers of English. *You've Made the Assignment. Now What?: An Annotated Bibliography on the Process of Teaching Composition.* Redlands, California: California Association of Teachers of English, 1977. ED 145 467.

Chatterjee, S. S. "Technical Writing Curricula and Teaching Methods; A Review of the Literature and an Identification of the Basic Issues." *DAI* 41 (1981): 3923-A.

Clay, M. M. "Research Update: Learning and Teaching Writing: A Developmental Perspective." *LA* 59 (1982): 65–70.

Collins, J. L. "Dialogue and Monologue and the Unskilled Writer." *EJ* 71, no. 4 (April 1982): 84–86.

Cronnell, B. *Punctuation and Capitalization: A Review of the Literature.* Los Alamitos, California: Southwest Regional Laboratory for Educational Research and Development, 1980. ED 208 404.

Crymes, R. *A Bibliographical Introduction to Sentence-Combining.* 1974. ED 115 130.

Cunningham, D. H., and V. Hertz. "An Annotated Bibliography on the Teaching of Technical Writing." *CCC* 21 (1970): 177–86.

Daly, J. A., and D. Wilson. *Writing Apprehension, Self-Esteem, and Personality.* 1980. ED 192 320.

Dieterich, D. J. "ERIC/RCS Report: Composition Evaluation: Options and Advice." *EJ* 61 (1972): 1264–71.

———. "ERIC/RCS Report: Teaching High School Composition." *EJ* 62 (1973): 1291–93.

Early, M. "Important Research in Reading and Writing." *Phi Delta Kappan* 57 (1976): 298–301.

Flower, L., and J. R. Hayes. "Process-Based Evaluation of Writing: Changing the Performance, Not the Product." Paper, Annual Meeting of AERA, 1981. ED 204 795.

Flynn, T. "Hierarchies of Skill in the Composing Process: A Review of Current Research." Paper, Annual Meeting of the Writing Centers Association, 1981. ED 208 422.

Frederick, A., ed. *Annotated Index to the English Journal, 1944–1963.* Champaign, Illinois: NCTE, 1964.

Gentry, L. A. *A New Look at Young Writers: The Writing Research of Donald Graves. Technical Note.* Los Alamitos, California: Southwest Regional Laboratory for Educational Research and Development, 1980. ED 192 354.

———. *Textual Revision: A Review of the Research. Technical Note.* Los Alamitos, California: Southwest Regional Laboratory for Educational Research and Development, 1980. ED 192 355.

Godwin, L. R. "Studies Related to the Teaching of Written Composition." *Canadian Education and Research Digest* 3, no. 1 (March 1963): 35–47.

Gregg, L. W., and E. R. Steinberg, eds. *Cognitive Processes in Writing.* Hillsdale, New Jersey: Lawrence Erlbaum Associates, Publishers, 1980.

Groff, Patrick. "The Effects of Talking on Writing." *English in Education* 13, no. 3 (1979): 33–37.

Gunderson, D. V. "U. S. Office of Education: Report on Cooperative Research Projects." *EJ* 56 (1967) 617–21.

———. "U. S. Office of Education: Report on Research Projects." *EJ* 59 (1970): 304–07.

Guthrie, J. T. "Processes of Writing." *Journal of Reading* 24 (1981): 764–66.

Haley-James, S. M., ed. *Perspectives on Writing in Grades 1–8.* Urbana, Illinois: NCTE, 1981.

Harvey, R. C., C. M. Kirkton, and the Staff of the ERIC Clearinghouse on the Teaching of English. *Annotated Index to the English Journal, First Supplement: 1964–1970.* Urbana, Illinois: NCTE, 1972.

Haynes, E. F. "Using Research in Preparing to Teach Writing." *EJ* 67, no. 1 (January 1978): 82–88.

Hoover, R. M. "Annotated Bibliography on Testing." *CCC* 30 (1979): 384–92.

Hoyer, L. E. "The Invention Process in Composition: A Selected Annotated Bibliography, 1950–1974." M. A. Thesis, Texas A & M University, 1974. ED 103 914.

Humes, A. *The Composing Process: A Review of the Literature. Technical Note.* Los Alamitos, California: Southwest Regional Laboratory for Educational Research and Development, 1980. ED 192 378.

Hunting, R. "Recent Studies of Writing Frequency." *RTE* 1 (1967): 29–40.

Jerabek, R., and D. Dieterich. "Composition Evaluation: The State of the Art." *CCC* 26 (1975): 183–86.

Kantor, K. J. "Research in Composition: What It Means for Teachers." 70, no. 2 (February 1981): 64–67.

Koch, R. "Syllogisms and Superstitions: The Current State of Responding to Writing." *LA* 59 (1982): 464–71.

Kolin, M. "Closing the Books on Alchemy." *CCC* 32 (1981): 139–51.

Larson, R. L. "Selected Bibliography of Writings on the Evaluation of Students' Achievements in Composition." *Journal of Basic Writing* 1, no. 4 (1978): 91–100.

Lawlor, J. *Improving Student Writing through Sentence Combining: A Literature Review. Technical Note.* Los Alamitos, California: Southwest Regional Laboratory for Educational Research and Development, 1980. ED 192 356.

Lindell, E. *Composition in the Intermediate Stage of the Comprehensive School (FRIS).* Stockholm, Sweden: Stockholm School of Education, Institute of Educational Psychology. 1971. ED 060 039.

———. *Six Reports on Free Writing: A Summary of the FRIS Project.* *"Didakometry" No. 61.* Malmo, Sweden: School of Education, Department of Educational and Psychological Research, 1980. ED 207 083.

Lundsteen, S. W., ed. *Help for the Teacher of Written Composition: New Directions in Research.* Urbana, Illinois: ERIC Clearinghouse on Reading and Communication Skills and the National Conference on Research in English, 1976. ED 120 731.

McDonell, G. M., and E. B. Osburn. "Beginning Writing: Watching It Develop." *LA* 57 (1980): 310–14.

McNutt, A. S. *An Annotated Bibliography for Teachers of Technical Writing.* 1977. ED 210 706.

Martin, F. "Close Encounters of an Ancient Kind: Readings on the Tutorial Classroom and the Writing Conference." *Writing Center Journal* 2, no. 2 (1982): 7–17.

Meckel, H. "Research on Teaching Composition and Literature." In *Handbook of Research on Teaching.* Edited by N. L. Gage, 966–1006. Chicago: Rand McNally, 1963.

O'Donnell, B. *"NCTE/ERIC:* Summaries and Sources." *EJ* 59 (1970): 134–38.

O'Donnell, R. C. "Research in the Teaching of Secondary English: Actuality and Potential." Paper, Annual Meeting of the Secondary School English Conference, 1976. ED 120 799.

———. "A Survey of *Research in the Teaching of English,* Volumes 1–10." *RTE* 14 (1980): 82–88.

Office of Education (Dept. of Health, Education, and Welfare). *Cooperative Research Projects. A Seven-Year Summary, July 1, 1956–June 30, 1963.* Washington, D.C.: Office of Education, Dept. of Health, Education, and Welfare, 1964. ED 064 251.

Pooley, R. C. "Curriculum Research and Development in English." *Journal of Experimental Education* 37 (1968): 56–64.

Shafer, R. E. "The Crisis in Knowing about Learning to Write." *ADE Bulletin* 6, no. 6 (1975): 52–57.

Shane, H. G., J. Walden, and R. Green. *Interpreting Language Arts Research for the Teacher.* Washington, D.C.: Association for Supervision and Curriculum Development, 1971.

Sherwin, J. S. *Four Problems in Teaching English: A Critique of Research.* Scranton, Pennsylvania: International Textbook Co., 1969.

Steinberg, E. R. "Research in the Teaching of English: Tactics and Logistics." *Universities Quarterly* 20 (1966): 267–74.

———. "Research on the Teaching of English under Project English." *Publications of the Modern Language Association* 79, no. 4, Part 2 (1964): 50–76.

Tate, G., ed. *Teaching Composition: 10 Bibliographical Essays.* Fort Worth, Texas: Texas Christian University Press, 1976.

VanDeWeghe, R. *"Research in Written Composition": Fifteen Years of Investigation.* 1978. ED 157 095.

Vukelich, C., and J. Golden. "The Development of Writing in Young Children: A Review of the Literature." *Childhood Education* 57 (1981): 167–70.

Wagner, E. "Developmental English: More Harm Than Good?" *Teaching English in the Two-Year College* 1 (1975): 147–52.

West. W. W. "Written Composition." *Review of Educational Research* 37 (1967): 159–67.

Note on ERIC Documents

Documents indexed in *Resources in Education (RIE)* are denoted by a 6-digit ED (ERIC Document) number. The majority of ERIC documents are reproduced on microfiche and may be viewed at ERIC collections in libraries and other institutions or can be ordered from the ERIC Document Reproduction Service (EDRS) in either paper copy or microfiche. For ordering information and price schedules write or call EDRS, 3900 Wheeler Avenue, Alexandria, VA 22304, 1-800-227-3742.

Index

In the entries below, an italicized page number next to an author's name indicates a table in which the author's study or studies appear.